# RENAISSANCE
# AND
# REFORMATION
## 1300–1648

# RENAISSANCE AND REFORMATION 1300–1648

THIRD EDITION

EDITED BY

# G. R. ELTON
The University of Cambridge

Macmillan Publishing Co., Inc.
New York

Collier Macmillan Publishers
London

Macmillan Publishing Co., Inc.
866 Third Avenue, New York, New York 10022

Collier Macmillan Canada, Ltd.

---

*Library of Congress Cataloging in Publication Data*

Main entry under title:

Renaissance and Reformation, 1300–1648.

1. Renaissance—History—Sources. 2. Reformation—History—Sources. I. Elton, Geoffrey Rudolph.
CB359.R46 1976        909.07        75-5718
ISBN 0-02-332840-1

---

Printing    7891011    year        56789

ISBN    0-02-332840-1

# PREFACE

In this new and much enlarged edition, I have added eighteen extracts to the ninety-one of the second edition. This helps to modify, though it does not remove, the insufficiency that must beset any selection covering 350 years of European history in one short volume—an insufficiency of which I have declared myself well aware in earlier prefaces. It still remains the case that I have been forced to omit some interesting and, no doubt, important topics, but several new ones are now introduced. As far as there could be a principle of selection, I have endeavored to choose something from the leading personalities and something on the leading issues, both of which must admittedly always remain, up to a point, a matter of personal opinion. Allowing for the fact that some pieces necessarily choose themselves, I have also tried to use unfamiliar material not commonly found in such collections, and I have throughout worked solely from the originals, with no reliance on other people's anthologies.

Where necessary, I have modernized the spelling and punctuation, even where modern editions preserved the old spelling. On a few occasions I have taken the liberty of amending sixteenth-century grammatical obscurities in the interest of clarity. Unless another translator's name is mentioned, I am myself responsible for all translations. For Bible passages, I have ordinarily used the King James Version (1611), the nearest convenient equivalent to what the original author had before him. Brackets surround editorial insertions.

G. R. E.

# CONTENTS

# RENAISSANCE
# AND
# REFORMATION
# 1300–1648

# I / THE CHURCH
# IN THE LATER
# MIDDLE AGES

*From about the year 1300 to the Reformation, the history of the Church in the main turned on the fortunes of the papacy. Despite his uncompromising assertion of the universal claim to supremacy established by the great popes of the previous 250 years, Boniface VIII really saw its end. In a world manifestly dominated by territorial princes and secular governments, the traditional pretensions of both papacy and empire ceased to have any reality. Marsiglio of Padua drew the logical conclusions, but he was alone in totally denying the right of the spiritualty to govern. Whatever doctrine might say, the facts were all against the papacy. From 1327 the popes were French clients resident at Avignon; and after 1377 things got worse still with the Great Schism, when first two, and in the end three, popes contended for the disappearing obedience of Christendom. Clearly a new agency was required to restore unity and peace to the Church. The answer seemed to be the long-defunct General Council of the Church to which a group of writers, the so-called conciliarists, now ascribed the ultimate government in the Church. The calling of a Council seemed the more necessary because these political problems were accompanied by a crisis of faith and doctrine. The fourteenth century witnessed the growth of a sceptical philosophy called nominalism, chiefly associated with William of Occam (see No. 3), whose philosophical and political radicalism helped to undermine the Thomist system upon which the Church had come to rest its orthodoxy. Occamism, nationalism, and resentment at the unspiritual state of the papal Church produced two major heretical movements. In England and Oxford, the home of nominalist speculation, John Wyclif (see No. 4) propounded ideas hostile to the established order of the clergy and thought to be hostile, too, to the settled order of society; and though his heresy was driven underground, it played its part in provoking the movement led by Jan Hus in Bohemia.*

whole existing order; and though Wycliffite heresy was driven underground, it played its part in provoking the movement led by Jan Hus in Bohemia.

Thus the calling of the General Council was finally achieved at Constance. That Council burned Hus, an act which led to prolonged war against his outraged followers, and healed the schism. Another met at Basel, but the momentum of conciliarism was slowing rapidly, and the reestablished papacy could attempt to restore its monarchic rule in the Church. Pius II and his successors left no doubt as to where the political center of gravity in the Church now lay. However, they could do this only by coming to terms with the world. On the one hand, this meant conceding considerable degrees of independence to national rulers and territorial churches; on the other, it involved the creation by the papacy of a territorial power of its own in central Italy. The popes of the period immediately preceding the Reformation were in effect Italian princes playing a political game both in the peninsula and in Europe at large, supporting their activities by an increasingly less real theory of supremacy over all Christians and an increasingly burdensome extraction of money from all Christians. Their private lives usually added to the anger they aroused.

All this does not mean that religion was dead, but it does mean that in these two centuries the most notable spiritual manifestations tended to be either disruptive heresies like those of Hus or movements of private devotion. Mysticism (a search for direct union with God) became the characteristic form of spiritual Christianity. One such tradition arose in Germany in the hands of Master Eckhart (1260–1327) and his disciple Johann Tauler (c. 1300–1361); another in England, where Richard Rolle and others manifested a profoundly religious and uninstitutional cast of mind. A little less profound, but quite as devotional and personal, were the movements in the Netherlands associated especially with the names of Gerhard Groot and Thomas à Kempis. All this was doctrinally orthodox, but in effect it denied the sufficiency of the Church's own behavior and methods, stressed the personal relation of the soul to God, and so helped to prepare the ground for a more drastic reaction to the spiritual malaise of Western Christendom.

# 1 / BONIFACE VIII (C. 1235-1303): THE BULL UNAM SANCTAM (1302)

*Pope from 1294, Boniface attempted to maintain the sovereign traditions of Innocent IV, but was badly defeated in a quarrel with Philip IV of France which arose out of that king's attempt to control the French clergy. This began in 1301. In November, 1302, Boniface issued this bull as a manifesto of papal claims; a few weeks later he was an ill-treated prisoner in French hands.[1]*

One holy Catholic and also apostolic Church we are compelled by faith to believe in and to hold to, and we so believe firmly and in simplicity; outside of which there is neither salvation nor remission of sins; as the bridegroom says in the Song of Songs, 6.9: "My dove, my undefiled one, is but one; she is the only one of her mother." Which Church represents one mystic body whose head is Christ, and Christ's head is God.

In this there is one lord, one faith, one baptism. For there was at the time of the Flood one ark of Noah, prefiguring the one Church, which, complete in one cubit, had the one single ruler and guide, that is to say Noah; outside of which ark, as we read, all other things existing on earth were destroyed.

This one we venerate alone, as the Lord says through the prophet (Psalm 22.20): "Deliver my soul from the sword; my darling from the power of the dog." For He prayed for His soul, that is for Himself, head and body together, which body He names, as it were, His only Church, through the unity of bridegroom, faith, the sacraments, and the charity of the Church.

She is the seamless garment of the Lord which was never rent but was awarded by lot (John 19.24).

Therefore the one and only Church has one body, one head, not two heads like a monster, that is to say Christ and Christ's vicar Peter, and Peter's successor; as the Lord said to the same Peter: "Feed my sheep" (John 26.17).

---

[1] Translated from J. H. v. Planck, *Die Bulle Unam Sanctam* (Munich, 1887).

Mine, He said, and in general; not particularly these or those; by which means it is clear that He committed everyone to him.

Thus if the Greeks or others say that they are not committed to Peter or his successors, they necessarily confess themselves not to be Christians; for the Lord says, in St. John's Gospel, that there is but one fold and one shepherd.

That in this Church and in her power there are two swords, namely the spiritual and the temporal, we are taught by the words of the gospel. For when the apostles said, "Lo, there are here two swords" (meaning in the Church); when they said this the Lord replied, not "It is too much," but "It is enough."

Surely he who denies that the temporal sword is in Peter's power ill attends the word of the Lord, who says: "Put up again thy sword into his place" (Matt. 26.52).

Therefore both swords, the spiritual as well as the material, are in the power of the Church. But the latter is to be exercised on the Church's behalf and the former by the Church; the former in the hand of the priest, the latter in that of kings and soldiers, but at the beck and sufferance of the priest.

One sword, however, must be beneath the other, and temporal authority must be subjected to spiritual. For when the apostle says (Rom. 13.1) "there is no power but of God; the powers that be are ordained of God," they would never be so ordained if one sword did not rest beneath the other, and if the inferior were not, so to say, brought to the heights by the other. For according to the blessed Dionysius [2] it is the law of God that the lowest shall by the intermediate be brought to the highest.

Therefore, by the order of the Universe, all things are not equally and immediately brought to order, but the lowest by the intermediate and the inferior by the superior.

That, however, the spiritual power excels in dignity and nobility any temporal power we must confess to be obviously true, in measure as matters spiritual excel matters temporal. And this we see clearly proved by the giving of tithe and the benediction and the sanctification, by the reception of that very power, and by the rule of things.

For the witness of truth the power spiritual must institute the power temporal and must judge it if it be not good. Thus the Church and its power render true the saying of Jeremiah (1.10), "See, I have this day set thee over the nations and over the kingdoms, etc."

Therefore, if the temporal power errs it shall be judged by the

---

[2] The so-called Pseudo-Dionysius, a sixth-century Byzantine compilation of allegedly first-century Christian documents, accepted as authoritative until the fifteenth century.

power spiritual; if the lesser spiritual power errs, its judge is its superior; but if the highest spiritual power errs, it can be judged by God alone and not by man, as the apostle testifies (1 Cor. 2.15): "he that is spiritual judgeth all things, yet he himself is judged of no man."

This authority, though it be given to a man and exercised by a man, is not human but rather divine, granted by God's words to Peter, confirmed to him and his successors in him whom Christ called the rock; as the Lord said to Peter (Matt. 16.19), "whatsoever thou shalt bind etc."

Therefore, whosoever shall resist the power so ordained by God resists God's ordinance, unless, following the Manichaeans, he pretends that there are two principles; which doctrine we judge to be false and heretical because, as Moses testifies, God created heaven and earth not in several but in one principle.

In consequence of which we declare, assert, define, and pronounce that it is entirely necessary for salvation that all human creation be subject to the pope of Rome.

Given at the Lateran, in the 8th year of our pontificate [1302].

# 2 / MARSIGLIO OF PADUA (C. 1275-C. 1342): DEFENSOR PACIS (1324)

*An Italian physician and philosopher, Marsiglio of Padua in 1313 was rector of the University of Paris and later espoused the imperial cause in the quarrel between Lewis IV (the Bavarian) and Pope John XXII. However, his real support was for the autonomy of any political unit—city state, kingdom, or empire – in matters spiritual and temporal. These views he elaborated in this work, one of the most original and striking productions of medieval political thought, which, however, made no immediate impact because it was condemned and banned by the papacy.*[3]

[I. 15.2] . . . Let us say, in accordance with the truth and the doctrine of Aristotle . . . that the efficient power to establish or elect the

---

[3] Reprinted from *The Defender of Peace*, translated by A. Gewirth, Vols. I and II (New York: Columbia University Press, 1956), by permission of Columbia University Press.

ruler belongs to the legislator or the whole body of citizens, just as does the power to make laws. . . . And to the legislator similarly belongs the power to make any correction of the ruler and even to depose him, if this be expedient for the common benefit. For this is one of the more important matters in the polity; and such matters pertain to the entire multitude of the citizens. . . . The method of coming together to effect the aforesaid establishment or election of the ruler may perhaps vary according to the variety of provinces. But in whatever way it may differ, this must be observed in each case, that such election or establishment is always to be made by the authority of the legislator, who, as we have very frequently said, is the whole body of the citizens, or the weightier part thereof. . . .

[II. 16.13–14] Moreover, every bishop is alike the successor of every apostle in intrinsic, that is, inseparable dignity, and has the same merit or perfection in this dignity or character. . . . The Roman bishop neither is nor ought to be called the particular successor of St. Peter on account of the laying on of hands, because the Roman bishop happens to be a man on whom St. Peter never laid his hands, either indirectly or directly; nor again is the Roman bishop St. Peter's particular successor because he occupies a certain seat or has been assigned a certain territory. For, in the first place, none of the apostles were assigned by divine law entirely to some one people or territory. . . . Moreover, we read that St. Peter was at Antioch before being at Rome. Again, even if Rome were to become uninhabitable, Peter's succession would not on that account cease. And besides, it cannot be proved by the divine law that Christ or any of the apostles decreed that the bishop of any determinate province or diocese is or ought to be called the special successor of Peter or any other apostle, and leader of the rest . . . ; the successors of St. Peter and the other apostles are, in a certain sense, that person or those persons who are most like them in their lives and holy morals. . . .

[II. 17.15] It is the sentence of judgment . . . of the legislator, or of the ruler by its authority, therefore, that must approve or disapprove candidates for ecclesiastic orders, and appoint them to a major or minor post or headship, and remove them therefore or prohibit them to exercise it, or even, if out of malice they refuse to exercise their office, compel them to do so. . . .

[II. 20.2] And now I am going to show that the principal authority, direct or indirect, for such determination of doubtful questions belongs only to a general council composed of all Christians or of the weightier part of them, or to those persons who have been granted such authority by the whole body of Christian believers. . . . Let all the notable provinces or communities of the world, in accordance with the determination of their human legislators whether one or many, and according to their proportion in quantity and quality of persons, elect faithful men, first priests and then non-priests, suitable persons of the most blameless lives and the greatest experience in divine law. . . .

[II. 23.2] In all the seizures of secular power and rulership which the Roman bishops have perpetrated in the past, and which, as everyone can plainly see, they are still striving with all their might, although wrongly, to perpetrate, no small role has been played in the past, and will be played in the future, by that sophistical line of argument whereby these bishops ascribe to themselves the title of "plenitude of power." This sophistry is also the source of the misreasoning whereby they try to prove that all kings, rulers, and individuals are subject to them in coercive jurisdiction.

[II. 25.20] And so by this new fiction, previously unheard of, the Roman bishop has the audacity openly to make an assertion which is as false as it is insolent . . . when he pertinaciously asserts that he "undoubtedly" has "superiority" (he means in coercive jurisdiction or rulership) over the Roman emperor. . . . For who would have the effrontery to declare shamelessly that a proposition is undoubtedly true which was unheard of throughout the ages, which is confirmed neither by divine nor human law nor by right reason, and the opposite of which not only does have this confirmation but has always been conceived and asserted as an example of a truth believed by all men?

# 3 / WILLIAM OF OCCAM (C. 1280-1349): POWERS SPIRITUAL AND TEMPORAL

*Occam, a Franciscan friar, though born in northern England and educated at Oxford, spent most of his life on the Continent. He became the leading theologian and philosopher of the early fourteenth century. His main achievement was the demolition of the reconciliation of revelation (Scripture) and reason (Aristotelianism) established in the system erected by St. Thomas Aquinas. Occam was the foremost exponent of nominalism, the philosophy that denied reality to universals, asserting the sole ascertainable existence of particulars. In consequence, it disallowed Aquinas's universal law of God, asserted that the mysteries of the faith cannot be apprehended by reason, and introduced voluntarism (divine willfulness and human will) into the problem of salvation. Nominalism was to exert great influence on Luther and the Reformation, both by attraction and repulsion. Occam's resistance to authority in the Church also involved him in political opposition to the papacy; in the quarrel between Emperor Lewis IV (the Bavarian) and Pope John XXII he wrote powerful pamphlets in support of the former, from one of which this extract is taken. It shows how Occam's relativist position led him to deny the papal claim to universal rule and to assert the rights of secular princes. Though starting from very different premises, he thus arrived at conclusions very similar to those of Marsiglio of Padua. The translation used here was produced by the champions of Henry VIII of England when he similarly came to quarrel with the papacy.*[4]

CLERK: I wonder, sir noble knight, that in few days times be changed, right is buried, laws be overturned, and statutes trodden under foot.

KNIGHT: Those words pass my capacity. I am a lewd[5] man, and though I went to school in my childhood yet got I not so profound learning that those your words can of me be understood. And therefore, worshipful clerk, if ye desire to have communication with me, ye must use a more homely and plainer fashion of speaking.

CLERK: I have seen in my time that kings, princes and other nobles have had the Church in right great worship. And now I see the contrary. The Church is made a prey to you all, and many things are challenged of us, and nothing is given us. If we give not our goods they be taken from us by strong hand. Our goods and chattels are destroyed; our laws and freedom be not holden but despised and withsaid.[6]

KNIGHT: I cannot lightly believe that the king (of whose council those of the clergy be) will deal unjustly with you, neither destroy your law.

CLERK: Yea truly, against all law we suffer innumerable wrongs.

KNIGHT: I would fain[7] know what you call law.

CLERK: I call law the statutes and ordinances of bishops of Rome and decrees of holy fathers.

KNIGHT: Whatever they ordain, or other have ordained in time past,

---

[4] From William of Occam, *A Dialogue Between a Knight and a Clerk Concerning the Powers Spiritual and Temporal* (London, 1530).

[5] simple

[6] denied

[7] gladly

of temporalty [8] may well be law to you, but not to us. For no man hath power to ordain statutes of things over which he hath no lordship. As the king of France may ordain no statutes upon the empire, neither the emperor upon the king of England. And likewise no princes of the world may ordain no statutes of your spiritualty, over the which they have no power: no more ye may ordain no statutes of their temporalty over the which ye have neither power nor authority. Wherefore it is a thing in vain whatever ye ordain of temporal things over which ye have received of God no power. And therefore of late I laughed well fast when I heard that Pope Boniface VIII had made a new statute that he himself should be above all secular lords—princes, kings and emperors—and above all kingdoms, and make law upon all things; [9] and that him needeth naught but write, for all things shall be his when he hath written: and so all things shall be yours. For to make a statute, his statute is naught else but to will that the decree be holden and kept, and ordain and write that it be holden. If he will have my castle, my town, my field, my money, or any other such things: him needeth naught but will it and write it and make a decree and write that it be holden; and when that is done, he hath right to all such things. Now, good clerk, thou wotest [10] well how worthy this jape is to be scorned.

CLERK: Sir knight, ye speak sharply, slily and wisely enough. All your talking and meaning is (as I perceive) that the pope hath no power to ordain and make statutes of your temporalties, for ye know not that he hath lordship, power and authority upon your temporalties. Though we would prove it by our law and by decrees written, ye account them for naught. For ye ween [11] that Peter had no lordship ne power over temporalty but by such law written. But if thou wilt be a true Christian man and of right belief, thou shalt not deny but that Christ is lord of all things. To him it was said in the psalter book: "ask of me and I shall give nations to thine heritage and all the world about to thy possession" (Psalms, 2). And also of him it is written . . . that he is king of kings and lord of lords (I Tim. 6). These be not ours but God's own words; nor we wrote them not, but God sent them and the Holy Ghost spake them. And who doubteth whether he may ordain and make statutes whom he knoweth to be lord of all things?

KNIGHT: I withsay not the majesty, lordship and might of our Lord God, for he may not be withsaid in no manner wise. But if it may be showed by Holy Writ that the pope is lord of all temporalties, then kings and princes must be subject to the pope as well in temporalty as in spiritualty.

[8] in matter secular
[9] *The Bull Unam Sanctam;* see No. 1.
[10] knowest
[11] think

CLERK: That may be showed lightly [12] . . . The faith of holy Church holdeth that Peter the Apostle was ordained Christ's full vicar for himself and his successors. And he that is full vicar may do the same as his lord may. . . . If ye cannot deny but that Christ that is lord of heaven and earth may ordain and make statutes of your temporalties, how can ye for shame deny Christ's vicar to have the same power?

KNIGHT: I have heard of holy and devout men that we should distinguish two divers times of Christ: one of his humility and another of his power and majesty. The time of his humility was from the time that he took flesh and blood unto his passion; the time of his power and majesty was and is after his Resurrection. . . . Peter was ordained Christ's vicar for the state of his humility and not for the state of his bliss and majesty. . . . Ergo, Christ committed thilk [13] power to his vicar which he as man mortal exercised, and not that power which after his glorification he received. [Cites Scripture to prove the point.] In the which first estate it is plain that Christ exercised no temporal power but put it clean away from him and used only that longed [14] to the governance of our salvation; and in that manner of doing he made Peter his vicar whom he neither made knight nor crowned king, but ordained him to be a priest and bishop. And if ye will yet strive that Christ's vicar should have that power in temporalty that Christ had after his Resurrection in heaven and used not here on earth, your strife shall not turn you to worship at length. For it is evident to every faithful man that if God should command him to give his money, his field, or his vineyard to any other man, without any provision or reasonable request and without any express studying, he ought forthwith to obey. Wherefore if ye will contend that the pope hath the same power, then of necessity ye must grant also that the pope may take from you and from us all the goods that ye and we have, and give them all to which of his nephews or cousins that he will, and tell not cause why; and also he may take away from princes and kings principalities and kingdoms at his own will and give them there as him liketh. But take heed how wrongfully that were done, and deemith your own self how that would mislike you if he did so to you. If that very reason constrain you to forsake your foolish argument, the pope shall also be constrained to give back.

[12] easily
[13] that
[14] belonged

# 4 / JOHN WYCLIF (C. 1330-1384): ATTACKS ON THE PRIESTHOOD

*Wyclif, an obscure Oxford scholar and exceptionally difficult theologian, became the inspirer of a heretical movement because he came to believe in the possibility of bringing religion directly to the people. In this regard, his chief tenets were two: he denied the special claims of an ordained priesthood in Christ's Church; and, by translating the Scriptures into the vernacular, he wished to make the grounds of the faith available to all. The heart of his beliefs was an intent Biblicism, but his moral theology joined disturbingly with the widespread social dissatisfaction of the day to disturb the beneficiaries of the existing order. Protected during his life by a powerful political faction, Wyclif died in peace, but his influence sparked off two movements that were energetically persecuted. In Bohemia, Wyclif's writings contributed to the heresy of Hus and his followers; in England, Wycliffite scholasticism came to be translated into the popular heretical movement called Lollardy, which, despite much persecution, survived among several groups of poor and obscure people to play its part in preparing the country for the reception of the Reformation. The following extracts illustrate Wyclif's belief in the vernacular (A) and his attacks on clerical exclusiveness (B).*[15]

## A. THE PATER NOSTER

Since the Pater Noster is the best prayer that is, for in it must all other prayers be [en]closed if they shall graciously be heard of God, therefore should men ken this prayer and study the wit [16] thereof. And since the truth of God standeth not in one language more than in another, but whoever liveth best teacheth best, pleaseth most God, of what language ever he be, therefore this prayer declared in English

---

[15] From *Select English Works of John Wyclif*, ed. T. Arnold (Oxford, 1871), iii. 98–9, 508–23.

[16] meaning

may edify the lewd [17] people as it doth clerks in Latin. And since it is the gospel of Christ, and Christ bade it be preached to the people, for the people should learn and ken it and work thereafter, why may we not write in English the gospel and other things declaring the gospel, to edification of Christian men's souls, as the preacher telleth it truly in English to the people? For by the same reason it should not be written, it should not be preached. This heresy and blasphemy should men put out from their hearts, for it springeth up by the fiend: as Christ sayeth, the fiend is father of lies. And so the kindred of Pharisees is cursed of God that loveth not Jesus, as St Paul says, but letteth [18] the gospel to be learned of the people. For if there be any subtlety lighter than other, for to ken a craft that is needful, he that can this subtlety and will not teach the learned able thereto, he is cause of his uncunning.[19] And so writing of the gospel in English, and of good lore according thereto, is a subtlety and a mean to the common people to ken it the better. . . . This wicked kindred would that the gospel slept.

## B. PETITION TO THE KING AND PARLIAMENT, 1383?

Please it to our most noble and most worthy King Richard, king both of England and of France,[20] and to the noble duke of Lancaster,[21] and to other great men of the realm, both to seculars and men of Holy Church, that be gathered in the Parliament, to hear, assent and maintain the few articles or points that be set within this writing and proved both by authority and reason; that Christ's faith and Christ's religion be increased, maintained and made stable, since our Lord Jesus Christ, very God and very man, is head and prelate of this religion and shed his precious blood and water out of his side on the cross, to make his religion perfect and stable and clean, without error.

The first article is this: that all persons of what kin, private sects, or singular religion, made of sinful men,[22] may freely without any letting or bodily pain leave that private rule or new religion, founded of sinful men, and stably [23] hold the rule of Jesus Christ, taken and given by Christ to his apostles, as far more perfect than any such new religion founded of sinful men.

.    .    .

The second point or article is this: that though men that unreason-

[17] ordinary
[18] hinders
[19] ignorance
[20] Richard II
[21] John of Gaunt, Duke of Lancaster
[22] members of religious orders
[23] firmly

ably and wrongfully have condemned the king and all his Council be amended of so great error, and that their error may be published to men dwelling in the realm. . . . Neither the king nor his Council did unrightfully forasmuch as he took away the possessions of some prelates that trespassed. . . . Some friars write thus in Coventry, among articles that they damn as heresy and error, that it is error to say that secular lords may lawfully and rightfully take away temporal goods given to men of the Church. But since our king hath done so, and other kings his predecessors have done so many times, by lawful cause, by counsel of peers of the realm, it follows that not only our king now present hath erred but also his predecessors, and generally all his councillors, as lords and prelates and all men of the Parliament counselling thereto.

. . .

The third article is this: that both tithe and offerings be given and paid and received by that intent, to which intent or end both God's law and the pope's law ordained them to be paid and received; and that they be taken away by the same intent and reason that both God's law and the pope's law ordain that they should be withdrawn. . . . The things that be due to [a] priest should not be asked by strength or violence or cursing, but be given freely, without exaction or constraining. And if the priest be reproved of God for his sins, he should be put out of his office, and their sacrifices should not be given to him but taken from him.

. . .

The fourth article is this: that Christ's teaching and belief of the sacrament of his own body, that is plainly taught by Christ and his apostles in gospels and epistles, may be taught openly in churches to Christ's people, and the contrary teaching and false belief, brought up by cursed hypocrites and heretics and worldly priests, uncunning [24] in God's law, distried.[25] . . . The false faith taught of Antichrist and of his false cursed disciples is this, that the sacrament that men see with bodily eye between the priest's hands is neither bread nor Christ's body but accidents without subject, and this is neither grounded in Holy Writ nor reason nor wit,[26] nor taught by the most wisest old saints. . . . The right faith of Christian men is this: that this worshipful sacrament is bread and Christ's body, as Jesus Christ is very God and very man. And this faith is grounded in Christ's own word. . . .

[24] unlearned
[25] discontinued
[26] sense

# 5 / JAN HUS (1369-1415): ON SIMONY

*The celebrated Czech heresiarch and national hero, Jan Hus, exercised his influence in the main through his preaching and pastoral work, but was also a considerable writer and scholar who built up an unorthodox and antipapal doctrine in part on Wycliffe's teaching and in part on his own view of positive Christianity. This resulted in his excommunication in 1409 and his burning at Constance in 1415, in spite of an imperial safe-conduct. Simony (the selling of ecclesiastical appointments from the papacy downwards) was justly one of the chief grievances against an unreformed Church; by inevitably introducing insufficient and corrupt men into places of power, it made virtually impossible any serious attempt to reform abuses.*[27]

Let us now enquire whether a pope may be a simoniac. It would appear that he cannot, since he is the lord of all the world, who by right takes whatever he wishes and does as he pleases; moreover, that he is the most holy father who cannot sin. But know that many popes were heretics or otherwise evil, and were deposed from the papacy. . . . If someone would defend him by saying that he cannot commit simony or other mortal sin, he would exalt him above Peter and the other apostles. As for the argument that he is the lord of all the world, who by right takes whatever he wishes and does as pleases, the answer is that there is only one Lord of all the world, who cannot sin and who has the right to rule the world and to do as he pleases, and that Lord is God the mighty One. Furthermore, as for the argument that the pope is the most holy father who cannot sin, I deny it; for it is our Father most holy, the Lord God, who alone cannot sin.

But perhaps you say, "In this world the pope is the most holy father." I answer that if you prove that he lives the most holy life, following Christ in His poverty, humility, meekness, and work, then I shall admit that he is most holy. But his manifest covetousness, pride, and other sins predispose men to believe that he is not the most holy father! But you retort: "The whole world calls him the most holy father except yourself! Why should you be more worthy of belief?" Thereupon I answer that you exaggerate when you speak of "the whole world," since hardly perhaps one in a hundred acknowledges him as

[27] From *Advocates of Reform*, Vol. XIV, pp. 211–19, Library of Christian Classics. Tr. M. Spinka. Published 1953, The Westminster Press. By permission.

the bishop of Rome. But even though all men were to call him holy and the most holy, if his acts be contrary to Christ he is not holy, whether or not he is called so. . . .

Furthermore, they put forth the excuse that he is most holy on account of his office. But the saints reply that office does not make a man holy, as is proved by the apostle Judas and by the bishops and priests who murdered Christ. Moreover, the saints affirm that the worthier the office the greater the damnation of the incumbent if he be sinful. . . .

But if any pope avoids simony and follows the Saviour in his manner of life, he has the right to make use of all things in the world, just as the apostles. . . . Besides this right to the use of the world, he has likewise the right to serve holy Church, and to order, teach, and direct it in accordance with the Word of God. But that is a different matter from the worldly rule in which men, particularly clerics, easily go astray. For the papal office, as well as the apostolic, consists in preaching the Word of God, in administering the sacraments, and in praying diligently to God on behalf of the people. To administer temporal possessions belongs to the lower estate, the secular. Consequently, the pope should observe that Christ and Peter did not meddle with ruling over worldly possessions. . . . When Pilate told him, "Thine own nation and bishops delivered thee unto me; what hast thou done?" Jesus answered: "My kingdom is not of this world; if my kingdom were of this world, then would my servants fight that I should not be delivered to the Jews. But now is my kingdom not hence." . . .

Finally, be it known to you that papal power is limited by God's law, the law of nature, and the pronouncements of saints which are grounded in God's Word. The law of God constrains the pope to do nothing contrary to it; consequently he should give spiritual gifts freely as the apostles have done. The law of nature, which is an intelligent being's reason, by which he should regulate his life, asserts that the pope should do nothing unworthy. . . . May the Lord grant that the present pope and his successors, instead of meddling in wars, bestow no benefice upon unworthy men for money but rather follow Christ! But it seems to me that but few of them will be willing to enter upon the way of Christ, the way of humility, poverty, and of work, until the work of Christ be fulfilled; for the miserable worldly possessions have blocked the way of Christ and have given birth to confusion among the priesthood, so that it is full of simony, avarice, and quarrels. Consequently, simony will not be expelled from the holy Church as long as priests do not surrender wealth and rule. . . .

# 6 / DIETRICH VON NIEHEIM (C. 1340-1418): THE UNION AND REFORM OF THE CHURCH BY A GENERAL COUNCIL (1410)

*Bishop of the north German see of Verden (1395–1401), Dietrich von Nieheim nevertheless spent most of his life from 1370 in the service of the papacy. His experiences made him a vigorous advocate of the calling of a General Council as the only hope for Christendom, and he therefore argued both the superiority of the Council to the pope and the right of others (especially the emperor) to call one if the pope should fail to do so.*[28]

Now take the pope. He is a man of the earth, clay of clay, a sinner liable to sin, a mere two days ago the son of a poor peasant. Then he is raised to the papacy. Does such a man, without any repentance of sin, without confession, without inner contrition, become a pure angel, become a saint? Who has made him a saint? Not the Holy Spirit, because it is not as a rule the office which confers the Holy Spirit but only the grace and love of God; nor his place of authority which may come to both the good and the wicked. Therefore, since the pope can be no angel, the pope as a pope is a man, and being a man he thus is pope: and as pope, and as a man, he can err. For a good many of them, as you may read in the chronicles, were not very spiritual. . . . It is absurd to say that one mortal man should claim the power to bind and to loose from sin in heaven and earth, even though he may be a son of perdition, a simoniac, miser, liar, oppressor, fornicator, a proud man and arrogant, one worse than the devil. Therefore human judgment neither can nor ought to assume one to be a saint who in that Seat, by his evil deeds, proclaims the contrary. . . .

[28] Translated from *De Unione et Reformatione Ecclesiae*, ed. H. Heimpel (Leipzig, 1933), pp. 2, 20, 25, 34–6, 43. By permission of H. Heimpel and B. G. Teubner Verlagsgesellschaft.

These various members [of the Church], however, stand diversely—higher and lower—in its mystical body. They must all be brought back to the unity of the Church in a double manner: by obedience as well as by withdrawal. That is to say, they must obey the one universal and undoubted vicar of Christ, and they must by common consent and with a single will withdraw their obedience from these two or three contenders for the papacy who are a scandal to the whole Church. This withdrawal, as I have said, is binding uniformly on all Christians under the pain of mortal sin. For supposing the Universal Church, whose head is Christ, have no pope, the faithful dying in charity shall yet be saved. For when two or more compete for the papacy and when the truth of the matter is not known to the universal Church, it is neither an article of faith, nor a deduction from one, that this man or that must be accepted as pope, nor can any faithful Christian be obliged to believe so. . . .

Now, since the General Council represents the Universal Church, I shall speak my mind about the assembling of this Council.

I have said elsewhere that when the issue is the reconstruction of the Church and the matter of the pope—whether to get him to resign, or whether he should be deposed for his evil living and the scandal in the Church—it by no means belongs to the pope, however sole, universal and undoubted he be, to call a General Council. Nor is it his place to preside as a judge, or to lay down anything concerning the state of the Church; but the duty belongs in the first place to the bishops, cardinals, patriarchs, secular princes, communities and the rest of the faithful. In equity no man of ill-fame can or may be a judge, particularly in his own cause. . . . I tell you, the prelates and princes of the world must, under pain of mortal sin, call and summon [a Council] as quickly as they can; they must cite to it this pope and those who strive with him for the papacy, and, if they will not obey, must depose and deprive them. . . . But is then such a Council, in which the pope does not preside, above the pope? Indeed it is: superior in authority, superior in dignity, superior in competence. For even the pope must obey such a Council in all things. Such a Council can limit the pope's power because to it, representing the Universal Church, are granted the keys to bind and to loose. Such a Council can abrogate the papal decrees. From such a Council there is no appeal. Such a Council can elect, deprive and depose the pope. Such a Council can make new laws and repeal old and existing ones. The constitutions, statutes and regulations of such a Council are immutable and cannot be dispensed from by anyone inferior to the Council. The pope cannot, nor ever could, issue dispensations contrary to canons made in General Councils, unless the Council, for good reason, specifically empowered him to do so. Nor can the pope alter the decisions of the Council, or even interpret them or dispense from them, for they are like Christ's gospels from which there is no dispensing and over which the pope has no jurisdiction. Thus there will come to the members the unity of the Spirit in the bonds of peace; thus we shall live in the Spirit and shall walk in the Spirit. . . .

Therefore, if a General Council, representing the Universal Church, is anxious to see an entire union and to repress schism, and if it wants to put an end to schism and exalt the Church, it must before all else, following the example of the holy fathers our predecessors, limit and terminate the coercive and usurped power of the pope.

# 7 / THE COUNCIL OF CONSTANCE (1414-1418)

*The first and most effective of the reforming Councils was the Council of Constance, called by the Emperor Sigismund but dominated by a French party of reformers (Jean Gerson, Pierre D'Ailly). The two decrees here printed define the two pillars of conciliar doctrine: the assertion of the General Council's omnicompetence within the* res publica Christiana, *and the arrangement for a regular convening of Councils in the future. The first was soon to be denied; the second lapsed after the calling of one more Council at Basel (1431–49).*[29]

## "SACROSANCTA"; APRIL, 1414

This holy Synod of Constance, constituting a General Council, legitimately assembled in the Holy Spirit for the extirpation of schism and the union and reform of God's Church in head and members, to the praise of Almighty God, for the greater ease in uniting and reforming the Church of God, ordains, defines, decrees and declares as follows:

First, that, legitimately assembled in the Holy Spirit and constituting a General Council and representing the Catholic Church, it has power directly from Christ which everyone, of whatever condition or dignity (including the pope's) he may be, is bound to obey in such things as

[29] Translated from J. Mansi, *Sacrorum Conciliorum nova et amplissima Collectio* (Venice, 1784), Vol. 27, pp. 590–1, 1159.

touch the faith and the extirpation of the said schism, and the reformation of the said Church in head and members.

Further, it declares that everyone of every condition, state or dignity (including the pope's) who shall contumaciously refuse to obey the mandates, statutes and ordinances, or the precepts made or to be made by this holy Synod, concerning the premises or pertaining to them, shall, unless he comes to his senses, be subjected to condign penance and suitably punished, with recourse, if need be, to the other sanctions of the law. . . .

## "FREQUENS"; OCTOBER, 1417

The frequent holding of General Councils ensures an excellent cultivation of the Lord's acre. It cleans out the thorns, brambles and spikes of heresies, errors and schisms, corrects excesses, reforms the deformed, and brings the Lord's vineyard to a state of abundant fruitfulness. Their neglect spreads and encourages the aforesaid evils, as the memory of times past and a study of the present make plain to our eyes. Therefore we by this perpetual edict confirm, decree and ordain that General Councils shall be held in the following fashion. Five years after the end of this Council, then seven years after the end of the next Council, and thereafter every ten years for ever, Councils shall be held in such places as, during the month before the closing of each Council, the pope, with the approval and consent of the Council, or failing him the Council itself, shall be bound to appoint and assign. . . . The pope may, with the advice of his brethren of the Holy Church of Rome,[30] shorten the interval [between Councils] if emergencies occur, but it shall on no account be extended. The place fixed for the next meeting of the Council shall not be altered without manifest necessity. If however, it should appear necessary to change the meeting place—for instance because of a siege, because of war, or because of plague, or some such reason—the pope may, with the written consent of his aforesaid brethren, or of two thirds of them, substitute another place for that previously chosen, apt in itself and within the same country. . . .

[30] the cardinals

# 8 / PIUS II:
# THE BULL EXECRABILIS
# (1460)

*Enea Silvio Piccolomini (1404–64), a leading humanist and diplomatist, prolific writer on history and geography, poet and playwright and letter writer, was one of the outstanding figures of the fifteenth-century Renaissance. He played an important part at the Council of Basel, but after 1442 deserted the Council for service with the Emperor Frederick III. Elected pope in 1458, he turned his back on his humanist and conciliarist past; enormously impressed by the fall of Constantinople to the Turks (1453), he devoted his energies to the restoration of papal control in the Church and the preparation of a crusade, being markedly more successful in the first. In this bull he denied that appeals could lie from a pope to a General Council; although this was made to appear as no more than a concern for ✓ffective justice, it was really an outright attack on the theories which had put the pope under conciliar control.*[31]

An execrable and in previous ages unheard of abuse has sprung up in our times, inasmuch as some men, imbued with the spirit of rebellion, presume to appeal to a future Council from the pope of Rome, the vicar of Jesus Christ . . . ; and that not from a desire for a sounder judgment but to avoid the consequences of sin. How far this contravenes the sacred canons and how harmful it is to the community of Christians, anybody not wholly ignorant of the canon law can readily see. For—not to mention other ways in which this abuse most manifestly contradicts justice—who would not judge it absurd to appeal to something which at the time does not exist and whose date in the future is unknown? The poor are in many ways oppressed by the powerful; crimes remain unpunished; rebellion is nourished against the Holy See; freedom to offend is granted; all ecclesiastical discipline and hierarchical order are confounded.

Wishing therefore to drive forth from Christ's Church this pestilent poison, to provide for the safety of the sheep committed to our care, and to keep from our Savior's fold all matter of scandal; we, by the

---

[31] Translated from *Magnum Bullarium Romanum* (Luxemburg, 1717), Vol. 1, pp. 369–70.

advice and assent of our venerable brethren the cardinals, all the prelates and the experts in the divine and human laws attending our court, and from our own certain knowledge, condemn appeals of this sort and denounce them as erroneous and detestable. . . . We further order that no one shall dare, for whatever reason, to interpose any such appeal from any of the ordinances, sentences or mandates of ourselves or of our successors, or to support anyone else's appeal. . . . No man may infringe this page of our will, condemnation, reprobation, cancellation, annulment, decree, declaration and mandate, or in an audacious spirit contravene it. Should anyone presume to attempt this, let him be aware that he will incur the indignation of Almighty God and of the blessed apostles Peter and Paul.

# 9 / THE GALLICAN CHURCH

*The quarrel between Boniface VIII and Philip IV had arisen over the "liberties" of the French Church, i.e., over its claim to some independence from papal rule and the king's desire to substitute his own control for the pope's. Defenders of "gallican" liberties were prominent in the Conciliar movement, and in 1438, in alliance with King Charles VII, they achieved a victory embodied in the* Pragmatic Sanction of Bourges (A). *This registered certain decrees of the Council of Basel, with additions that enlarged the freedom of the French Church but also recognised royal claims.[32] Neither the papacy nor the crown were content with an arrangement which gave the French clergy so much self-government; kings of France began to view with envy the treaties (concordats) made between popes and other kings in the later fifteenth century. In 1516, Francis I, recently victorious at Marignano (1515) and for a time the dominant figure in Italy, came to terms with Pope Leo X in the* Concordat of Bologna (B), *in form a grant by the pope, which abrogated the Pragmatic Sanction and put the French Church under a codominium of pope and king in which the latter predominated.[33]*

[32] Translated from *Ordonnances des Rois de France de la troisième race* (Paris, 1782), p. 274.

[33] Translated from *Ordonnances des Rois de France: Règne de François I* (Paris, 1902), Vol. 1, pp. 441 ff.

## A. PRAGMATIC SANCTION OF BOURGES

[This Assembly also accepts] a fourth decree, beginning: "Furthermore, this holy Council [of Basel], having abolished the general reservation of all elective benefices and dignities, has recently decreed that provision to the aforesaid benefices and dignities shall be by canonical election and confirmation. It was its will also to prohibit special or particular reservation of the same elective benefices and dignities by which the free power of electing and confirming to them might be impeded, and that the pope of Rome attempt nothing contrary to this order except for a weighty, reasonable and evident cause to be expressly stated in his apostolic letters. Yet not a few contraventions of the tenor of this same decree, there being no such cause of exception, have taken place, whereby grave scandals have already occurred and graver yet, it is feared, may occur in the future. This Council, desirous to prevent these and determined that the purpose of that decree (which was to remove every hindrance from canonical elections and confirmations) shall not be frustrated, has ordered that elections to the said benefices shall be held without impediment or obstacle of any kind whatsoever, and that after notification had they shall be confirmed according to the meaning of the common law [of the Church] and of our said decree. However, if it should some time happen that some election be held which, though otherwise canonical, may, it is feared, lead to a disturbance in the Church or state or the public weal, the pope, having received the application for confirmation, may, if he knows the case to be extremely urgent, after thorough discussion and full defense made by the party, and with the signed assistance of the cardinals of the Church of Rome . . . reject such an election and remit it to the chapter or convent, in order that they may proceed to another election from which such consequences are not to be feared, within the time fixed by the law, or otherwise according to the distance of the place."

However, the aforesaid Assembly [of Bourges] holds that the pope shall be compelled to send any person (to be promoted, as stated above, by himself or by his authority) back to that person's immediate superior, to receive there his consecration and blessing, unless the said person so promoted is present in the Court [of Rome] and wants to be consecrated there. Notwithstanding which, he shall send back to their immediate superiors all persons consecrated or blessed in the Court of Rome, so that they may render to these superiors, or in their absence to their vicars, the oath of due obedience. If anyone presumes to receive consecration or blessing outside that Court, even by force of an apostolic commission, from someone other than his immediate superior or by that superior's authority, he shall be fined 100 ducats to the use of the ordinary [34] and the fabric of that ordinary's church, any dispensations to the contrary whatsoever being void. Also: this assembly does not think it will be improper if the king and the princes of his realm, avoiding all threats or violence of any sort, occasionally intervene with gentle and well intentioned requests, on behalf of deserving persons zealous for the good of the commonwealth. . . .

## B. CONCORDAT OF BOLOGNA

And the elections which for many years have taken place in churches, cathedrals and metropolitan sees have been the cause of grave perils to souls. Many have been decided by the interference of the secular power; some others by unlawful precedents and simoniac practices; others again by special favor and the ties of blood. Nor has the crime of perjury been absent, for though the electors, having been instructed before the election to procure a more suitable choice and one not influenced by the promise or gift of any temporal thing, or by their own or anyone else's prayer or prayers, have sworn to make a free choice, they have not observed their oath but have, to the prejudice of their souls, proceeded contrary to it. This we well know from the frequent absolutions and rehabilitations requested and obtained from us and our predecessors. Thus the same King Francis, ready like a good and obedient son to give heed to our paternal warning, has accepted . . . the laws and constitutions recited below, in place of the said Pragmatic Sanction, both for the promotion of obedience, in which there is in truth great merit, and for the common and public weal of his kingdom. . . .

We order and decree from henceforth, for all future times, in place of the said Pragmatic Constitution and all and singular chapters contained in it, as follows. In future, when any cathedrals or metropolitan sees in the said kingdom . . . shall be vacant . . . their chapters and canons shall not be entitled to proceed to the election or preelection of a new prelate there. But when such a vacancy occurs, the king of France for the time being shall within six months reckoned from the day of the vacation of the same churches nominate to us and our successors as popes of Rome, or to the aforesaid Holy See, one worthy master or licentiate in theology, or a doctor of both or either laws, or a licentiate in a reputable university employing a proper standard of examinations, which nominee shall have attained the age of 27 years at least and is otherwise suitable. And the person so nominated by the

---

[34] the head of the ecclesiastical organization within which the benefice is situated

king shall be provided [35] by us and our successors, or by the said Holy See. And if the aforesaid king should happen to nominate for such a vacant living a person not so qualified, we and our successors, or the Holy See, shall in no way be obliged to provide a person so nominated to the same sees. But within three months after the refusal of an unqualified person has been intimated in the proper form to the [French king's] agent responsible for making the nomination, the king shall be bound to nominate another candidate qualified as set out above. Failing which, in consideration of the need to proceed quickly in such burdensome cases of vacancy, we and our successors, or the Holy See, shall be free to provide a person qualified as stated; and shall always be able to do so in the case of vacancies occurring through death at the Court of Rome, without nomination by the king. . . .

# 10 / HERESY IN THE NETHERLANDS

*The territories united in the fifteenth century by the Valois dukes of Burgundy provided in the later middle ages fertile ground for various forms of deviation from the official religion of the Church. Some of it was peaceful and rather noble, some wild and barely sane, some distinctly subversive and even professedly revolutionary; but all of it derived from a desire to substitute a personal experience of God for the formal exercises of the Church. At their most extreme (A), sectaries refused earthly authority on the ground that they had been saved by the Holy Spirit within themselves. This, they claimed, had freed them from all law except that of their own liberated will. (One should, however, note that this extract embodies charges brought by their enemies that should not necessarily be taken at face value. Still, the evidence is strong that many such Brethren held to total sexual freedom and general license.) The sectaries' inclination to extreme views and licentious behavior accounts for the authorities' pursuit of even the more harmless brands. The experiences of the fifteenth century played their part in the persecutions of the early sixteenth century as the Reformation came to reinvigorate native dissent; but what made attitudes more inflexible was not any success the*

---

[35] i.e., appointed by papal letter

*sects might have had so much as the arrival of Habsburg rule and especially the arrival of the Archduke Charles (later the Emperor Charles V), who meant to enforce orthodoxy ruthlessly (B). His methods proved too much at times, even for local conformists. However, as the Reformation spread, Charles's extremism gained more support.[36]*

## A. A SECT OF THE FREE SPIRIT (c. 1450)

The adherents of the underwritten sect or heretical perversion call one another "people of the knowledge." [37] They have two leaders from whom the infection has spread to their various members. One of the said leaders is called Brother William of Hildernes, a friar carmelite. The other is an illiterate layman, about sixty years of age, called Giles the Cantor, who regards himself as superior to the said Brother William; some of the sect agree with this, while some prefer William.

1. The said lay traducer has said several times to several audiences: I am the saviour of men, and through me they shall see Christ, and through Christ they shall see the Father.

2. He has said that the devil shall in the end be saved, but that then he will be no devil—proud Lucifer shall be humble, and at the last all men shall be saved.

3. The devil did not carry the Lord Jesus to the pinnacle of the temple.

4. The said Giles has said that as he was going along the road the Holy Spirit whispered these words to him, "thou art rendered in the state of a three-year-old boy; don't fast, but eat tripe in Lent." Which he has done, with others of his sectaries, male and female. . . .

5. They pay no heed to the laws, precepts and ordinances of the Church nor to prayer, saying that God does what he has resolved to do and what he wills, and that there is no need of prayer.

6. They ignore confession. But solely to avoid trouble they sometimes present themselves to a priest, confessing a few things venial in themselves and keeping silence about criminal acts of lechery and other mortal sins which would convict them of breaches of the faith, as other people report of them.

7. They will admit no serious penance, holding that we have no need of such.

8. There is one among the women of that sect who will not allow

---

[36] Translated from *Corpus Documentorum Inquisitionis hereticae pravitatis Neerlandicae*, ed. P. Fredericq (Brussels, 1889), i. 217–3, 516–7.

[37] "homines intelligentiae," meaning those who had a special and secret understanding of the power of the "free spirit" to save men

herself to be known by any man. For which reason she suffers much molestation from members of the sect of both sexes who upbraid her for not using sexual intercourse.

9. The said Giles practises a special form of the sex act (though not contrary to nature) which he says was used by Adam in paradise. The foresaid Brother William does not follow this practice.

10. Inventing private expressions among themselves, they call sexual intercourse "the joys of paradise" or "climbing." And so they freely converse of that lustful act without other people understanding what they are talking about.

11. An old woman whom the said layman has named Seraphim has stated publicly that the sex act is permitted outside marriage without taint of sin: the act (she says) is simply natural, like eating and drinking. And yet (she says) that act is frowned upon and not those others; for which reason she marvels with others at the blindness of people who will hold these common opinions.

12. There is a married woman who makes no distinction between one man and another but indifferently admits anybody according to their time and place. And this is quite common among their women.

13. The said Brother William has no respect for anybody unless they engage in sexual intercourse without fear of God or scruple of conscience.

14. Brother William holds that all their actions can be justified or coloured by Holy Scripture, except intercourse condemned by the Church. And therefore he has been in the habit of warning his followers to be careful in speaking of illicit sexual relationships.

15. The aforesaid Seraphim, hearing others say that Brother William had been forced to recant his preaching, answered that so far from recanting he asserted "I didn't say this, but that," adding and subtracting in the text of his sermon; and thus he escaped scot free. For which reason he has the reputation of having confirmed his sayings rather than withdrawn them.

16. They rest all their deeds, even the most nefarious, on the will of God, saying that God wills such things. . . .

17. Outside the walls of Brussels there is a tower belonging to a bailiff of the town where they meet to hold their gatherings.

18. They say that the time of the old law was the time of the Father, and the time of the new law the time of the Son, and now is the time of the Holy Spirit. . . . What before this has been thought true will now be rejected, including Catholic doctrine, as for instance the Catholic verities which have used to be preached touching poverty, chastity and obedience. The opposite of these verities, they maintain, must be preached in this present time of the Holy Spirit.

19. Whatever comes into their minds or suggests itself to them, they hold it proceeds from the Holy Spirit. For which reason the oft-men-

tioned layman has done some pretty stupid things. After one such "inspiration" he went for a long walk, totally naked, carrying on his head a dish with meat in it to give to some poor man.

20. They marvel that some people should cross themselves, demanding "Do you still require blessing?"

21. The adherents of the sect, and especially the women, have persuaded some upright men to cease in future from preaching chastity and virginity and from recommending continence—asserting that there is no virgin except one, who, they say, is Wisdom.

22. Touching purgatory, they hold contrary to the Church. Similarly, touching hell. And they have a singular and contrived way of speaking of that matter.

## B. PERSECUTION

Where by our letters in form of a proclamation we have caused it to be published and announced that no one shall venture to swear and blaspheme by the name of God and that of God's glorious mother, the Virgin Mary, under pains and fines contained and declared in our said other letters: [38] Nevertheless we hear that no efforts have been made to punish such. And it might seem that the judges and men of the law have put off and are putting off proceeding to their punishment under the pretence that the said penalties are too rigorous and excessive; by which means the said blaspheming continues more and more, to the great contempt of God's name and our catholic faith; and so it will further be if we do not proceed otherwise.

For which reason, We (these matters considered), anxious to root out these blasphemies and cause them to cease, give you express commandment that incontinent and without delay you cause to be again published and proclaimed as on our behalf throughout all our land and county of Flanders, wherever it is customary to make and cry such proclamation, that all persons of whatsoever estate or condition shall take care to avoid blaspheming the name of God and of his glorious Virgin Mother, on pain of forfeiting, on the first occasion, 60 pence at 2 groats' value Flemish; for a second time, double; for a third time, three times that fine with six whole days' imprisonment on bread and water; for the fourth time he shall be put in the pillory in some public place for the space of at least two hours. Proceeding and causing to proceed against transgressors and wrongdoers by the execution of the said penalties rigorously and without partiality, favour or dissimulation. . . .

[38] The earlier letter of November 30, 1517 (ibid., pp. 513–4) had decreed these penalties: first offence—fine at the judge's discretion; second offence—pillory and boring of tongue; third offence—whipping and exile.

# 11 / RICHARD ROLLE
# (C. 1300-1349):
# THE FIRE OF LOVE

*The most influential of the English fourteenth-century mystics, Richard Rolle was a Yorkshireman who, after trying both the study and the cloister, found that he could best satisfy his spiritual longings by living as a hermit. However, he led a productive literary life. His teaching was that the soul comes to true knowledge of God in a mystical union achieved by that complete surrender to the Divine Being which he called love. He was also active as a spiritual adviser, especially to nuns.*[39]

### CHAPTER 5

In all our actions and thoughts let us give greater weight to divine love than to learning and argument. For love delights the soul and sweetens the conscience, drawing it away from the attraction of lesser delights and the appetite for personal distinction. Learning without charity contributes nothing to eternal salvation but blows a man up to miserable perdition. May our spirit therefore be strong in taking upon itself hard labors for God; may it be wise with heavenly wisdom, not with that of the world; may it yearn to glow with wisdom eternal and to burn with that sweet flame which excites man to love and desire solely his Maker and be given powerful strength to despise all transitory things. Thus [the soul] puts away trust in the solace of things which do not endure, as one having there no dwelling place, but incessantly seeks that place to come which is not made by hands, and cries "For me to live is Christ and to die is gain" (Phil. 1.21).

### CHAPTER 13

There have been some men, and perhaps they still exist, who altogether prefer the communal to the solitary life; they hold that we must run in crowds if we desire to reach the highest perfection. One cannot seriously argue with such men because they praise only that kind of life which they would wish to follow or at least have known a little.

[39] Translated from Richard Rolle, *Incendium Amoris*, ed. M. Deanesley (Manchester: Manchester University Press, 1915). By permission of Manchester University Press.

They fail to praise the solitary life simply because they do not know it. For it is a life which no one living in the flesh can know except he to whom God grants that he live it, and no one assuredly judges rightly of this matter who remains uncertain what it is and how it works. I know beyond doubt that if they knew it they would praise it more to others. Others err more dangerously by unceasingly denouncing and slandering the solitary life. They say, "Woe to the solitary," meaning not only "man without God" but "man without fellows." For he is alone with whom God is not. When he shall fall into death he shall at once be taken to the torments and shall for ever be cut off from the sight of God's glory and the saints'. Indeed, he who chooses the solitary life for God and lives it rightly shall be full not of "Woe" but of "Wonderful Virtue" and shall continuously delight in thinking of the name of Jesus.

## CHAPTER 38

With an indissoluble knot, I bind thy love within me, sweet Jesus, seeking the treasure which I covet; and I experience a permanent longing because I cannot cease to think of thee. And thus, my sorrow vanishes like the wind, for my reward is a melody which no man perceives; my inner nature turns into most sweet song and I long to die for love. . . .

In the rational soul love works in such fashion that whether it be good or bad shall be judged from its own nature. Nothing is so effective in gaining the joy of eternity as the love of Christ, nor does anything more certainly lead to the last damnation than love of the world. Therefore let love of the eternal inflame our minds, and let the vicious and hateful delight of carnal desires be driven far away. May the glory of heavenly life enrapture us so that we no longer want to delight in the bitter sweetness of the present life. . . . So, if ever evil or unclean thoughts shake their spirits and by force wish to enter, the chosen who burn with divine love to the depth of their being and inseparably adhere to Christ, look up to heaven and at once throw off and smother with the ardor of their devotion [all such thoughts]. . . . For he who burns with perfect charity feels neither sin nor wicked delight, but exults more greatly in his God, and neither anger nor uncleanness can make him sad.

## CHAPTER 42

No sweeter delight I know, O beloved Jesus, than to sing to thee in my heart a song of thy praise. I know no better and more abundant happiness than to feel in my mind the sweet ardor of love. Of all things I think it best to set Jesus in my heart and to wish for absolutely nothing else. . . . Come, my Savior, and solace my soul! Make me firm in love that I may never cease to love. Abolish sorrow when I must depart, for there is no sinner who shall not be able to rejoice if he is truly turned to thee. . . . In the beginning of my conversion and my singular intent I thought I wanted to be like a little bird that languishes for the love of its beloved but even in languishing is gladdened by the coming of him whom he loves; and in his joy he sings, languishing even in his song but in sweetness and ardor. . . . Fainting I shall be restored and nourished with love. . . . O good Jesus, thou hast bound my heart in the contemplation of thy name and now I have no strength to sing it. Therefore take pity upon me and finish what thou hast begun.

# 12 / THOMAS A KEMPIS (C. 1380-1471): THE IMITATION OF CHRIST

*The authorship of this famous book is not quite certain, but best opinion inclines to ascribe it to Thomas, a monk at Zwolle in the Netherlands and a follower of the Flemish mystic and teacher Gerhard Groot (1340–84), at whose Deventer school he taught for a while. Thomas' long life was spent in writing and devotion; he was a thoroughly unworldly man of great charm and simplicity. This Dutch mysticism (Brethren of the Common Life, devotio moderna) lacked the intellectual intensity which distinguished the German, English, and later Spanish kinds. The* Imitation *both recorded a private search for God and instructed in the way there; it was one of the most successful and influential works ever written, appearing in six thousand editions. An English translation appeared in 1517, in which the fourth book, dealing with the sacraments, was translated by Lady Margaret Beaufort, mother of King Henry VII; that translation is used here.*

## BOOK 4, CHAPTER 2

O my God, I come unto thee, putting my confidence in thy mercy and bounty. I [am] sick and come unto my Saviour; hungry and thirsty, unto the fountain of life; poor and needy, unto the King of Heaven; the servant unto his lord; the creature unto his maker; the person desolate unto his piteous comforter. But whereof is this that thou comest unto me? Who am I that thou wilt thus give thine own self to? How dare I, a sinner, behold to appear before thee? And how may it please thee to come unto such a wretch? Thou knowest thy servant and well understandest that nothing good is in him. Wherefore shouldst thou do this grace unto me? Then I confess mine unworthiness and acknowledge thy bounty and praise thy charity. Thou dost this for thyself, good Lord, and not for my merit, to the end that thy bounty may the more be known unto me. Thy charity is more largely verified and thy meekness commended more perfectly, since that it thus pleases thee, and so thou hast commanded it to be done. This thy pleasure contents me, and with my will my wickedness shall not resist thee.

O sweet and benign Jesus! How great reverence and giving [of] thanks with perpetual praises be due unto thee, my good Lord Jesus Christ, that by thy pleasure and will I may receive thy blessed body. Whose worthiness no man is found able to declare or express. But what shall I think of this communion when I shall come unto thee, my Lord God, which I cannot duly honour? And yet I desire devoutly to receive thee. What may I think better and more profitable for me than to make myself holy before thee and to praise thy infinite bounty above all things. I praise thee, my Lord God, everlastingly, and dispraise and submit me unto the deepness of my wretchedness. O my God, thou art saint of all saints, and I the filth of all sinners; yet thou inclinest thyself unto me that am not worthy to behold thee.

Alas my sweet creature that so meekly comest unto me, and willest to be with me, and desirest me unto thy dinner, and givest unto me the meat of heaven and the bread of angels, which is bread of life, and no less thing than thyself which is descended from heaven and gave life to the world. Let me see here what great love proceeds from thee and what gentleness does shine upon us. . . . Thou Lord of all hast no need of anything, yet thou hast willed to inhabit within us by this thy holy sacrament. . . .

O my soul, rejoice and give thanks unto thy God for his noble gift and singular comfort, that it list him here in this vale of tears thus to comfort thee. For as oftentimes as thou rememberest this mystery and receivest thus the blessed body of our Lord: so often thou receivest the work of thy redemption and art made partner of all the merits of our Lord Jesus Christ. . . .

# II / THE HUNDRED YEARS' WAR AND CHIVALRY

*From 1338 to 1453 the history of Western Europe was dominated by the intermittent war between France and England. The conflict at times drew in others, especially the Spanish kingdoms, the territories of the Netherlands, and Burgundy. Ostensibly arising out of the English monarchy's claim to the French crown, it was in fact a war for territory, for economic advantage, and above all for national and chivalric prestige. It brought ruin to France, but a good deal of prosperity to England through ransoms and booty. It consolidated national feeling on both sides of the English Channel and prepared opinion for the emergence of powerful nation states, though in England one existed even before the outbreak of war. It first destroyed, but finally promoted, the power of the Valois monarchy; it assisted the emergence of Burgundy as a great power (for this, see also No. 32); in England its disastrous conclusion, after many successes, led directly to the collapse of the Plantagenet dynasty in the civil war from which the House of Tudor emerged as victor and national savior (1485). Those 115 years saw many changes in the art of war: gunpowder came to be more widely used, infantry and missile weapons established an acknowledged superiority over the heavily armed and lumberingly mounted knight, the prevalence of siege warfare increased skill in fortifications.*

*Nevertheless, in the realm of ideas the astonishing thing is that this long and sordid war, so full of misery and trickery, should have been seen by many, both participants and onlookers, as the embodied reality of chivalry. The aristocracies of all the countries involved, trained for war and little else, eagerly welcomed each renewal not only because it might bring wealth, but mainly be-*

*cause it would give them the chance of glory. Chroniclers wrote it up in the spirit of the modern movie magazine: here at last were the real heroes to set beside the legendary giants of King Arthur and the rest. The trappings of chivalry grew ever more wonderful and more admired, although reality quite evidently had parted company with them. This was the age when orders of knighthood, in conscious imitation of the Round Table, were founded by princes whose political actions proved that they recognized less heroic and less childish criteria (the English Garter in 1346, the Burgundian Golden Fleece in 1430). But one must not overplay the obvious irony of the contrast. Not only was the whole code and notion of chivalry a way of providing standards of behavior and manners which did something to soften the horrors of war; but no interpretation of the period or its leading personalities will come near the historical truth if it forgets that knighthood was to them a much more real and much more obvious concern than the economic considerations and dynastic preoccupations which modern historians quite rightly recognize.*

# 13 / JOHN FROISSART (1338-1410?): THE BATTLE OF CRECY (1346)

*The chronicler of the Hundred Years' War was born at Valenciennes in the Walloon parts of the Low Countries, of burgher stock. It is clear that from an early age he was captivated by the glamor of battles and chivalry, and he spent his life in traveling all over Western Europe, from Gascony to Scotland, collecting materials for his voluminous History. Besides his passionate interest in the life and habits of a class not his own, he displays commendable accuracy in reporting and splendid skill in describing. The English victory at Crecy led directly to the capture of Calais, a town which was to remain in English hands for over two hundred years, and established the fame of Edward III, his son the Black Prince, and the English archers.*[1]

The Englishmen who were in three battles,[2] lying on the ground to rest them, as soon as they saw the Frenchmen approach they rose upon their feet, fair and easily without any haste, and arranged their battles. The first, which was the prince's [3] battle, the archers there stood in manner of a hearse and the men at arms in the bottom of the battle. The earl of Northampton and the earl of Arundel with the second battle were on a wing in good order, ready to comfort the prince's battle, if need were. The lords and knights of France came not to the assembly together in good order, for some came before and some came after, in such haste and evil order that one of them did trouble another. When the French king saw the Englishmen, his blood changed, and [he] said to his marshals, "Make the Genoese go on before, and begin the battle in the name of God and St. Denis." There were of the Genoese crossbows about 15,000, but they were so weary of going on foot that day a six leagues armed with their crossbows that they said to their constables, "We be not well ordered to fight this day, for we be not in the case to do any great deed of arms, we have more need of rest." These words came to the earl of Alençon who said, "A man is well at ease to be charged with such a sort of rascals, to be faint and fail now at most need." Also the same season there fell a great rain . . . with a terrible thunder, and before the rain there came flying over both battles a great number of crows, for fear of the tempest coming. Then anon the air began to wax clear and the sun to shine fair and bright, the which was right in the Frenchmen's eyes and on the Englishmen's backs.

When the Genoese were assembled together and began to approach, they made a great leap and cry to abash the Englishmen, but they stood still and stirred not for all that. Then the Genoese again the second time made another leap and a fell [4] cry and stepped forward a little, and the Englishmen removed not a foot. Thirdly again they leapt and cried and went forth till they came within shot; then they shot fiercely with their crossbows. Then the English archers stepped forth one pace and let fly their arrows so wholly and so thick that it seemed snow. When the Genoese felt the arrows piercing through

---

[1] From Froissart's *Chronicle,* translated by Lord Berners in 1525 and edited by W. P. Ker, Tudor Translations (London, 1901), Chapter 130.

[2] divisions

[3] Edward, Prince of Wales (the Black Prince)

[4] dreadful

heads, arms and breasts, many of them cast down their crossbows and did cut their strings, and returned discomfited. When the French king saw them fly away he said, "Slay the rascals, for they shall let [5] and trouble us without reason." Then you should have seen the men-at-arms dash in among them, and killed a great number of them; and ever still the Englishmen shot whereas they saw the thickest press. The sharp arrows ran into the men-at-arms and into their horses, and many fell, horse and men, among the Genoese, and when they were down they could not relieve [6] again; the press was so thick that one overthrew another. And also among the Englishmen there were certain rascals that went on foot with great knives, and they went in among the men-at-arms and slew and murdered many as they lay on the ground, both earls, barons, knights and squires, whereof the king of England was after displeased, for he had rather they had been taken prisoners.

The valiant king of Bohemia, called Charles [7] of Luxemburg, son to the noble emperor Henry of Luxemburg,[8] for all that he was nigh blind, when he understood the order of the battle, he said to them about him, "Where is the lord Charles, my son?" His men said, "Sir, we cannot tell, we think he be fighting." Then he said, "Sirs, you are my men, my companions and friends in this journey, I require you to bring me so far forward that I may strike one stroke with my sword." They said they would do his commandment, and to the intent that they should not lose him in the press they tied all their reins of their bridles each to other and set the king before to accomplish his desire; and so they went on their enemies. The lord Charles of Bohemia, who wrote himself king of Almain [9] and bore the arms, he came in good order to the battle; but when he saw that the matter went awry on their part he departed, I cannot tell you which way. The king his father was so far forward that he struck a stroke with his sword, yea and more than four, and fought valiantly and so did his company; and they adventured themselves so forward that they were all slain, and the next day they were found in the place about the king, and all their horses tied each to other.

The earl of Alençon came to the battle right ordinately [10] and fought with the Englishmen; and the earl of Flanders also on his part; these two lords with their companies coasted [11] the English archers and

[5] hinder
[6] rise
[7] correctly John
[8] the Emperor Henry VII (1269–1313)
[9] later the Emperor Charles IV (1316–78). Almain is Germany.
[10] orderly
[11] passed by

came to the prince's battle and there fought valiantly long. The French king would fain have come thither when he saw their banners, but there was a great hedge of archers before him. The same day the French king had given a great black courser to Sir John of Hainault, and he made the Lord John of Senzeille to ride on him and to bear his banner. The same horse took the bridle in the teeth and brought him through all the curriers [12] of the Englishmen, and as he would have returned again he fell in a great ditch and was sore hurt and had been there dead, an [13] his page had not been who followed him through all the battles and saw where his master lay in the ditch, and had none other let [14] but for his horse; for the Englishmen would not issue out of their battle for taking of any prisoner. Then the page alighted and relieved his master; then he went not back again the same way that they came, there was too many in his way.

This battle between Brois and Crecy this Saturday was right cruel and fell, and many a feat of arms done that came not to my knowledge. In the night diverse knights and squires lost their masters and sometimes came on the Englishmen who received them in such wise that they were ever nigh slain, for there was none taken to mercy nor to ransom; for so the Englishmen were determined. In the morning [of] the day of the battle certain Frenchmen and Almains perforce opened the archers of the prince's battle and came and fought with the men-at-arms hand to hand. Then the second battle of the Englishmen came to succour the prince's battle, the which was time, for they had then much ado; and they with the prince sent a messenger to the king who was on a little windmill hill. Then the knight said to the king, "Sir, the earl of Warwick and the earl of Oxford, Sir Reginald Cobham and other, such as be about the prince your son, are fiercely fought withal and are sore handled; wherefore they desire you that you and your battle will come and aid them; for if the Frenchmen increase, as they doubt [15] they will, your son and they shall have much ado." Then the king said, "Is my son dead or hurt, or on the earth felled?" "No," quoth the knight, "but he is hardily matched, wherefore he has need of your aid." "Well," said the king, "return to him and to them that sent you hither, and say to them that they send no more to me for any adventure that falls [16] as long as my son is alive; and also say to them that they suffer him this day to win his spurs; for if God be pleased, I will this journey be his and the honour thereof, and to them that be about him." Then the knight returned again to them and

12 ranks
13 if
14 obstacle
15 expect
16 no matter what may happen

showed them the king's words, the which greatly encouraged them, and repined in that they had sent to the king as they did.

Sir Geoffrey of Harcourt would gladly that the earl of Harcourt, his brother, might have been saved; for he heard say by them that saw his banner how that he was there in the field on the French party, but Sir Geoffrey could not come to him betimes, for he was slain or [17] he could come at him; and so also was the earl of Aumâle, his nephew. In another place the earl of Alençon and the earl of Flanders fought valiantly, every lord under his own banner; but finally they could not resist against the puissance [18] of the Englishmen, and so there they were also slain and divers other knights and squires. Also the earl Louis of Blois, nephew to the French king, and the duke of Lorraine fought under their banners; but at last they were closed in among a company of Englishmen and Welshmen, and there were slain, for all their prowess. Also there was slain the earl of Ausser, the earl of St. Pole, and many other.

In the evening the French king, who had left about him no more than a threescore persons, one and other, whereof Sir John of Hainault was one who had remounted once the king, for [the king's] horse was slain with an arrow. Then he said to the king, "Sir, depart hence, for it is time; lose not yourself wilfully; if you have loss at this time, you shall recover it again another season." And so he took the king's horse by the birdle and led him away in a manner perforce. Then the king rode till he came to the castle of Brois. The gate was closed because it was by that time dark. Then the king called the captain who came to the walls and said, "Who is that calls there this time of night?" Then the king said "Open your gate quickly, for this is the fortune of France." The captain knew then it was the king and opened the gate and let down the bridge. Then the king entered, and he had with him but five barons—Sir John of Hainault, Sir Charles of Montmorency, the lord of Beaujeu, the lord D'Aubigny, and the lord of Montfort. The king would not tarry there, but drank and departed thence about midnight and so rode by such guides as knew the country, till he came in the morning to Amiens, and there he rested. This Saturday the Englishmen never departed from their battles for chasing of any man, but kept still their field, and ever defended themselves against all such as came to assail them. This battle ended about evensong time.

[17] before
[18] might

# 14 / TRIAL OF JEANNE D'ARC (1412-1431)

*The story of the peasant girl who was urged by the voices of saints to take up arms and drive the English from France is sufficiently well known, as is her triumph at Orleans. Captured at Compiègne in 1431, handed over to the English, deserted by the king of France whom she had virtually made, and tried for heresy and witchcraft by a commission presided over by an enemy (Pierre Cauchon, bishop of Beauvais), she was condemned and burned, only to be rehabilitated in 1456 and sainted in 1920. The record of her trial illumines her own character and tells much of that of the age; many, even among her own side, doubted whether her inspiration might not be from the devil and felt that her insistence on wearing men's clothes and armor somehow proved her a witch. A is from the preliminary interrogation, B from the Articles of Accusation.*[19]

## A. PRELIMINARY INTERROGATION

She also says that the aforesaid English shall have a greater loss than ever they had in France, and that this will be by a great victory which God will send the French.

Asked how she came to know this, answers: "I know this well by the revelation made to me, and that it will happen within seven years; and I should be well angry if it were to take so long." She also said that she knew this revelation as well as she knew that we were there in front of her.

Asked when it would happen, answers that she knows neither the day nor the hour. . . .

Asked by whose means she thus knew the future, answers that she knows it from St. Catherine and St. Margaret.

Asked if St. Gabriel was with St. Michael when he came to her, answers that she does not remember. . . .

Asked if she always sees them in the same dress, answers that she always sees them in the same shape and that their figures are most resplendently crowned. Of other garments she speaks not. Also she says that she knows nothing of their mantles.

[19] Translated from *Procès de condamnation de Jeanne d'Arc*, ed. P. Champion (Paris: Librairie Honoré Champion, 1920–1), Vol. 1, pp. 63–7, 169–78.

Asked how she knows whether the apparition be a man or a woman, answers that she well knows and recognises them by their voices and that they had revealed themselves to her; nor does she know anything except by the revelation and direction of God.

Asked what shape she sees there, answers that she sees a face.

Asked if the saintly apparition have hair, answers "That is worth knowing!"

Asked if there was anything between their crowns and their hair, answers no. . . . Also she says that they spoke extremely well and beautifully, and that she understood them easily.

Asked in what manner they spoke, having no organs, answers: "I refer myself to God." She also says that their voices are beautiful, sweet and low, and that they speak in French.

Asked if St. Margaret did not speak in English, answers: "Why should she speak English since she does not come from England?"

Asked if the aforesaid crowned heads had rings in their ears or elsewhere, answers "I do not know about that."

Asked if she, the same Joan, had certain rings, answers, speaking to us the aforesaid bishop: "You have one of mine; give it back to me." She also says that the Burgundians have another ring. And asked us, if we had the said ring, to show it to her.

Asked who gave her the ring which the Burgundians have, answers her father or mother: and she thinks that it had the words "Jesus Maria" inscribed; she knows not who caused them to be written there, nor, as she thinks, is there a stone; and the same ring was given her in the village of Domremy. She also says that her brother gave her the other ring which we had and that she charged us to give that one to the Church. She also says that she never healed any person by any of her rings. . . .

Asked if her voice had told her that within three months she should be freed from prison, answers: "That is nothing to do with your process; however, I do not know when I shall be free." And she said that those who wished to remove her from this world could well go ahead of her.

Asked if her counsel had not told her that she would be freed from her present prison, answers: "You keep speaking to me of three months; I shall answer you concerning this." Further she said: "Ask your assessors on oath whether this touches the process."

Later, after consultation with the assesors who all held that it did touch the process, she said: "I have always told you that you shall not know everything." . . .

Asked if her voices forbade her to tell the truth, answers: "Do you want me to tell you what shall happen to the king of France? There are many things there which do not concern the process." She also said that she knew well that her king should win the kingdom of France; and this she knew as well as she knew that we were sitting there before her in judgment. She also said she would have died but for this revelation which daily comforted her.

Asked what she had done with her mandrake, answers that she had none nor ever had; but she had heard it said that there was one near her village, but she never saw one. She also said that she had heard it said that it was a dangerous thing and ill to keep. . . .

Asked in what shape St. Michael was when he appeared to her, answers she saw no crown on him; of his garments she knew nothing.

Asked if he was naked, answers: "Do you think God has not the means to clothe him?"

Asked if he had hair, answers: "Why should it have been cut off?" Also says that she did not see St. Michael after leaving the castle of Crotoy, nor ever saw him after. In the end she says she does not know whether he had hair. . . .

## B. ARTICLES OF ACCUSATION

### II

That the said accused, not only in the present year but from the days of her youth, and not only in your said diocese [of Beauvais] and jurisdiction but also in the adjoining parts in many other and diverse places in this realm, has made, composed, mixed and provided many sorceries and superstitions; she has been deified and has allowed herself to be adored and venerated; she has invoked daemons and malignant spirits, has consulted them, has had converse with them, has entered into pacts, treaties and agreements with them, and has made use of them; to others doing the same she has offered counsel, aid and favor, and has induced them to do such and similar things, by saying, believing, asserting and maintaining that to do so and to believe in such sorceries, prophecies and superstitious acts and to use them is no sin nor forbidden; but rather has asserted that it is permitted, laudable and worthy of commendation; bringing as many persons as possible of varying degree and either sex into these errors and evils, and impressing on their hearts such and similar sayings. . . .

To this second article Joan replies: she denies the charge of sorcery and superstitious acts and prophecy; of the adoration she says that if some people kissed her hands or dress, this did not happen by her will, and moreover she tried to avoid it to the best of her power. The rest of the article she denies. . . .

### IV

And the better and more fully to inform the Court concerning the beforementioned offenses, excesses, crimes and delicts committed, as is alleged, by the said accused . . . it is true that the said accused was born in the village of Greux, her father being Jacques d'Arc and her mother Isabelle, his wife; she was raised in youth till her eighteenth year or thereabouts in the village of Domremy on the Meuse, in the diocese of Toul. . . . Which Joan was in her youth not instructed in true belief and the elements of the faith; but was by some old women accustomed and trained to the use of sorcery, divination and other superstitious works or magic arts; and several inhabitants of those villages are noted of old for using the said evils. And from several people—especially, as the said Joan herself says, from her godmother— she has heard much concerning visions and appearances of certain spirits, vulgarly called fairies, and was also by others instructed and taught in evil and pernicious errors concerning these spirits, so much so that in the process before you she has confessed that to this day she does not know whether these fairies are evil spirits.

To this article she answers that she confesses the first part, that is to say touching her father, mother and birthplace; and as regards the fatal ladies called fairies, she knows not what that might be. With respect to her instruction, she learned the creed and was well and properly taught to do as a good child should do. As concerns her godmother, she refers herself to what she has said elsewhere. . . .

### XII

In order the better and more openly to carry out her purpose, the said Joan demanded . . . men's clothing with the appropriate weapons. . . . The said clothing and weapons having been made and provided, the aforesaid Joan, having rejected and cast off all womanly dress, her hair cut short in a page-cut, put on and armed herself with a shirt, breeches, doublet, single joined hose (long and tied to the doublet by twenty points), high laced shoes, a short tunic reaching to the knees or thereabouts, a docked hat, topboots, long spurs, sword, dagger, hauberk, lance and other weapons, in the manner of men's arms; and with these she did deeds of war, asserting that in this she was fulfilling God's command given to her by revelations and was acting in this in God's cause. . . .

### XIII

The said Joan alleges of God, his angels and saints that they ordered her to do what is contrary to the honesty of the female sex, prohibited by divine law, abominable to God and men, and by the canons of the Church forbidden under pain of excommunication, inasmuch as she dressed up in men's clothing, short, abbreviated and indecent . . . ; and dressed herself in sumptuous and showy garments of fine stuffs and cloth of gold and even furred; and not only in short tunics but also gowns and mantles slit up on either side. . . .

### XIV

And the said Joan maintains that she did well in wearing such like indecent male garments and dress; and means to persist in doing so, saying she will not put them off unless she has express permission from God by revelation. . . .

### XVIII

While the said Joan stayed with King Charles, she used all her powers to dissuade him and his followers from attending any peace negotiations or conferences with his enemies, always inciting them to killing and the shedding of human blood; asserting that peace could only be gained by the stroke of lance or sword, and that this was so appointed by God because the king's enemies would not otherwise surrender the parts of the realm which they occupied: whom so to overcome in battle was, she said, one of the great benefits that could come to all Christendom.

To this Joan answers: as regards the duke of Burgundy, she herself asked him by letter and through his ambassadors that peace be made between the king and the said duke, as regards the English, the peace which had to be was bound up with their going home to England. . . .

### XXII

[Joan's letter sent to the English during the siege of Orleans, included in the indictment against her] "King of England, and you, duke of Bedford who call yourself regent of France; you, William de la Pole, earl of Suffolk, John Talbot, and Thomas Lord Scales, calling yourselves lieutenants of the said duke of Bedford; give ear to the King of Heaven. Render to the Maid, who is sent here by God, the

King of Heaven, the keys of all the fair towns which you have taken and violated in France. She is come here in God's cause to reclaim the blood royal. She is quite ready to make peace if you will see reason, provided you leave France and pay for that which you have taken. And as for you, archers, men-at-arms, gentlemen and others who lie before the city of Orleans, go with God to your country; and if you will not do so, listen to news of the Maid who will shortly come to see you, to your great ruin. King of England, if you do not do this, I am captain of the wars, and wherever I shall find your people in France I shall make them to go, whether they like it or not; and if they will not obey I shall cause them to be killed. I am sent here by God, the King of Heaven, body for body, to throw you out of all France. . . ."

# 15 / WILLIAM CAXTON (C. 1422-1491): THE ORDER OF CHIVALRY (1484)

*Caxton, who introduced printing into England, spent the last twenty-five years of his life in putting out works of religion, instruction and entertainment, many of which he translated himself. He usually found room in his editions for expressing views of his own. The Order of Chivalry, Caxton's epilogue to which is given here, was a French book describing the duties, ceremonies and circumstances of a knight's way of life.[20]*

Here ends the book of *The Order of Chivalry;* which book is translated out of French into English at a request of a gentle and noble esquire by me, William Caxton, dwelling in Westminster beside London, in the most best wise that God has suffered me, and according to the copy that the said squire delivered to me. Which book is not requisite to every common man to have, but to noble gentlemen that by their virtue intend to come and enter into the noble order of chivalry, the which in these late days has been used according to this book

[20] From *The Prologues and Epilogues of William Caxton,* ed. W. J. B. Crotch (London: Early English Text Society, 1928), pp. 82–4. Reprinted by permission of Early English Text Society and Oxford University Press.

heretofore written but forgotten, and the exercises of chivalry not used, honoured, nor exercised as it has been in ancient time; at which time the noble acts of the knights of England that used chivalry were renowned through the universal world. As, for to speak before the incarnation of Jesus Christ, where were there ever any like to Brennius and Belinus [21] that from the Great Britain now called England, unto Rome and far beyond, conquered many realms and lands? Whose noble acts remain in the old histories of the Romans. And since the Incarnation of our Lord, behold that noble king of Britain, King Arthur, with all the noble knights of the Round Table, whose noble acts and noble chivalry of his knights occupy so many large volumes that [it] is [as] a world or as a thing incredible to believe.

Oh, ye knights of England, where is the custom and usage of noble chivalry that was used in the days? What do ye now but go to the bains [22] and play at dice? And some, not well advised, use not honest and good rule, against all order of knighthood. Leave this, leave it, and read the noble volumes of Saint Grail, of Lancelot, of Galahad, of Tristram, of Perceforest, of Parsival, of Gawain, and many more. There ye shall see manhood, courtesy, [23] gentleness. [24] And look in later days of the noble acts since the Conquest, as in King Richard's days, Coeur de Lion; Edward I and III and his noble sons; Sir Robert Knowllys, Sir John Hawkwood, Sir John Chandos, and Sir Gaultier Manuy—read Froissart! And also behold that victorious and noble king, Harry the Fifth, and the captains under him—his noble brethren, the earl of Salisbury, Montague, and many others whose names shine gloriously by their virtuous noblesse and acts that they did in honour of the order of chivalry. Alas, what do ye but sleep and take ease, and are all disordered from chivalry. I would demand a question, if I should not displease: how many knights be there now in England that have the use and the exercise of a knight? That is to wit, that he knows his horse and his horse him, that is to say, he being ready at a point to have all things that belong to a knight, a horse that is according and broken after his hand, his armour and harness meet and fitting, and so forth, etc. I suppose, an [25] a due search should be made, there should be many found that lack. The more pity [it] is. I would it pleased our sovereign lord that twice or thrice a year, or at the least once, he would do cry jousts of peace, [26] to the end that every knight should have horse and harness, and also the use and craft of a knight;

[21] legendary heroes
[22] baths
[23] courtly behaviour
[24] gentility
[25] if
[26] arrange tournaments

and also to tourney one against one, or two against two, and the best to have a prize, a diamond or jewel such as should please the prince. This should cause gentlemen to resort to the ancient customs of chivalry to great fame and renown. And also to be always ready to serve their prince when he shall call them or have need. Then let every man that is come of noble blood and intends to come to the noble order of chivalry read this little book, and do thereafter in keeping the lore and commandments therein comprised. . . .

# 16 / COMMENT: JOHAN HUIZINGA (1872-1945) ON CHIVALRY

*The celebrated Dutch historian specialized in that field of history in which politics, culture, and ideas meet—usually called the history of civilization. His best-known work, from which this passage is taken, is* The Waning of the Middle Ages.[27]

Medieval thought in general was saturated in every part with the conceptions of the Christian faith. In a similar way and in a more limited sphere the thought of all those who lived in the circles of court or castle was impregnated with the idea of chivalry. Their whole system of ideas was permeated by the fiction that chivalry ruled the world. This conception tends to invade the transcendental domain. The primordial feat of arms of the archangel Michael is glorified by Jean Molinet as "the first deed of knighthood and chivalrous prowess that ever was achieved." From the archangel "terrestrial knighthood and human chivalry" take their origin, and in so far are but an imitation of the host of the angels around God's throne.

This illusion of society based on chivalry curiously clashed with the reality of things. The chroniclers themselves, in describing the history of their time, tell us far more of covetousness, of cruelty, of cool calculation, of well-understood selfinterest, and of diplomatic subtlety, than of chivalry. None the less, all, as a rule, profess to write in honour of chivalry, which is the stay of the world. . . . History, to them, is illumined throughout by this their ideal. Later, when writing, they for-

---

[27] Johan Huizinga, *The Waning of the Middle Ages*, trans. F. Hopman (London: Edward Arnold Ltd., 1924), pp. 56–60. Reprinted by permission of Robert Harben.

get it more or less. Froissart, himself the author of a superromantic epic of chivalry, *Meliador,* narrates endless treasons and cruelties, without being aware of the contradiction between his general conceptions and the contents of his narrative. Molinet, in his chronicle, from time to time remembers his chivalrous intention, and interrupts his matter-of-fact account of events, to unbosom himself in a flood of high-flown terms.

The conception of chivalry constituted for these authors a sort of magic key, by the aid of which they explained to themselves the motives of politics and history. The confused image of contemporaneous history being much too complicated for their comprehension, they simplified it, as it were, by the fiction of chivalry as a moving force (not consciously, of course). A very fantastic and rather shallow point of view, no doubt. How much vaster is ours, embracing all sorts of economic and social forces and causes. Still, this vision of a world ruled by chivalry, however superficial and mistaken it might be, was the best they had in the matter of general political ideas. It served them as a formula to understand, in their poor way, the appalling complexity of the world's way. What they saw about them looked primarily mere violence and confusion. War in the fifteenth century tended to be a chronic process of isolated raids and incursions; diplomacy was mostly a very solemn and very verbose procedure, in which a multitude of questions about juridical details clashed with some very general traditions and some points of honour. All notions which might have enabled them to discern in history a social development were lacking to them. Yet they required a form for their political conceptions, and here the idea of chivalry came in. By this traditional fiction they succeeded in explaining to themselves, as well as they could, the motives and the course of history, which was thus reduced to a spectacle of the honour of princes and the virtue of knights, to a noble game with edifying and heroic rules. . . .

The conception of chivalry as a sublime form of secular life might be defined as an aesthetic ideal assuming the appearance of an ethical ideal. Heroic fancy and romantic sentiment form its basis. But medieval thought did not permit ideal forms of noble life, independent of religion. For this reason piety and virtue have to be the essence of a knight's life. Chivalry, however, will always fall short of this ethical function. Its earthly origin draws it down. For the source of the chivalrous idea of pride is aspiring to beauty, and formalized pride gives rise to a conception of honour, which is the pole of noble life. The sentiment of honour, Burckhardt says, this strange mixture of conscience and of egotism, "is compatible with many vices and susceptible of extravagant delusions; nevertheless, all that has remained pure and noble in man may find support in it and draw new strength from it."

. . . According to the celebrated Swiss historian, the quest for personal glory was the characteristic attribute of the men of the Renaissance. The Middle Ages proper, according to him, knew honour and glory only in collective forms, as the honour due to groups and orders of society, the honour of rank, of class, or of profession. It was in Italy, he thinks, under the influence of antique models, that the craving for individual glory originated. Here, as elsewhere, Burckhardt has exag-gerated the distance separating Italy from the Western countries and the Renaissance from the Middle Ages.

The thirst for honour and glory proper to the men of the Renaissance is essentially the same as the chivalrous ambition of earlier times, and of French origin. Only it has shaken off the feudal form and assumed an antique garb. The passionate desire to find himself praised by con-temporaries or by posterity was the source of virtue with the courtly knight of the twelfth century and the rude captain of the fourteenth, no less than with the beaux-esprits of the *quattrocento*. When Beau-manoir and Bamborough fix the conditions of the famous combat of the Thirty, the English captain, according to Froissart, expresses him-self in these terms: "And let us right there try ourselves and do so much that people will speak of it in future times in halls, in palaces, in public places and elsewhere throughout the world." The saying may not be authentic, but it teaches us what Froissart thought.

The quest of glory and of honour goes hand in hand with a hero-worship which also might seem to announce the Renaissance. The somewhat factitious revival of the splendour of chivalry that we find in European courts after 1300 is already connected with the Renaissance by a real link. It is a naive prelude to it. In reviving chivalry the poets and princes imagined that they were returning to antiquity. In the minds of the fourteenth century, a vision of antiquity has hardly yet disengaged itself from the fairyland atmosphere of the Round Table. Classical heroes were still tinged with the general colour of romance. On the one hand, the figure of Alexander had long ago entered the sphere of chivalry; on the other, chivalry was supposed to be of Roman origin. "And he maintained the discipline of chivalry well, as did the Romans formerly," thus a Burgundian chronicler praised Henry V of England. The blazons of Caesar, of Hercules, and of Troilus, are placed in a fantasy of King René, side by side with those of Arthur and Lancelot. Certain coincidences of terminology played a part in tracing back the origin of chivalry to Roman antiquity. How could people have known that the word *miles* with Roman authors did not mean a *miles* in the sense of medieval Latin, that is to say, a knight, or that a Roman *eques* differed from a feudal knight? Consequently, Romulus, because he raised a band of a thousand mounted warriors, was taken to be the founder of chivalry. . . .

# III / RENAIS-SANCE AND HUMANISM

*The term "Renaissance" has been so much bandied about by historians that it is difficult to know today how to use it, or whether to use it at all. Yet after the disputes, after all the discovery of other "renaissances" at various times, it seems to me that the name still deserves its place in the historical vocabulary and can have a precise meaning. It is an illusion to suppose that any event or phenomenon in politics, administration, or diplomacy is explained by being called Renaissance; a "Renaissance state" or "Renaissance monarchy" means nothing, because here the term begs questions which need a specific answer. However, it can usefully denote a particular complex of ideas and a definable civilization. In the realms of thought, literature, art, and scholarship the three centuries after 1300 have a reasonably coherent character of their own. This is least easily demonstrated for the fine arts; the two extracts given here (Nos. 21 and 22) must be accepted as a minute token of a great and wonderful outburst which cannot be in the least appreciated without a good look at paintings, statues, and buildings.*

*For the rest, the Renaissance may be described as a period during which a self-conscious recovery of the achievements of the ancient world produced new intellectual and artistic attitudes and results. It is marked by a hostile reaction against the scholastic philosophy, Aristotelianism, predominantly theological interests, and debased (if alive) Latinity which ruled in the universities, and also, outside the present purpose, by a flowering of poetry and imaginative writing in rapidly developing vernacular languages. It expressed itself in a refinement of philological tools, in a thorough exploration of ancient authors, many of them newly discovered or newly edited, and in an often slavish admiration for classical Latin and Greek; it involved the growth of new literary forms, like the dialogue, the essay, the informal treatise; it promoted a more critical approach to all forms of study, whether history, geography, natural history, or divinity. Above all, it insisted on the autonomy of the human being, on man's right to be treated with intellectual respect, an attitude summed up in the word "humanism." Humanism did not necessarily mean the glorification of man; few humanists even in Italy, where pagan influences were strong, either abandoned religion or regarded man as master of his fate, even though they often liked to conceal the God of the Christians behind the blind Fortune of the ancients. The Renaissance and humanism quarrelled with the scholarship of preceding generations, but not with the Christian religion; this they wished to purify and free from what they regarded (often rightly) as the stultifying accretions of pointless subtleties expressed in barbaric Latin.*

*The movement began and centered in Italy, where it claimed the allegiance both of numerous pure scholars and of innumerable gifted amateurs. North of the Alps it exercised profound influence from about the middle of the fifteenth century and produced in Erasmus the most complete type of the dedicated scholar. Humanist influences are easily traced among the reformers of the Church, whether they remained faithful to the papacy or broke away from it; and humanism as the basis of learning not only swamped the universities and schools of the sixteenth century, but may be said to have remained the dominant factor in European education until, in the nineteenth century, the rise of history and the natural sciences undermined humanism's reliance on the study of language and literature as the means to a full development of the human intellect.*

*Two points of importance must be made in even so brief and inadequate a summary. One is that although the Renaissance, as was natural, often expressed unjustified contempt for what it came to attack and displace, one may well accept the existence of a genuine new movement of thought and learning without sharing that contempt. The fact of the Renaissance is not disproved by demonstrating the beauty of Gothic architecture, the profundity of medieval theology, or the width of learning and originality manifested in the twelfth and thirteenth centuries. Secondly, although humanism is most easily defined as the activities of a body of scholars and intellectuals, it was always distinguished by a firm involvement in the world at large. Humanists of every kind believed that their work must, and did,*

*contribute to life itself, not only to scholarship. This did not al-*
*ways save them from pedantry—far from it; at times it gave their*
*thinking a dilettante air. But it also resulted in a genuine re-*
*thinking of such human problems as politics, society, education,*
*law, or the art of war. A schematic adherence to the ancients*
*could be disastrous, but among the best men—and, like any in-*
*tellectual movement, humanism deserves to be judged by its best*
*men—the transmitted experience of the ancient world was mar-*
*ried to independent thought and direct experience to produce a*
*genuine liberation of the human spirit.*

# 17 / FRANCESCO PETRARCA (1304-1374)

*If any single man may be said to have "begun" the Re-*
*naissance, Petrarch (to use the anglicized version of his name),*
*with his enormous published output—poetry, history, reflections,*
*letters and controversy—and his huge contemporary reputation,*
*was that man. He perfected the sonnet and with Dante and Boc-*
*caccio created the first literary vernacular of modern Europe, but*
*here he must appear rather as the thinker and man of letters. A,*
*from the first of two "Dialogues of True Wisdom," displays his*
*ease of style as well as the significant stress he laid on looking at*
*reality rather than books. B, a letter to Thomas Caloria of Messina*
*in Sicily, shows Petrarch fully aware of the innovations in schol-*
*arly method which he and his associates were introducing; the*
*dialectician attacked is an exponent of the formal Aristotelian*
*logic which the new learning regarded as unreal. The letter also*
*indicates the importance of a correspondence which linked several*
*generations of scholars in fruitful interplay.*[1]

## A. TRUE WISDOM

A certain simpleton met a very rich orator in the main square of
Rome and addressed him thus with a touch of mockery.

SIMPLETON: I wonder at your assurance. You tire yourself with continuous reading and working through innumerable books, and yet you

[1] Translated from Petrarca's *Opera* (Basel, 1554), pp. 364 ff., 644 ff.

have so far got nowhere near humility. Surely this is because the learning of this world in which you think you excel all others is only stupidity before God and just blows one up. And out of that inflation grows a swollen pride which, being sky-born, always rises upwards only to fall the more heavily. True knowledge makes humble, for since it is not troubled with inflation it does not ride high for a fall. I could therefore wish that you would change over to this second kind where the treasure of joy lies.

ORATOR: You are being rather presumptuous—you, a poor, dumb, ignorant type, to belittle the study of letters without which no one can do well for himself.

s: My dear sir, not presumption but charity compels me to speak. I see you are devoted to a search for wisdom involving much useless labour from which, if I can, I should like to save you. If you think carefully about your mistake, I think you will be glad to escape from the opposite snare. You are so bewitched by authority that you are like a horse—free by nature but so tied by its halter to the manger that it will eat only what is given to it.

o: If the food of wisdom is not found in wise men's books, where would you find it?

s: I do not say it is not there, but I maintain it is not found there naturally. The first people to put wisdom on paper did not live on a diet of books (there were none as yet), but built themselves into perfect specimens on natural nourishment. And they were far ahead in wisdom of those who thought to get profit from books.

o: Though it is possible to know some things without studying the literature, this does not apply to difficult and really weighty matters. Knowledge goes by accretion. . . . I call myself wise.

s: Things would be fine if there were as many wise men as there are pretenders to wisdom. The one is very difficult, the other very easy.

o: I have come to wisdom by study.

s: If only one came to it that way. But think again whether you have arrived, for it is not a matter of a few years' brief study, like the other arts; it takes all of the longest life. If a man were to run all day and get there in the evening, he might do . . .

o: I am called wise.

s: Neither your voice nor that of others will ever make a wise man; only the thing itself.

o: I am *generally* called wise.

s: The generality call madmen wise and wisdom mad, after their principle which is to think truth false and falsehood true. Nothing is farther removed from truth than the general opinion.

o: Everybody proclaims me wise!

s: That may prove your fame but in no way your wisdom.

o: I know myself to be wise.

s: Learned, you mean. Evidently there are some learned men—even quite a few—but hardly any wise men. To talk wisely and live wisely, to be called wise and really be it—these are not at all the same things. Some people have maintained that there are no wise men; I will not argue whether that is true or false. . . .

o: I hear you call yourself a simpleton, but you seem to know quite a bit.

s: Perhaps that is the difference between us. You think you are wise though you are not; that is why you are proud. I recognise I am a simpleton and therefore am humbler; and perhaps am for all that the better instructed.

o: How can you have been brought to a knowledge of your ignorance when you are a simpleton?

s: Not by your book but by God's.

o: What book?

s: Those He has written with His finger.

o: Where may they be found?

s: Everywhere.

o: How do you mean—here in the market place?

s: Indeed yes, and at the head of the book it says that wisdom shouts in the street.

o: I should like to hear this explained.

s: If I thought you were really driven by a desire to know, I should tell you at length.

o: Could you not quite shortly give me an idea of what you mean?

s: Yes, I could.

o: Well, let us move over here into this barber's shop, to talk more peacefully sitting down.

The simpleton agreed: and as they entered and turned to look out on the square, he resumed the argument. . . .

## B. SCHOLARLY METHOD

It takes nerve to engage an enemy who is less interested in victory than in a fight. You tell me of an elderly dialectician who has got violently excited over a letter of mine, thinking I had denounced his craft. So he fumes and rages in public, with threats to attack our method in a letter of his, and you have been waiting for many months for this letter. Do not any longer expect it; believe me, it will never materialise. He has so much sense left: whether in embarrassment at their clumsy style or in confession of their ignorance, these adversaries, so implacable with their tongues, never fight with their pens. They do not like to show up the feebleness of their armament and therefore use the Parthian tactics of battling in flight, throwing their light words about as though committing arrows to the winds. Well, as I said, it takes nerve to engage with such people in their own kind of warfare, especially because they derive supreme satisfaction from the struggle; they do not mean to get at the truth but to enjoy the debate. However, as one of Varro's sayings has it, "In excess of debate the truth is lost." . . . You need not fear that they will descend to the open ground of written papers and scholarly discussion. . . .

There is one thing, my friend, that I want to tell you: if you wish to follow virtue and truth, avoid such people. But where shall we find refuge from this gang of madmen if not even islands are safe any more? Not even Scylla and Charybdis can stop this plague from swimming across to Sicily. Indeed, it would seem to be a disease to which islands are particularly susceptible, seeing that the British army of dialecticians [2] now finds itself rivalled by a new race of one-eyed Cyclopses on the slopes of Etna. . . . One thing of which you remind me I had indeed noticed before: they use the glorious name of Aristotle to protect their sect, maintaining that Aristotle employed their method of argument. Admittedly it is a sort of excuse to follow in the footsteps of famous leaders, and even Cicero says that, if need be, he would not mind erring in company with Plato. But this is a mistake. Aristotle was a fiery spirit who discussed and wrote about the ultimate problems. . . . And why do these gentry stray so variously from their alleged leader? Why, I ask you, do they like to be called Aristotelians when they should be ashamed of using the name? Nothing is more entirely unlike that great philosopher than a man of their kind who writes nothing, knows little, but yells much and off the point.

How utterly ridiculous these allegedly educated men are, with their futile points of argument with which they bore themselves and others. . . . You know that story of Diogenes when a troublesome dialectician started arguing with him. Says he: "What I am you are not," and Diogenes nodded. He continued: "But I am a man." When Diogenes did not deny this either, the sophister slipped in this conclusion: "Thus you are not a man." "This last bit," replied Diogenes, "is unhappily false; if you want to make the syllogism come true, start with me." Much of their logic is as utterly absurd as this. What they hope to gain by it—fame, amusement, help towards a good and bounteous life— they themselves perhaps know; I have no idea. To noble minds money is no fit reward for intellectual pursuits. Manufacturers are quite right to look for cash: the liberal arts have a finer end in view. When they hear this they get wild, for the volubility of quarrelsome men is always very close to anger. "So you write off the dialectic method," they say.

2 William of Ockham and his followers

Of course not. I know how much it was valued by the Stoics, a strong and masculine race of philosophers of whom our Cicero has much to say, especially in his book on "The Last Things." I know it is one of the liberal arts, a step along the road to higher accomplishments and not at all a useless weapon for those who wish to penetrate the thickets of philosophical enquiry. It trains the intellect, shows the way to the truth, teaches one to avoid fallacies; lastly, if it does nothing else, it makes people quick and sharp.

That this is true I do not deny. However, an honorable road is not necessarily a praiseworthy dwelling-place, and surely a traveller who over the attractions of the road forgets his destination is a bit of a fool. The right approach to travel involves a rapid journey through long distances without any stops before the end. And who among us is not a traveller? We are all on a long and difficult journey, to be finished in a short time and in adverse weather, as it were on one rainy winter's day; and of this journey dialectic can be a part, provided it be not the goal. It can be a part of that day's morning, not of its evening. In our time we have done many things quite properly which it would now be quite improper still to be doing. If in our old age we cannot get away from the schools of dialectic just because we played in them as boys, we should not by the same token blush still to play hopskotch, or ride a hobby-horse, or let ourselves be rocked in a cradle. . . . Not a man but would dislike and despise an old fellow playing like a child, or marvel at a grey-haired boy with gout. I ask you, what is more useful, even necessary, than a first attempt at learning to read, the absolute foundation of all studies? On the other hand, what more laughable than an old man still engaged in that exercise?

Do you therefore work on that old man's pupils with my words. Do not scare them off; rather encourage them to make haste, not indeed just to study dialectic but to pass through it to higher things. And tell the old man himself that I condemn not the liberal arts but childish old men. For if, as Seneca says, there is nothing more disgraceful than an elderly schoolboy, so there is nothing more unpleasing than an ancient logic-chopper. And if he starts spewing syllogisms, I should advise you to run away and tell him to argue with Encheladus.[3]

---

[3] a mythical giant buried by Jupiter under Mount Etna

# 18 / LEONARDO BRUNI (1370-1444): A LETTER TO NICCOLÒ STROZA

*Bruni, who wrote a useful* History of Florence, *is a typical rather than outstanding product of the Renaissance, a stylist and publicist rather than an original spirit. This letter, which may have been only a literary exercise, was written in the course of a scholars' controversy concerning the rival advantages of humane and legal studies.*[4]

Your recent letter gave me the greatest pleasure. For it demonstrated both the excellence of your spirit and your vigorous and intelligent schooling, the product of study and diligence. Considering your age and the penetration of that letter, it is clear to me that your maturity appears admirable and plainly beyond your years. Nor do I doubt, unless you should be untrue to yourself, that you will become a most distinguished man. Therefore, I beg you, take care, add a little every day and gather things in: remember that these studies promise you enormous prizes both in the conduct of your life and for the fame and glory of your name. These two, believe me, are the way to those ample riches which have never yet been lacking to famous and accomplished men, if only the will was present. You have an excellent teacher whose diligence and energy you should imitate. Devote yourself to two kinds of study. In the first place, acquire a knowledge of letters, not the common run of it, but the more searching and profound kind in which I very much want you to shine. Secondly, acquaint yourself with what pertains to life and manners—those things that are called humane studies because they perfect and adorn man. In this kind of study your knowledge should be wide, varied, and taken from every sort of experience, leaving out nothing that might seem to contribute to the conduct of your life, to honor, and to fame. I shall advise you to read authors who can help you not only by their matter but also by the splendor of their style and their skill in writing; that is to say, the works of Cicero and of any who may possibly approach his level. If

---

[4] Translated from *La disputa delle Arti nel Quattrocento,* ed. E. Garin (Florence: Vallechi Editore, 1947), pp. 5–6. By permission of Vallechi Editore.

you will listen to me, you will thoroughly explore the fundamental and systematic treatment of those matters in Aristotle; as for beauty of expression, a rounded style, and all the wealth of words and speech, skill in these things you, if I may so put it, borrow from Cicero. For I would wish an outstanding man to be both abundantly learned and capable of giving elegant expression to his learning. However, no one can hope to achieve this without reading a lot, learning a lot, and taking a lot away from everywhere. Thus one must not only learn from the scholars (which is the foundation of all study) but must also get instruction from poets, orators and historians, so that one's style may become eloquent, elegant, and never crude in substance. . . . If you do obtain that excellence which I expect of you, what riches will compare with the rewards of these studies? Perhaps the study of law will more easily get you a job, but it is a long way behind those others in utility and dignity. For they combine to produce a good man, than which nothing can be thought more useful; the law does nothing of the sort. . . . Apart from everything else, goodness and virtue are absolute, while the law varies so much in place and time that what is lawful in Florence may be illegal in Ferrara. Great and famous men do not consider this mercenary traffic in law-suits and disputes sufficiently honorable. Thus those distinguished by rank and wealth take pride in military office but are inclined to treat a law degree rather as a form of disgrace. On the other hand, the standing of those other studies is so high that no prince or even king would think it beneath him to display knowledge and eloquent skill in them. Assuredly Philip of Macedonia put his son Alexander with Aristotle, not that he might learn law (which so powerful a king would have thought a mean thing), but for a thorough grounding in the arts of life and manners, and in eloquence. I say nothing of the joy and delight of these studies which make it difficult to tear oneself away from them. On the other hand, what except boredom is found in the study of law—so much so that the ancients not unfairly called it the yawning science? Enough of this. In writing to you, I find it pleasanter to talk of these things rather than about my friendship with your family and father. That can await its time and has not been unmentioned before this. But the encouragement to pursue these studies will brook no delay. Farewell.

# 19 / LORENZO VALLA (1407-1457): ON THE DONATION OF CONSTANTINE

*Though also notable for his Latinity and literary elegance, Valla must be chiefly remembered as a brilliant critical scholar whose attacks on tradition got him into much trouble with the Church. His most famous book exposed as a forgery one of the fundamental documents on which the papacy then rested its claim to supremacy, the so-called "Donation of Constantine." This purported to be a grant of territorial sovereignty over the Western half of the Roman empire, allegedly made by Constantine the Great (312–37) to Pope Sylvester I (314–35). The document was in fact composed in the eighth century. Valla's exposure displays high powers of rational analysis and linguistic criticism.*[5]

I shall show that that Donation from which the popes wish to derive their titles was equally unknown to Sylvester and Constantine. Before, however, I turn to the refutation of the document itself—their only defense, and that not only forged but stupid—good order demands that I start some way back. I shall develop these arguments: first, that neither Constantine nor Sylvester fits the picture presented; the first had neither the will nor the legal right to make such a donation, nor was empowered to hand over those lands to another, while the latter could not either have wanted to accept them or have the right to do so. Secondly—supposing these absolutely true and evident facts to have been otherwise—Sylvester did not accept nor Constantine bestow possession of what is alleged to have been granted; this [territory] always remained under the control and rule of the emperors. Thirdly, Constantine gave nothing to Sylvester but something to an earlier pope, having been baptised earlier still; and these were gifts of little import, being simply designed to meet the pope's ordinary needs. Fourthly, it is not true that a copy of the Donation is found in Gratian's

---

[5] Translated from *De Donatione Constantini*, ed. C. B. Coleman (New Haven, Conn.: Yale University Press, 1922). By permission of Yale University Press.

*Decretum* [6] or that it was taken from the *History of Sylvester*,[7] being found neither in that nor in any other history. The document itself contains inconsistencies, improbabilities, idiocies, barbarisms, and some nonsense. Further I shall speak of the pretended or mock donations of some other emperors. By way of supererogation I shall add that even if Sylvester had been possessed of the lands, yet, he or any other pope having been ejected, recovery is impossible after so long an interval of time under either divine or human law. Lastly, the present extent of the pope's claims cannot be justified by prescription, however ancient. . . .

I appeal to you, kings and princes: for hard it is for a private person to imagine himself into the mind of a king. I search your thoughts, I study your conscience, I ask your testimony. Would any one of you, if he had been in Constantine's place, have thought himself bound, in sheer generosity, to grant to another the city of Rome, his fatherland, the head of the world, of cities the queen, among all peoples the most powerful, most noble and the richest, triumphant among the nations, and sacred in her very aspects—to do this and then take himself off to that humble township, Byzantium? To grant moreover with Rome all Italy (no province but the conqueror of provinces); to grant three Gauls, two Spains, the Germans and Britons: to grant the whole West and rob himself of one of the two eyes of his empire? I cannot bring myself to believe that anyone in his senses would do this. . . .

They say the reason was that he had turned Christian. Would he therefore give up the best part of his empire? I suppose it was a crime, an outrage, a sin, to continue reigning at all; kingship was incompatible with the Christian religion! The practitioners of adultery, the beneficiaries of usury, the successful robbers, these usually after baptism return the stolen wife, the stolen money, the stolen goods. If this was your idea, Constantine, you must restore the cities to liberty, not change their masters. But that does not arise; you are simply moved to act for the honor of religion. As though it were more pious to renounce a realm than to govern it to the well-being of religion! . . .

The next point. If we are to give credit to the donation mentioned by the document, there ought to be some evidence that Sylvester accepted it. There is none. But it is believable, you say, that he took the donation for granted. I do not doubt it: one may well believe that he would not only have taken it for granted, but would have hunted for it, begged for it, extorted it with prayers. But why call that credible which is contrary to human experience? The fact that the document

[6] the basic document of the canon law, a compilation made in the twelfth century which initiated the independent study of the law of the Church

[7] the *Legend of Sylvester,* a fifth-century life of the pope

makes mention of the donation is no proof that it was received; on the contrary, the fact that there is no mention of reception strongly suggests that there was no donation. The argument against you is the stronger: there is more to show that Sylvester refused the gift than that Constantine wanted to make it; and no benefaction is conferred upon a man against his will. Indeed, we must suspect not only that Sylvester refused the donation, but also from his silence that in his view Constantine could not in law make it, nor he in law accept it. . . .

But grant that this, too, is no obstacle, that notwithstanding Sylvester be thought to have been in possession, and let us suppose that the whole affair took place, though contrary to custom and nature. After the emperor went off, what governors did Sylvester appoint for provinces and cities, what wars did he wage, what armed national risings did he subdue, through whom did he govern? We know nothing about all this, you will answer. I see: it was all done at night and no one therefore saw it.

Was Sylvester ever in possession? Who deprived him of it? For he certainly was not permanently in possession, nor were his successors, at least till Gregory the Great,[8] and it is not clear that he was. One who lacks possession and cannot prove deprivation assuredly never did possess; and if he says he did he must be out of his mind. You see, the argument now shows you to be out of your mind. Or else tell me who did dispossess the pope? Constantine himself, perhaps, or his son, or Julian,[9] or some other emperor? Give the expeller's name, the date, the first and second and later occasions of deprivation. Was it done by sedition or murder, or without these? Did all the nations conspire against him, or which first? What, did no one help him, not even one of those whom Sylvester or some other pope had put in charge of cities and provinces? On one single day he lost everything: or perhaps gradually and by stages? He and his officers resisted: or did they abdicate at the first disturbance? . . . The Roman empire, created by such labors and so much bloodshed, was won and lost so peacefully, so quietly by Christian priests that no bloodshed, no war, no uproar took place; and, no less remarkable, by whom this was done, when and how and during what time, remains entirely unknown. . . .

In the first place, not only must the fellow who would take the part of Gratian and add passages to Gratian's work stand convicted of dishonesty, but those who believe that the document was transcribed into Gratian prove their ignorance. No scholar has ever thought so, and it is not to be found in the earliest editions of the *Decretum*. If Gratian had referred to the matter anywhere he would not have done

[8] Pope Gregory I (590–604)
[9] the Emperor Julian the Apostate (361–63)

so in the place where they put it, interrupting his argument, but where he treats of the agreement made with Louis the Pious.[10] Besides, there are thousands of places in the *Decretum* which go counter to the sense of that passage. . . . It is well and enough: we have won. First because Gratian does not say what they lyingly assert; more particularly because one may see from innumerable passages that he denies and refutes it; lastly because they bring forward an ignorant and totally insignificant man, so stupid that he adds to Gratian what cannot be reconciled with his other statements. . . .

What say you, you forger? Why cannot we read this document in the *History of Sylvester*? This book, I daresay, is rare, hard to find, not widely known. . . . It is written, no doubt, in Greek or Syrian or Chaldaean. Gelasius [11] testifies that it was read by many of the orthodox; Voraginus [12] mentions it; we have seen a thousand anciently written copies of it; in just about every cathedral they read from it every Sylvester's day. And yet no one says that they have read there what you have put in it; no one has heard or dreamt of it. Or is there perhaps another *History*? And what might that be? I know of no other, nor do I understand that you have one in mind, for you speak of the one which Gelasius says is read in many churches. But in that we cannot find your grant. . . .

[The rest of the treatise analyzes the Donation in detail, demonstrating historical errors both in content and in phrasing.]

# 20 / GIOVANNI PICO DELLA MIRANDOLA (1463-1494): TREATISE AGAINST ASTROLOGY

*The young genius of the high Renaissance, together with Marsilio Ficino (1433–99) the leading exponent of the Renaissance rediscovery of Plato, was that unusual combination of an aristocratic dilettante with the instincts and abilities of a professional scholar. His best-known work, a disquisition on human*

---

[10] the Carolingian emperor (816–840)
[11] Pope Gelasius I (d. 496)
[12] author of the *Golden Legend,* a collection of saints' lives (d. 1298)

*dignity, adorns a somewhat conventional fifteenth-century humanism with a youthful splendor of language; but the passage here chosen gives a better idea of both his powers of rational argument and of his remarkable erudition. As to this last, it should, however, be said that he appears to have met some of his authorities only in Cicero's* On Divination. *Pico's attitude to astrology was not typical of Renaissance humanism. A very large number of otherwise rational men firmly believed that the stars had a direct and discoverable influence on human fate.*[13]

## CHAPTER 1

First of all I want the reader to know that this plan of mine to reject and confute astrology is no innovation and impertinence on my part, but that from ancient times good judges have always held that what contained so much discomfort to mankind, so much insanity under the pretence of science and usefulness, was not really a true art. For that reason the laws of emperors and sages exclude it from public life, as something harmful to society; the words of prophets, the commands of priests, the voices and teachings of the most holy men, condemn it as disastrous to morals and religion; it stands despised or refuted by philosophers and mathematicians, insofar as their books have taught them wisdom and not merely rhetoric, as being false, useless, impossible, the enemy of philosophy. This I propose to demonstrate in this first book, before entering upon my own analysis and for the benefit of the ignorant or the hostile, so that this my accusation, following after such accusers, may not seem to rise from malice but serve to save the faces of any who might take issue with it.

Let me begin with the professional philosophers, whose authority as a rule carries more weight than that of men of sense and is more widely acknowledged than that of the prophets. That Pythagoras [14] gave no credit to astrology is avowed by Theodoretus,[15] while Diogenes Laertius [16] and Plutarch [17] suggest the same. Democritus [18] is reported as saying that "no one looks at what is in front of his nose—people prefer to scan the fields of heaven." The academic Favorinus [19]

---

[13] Translated from *Disputationes adversum astrologiam divinatricem*, ed. E. Garin (Florence: Vallechi Editore, 1946), from Book 1. By permission of Vallechi Editore.

[14] Greek philosopher (sixth century B.C.)

[15] Byzantine lexicographer (third century A.D.)

[16] historian of philosophy (third century A.D.)

[17] Greek historian (c. 46–120 A.D.)

[18] originator of the atomic theory of the universe (c. 470–380 B.C.)

[19] a philosopher of the second century A.D.

and the stoic Panaetius [20] battled against astrology; Seneca [21] ridiculed it and Cicero confuted it; who can fail to recall Carneades [22] arguing against it and the philosopher Bio [23] recording his opposition to divination? Must not something to which even the insane Orestes [24] refused assent surpass all madness; and how much delirium must astrology contain if even the often delirious Epicurus [25] would have nothing to do with it!

Plato and Aristotle, the leaders of the profession, considered astrology unworthy of discussion, condemning it in their whole teaching more effectively by their silence than anyone else might have done in speech and writing. Those who hold otherwise must please discuss this question: why, in all the corpus of their treatises, do they never once use an argument from astrology when explaining the properties of celestial bodies or seeking to understand the causes of terrestrial affairs? Is it to be supposed that they thought it no matter for philosophers to consider the first and noblest parts of the universe, how bodies move and in turn move others, the efficient causes without which nothing can happen or be understood in nature—if, that is, all these may be believed to be what astrologers make them? . . . If this be not proof enough, let us turn to the pupils of both philosophers who explicitly testify to the opinion which their masters pronounced by their silence. Plotinus [26] is reckoned the first in authority in Plato's family. Of him Porphyrius [27] records that, after laboring much in astrology and discovering the vanity and falsity of that art, he disavowed all belief in astrological predictions and wrote a book *On the Action of the Stars* in which he derided and refuted the teachings of astrologers. . . .

## CHAPTER 3

Astrology offers no help in discovering what a man should do and what avoid.

As I said above, another use may be attributed to astrology: namely that it enables us to do whatever the astrologer advises and avoid

[20] (180–109 B.C.) introduced the stoic school of philosophy at Rome

[21] stoic philosopher (c. 4 B.C.–A.D. 65)

[22] Greek Platonist (214–129 B.C.)

[23] probably Bio of Abdera, a mathematical philosopher of the fourth century B.C.

[24] an unidentified reference to the legend of Orestes, son of Agamemnon, driven mad by the Furies after his part in the murder of his father.

[25] Greek philosopher of ethics and physics (341–270 B.C.)

[26] eminent Greek philosopher and founder of Neoplatonism (A.D. 205–270)

[27] Greek scholar and biographer of Plotinus (A.D. 233–c. 300)

that which he prohibits. I shall show that this [opinion] is either superfluous or harmful. The astrologer's predictions deal with matters of man's body, or with external and contingent events. Turning to the first: supposing they concern health, we may ask whether his judgment agrees with that of a physician or differs greatly from it. If they both agree, the astrologer does nothing that the doctor could not do alone; if they disagree, which of the two, we may well enquire, deserves greater confidence? Surely, if a man ignores his doctor and entrusts himself to his astrologer, he deserves the penalty of his folly. Similarly, with respect to actions, the question is: does common prudence support whatever advice astrology may offer, or does its judgment go strictly the other way? If they agree, why seek among the far heavens what we can find at home; if they disagree, how can one defend as right and rational an action which in the process would ignore prudence—that prudence which, after all, amounts only to right reason applied to the doing of things?

An example will make this clear. Suppose an astrologer tells you that Mars will be very hostile to you, that with the power which his annual revolution provides he will raise your bile; that therefore you should use cold things and regulate your life against the heat of Mars. He tells you this from his reading of the skies; and the symptoms of your body, on which doctors rely in their diagnosis, either will or will not demonstrate the same. If they do demonstrate it, that will suffice to make you take precautions against future ill health. If they do not—if there is no sign of overheated bile but instead you have traces of albumen and fat in your urine, a sluggish pulse, pale complexion, weariness of the limbs, and all the other symptoms from which medical men deduce a preponderance of phlegm, not of bile—would you nevertheless think it right to evacuate bile because some astrologer pretends that Mars threatens you from the skies? . . .

Now let us take a similar example from the field of action. Suppose some mathematician advises a prince not to engage in war with his enemies because Mars is not favourable enough to him. One would like to know whether, when this counsel was given, the prince had no just cause to go to war, or (if he had one) was yet without prospect or chance of victory; or whether, on the other hand, a just cause of war was present and all the means of victory supplied. In the former case, he would rightly avoid war, but he would do so because his prudence guided him, no matter though the mathematician had never spoken. In the latter, even the astrologer himself, if his science were not involved, would not judge it necessary to refrain from war; and if he did refrain, what were this but a surrender of common sense and the obvious to specious and conjectural reasoning? . . .

# 21 / GIORGIO VASARI (1511-1574): LIFE OF GIOTTO

*Himself a painter of some distinction, Vasari is chiefly re-membered as an art historian. His voluminous work on the Italian painters from the late thirteenth century to his own day combines reliable, if sometimes rather anecdotal, biography with a shrewd and practical assessment of their work. Giotto (1266–1337) was then and is now regarded as the first genuine Renaissance artist.*[28]

This great man was born at the village of Vespignano, in the district of Florence, fourteen miles distant from that city, in the year 1276, from a father named Bondone, a tiller of the soil and a simple fellow. He, having had this son, to whom he gave the name Giotto, reared him comformably to his condition. . . . Bondone gave some sheep into his charge, and he, going about the holding, now in one part and now in another, to graze them, and impelled by a natural inclination to the art of design, was for ever drawing, on stones, on the ground, or on sand, something from nature, or in truth anything that came into his fancy. Wherefore Cimabue,[29] going one day on some business of his own from Florence to Vespignano, found Giotto, while his sheep were browsing, portraying a sheep from nature on a flat and polished slab, with a stone slightly pointed, without having learned any method of doing this from others, but only from nature; whence Cimabue, standing fast in a marvel, asked him if he wished to go to live with him. The child answered that, his father consenting, he would go willingly. . . . In a short time, assisted by nature and taught by Cimabue, the child not only equalled the manner of his master, but became so good an imitator of nature that he banished completely that rude Greek[30] manner and revived the good and modern art of paint-ing, introducing the portraying well from nature of living people, which had not been used for more than two hundred years. . . .

[28] From Giorgio Vasari, *Lives of the Most Eminent Painters, Sculptors and Architects*, transl. G. du C. de Vere (London: Macmillan & Co., Ltd., 1912–14), Vol. 1, pp. 71 ff. By permission of Macmillan & Co., Ltd.

[29] Giovanni Cimabue (c. 1240–c. 1302), the last notable pre-Renaissance painter in Italy

[30] i.e., Byzantine

[At Rimini] he painted in fresco the story of the Blessed Michelina, which was one of the most beautiful and excellent works that Giotto ever made, by reason of the many and beautiful ideas that he had in working thereon; for besides the beauty of the draperies, and the grace and vivacity of the heads, which are miraculous, there is a young woman therein as beautiful as ever a woman can be, who, in order to clear herself from the false charge of adultery, is taking an oath over a book in a most wonderful attitude, holding her eyes fixed on those of her husband, who was making her take the oath by reason of mistrust in a black son born from her, whom he could in no way bring himself to believe to be his. She, even as her husband is showing disdain and distrust in his face, is making clear with the purity of her brow and her eyes, to those who are most intently gazing on her, her innocence and simplicity and the wrong that he is doing to her in making her take oath and in proclaiming her wrongly as a harlot. . . .

The foreshortenings, next, that are seen in another picture among a quantity of beggars that he portrayed, are very worthy of praise and should be held in great price among craftsmen, because from them there came the first beginning and method of making them, not to mention that it cannot be said that they are not passing good for early work. . . .

# 22 / LEONARDO DA VINCI (1452-1519): ON PAINTING

*No other man of the Renaissance came so near as Leonardo to the contemporary ideal of the "universal man." Painter, sculptor, architect, anatomist, engineer, inventor, and writer, he excelled in everything he touched, but, afflicted by a neurotic search for perfection, completed little and left hardly more than fragments behind. Less daemonic than his younger contemporary Michelangelo Buonarotti (1475–1564), he was much the worse poet and much the better scientist. His book on the painter's art exemplifies the highly professional attitude of Renaissance artists.*[31]

[31] Reprinted from Leonardo da Vinci, *Treatise on Painting*, transl. A. Philip McMahon (Princeton, N.J.: Princeton University Press, 1956), by permission of Princeton University Press.

## PART 1

If you disparage painting, which alone can portray faithfully all the visible works of nature, you certainly disparage a discovery which considers all manner of forms with subtle and philosophical attention: the sea, places on land, plants, animals, grass, flowers, all of which are surrounded by shadow and light. Truly this is a science and the legitimate daughter of nature, since painting is born of nature. To speak more accurately, we would say the grandchild of nature, for all visible things are born of nature, and painting is born of these. Therefore, we rightly call painting the grandchild of nature and related to God. . . .

That science is most useful the results of which are most communicable, and, conversely, that is less useful which is less communicable.

Painting makes its end result communicable to all the generations of the world, because it depends on the visual faculty; not reaching the understanding through the ear, it does not proceed in the same way that impressions of [hearing] do.

Thus painting does not have need of interpreters for different languages as does literature and at once satisfies mankind, no differently than do things produced by nature; and not mankind alone, but other living creatures also. This was shown by a painting, representing the father of a family, which was caressed not only by the little children when still in swaddling clothes, but likewise by the dog and the cat of the household, a marvellous thing and an extraordinary spectacle to behold. . . .

I do not find any difference between painting and sculpture except that the sculptor pursues his work with greater physical fatigue than the painter, and the painter pursues his with greater mental fatigue. This is proved to be true, for the sculptor in producing his work does so by the force of his arm, striking the marble or other stone to remove the covering beyond the figure enclosed within it. This is a most mechanical exercise accompanied many times with a great deal of sweat, which combines with dust and turns into mud. The sculptor's face is covered with paste and all powdered with marble dust, so that he looks like a baker, and he is covered with minute chips, so that he looks as though he had been out in the snow. His house is dirty and filled with chips and dust of stones. In speaking of excellent painters and sculptors we may say that just the opposite happens to the painter, since the well-dressed painter sits at great ease in front of his work, and moves a very light brush, which bears attractive colours, and he is adorned with such garments as he pleases. His dwelling is full of fine paintings and is clean and often filled with music, or the sound of different beautiful works being read, which are often heard with great pleasure, unmixed with the pounding of hammers or other noises. . . .

Painting is a matter of greater mental analysis, of greater skill, and more marvellous than sculpture, since it compels the mind of the painter to transform itself into the very mind of nature, to become an interpreter between nature and art. It explains the causes of nature's manifestations as compelled by its laws: in what ways the images of objects before the eyes come together in the pupil of the eye; which, among objects equal in size, looks larger to the eye; which, among equal colours, will look more or less dark or more or less bright; which, among things of the same depth, looks more or less low; which, among those objects placed at equal height, will look more or less high, and why, among objects placed at various distances, one will appear less clear than the other. . .

## PART 2

. . . The young should first learn perspective, then the proportions of all objects. Next, copy work after the hand of a good master, to gain the habit of drawing parts of the body well; and then work from nature, to confirm the lessons learned. View for a time works from the hands of various masters. Then form the habit of putting into practice and working what has been learned. . . .

I declare and affirm that it is much better for many reasons for a student to draw in company than alone. First, because if you are inadequate, you will be ashamed to be seen among the number of men drawing, and this mortification is a motive for studying well. Secondly, a sound envy will stimulate you to become one of the number who are praised more than you, and the praise of others will spur you on. Another reason is that you will get something from the way in which they draw, who do this better than you. If you are better than the others, you will benefit by despising their defects, while the praise of others will increase your efficacy. . . .

I shall not fail to include among these precepts a new discovery, an aid to reflection, which, although it seems a small thing and almost laughable, nevertheless is very useful in stimulating the mind to various discoveries. This is: look at walls splashed with stains or stones of various mixed colours. If you have to invent some scene, you can see there resemblances to a number of landscapes, adorned in various ways with mountains, rivers, rocks, trees, great plains, valleys and hills. Moreover, you can see various battles, and rapid actions of figures, strange expressions on faces, costumes, and an infinite number of things, which you can reduce to good, integrated form. . . .

# 23 / DESIDERIUS ERASMUS (1466?-1536)

*No short note can do justice to this famous Dutchman, the prince of professors, the very epitome of learned men. His nervous constitution, hypochondria, and touchiness did not prevent him from dominating the scholarly world of north and west Europe for thirty years. Even a great hebraist like the German Johann Reuchlin (1455–1522) or a great classicist like the Frenchman Guillaume Budé (1467–1540) sit in his shadow. Erasmus edited many of the early Fathers as well as classical texts; his most influential achievement was his edition of the New Testament in Greek (1516) which demonstrated the inaccuracy of the Latin Vulgate and questioned the ascendancy of the priesthood. However, brought up in the* devotio moderna *(see p. 30), Erasmus remained all his life a devout Christian and spent much time and ink on theological questions and the reform of the Church. His bitter battle against the ossified scholasticism of universities and monasteries showed the world his powers of satire. A selection from his enormous output can hardly be representative, but the passages here included show him in three of his several aspects. A, from the* Praise of Folly *(1510), displays Erasmus the satirist.[32] B,* The Manual of a Christian Soldier *(1504), a devotional treatise which had very wide influence, shows his personal, quite uninstitutional, and somehow rather rational piety.[33] C,* Of the Two Kinds of Style, *an educational textbook on rhetoric, gives some idea of Erasmus the scholar and pedagogue.[34]*

## A. PRAISE OF FOLLY

### Chapter 1

Folly speaking: However men may commonly talk of me (as though I did not know), however badly Folly is thought of even among the most foolish, it is I and I alone, I tell you, who by my presence cheer

---

[32] Translated from *Moriae Encomium,* ed. I. B. Kan (The Hague, 1898).

[33] From *Enchiridion Militis Christiani,* translated by William Tyndale, the English reformer (London, 1534).

[34] Translated from *De Duplici Copia Verborum* (Basel, 1516).

both gods and men. And here is proof truly large enough: when just now I stepped forth into this notable assembly to have my say, all your faces lit up with such a new and unwonted hilarity, you so smoothed your brows and applauded with such pleased and pleasant laughter, that all of you that I see before me would in truth seem to me to be drunk with the nectar of Homer's gods laced with the herb of forget-fulness. For before this you were sitting here all glum and worried, as though you had just come back from Trophonius' cave.[35] It was just like those occasions when the sun first shows its fair and golden face to the earth, or when after a hard winter the new spring blows its gentle airs: then suddenly things take on a new appearance, a new color, and, aye, a new youth. In like wise you got new faces as soon as you saw me. And thus, what all those great rhetoricians can hardly achieve with their long and long-pondered speeches, I have done at one blow merely by showing myself: I have driven away the heavy cares of the mind. . . .

### Chapter 3

And so away with all those moralists who preach that self-praise is the height of folly and insolence. Or rather, let them by all means call it folly as long as they admit it to be proper. For what could be more fitting than for Folly to blow her own trumpet? Who can speak better for me than I myself? Unless perchance I am better known to someone else than I am to myself. However, I reckon even this self-praise is a good deal more modest than the practice of some men great in affairs or learning who, in a kind of backward bashfulness, hire for money a syrup-pouring speaker or fine-talking poet from whom they may learn their praises, or rather some bare-faced lies. . . . In short, I follow the common saying by which it appears that he whom no one else will praise may rightly praise himself. Though I must say, I wonder at the ingratitude (if that is the right word) of men, at their lack of appreciation. Everybody courts me most eagerly and freely tastes of my benefits; yet in all these centuries no one has thought to celebrate the praise of Folly in words of gratitude; and this even though there has been no shortage of men to sweat at praises, with much waste of midnight oil and sleep, for bloody tyrants, quartan fevers, flies, bald pates, and nonsense of that kind. From me you shall hear a speech improvised and unprepared, but the truer for that. . . .

---

[35] a famous oracle in ancient Boeotia. Consulting it involved a depressing ritual and an underground descent.

## Chapter 35

Again, among men, Pythagoras [36] greatly preferred the feeble-minded to the learned and great; and Gryllus [37] judged a good deal more wisely than the 'deep-thinking' Ulysses when he preferred to grunt in a sty rather than join that traveller in encountering so many dangerous situations. I think, Homer, the father of fiction, agrees with me in this: though time and again he calls all mortals miserable and wretched, he frequently terms Ulysses, his model of wisdom, a pessimist, a word nowhere applied to Paris or Ajax or Achilles. Why this, then? Surely only because that crafty and cunning character, withdrawing as far as he might from nature's path, did nothing except by Athene's advice and was too clever by half. And thus among men those are furthest from bliss who devote themselves to wisdom; indeed, they are doubly foolish in that, being mortals born, they yet forget their condition, hanker after the life of the immortal gods, and, after the example of the titans, make war on nature with the engines of their science. By the same token those seem least miserable who come nearest to the spirit and stupidity of beasts and never attempt anything beyond man's proper station. . . . By the immortal gods, is there any sort of men more happy than those who get called morons, fools, idiots and turnips—names, in my view, of great splendor? At first sight I may seem to be talking absurd nonsense, but it will soon appear to be the entire truth. For first of all, they do not know the fear of death, no little evil in all conscience. They do not know the torments of conscience. They are not troubled by tales of ghostly visitations. They are not frightened by spectres and goblins, not plagued by the dread of impending ills or by hopes of good things to come. In short, they are not torn to pieces by the thousand cares to which life is subject. They know neither shame nor fear nor ambition nor envy nor love. And lastly, if they come closer to the stupidity of beasts, they cannot sin, according to the theologians.

## Chapter 49

I should myself be more than foolish . . . if I tried to enumerate the forms which folly and madness take among the general herd. Rather will I turn to those who enjoy some reputation for wisdom among men and seek to win, as the saying is, the golden bough. Among these schoolmasters come high, surely a tribe whose lot would seem

[36] See p. 62.
[37] author of a work praising animal before human existence

the most disastrous, the most wretched, the most godforsaken, if I did not soften the horrors of that miserable profession with a sweet touch of madness. For they are afflicted not with five but with six hundred furies, always starving, filthy in their pastimes—their pastimes indeed? rather on their treadmill and rack, among the hordes of boys. Yet while they grow grey with labor, deaf with the noise, haggard with stench and filth, they think themselves, thanks to my good offices, princes among men. So they take their pleasure, terrorising their cowed flock with threats of voice and countenance, cutting those wretched boys to pieces with cane and rod and whip, and raging at their sweet will in all the ways they can think of. . . . Would you prefer to call this madness or folly? No odds to me, as long as you admit the value of my offices by means of which an animal so far more wretched than any other is brought to such felicity that it would not exchange its lot for that of the great kings of Persia. . . .

### Chapter 51

Among the learned, lawyers claim a high place for themselves; no other profession has a higher self-esteem. Rolling Sisyphus' rock diligently uphill, they spin a web of six hundred laws in the same spirit, indifferent whether there is any relevance to the case; piling gloss upon gloss and opinion upon opinion, they make their study appear the most difficult of all. For they reckon that degree of labor proves degree of excellence. To them we will add logical philosophers, a class of men . . . so given to talking that any one of them could undo twenty picked women in loquacity; and it will be a lucky day if they confine themselves to talking and do not branch out into brawls, faithful to the example of those who battle like the devil for the moon in the water and in their great struggle lose the best part of the truth. . . .

### Chapter 61

Fortune loves the imprudent, she loves the reckless and those who like taking chances. Wisdom makes men wary, and you therefore see men of sense always burdened with poverty and hunger and mere depression, living their lives in neglect, disregard and obscurity. Fools get all the money and hold the high places in the state; in short, they flourish in every way. For surely, if to stand well with the rulers of this world and move among our jewelled images is to be thought a blessed condition, what then has less value than wisdom, what is more fatal among men of that sort? Are riches in question? What profit shall come to the merchant who follows the path of wisdom, jibbing at perjury, blushing at the detected lie, worried even the tiniest bit by those anxious scruples with which wise men regard theft and usury? As for those who hanker after the honors and distinctions of the Church: an ass or an ox shall sooner get them than a man of sense. If it is love you want, well, the girls—the biggest part of that story—lavish themselves wholeheartedly on fools and flee in horror from any wise man as from a scorpion. To clinch the point: when people want to enjoy themselves a bit more freely, they first shut out the sage and admit in preference any sort of animal. In short, wherever one turns, to prelates, princes, judges, magistrates, friends and enemies, the greatest and the least, all is got for ready cash; and as the wise man despises cash, it usually escapes him only too easily. But though there is neither measure nor end to my praises, yet must my discourse some time have its conclusion.

## B. THE MANUAL OF A CHRISTIAN SOLDIER

### Chapter 1

The first point is, we must needs have in mind continually that the life of mortal men is nothing but a certain perpetual exercise of war. . . . The most part of men be overmuch deceived whose mind this world as a juggler holds occupied with delicious and flattering pleasures; which also departing from war, as though they had conquered all their enemies, make holiday out of season and give themselves to rest out of time none otherwise truly than in a very assured peace. It is a marvellous thing to behold how without care and circumspection we live, how idly we sleep, now upon the one side and now upon the other, when without ceasing we are besieged by so great a number of armed vices sought and hunted for with so great craft, invaded daily with so great lying-in-wait. Behold, over thy head wicked devils that never sleep but keep watch for our destruction, armed against us with a thousand deceits. . . . Oh thou Christian man, rememberest thou not when thou wert professed and consecrate with the holy mysteries of the fountain of life? How thou boundest thyself to be a faithful soldier unto they captain Christ? To whom thou owest thy life twice, both because he gave it thee and also because he restored it again to thee; to whom thou owest more than thou art able to pay. . . . Our hearts arise and grudge at the remembrance of death of the body, as at a terrible and outrageous thing, because it is seen with bodily eyes. The soul to die—because no man sees and few believe, therefore very few fear it. And yet is this death more cruel than the other. . . . The bodies of holy people be the temples of the holy ghost. And lewd men's bodies be the sepulchres of dead corpses . . . the grave of the soul. The breast is the sepulchre, the mouth and throat is the gaping of the sepulchre; and the body destitute of the soul is not so dread as is the soul when she is forsaken of Almighty God. Neither any corpse sticks in the nose of man so sore as the stench of a soul buried four days offends the nose of God and all the saints. . . . In thyself thou are very weak; in Him thou are valiant, and nothing is there that thou art not able to do. Wherefore the end of our war is not doubtful, because the victory depends not of fortune but is put wholly in the hands of God and by him in our hands. No man is here that has not overcome but he that would not. . . .

### Last Chapter

. . . These be the only enemies of Christ's soldiers against whose assault the mind must be armed long beforehand with prayer, with noble sayings of wise men, with the doctrine of Holy Scripture, with example of devout and holy men, and specially of Christ. Though I doubt not that the reading of Holy Scripture shall minister all these things to thee abundantly, nevertheless charity, which one brother owes to another, has moved and exhorted me that at the least with these this sudden [38] and hasty writings I should further and help thy holy purpose, as much as lies in me. A thing which I have done somewhat the rather because I somewhat feared lest thou shouldst fall into that superstitious kind of religious men [39] which partly waiting on their own advantage, partly with great zeal but not according to knowledge, walk round about both by sea and land; and if anywhere they get a man recovering from vices into virtue, him straightway with most importunate and lewd [40] exhortations, threatenings and flatterings they enforce to thrust into the order of monks, even as though without a cowl there were no Christendom. Furthermore when they have filled his breast with pure scrupulosity and doubts insoluble, then they bind him to certain traditions found by man, and plainly thrust the wretched person headlong into a certain bondage of ceremonies, like unto the manner of the Jews, and teach him to tremble and fear, but not to love. The order of monkship is not piety but a kind of living . . . whereunto verily as I do not encourage thee, so likewise I counsel not from it. This thing only I warn thee of: that thou put piety neither in meat,[41] nor in raiment or habit,[42] nor in any visible thing, but in those things which have been declared and showed thee afore. And in whatsoever persons thou shalt find or perceive the true image

[38] unpremeditated
[39] monks
[40] rude
[41] food
[42] special dress

of Christ, with them couple thyself. Moreover, when such men be lacking whose conversation [43] should make thee better, withdraw thyself as much as thou mayest from the company of man and call the holy prophet Christ and the apostles into communication; but specially make Paul of familiar conversation with thee. . . .

## C. TWO KINDS OF STYLE

### Introduction

There is nothing more admirable or splendid than oratory, tumbling along like a golden river with its mass of sentences and words; but by the same token the thing is assuredly not to be attempted without a fair measure of danger. For, as the proverb has it, not every man may come to Corinth. Thus we see it happen to quite a few men that in their energetic but far from happy endeavor to achieve this divine accomplishment they produce only a futile and ugly garrulity, both obscuring the issue and burdening the suffering ears of their audience with a meaningless and uncritically heaped-up confusion of words and phrases. The outcome is that certain teachers, trying, with God's help, to hand on the rules of their craft, in preaching an expansive style only succeed in betraying their own narrow incompetence. All this has moved me to propound certain arguments, examples and formulae concerning both kinds of style, choosing on the one hand from the rules of rhetoric such precepts as fit the purpose, and applying on the other the lessons I have learned in an extended practice of speaking and writing and in the varied study of a good many authors. Of course, it is not my ambition to exhaust the subject in one single book; in this brief outline I shall be content to have opened the road to the learned and the learners and, so to speak, to have assisted a trifle towards raising the forest of work to come. Persuaded as I am to undertake this labor solely by a desire to help, I shall not grudge it if all the glory comes to another, as long as young men eager to learn derive some advantage from me. At the same time, I am committed to more serious studies than would justify devoting too much labor to these which, however exceedingly useful they may be in contributing to quite possibly great things, are yet in appearance rather petty.

### Conclusion

Now both [types of orator] must take care not to allow ambition to drag them into the error which lies in wait for each style. The lover of the spare style must beware of simply doing no more than say

---

[43] companionship

little: he must say the best he can with the fewest words. . . . For nothing makes pithy speech acceptable except the suitability and elegance of the words used. By sticking to straightforwardness, it will be easy to avoid the fault of obscurity, too common a companion to conciseness. Again, he must see to it that his oration, altogether unheated by passion as it is, does not congeal. The matter must therefore be so presented that by itself, and without a word being said, it imparts several kicks to the mind: everything must be seasoned with Attic wit. The greatest care must be taken that in the search for brevity nothing essential to the argument is forgotten. On the other hand, the practitioner of the eloquent style must apply selectivity to his words, points and images, lest his argument be worthless, his examples misplaced, his thoughts trivial, his asides long beyond bearing and inopportune, and his gestures too awkwardly affected. In respect of order and arrangement be must carefully avoid making his whole speech muddled and confused by an accumulation of ill-digested matter. All the time he must skirt tedium by the use of variety, pleasantries and humor. Variety, and also pleasantry, are particularly necessary in his similes. . . . In addition a warning: one must not seek to be eloquent all the time. Certain things simply are uninspiring; but leaving aside matters which by their nature do not permit the use of magniloquence, look for those parts which are most susceptible to eloquent treatment. Unless it is done for the sake of experiment, or by way of proving one's cleverness, it is occasionally quite a good idea to—as they say—make a mountain out of a molehill. . . . A young man may be forgiven luxuriance of expression. For the rest, where things are done not in play but in all seriousness and in conditions of real contests, a speaker, thinking the matter over sensibly, will for good practical reasons avoid all extravagance.

# 24 / SIR THOMAS MORE (1478-1535)

*The greatest English humanist was many things. Trained as a lawyer (his father was a judge), he followed a successful career in the service of his king, Henry VIII, reaching the exalted place of lord chancellor (1529–32). A devoted student and reader, he was Erasmus' special friend and one of the leading lights of what is usually called the new learning. A devout Catholic, he wrote and acted vigorously against the influence of Lutheranism in early Tudor England. At the last, opposing Henry VIII's break from Rome, he was executed on a trumped-up charge of treason and died a martyr for the papacy, which in 1935 paid a debt by canonizing him. But what made him memorable was a character of unusual sweetness, generosity, good sense and fortitude, a gift of gentle humor, and a penetrating intelligence. The, fact that he persecuted heretics and encouraged their burning must not be glossed over, as so often it is. His writings reflect the man. A comes from his famous* Utopia *(1516), the description of an imaginary island state; the first book contains a sharp criticism of contemporary England, the second by contrast the account of an ideal "natural" society—one, that is, which had everything excellent except the Christian religion.*[44] *B represent More the controversialist in extracts from his writings against the English Lutheran, William Tyndale (d. 1536).*[45] *C, a letter to his daughter Margaret Roper, written in 1534 from the Tower of London where he lay in his last imprisonment, shows More the spiritual Christian.*[46]

## A. UTOPIA

The city is compassed about with a high and thick stone wall full of turrets and bulwarks. A dry ditch, but deep and broad and over grown with bushes, briars and thorns, goes about three sides or quarters of the city. To the fourth side the river itself serves for a ditch. The streets be appointed and set forth very commodious and handsome, both for carriage and also against the winds. The houses be of fair and gorgeous building, and on the street side they stand joined together in a long row through the whole street without any partition or separation. The streets be twenty feet broad. On the back side of the houses, through the whole length of the street, lie large gardens enclosed round about with the back part of the streets. Every house has two doors, one into the street and a postern door on the back side into the garden. These doors be made with two leaves never locked nor bolted, so easy to be opened that they will follow the least drawing of a finger and shut again alone. Whoso will may go in, for there is

[44] From the translation by Ralph Robinson, 1551, Book 2.

[45] From Sir Thomas More, *English Works* (London, 1557), pp. 329, 420, 867, 927.

[46] Reprinted from *The Correspondence of Sir Thomas More*, ed. Elizabeth F. Rogers (Princeton, N.J.: Princeton University Press, 1947), pp. 542–4, by permission of Princeton University Press.

nothing within the houses that is private or any man's own. And every tenth year they change their houses by lot.

They set great store by their gardens. In them they have vineyards, all manner of fruit, herbs and flowers, so pleasant, so well furnished, and so finely kept that I never saw thing more fruitful nor better trimmed in any place. Their study and diligence herein comes not only of pleasure but also of a certain strife and contention that is between street and street concerning the trimming, husbanding and furnishing of their gardens, every man for his own part. . . .

But now I will declare how the citizens use themselves one towards another, what familiar occupying and entertainment there is among the people, and what fashion they use in the distribution of everything. First, the city consists of families; the families most commonly be made of kindreds. For the women, when they be married at a lawful age, they go into their husbands' houses, but the male children, with all the whole male offspring, continue still in their own family and be governed of the oldest and ancientest father, unless he dote for age, for then the next to him in age is placed in his room. But to the intent the prescript number of citizens should neither decrease nor above measure increase, it is ordained that no family, which in every city be six thousand in the whole besides them of the country, shall at once have fewer children of the age of fourteen years or thereabout than ten or more than sixteen, for of children under this age no number can be prescribed or appointed. This measure or number is easily observed and kept by putting them that in fuller families be above the number into families of smaller increase. But if chance be that in the whole city the store increase above the just number, therewith they fill up the lack of other cities. But if it so be that the multitude throughout the whole island pass and exceed the due number, then they choose out of every city certain citizens and build up a town under their own laws in the next land where the inhabitants have much waste and unoccupied ground, receiving also the same country-people to them if they will join and dwell with them. . . . And if they resist and rebel, then they make war against them. For they count this the most just cause of war, when any people holds a piece of ground void and vacant to no good nor profitable use, keeping others from the use and possession of it which notwithstanding by the law of nature ought thereof to be nourished and relieved. If any chance do so much diminish the number of any of their cities that it cannot be filled up again without the diminishing of the just number of the other cities . . . they fulfill and make up the number with citizens fetched out of their foreign towns; for they had ·rather suffer their foreign towns to decay and perish than any city of their own island to be diminished.

But now again to the conversation of the citizens among themselves.

The eldest (as I said) rules the family. The wives be ministers to their husbands, the children to their parents, and to be short, the younger to their elders. Every city is divided into four equal parts or quarters. In the midst of every quarter there is a market-place of all manner of things. Thither the works of every family be brought into certain houses, and every kind of thing is laid up several [47] in barns or storehouses. From hence the father of every family or every householder fetches away whatsoever he and his have need of, and carries it away with him without money, without exchange, without any gage, pawn or pledge. For why should anything be denied unto him, seeing there is abundance of all things, and that it is not to be feared lest any man will ask more than he needs? For why should it be thought that that man would ask more than enough which is sure never to lack? Certainly in all kinds of living creatures either fear of lack does cause covetousness and ravin, or in man only pride, which counts it a glorious thing to pass and excel other in the superfluous and vain ostentation of things. The which kind of vice among the Utopians can have no place. . . .

They begin every dinner and supper by reading something that pertains to good manners and virtue; but it is short because no man shall be grieved [48] therewith. Hereof the elders take occasion of honest communication, but neither sad nor unpleasant. Howbeit, they do not spend all the whole dinner time themselves with long and tedious talks, but they gladly hear also the young men, yea and purposely provoke them to talk, to the intent that they may have proof of every man's wit and towardness [49] or disposition to virtue, which commonly in the liberty of feasting does show and utter itself. Their dinners be very short, but their suppers be somewhat longer, because that after dinner follows labour, after supper sleep and natural rest. . . . No supper is passed without music, nor their banquets lack not conceits [50] and junkets.[51] They burn sweet gums and spices or perfumes and pleasant smells, and sprinkle about sweet ointments and waters, yea they leave nothing undone that makes for the cheering of the company. For they be much inclined to this opinion, to think no kind of pleasure forbidden whereof comes no harm. . . .

The sick, as I said, they see to with great affection and let nothing at all pass concerning either physic [52] or good diet whereby they may be restored again to their health. Such as be sick of incurable diseases

[47] separately
[48] bored
[49] aptitude
[50] amusements
[51] play
[52] medicine

they comfort with sitting by them, with talking with them, and, to be short, with all manner of helps that may be. But if the disease be not only incurable but also full of continual pain and anguish, then the priests and the magistrates exhort the man (seeing he is not able to do any duty of life and by overliving his own death is noisome and irksome to other and grievous to himself) that he will determine with himself no longer to cherish that pestilent and painful disease; and, seeing his life is to him but a torment, that he will not be unwilling to die but rather take a good hope to him and either dispatch himself out of that painful life, as out of a prison or a rack of torment, or else suffer himself willingly to be rid out of it by other. And in so doing they tell him he shall do wisely, seeing by his death he shall lose no commodity but end his pain. . . .

There be divers kinds of religion not only in sundry parts of the island but also in divers places of every city. Some worship for god the sun, some the moon, some some other of the planets. There be those that give worship to a man who was once of excellent virtue or of famous glory, not only as god but also as the chiefest and highest god. But the most and the wisest part, rejecting all these, believe that there is a certain godly power unknown, everlasting, incomprehensible, inexplicable, far above the capacity and reach of man's wit, dispersed throughout all the world, not in bigness but in virtue and power. Him they call the father of all. To him alone they attribute the beginnings, the increasings, the proceedings, the changes and the ends of all things. . . . But after they heard us speak of the name of Christ, of His doctrine, laws, miracles, and of the no less wonderful constancy of so many martyrs whose blood willingly shed brought a great number of nations throughout all parts of the world into their sect, you will not believe with how glad minds they agreed unto the same. . . . They also which do not agree to Christ's religion fear no man from it nor speak against any man that has received it, saving that one of our company in my presence was sharply punished. He, as soon as he was baptized, began against our will, with more earnest affection[53] than wisdom to reason of Christ's religion and began to wax so hot in his matter that he did not only profess our religion before all other but also did utterly despise and condemn all other, calling them profane and the followers of them wicked and devilish and the children of everlasting damnation. When he had thus long reasoned the matter they laid hold on him, accused him and condemned him into exile, not as a despiser of religion but as a seditious person and a raiser up of dissension among the people. For this is one of their ancientest laws

53 passion

among them, that no man shall be blamed for reasoning in the maintenance of his own religion. . . .

In other places they speak still of the commonwealth, but every man procures his own private gain. Here, where nothing is private, the common affairs be earnestly looked upon. . . . Is not this an unjust and an unkind public weal [54] which gives great fees and rewards to gentlemen, as they call them, and to goldsmiths and to such other, which be either idle persons, or else flatterers and devisers of vain pleasures; and of the contrary part makes no provision for poor ploughmen, colliers, labourers, carters, ironsmiths and carpenters without whom no commonwealth can continue? But after it has abused the labours of their lusty and flowering age, at the last, when they be oppressed with old age and sickness, being needy, poor and indigent of all things, then . . . recompenses and acquits them most unkindly with miserable death. And yet beside this the rich men, not only by private fraud but also by common laws, do every day pluck and snatch away from the poor some sort of their daily living. . . . Therefore, when I consider and weigh in my mind all these commonwealths which nowadays anywhere do flourish, so God help me, I can perceive nothing but a certain conspiracy of rich men procuring their own commodities under the name and title of the commonwealth. . . .

## B. TRUE FAITH AND FALSE HERESY

### *"Confutation of Tyndale's 'Answer'"* (1532)

. . . Our Lord send us now some years as plentuous of good corn as we have had some years of late plentuous of evil books. For they have grown so fast and sprung up so thick, full of pestilent errors and pernicious heresies, that they have infected and killed, I fear me, more silly simple souls than the famine of the dear years have destroyed bodies. And surely no little cause there is to dread that the great abundance and plenty of the one is no little cause and occasion of the great dearth and scarcity of the other. For since that our Lord of his especial providence uses temporarily to punish the whole people for the sins of some part to compel the good folk to forbear [55] and abhor the naughty, whereby they may bring them to amendment and avoid themselves the contagion of their company: wisdom were it for us to perceive that like as folk begin now to delight in feeding their souls of the venomous carrion of those poisonous heresies . . . our

[54] society
[55] avoid

Lord likewise againward to revenge it withal begins to withdraw his gracious hand from the fruits of the earth, diminishing the fertility both in corn and cattle and bringing all in dearth much more than men can remedy or fully find out the cause. And yet beside this, somewhere he sends war, sickness and mortality, to punish in the flesh that odious and hateful sin of the soul that spoils the fruit from all manner of virtues, I mean unbelief, false faith and infidelity; and to tell all at once in plain English, heresy. . . .

. . . I have diverse good and true witnesses to bring forth when time requires, St Augustine, St Jerome, St Cyprian, St Chrisostom, and a great many more, which have also testified for my part in this matter more than a thousand years ago. Yet have I another ancient sad [56] father also, one that they call Origen. And when I desired him to take the pain to come and bear witness with me in this matter, he seemed at the first very well content. But when I told him that he should meet with Tyndale, he blessed himself and shrank back and said, he had liever go some other way many a mile than once meddle with him. "For I shall tell you, sir," quoth he, "before this time a right honourable man, very cunning [57] and yet more virtuous, the good bishop of Rochester, [58] in a great audience brought me in for a witness against Luther and Tyndale even in this same matter, about the time of the burning of Tyndale's evil translated testament. But Tyndale, as soon as he heard of my name, without any respect of honesty fell in a rage with me and all berated me and called me stark heretic, and that the starkest that ever was." This tale Origen told me and swore by St Simpkin that he was never so said unto of [59] such a lewd fellow since he was first born of his mother; and therefore would never meddle with Tyndale more. . . .

### "Apology" (1533)

. . . But where the brethren [60] say that I am not indifferent [61] in the matter, therein do they the thing they seldom do, that is to wit, say the truth. For if they call the matter either the vice or virtue of the persons (which *I* take not for the matter), yet therein am I not indifferent indeed between a temporal man and a spiritual. For as for vice I hold it much more damnable in a spiritual person than in a temporal man. And as for virtue, equal virtue, I hold it yet much more if it

[56] worthy
[57] learned
[58] John Fisher (1459–1535), later executed for opposition to the Reformation
[59] by
[60] the reformers
[61] impartial

happen in the temporal man than in the spiritual because, though the thing be equal, they be not both equally bound thereto. And therefore if they take this for the matter, in this wise I am not indifferent.

Now if they take for the matter the thing that I take for the matter, that is to wit the true faith and false heresies, then I am much less indifferent. For God keep me from being indifferent between those two sorts. For every good man is bound between truth and falsehood, the Catholic Church and heretics, between God and the devil, to be partial and plainly to declare himself to be full and whole upon the one side and clear against the other. . . .

They reprove that I bring in, among the most earnest matters, fancies and sports and merry tales. For as Horace says, a man may sometimes say full sooth [62] in game. And [one] that is but a layman, as I am, it may better haply become him merely to tell his mind than seriously and solemnly to preach. . . .

### C. THE DUTIES OF CONSCIENCE

Now have I heard since that same day that this obstinate manner of mine, in still refusing the oath, shall peradventure force and drive the King's Grace to make further law for me. I cannot let [63] such a law to be made. But I am very sure that if I died by such a law I should die for that point innocent afore God. . . . Albeit, mine own good daughter, that I found myself (I cry God mercy) very sensual and my flesh much more shrinking from pain and from death than me thought it the part of a faithful Christian man, in such a case as my conscience gave me that in the saving of my body should stand the loss of my soul, yet I thank our Lord that in that conflict the spirit had in conclusion the mastery; and reason with help of faith finally concluded that for to be put to death wrongfully for doing well (as I am very sure I do in refusing to swear against mine own conscience, being such as I am not upon peril of my soul bound to change, whether my death should come without law or by colour of law), it is a case in which a man may lose his head and yet have no harm, but instead of harm inestimable good at the hand of God.

And I thank our Lord, Meg, since I am come hither I set by death every day less than other. For though a man lose of his years in this world, it is more than manifold recompensed by coming the sooner to heaven. And though it be a pain to die while a man is in health, yet I see very few that in sickness die with ease. And finally, very sure am I that whensoever the time shall come that may hap to come—God

[62] truth
[63] prevent

wot [64] how soon—in which I should be sick in my deathbed by nature, I shall then think that God had done much for me if he had suffered me to die before by the colour of such a law. And therefore my reason shows me, Margaret, that it were great folly for me to be sorry to come to that death which I would after wish that I had died. Beside that, that a man may hap with less thanks of God and more adventure of the soul to die as violently and as painfully by many other chances, as by enemies or thieves. And therefore, mine own good daughter, I assure you (thanks be to God) the thinking of any such, albeit it has grieved me ere this, yet at this day grieves me nothing. And yet I know well, for all this, mine own frailty, and that St Peter (which feared it much less than I) fail in such fear soon after that at the word of a simple girl he forsook and forswore our Saviour. And therefore am I not, Meg, so mad as to warrant myself to stand. But I shall pray, and pray thee mine own good daughter to pray with me, that it may please God that has given me this mind to give me the grace to keep it.

And thus have I, mine own good daughter, disclosed unto you the very secret bottom of my mind, referring the order thereof only to the goodness of God, and that so fully that I assure you, Margaret, on my faith, I have never prayed God to bring me hence nor deliver me from death; but referring all things wholly unto His only pleasure, as to Him Who sees better what is best for me than myself does. Nor never longed I since I came hither to set my foot in mine own house, for any desire of or pleasure of my house; but gladly would I sometime somewhat talk with my friends, and specially my wife and you that pertain to my charge. But since that God otherwise disposes, I commit all wholly to His goodness and take daily great comfort in that I perceive that you live together so charitably and so quietly: I beseech our Lord to continue it. And thus, mine own good daughter, putting you finally in remembrance that—albeit if the necessity so should require, I thank our Lord in this quiet and comfort is mine heart at this day, and I trust in God's goodness so shall have grace to continue—yet, as I said before, I verily trust that God shall so inspire and govern the King's heart that he shall not suffer his noble heart and courage to requite my true faithful heart and service with such extreme, unlawful and uncharitable dealing, only for the displeasure that I cannot think so as others do. But his true subject will I live and die, and truly pray for him will I, both here and in the other world too. . . .

[64] knows

# 25 / BALDASSARE CASTIGLIONE (1478-1529): THE COURTIER (1528)

*The Renaissance produced quite a crop of works dealing with the duties of princes and their servants; of these Castiglione's* Courtier *was the best and most influential. The author served a number of Italian princes—including the duke of Urbino, at whose court the conversations in which the work is cast are imagined to have taken place. The book teaches success to gentlemen wishing to learn the very important art of sixteenth-century courtierdom; it instructs in the physical and intellectual exercises required and outlines the proper behavior toward one's employer. It demonstrates the civilizing influence of the Renaissance on the aristocracies of Europe.*[65]

### BOOK 1

. . . I will have this your courtier therefore to be a gentleman born and of a good house. For it is a great deal less dispraise for him that is not born a gentleman to fail in the acts of virtue, than for a gentleman. If he swerve from the steps of his ancestors he stains the name of his family. . . . Therefore it chances always (in a manner) both in arms and in all other virtuous acts that the most famous men are gentlemen. Because nature in everything has deeply sowed that privy seed which gives a certain force and property of her beginning unto whatsoever springs of it, and makes it like herself. As we see by example not only in the race of horses and other beasts, but also in trees whose slips and grafts always for the most part are like unto the stock of the tree they came from; and if at any time they grow out of kind, the fault is in the husbandman. And the like is in men: if they be trained up in good nurture, most commonly they resemble them from whom they come and often times [sur]pass them; but if they have not one that can well train them up, they grow, as it were, wild and never come to their ripeness. Truth it is, whether it be through the favour of the stars or of nature, some there are born endowed with such graces that they seem not to have been born but rather fashioned with the very hand of some god and abound in all goodness both of

[65] Taken from *Il Cortegiano*, transl. Sir Thomas Hoby (London, 1561).

body and mind. As again we see some so unapt and dull that a man will not believe but nature has brought them into the world for a spite and mockery. And like as these with continual diligence and good bringing up for the most part can bring small fruit, even so the other with little attendance climb to the full perfection of all excellency. . . .

I judge the principal and true profession of a courtier ought to be in feats of arms, the which above all I will have him to practise lively, and to be known among other for his hardiness,[66] for his achieving of enterprises, and for his fidelity toward him whom he serves. . . . The more excellent our courtier shall be in this art, the more shall he be worthy [of] praise; albeit I judge it not necessary in him so perfect a knowledge of things and other qualities that is requisite in a captain. But because this is over large a scope of matters, we will hold ourselves contented, as we have said, with the uprightness of a well-meaning mind and with an invincible courage, and that he always show himself such a one; for many times men of courage are sooner known in small matters than in great. . . . Yet will we not have him for all that so lusty to make bravery in words, and to brag that he has wedded his harness for his wife, and to threaten with such grim looks. . . . A worthy gentlewoman in a noble assembly spoke pleasantly unto one that shall be nameless for this time, whom she—to show him a good countenance—desired to dance with her; and he refusing both that and to hear music and many other entertainments offered him, always affirming such trifles not to be his profession, at last the gentlewoman demanding him, "what is then your profession?", he answered with a frowning look, "to fight." Then said the gentlewoman, "Seeing you are not now at the war or in place to fight, I would think it best for you to be well besmeared [67] and set up in an armory with other implements of war, till time were that you should be occupied, lest you wax more rustier than you are." . . .

I think also it will serve his turn greatly to know the feat of wrestling, because it goes much together with all weapons on foot. Again it is behoveful both for himself and his friends that he have a foresight in the quarrels and controveries that may happen . . . neither let him run rashly to these combats but when he must needs to save his estimation. . . . It is meet for him also to have the art of swimming, to leap, to run, to cast the stone; for beside the profit that he may receive of this in the wars, it happens to him many times to make proof of himself in such things, whereby he gets him a reputation especially among the multitude unto whom a man must sometimes apply him-

[66] courage
[67] oiled

self. Also it is a noble exercise and meet for one living in court to play at tennis, where the disposition of the body, the quickness and nimbleness of every member, is much perceived. . . . And I reckon vaulting of no less praise, which (for all it is painful and hard) makes a man more light and quicker than the rest. . . . He may set aside tumbling, climbing upon a cord, and other such matters that taste somewhat of the juggler's craft and do little beseem a gentleman. . . .

. . . Eschew as much as a man may . . . affectation or curiosity [68] . . . ; use in everything a certain recklessness to cover art withal, and seem whatsoever he does and says to do it without pain and (as it were) not minding it. And of this do I believe grace is much derived, for in rare matters and well brought to pass every man knows the hardness of them, so that a readiness therein makes great wonder. . . . Therefore that may be said to be a very art that appears not to be art; neither ought a man to put more diligence in anything than in covering it. . . .

That therefore which is the principal matter and necessary for a courtier to speak and write well, I believe is knowledge. For he that has not knowledge and the thing in his mind that deserves to be understood can neither speak nor write it. Then must he couch in a good order that [which] he has to speak or to write, and afterward express it well with words; the which (if I be not deceived) ought to be apt, chosen, clear and well applied, and above all in use also among the people. . . . And this do I say as well of writing as of speaking wherein certain things are requisite that are not necessary in writing: as a good voice, not too subtle and soft as in a woman, nor yet so boisterous and rough as in one of the country, but shrill, clear, sweet and well framed with a prompt pronunciation and with fit manners and gestures which (in my mind) consist in certain motions of all the body, not affected or forced but tempered with a mannerly countenance and with a moving of the eyes that may give a grace and accord with the words. . . . Neither will I have him to speak always in gravity, but of pleasant matters, of merry conceits, of honest devices, and of jests according to their time, and in all notwithstanding after a pithy matter. . . . And when he shall then common [69] of a matter that is dark and hard I will have him both in words and sentences well pointed, to express his judgment and to make every doubt clear and plain, after a certain diligent sort without tediousness. Likewise, when he shall see time, to have the understanding to speak with dignity and vehemence, and to raise those affections which our minds have in them, and to inflame or stir them according to the matter. . . .

[68] eccentricity
[69] speak

### BOOK 2

I suppose the conversation which the courtier ought chiefly to be pliable unto with all diligence to get him favour is the very same that he shall have with his prince. And although this manner of conversation brings with it a certain equality that a man would not judge can reign between the master and the servant, yet will we so term it for this once. I will have our courtier therefore—beside that he has and does daily give men to understand that he is of the prowess which we have said ought to be in him—to turn all his thoughts and force of mind to love and (as it were) reverence the prince he serves above all other things, and in his will, manners and fashions to be altogether pliable to please him. . . . And to this will I have the courtier to frame himself, though he were not by nature inclined to it, so that whensoever his lord looks upon him he may think in his mind he has to talk with him of a matter that he will be glad to hear. . . . He shall never be sad before his prince nor melancholy, nor so solemn as many that a man would ween [70] were at debate with their lords, which is truly a hateful matter. He shall not be ill-tongued, and especially against his superiors, which happens oftentimes. . . . Our courtier shall use no fond sauciness. He shall be no carrier about of trifling news. He shall not be overseen in speaking otherwise words that may offend, where his intent was to please. He shall not be stubborn and full of contention, as some busibodies that a man would ween had none other delight but to vex and stir men like flies and take upon them to contrary every man spitefully without respect. He shall be no babbler, not given to lightness, no liar, no boaster, nor fond flatterer, but sober and keeping him always within his bounds, use continually and especially abroad the reverence and respect that becomes a servant toward the master. . . . In suing for others he shall discreetly observe the times, and his suit shall be for honest and reasonable matters; and he shall so frame his suit, in leaving out those points that he shall know will trouble him . . . that his lord will ever more grant it to him. . . . He shall not covet to press into the chamber or other secret places where his lord is withdrawn . . . for great men oftentimes when they are privately gotten alone love a certain liberty to speak and do what they please and therefore will not be seen or heard of any person that may lightly deem of them; and reason wills no less. . . .

[70] think

## SUMMARY

The final end of a courtier, whereto all his good conditions and honest qualities tend, is to become an instructor and teacher of his prince or lord, inclining him to virtuous practices; and to be frank and free with him, after he is once in favour, in matters touching his honour and estimation, always putting him in mind to follow virtue and to flee vice, opening unto him the commodities of the one and the inconveniences of the other; and to shut his ears against flatterers which are the first beginning of self-liking and all ignorance. . . .

# 26 / ROGER ASCHAM (1516-1568): THE SCHOOLMASTER (1564)

*The humanists were naturally very much concerned with problems of education; Erasmus, the Spaniard Juan Vives (1492–1540), and many others wrote in that field. Nevertheless, the most attractive treatise on the subject is by Roger Ascham, a Cambridge scholar and experienced teacher who was tutor to, among others, the young Princess Elizabeth. His book, not published until 1570, is in the main an outline program for the teaching of Latin grammar and literature and, as such, one of the foundation stones of the long-enduring humanist educational tradition; its most interesting part deals with the different capacities encountered in boys and, contrary to the practice of the day, advocates patience as a better method than violence.*[71]

I have now wished, twice or thrice, this gentle nature to be in a schoolmaster; and that I have done so neither by chance nor without some reason I will now declare at large, why in my opinion love is fitter than fear, gentleness better than beating, to bring up a child rightly in learning. With the common use of teaching and beating in common schools in England I will not greatly contend; which if I did, it were but a small grammatical controversy, neither belonging

[71] From *The Scholemaster*, Arber's English Reprints (London, 1870), pp. 31–5, 39.

to heresy nor treason, nor greatly touching God nor the prince; although in very deed the good or ill bringing up of children does as much serve to the good or ill service of God, our prince and our whole country as any one thing does beside.

I do gladly agree with all good schoolmasters in these points: to have children brought to good perfectness in learning, to all honesty in manners, to have all faults rightly amended, to have every vice severely corrected. But for the order and way that leads rightly to these points, we somewhat differ. For commonly many schoolmasters—some as I have seen, more as I have heard tell—be of so crooked a nature as when they meet with a hard-witted [72] scholar they rather break him than bow him, rather mar him than mend him. For when the schoolmaster is angry with some other matter, then will he soonest fall to beat his scholar; and though he himself should be punished for his folly, yet he must beat some scholar for his pleasure, though there be no cause for him to do so, nor yet fault in the scholar to deserve so. These, ye will say, be fond [73] schoolmasters, and few they be that be found to be such. They be fond indeed, but surely over-many such be found everywhere. But this will I say that even the wisest of your great beaters do as often punish nature as they do correct faults. Yea, many times the better nature is sorer punished. For if one, by quickness of wit,[74] take his lesson readily, another, by hardness of wit, takes it not so speedily. The first is always commended, the other is commonly punished, when a wise schoolmaster should rather discreetly consider the right disposition of both their natures and not so much weigh what either of them is able to do now as what either of them is likely to do hereafter. For this I know, not only by reading books in my study but also by experience of life abroad in the world, that those which be commonly the wisest, the best learned, and best men also when they be old were never commonly the quickest of wit when they were young. The causes why, amongst other, be these few which I will reckon. Quick wits commonly be apt to take, unapt to keep; soon hot and desirous of this and that, as cold and soon weary of the same again; more quick to enter speedily than able to pierce far; even like oversharp tools whose edges be very soon turned. Such wits delight themselves in easy and pleasant studies and never pass far forward in high and hard sciences. And therefore the quickest wits commonly may prove the best poets, but not the wisest orators: ready of tongue to speak boldly, not deep of judgment either for good

---

[72] slow to learn
[73] stupid
[74] intelligence

counsel or wise writing. Also for manners and life quick wits commonly be in desire newfangled, in purpose unconstant, light to promise anything, ready to forget everything, both benefit and injury; and thereby neither fast to friend nor fearful to foe; inquisitive of every trifle, not secret in greatest affairs; bold with any person, busy in every matter; soothing such as be present, nipping any that be absent; of nature also always flattering their betters, envying their equals, despising their inferiors; and by quickness of wit very ready to like none so well as themselves.

Moreover, men very quick of wit be also very light of conditions; and thereby very ready of disposition to be carried over quickly by any light company to any riot and unthriftiness when they be young; and therefore seldom either honest of life or rich in living when they be old. For quick in wit and light in manners be either seldom troubled, or very soon weary, in carrying a heavy purse. Quick wits also be in most part of all their doings overquick, hasty, rash, heady and brainsick. These two last words, heady and brainsick, be fit and proper words rising naturally of the matter and termed aptly by the condition of over-much quickness of wit. In youth also they be ready scoffers, privy mockers, and ever over-light and merry. In age, soon testy, very waspish, and always over-miserable; and yet few of them come to any great age by reason of their misordered life when they were young; but a great deal fewer of them come to show any great countenance or bear any great authority abroad in the world, but either live obscurely, men know not how, or die obscurely, men mark not when. They be like trees that show forth fair blossoms and broad leaves in spring time, but bring out small and not long-lasting fruit in harvest time, and that only such as fall and rot before they be ripe, and so never or seldom come to any good at all. For this ye shall find most true by experience that amongst a number of quick wits in youth few be found in the end either very fortunate for themselves or very profitable to serve the commonwealth, but decay and vanish, men know not which way; except a very few to whom peradventure blood and happy parentage may perchance purchase a long standing upon the stage. . . .

Some wits, moderate enough by nature, be many times marred by over-much study and use of some sciences, namely music, arithmetic and geometry. These sciences, as they sharpen men's wits over-much so they change men's manners over-sore if they be not moderately mingled and wisely applied to some good use of life. Mark all mathematical heads which be only and wholly bent to those sciences, how solitary they be themselves, how unfit to live with others, and how unapt to serve in the world. This is not only known now by common experience, but uttered long before by wise men's judgment and sentence. Galen says, much music mars men's manners; and Plato has a notable place of the same thing in his books *De Republica*. . . .

Contrariwise, a wit in youth that is not over-dull, heavy, knotty, and lumpish, but hard, rough and though somewhat stiffish, . . . if it be at the first well handled by the mother and slightly smoothed and wrought as it should—not overthwartly [75] and against the wood—by the schoolmaster, both for learning and whole course of living proves always the best. In wood and stone not the softest but the hardest be always aptest for portraiture, both fairest for pleasure and most durable for profit. Hard wits be hard to receive, but sure to keep; painful [76] without weariness, heedful without wavering, constant without new-fangledness; bearing heavy things though not lightly yet willingly; entering hard things though not easily yet deeply; and so come to that perfectness of learning in the end that quick wits seem in hope but do not in deed, or else very seldom, ever attain unto. Also for manners and life, hard wits commonly are hardly carried either to desire every new thing or else to marvel at every strange thing; and therefore they be careful and diligent in their own matters, not curious and busy in other men's affairs; and so they become wise themselves and also are counted honest by others. They be grave, steadfast, silent of tongue, secret of heart. Not hasty in making but constant in keeping any promise. Not rash in uttering but wary in considering every matter; and thereby not quick in speaking but deep of judgment, whether they write or give counsel in all weighty affairs. And these be the men that become in the end both most happy for themselves and always best esteemed abroad in the world.

I have been longer in describing the nature, the good or ill success, of the quick and hard wit than perchance some will think this place and matter does require. But my purpose was hereby plainly to utter what injury is offered to all learning, and to the commonwealth also, by the fond father in choosing, but chiefly by the lewd [77] schoolmaster in beating and driving away the best natures from learning. A child that is still, silent, constant, and somewhat hard of wit, is either never chosen by the father to be made a scholar; he is smally regarded, little looked unto, he lacks teaching, he lacks encouraging, he lacks all things only he never lacks beating nor any word that may move him to hate learning, nor any deed that may drive him from learning to any other kind of living. . . .

[75] against its nature
[76] painstaking
[77] wicked

If a father have four sons, three fair and well-formed both in mind and body, the fourth wretched, lame and deformed, his choice shall be to put the worst to learning, as one good enough to become a scholar. I have spent the most part of my life in the University, and therefore I can bear good witness that many fathers commonly do thus. . . .

# 27 / COMMENT: JACOB BURCKHARDT (1818-1897) ON THE RENAISSANCE AND THE INDIVIDUAL

*The great Swiss historian, a university professor at Basel from 1844, wrote relatively little—he spent much time on his teaching—but produced in* The Civilization of the Renaissance in Italy *(1860) one of the remarkable books of the nineteenth century. In it he showed how an understanding of ideas and art can be used to give a depth to the writing of history which the then almost universal concentration on political and constitutional studies could not achieve. Burckhardt's stock has risen greatly since his death, in part because he wrote the sort of social history which has become fashionable in recent times, and in part because his distrust of the future seems today greater wisdom than the often naive optimism of so many of his contemporaries. While his book on the Renaissance remains a splendid work, a hundred years of research and reflection—much of it touched off by this book itself—have naturally altered many views and demolished many of Burckhardt's most firmly held positions (see, e.g., No. 16). Above all, he neither knew enough nor sympathized enough with the Middle Ages proper. None of this, however, detracts from the insight and power of synthesis which mark the book.*[78]

[78] Translated from *Die Kultur der Renaissance in Italien*, 2nd ed. (Leipzig, 1869), pp. 104–6, 109–10, 113–15, 121–2.

In the Middle Ages, the two sides of man's consciousness—the one directed at the world and the other to his inner self—lay dreaming or half-awake as under a common veil. That veil was woven out of faith, childlike immaturity and illusion; seen through it, the world and history appeared strangely colored, and man was aware of himself only in terms of race, people, faction, corporation, family, or some other form of communal existence. It was in Italy that this veil first vanished into air; an *objective* consideration and treatment of the state and of all the things of this world became possible; at the same time *subjective* attitudes grew to full power, man became intellectually *individual* and saw himself as such. In just this way the Greek had once thought himself superior to the barbarian, and the Arab, an individualist, to other Asiatics seen only as particles of a race. It will not be difficult to prove that political conditions played the major part in this.

Even in very much earlier days the growth of an independent personality is at times visible, in ways which do not occur—or do not reveal themselves—in the north. That circle of energetic miscreants described by Liudprand in the tenth century,[79] a few contemporaries of Gregory VII,[80] some adversaries of the early Hohenstaufen [81]—these display characteristics of that sort. But towards the end of the thirteenth century Italy began to teem with personalities; the interdict which had lain on individualism was here completely broken; a thousand faces become distinguishable with no sort of obstacle in the way. Dante's great epic would have been impossible in any other country, if only because the rest of Europe still lay under the spell of the community; in Italy that noble poet, through the abundance of his individualism, became the most entirely national herald of his day. However, the representation of human abundance in literature and art, with its many-sided characterizations, will be discussed in separate sections; here we are concerned only with the psychological fact itself. It now entered history totally and determinately; fourteenth-century Italy knew little of false modesty, or indeed of any kind of hypocrisy; no one was afraid of being and seeming different from everyone else.

Despotism, as we have seen, fostered in the first place the individualism of the despot, the condottiere, himself, but also that of the talented men he promoted or ruthlessly exploited—secretaries, officials, poets and courtiers. Pressed by necessity, the minds of such men came to know their inward resources, the permanent ones as well as those of the moment; they too, endeavoring to obtain the greatest

[79] tenth-century Italián chronicler
[80] pope, 1073–85
[81] German imperial house, 1138–1208 and 1214–54

value from what might be only a brief period of power and influence, found in things of the mind a more intense and concentrated means to the enjoyment of life.

However, their subjects did not entirely escape this impetus. We pass over those who wasted their lives in secret opposition and conspiracies, considering only those who acquiesced in a purely private existence, as did for instance most of the urban populations in the Byzantine empire and the Muslim states. True, the subjects of the Visconti, to take an example, often found it difficult to maintain the dignity of their family and person; a good many will have suffered in servitude a decline of moral character. But not so much of what may be called their individual character; for just because of their general political impotence, the many possibilities and enterprises of private life acquired a special vigor and variety. Wealth and education, in so far as they were allowed to manifest themselves in competition, together with strong surviving elements of municipal freedom and with the presence of a Church which, unlike that of the world of Byzantium and Islam, was not identical with the state—all these elements undoubtedly favored the rise of individual attitudes; and the absence of party struggles added the necessary leisure. The figure of the private individual, indifferent to politics and engaged in his sometimes serious, sometimes dilettante, occupations, probably first made its fully developed appearance in these fourteenth-century despotisms. . . .

When this impulse to develop the personality to the utmost encountered a truly powerful and at the same time many-sided nature which had mastered all the elements of contemporary culture, the result was the "universal man" (*uomo universale*), an exclusively Italian phenomenon. Men of encyclopaedic knowledge are found throughout the middle ages in various countries, because then that knowledge covered closely related fields; as late as the twelve century one finds artists who were universal because the problems of architecture were relatively simple and of one kind, while in sculpture and painting the matter to be represented took precedence over the manner. In Renaissance Italy, on the other hand, we meet individual artists who in all fields produced works which are both altogether original and perfect of their kind, and who in addition leave their greatest impression as human beings. Outside the sphere of the fine arts, other men developed universality in an astonishingly wide range of intellectual pursuits. . . .

The fifteenth century is preeminently the age of many-sided men. No biography but stresses notable sidelines pursued by its subject well beyond the limits of dilettantism. The merchant or statesman of Florence is often at the same time a scholar in both ancient languages; the most famous humanists are called upon to lecture to him or his sons on the *Politics* or *Ethics* of Aristotle; the daughters even of the house receive a higher education; indeed, it is in these circles that one must look for the beginnings of a higher private education. The humanist for his part is bidden to be universal, since for a long time his philological learning has to serve a daily use in real life, not testify (as it does today) only to his objective knowledge of classical antiquity. Thus while studying Pliny he will collect a museum of natural history; starting from the geography of the ancients he will turn to modern cosmography; following the pattern of their historiography, he will compose histories of his own times; the translator of Platus' comedies will also produce them on the stage; all forms of ancient literature with any sort of relevance, even down to Lucian's *Dialogues*, he will imitate as best he can; and in addition to all this he will practise as a secretary or diplomatist, not always to his advantage. . . .

The development of the individual described so far produced its new form of outward assertion—the modern concept of fame.

Outside Italy the individual estates of society lived each by itself with its particular medieval notion of honor. The poetic fame of *troubadours* and *minnesänger*, for instance, was known only to the knightly estate. In Italy, on the other hand, all estates were levelled by either despotism or democracy; one observes the beginnings of a universal society which (to anticipate) finds a common ground in Italian and Latin literature, a soil needed for the new element of life to grow in. In addition, those Roman authors who were beginning to be diligently studied are quite filled and saturated with the idea of fame; even their subject matter—Rome's empire of the world—contained all sorts of parallels ever present to the Italian mind. Henceforth all the desires and achievements of Italy were governed by a moral presupposition so far unknown in the rest of Europe.

Again, as in all significant issues, Dante must be the first to receive a hearing. With all the power of his soul he strove for the poet's laurel-wreath; even as a publicist and journalist he insisted on the essential novelty of his achievements, claiming not only to be but also to be recognised as the first man on his road. . . . Dante's successors, a new generation of poet-philologers, quickly took possession of fame in two senses: they themselves became the most renowned celebrities of Italy, and at the same time as poets and historians they self-consciously disposed of the fame of others. . . . Petrarch, too, enjoyed to the full the new incense, once available only to heroes and saints, even persuading himself in his later years that it seemed to him a useless and troublesome accompaniment. His letter "To Posterity" embodies the testament of an old and famous man compelled to satisfy public curiosity; he would wish to enjoy fame with posterity but would rather be free of it in his lifetime; when in his dialogue on fortune and misfortune he touches on fame, it is the opponent, who proves fame to be void, who has the better of the argument. But how seriously is one to take this when Petrarch shows pleasure at being as well known to the ruler of Byzantium through his writings as he is known to the Emperor Charles IV? For his fame did indeed extend beyond Italy in his own day. And he was justly moved when in 1370, during a visit to his birthplace Arezzo, his friends showed him the house where he was born and told him that the city was making sure that nothing in it was changed. . . .

Apart from such doings designed to provide an outward guarantee of fame, a veil is occasionally drawn aside to show us the most outrageous ambition and thirst for greatness, independent of object or success, in frighteningly true colours. Thus in the preface of his *History of Florence,* Machiavelli reproves his *predecessors* ( Leonardo Aretino [82] and Poggio [83] ) for keeping too tactful a silence about the factions of the city. "They much erred and proved that they had no idea of men's ambition and their avidity to perpetuate their names. Quite a few, unable to claim praiseworthy distinction, have sought to gain it through infamous actions. These writers failed to consider that deeds which have a touch of greatness about them—as is the case with the deeds of rulers and states—would always seem to earn fame rather than blame, irrespective of their character or their consequences." Thoughtful historians more than once ascribed some striking and terrible enterprise to a burning desire to do something great and memorable. All this manifests not just a perverted form of ordinary vanity, but something truly daemonic: unfreedom of the will linked with the use of the most extreme measures and with indifference to success as such. . . .

---

[82] Leonardo Bruni, for whom see p. 56.
[83] Gian Francesco Poggio ( 1380–1459 ), a leading scholar of the Renaissance

# IV / THE
# SECULAR STATE

*The period covered in this volume witnessed the end of universal empires, imperial or papal, and the rise of sovereign states and territorial churches. This generalization holds good even for those regions which remained Roman Catholic in religion; and it holds good not only for the powerful nation states of the western seaboard but also for the fragments into which both the German and Italian parts of the Holy Roman Empire broke up. Charles IV was forced to recognize the powers of the great German princes (see No. 28); Frederick III and Maximilian I in effect admitted that the imperial crown had lost all political reality; and even Charles V, though he saw himself as another Charlemagne, was really the ruler of too many disconnected territorial states. The Reformation was to exploit and confirm this breakup of Germany, and the settlement of 1648 (No. 85) acknowledged the fact. In Italy the age of republics was followed by the age of despots (signoria: e g., No. 29), and this in its turn by the foreign domination, first French then Spanish, over which patriots like Machiavelli wept bitter tears. A more characteristic form of polity grew up around the lower Rhine, as the dukes of Burgundy built up and lost their artificial realm; the Habsburgs inherited most of it, but the essential lack of cohesion of this complex of principalities was to be demonstrated in the war of independence (1560–1609) which left the northern provinces free, the middle ones Spanish, and the Burgundian homeland French.*

*Nevertheless, Burgundy played a significant part in the story; because of its enormous wealth (the product of Flemish industry and trade) and the personal ascendancy of the dukes, it led the way in several characteristic features of sixteenth-century politics—personal monarchy, lavish courts, administrative reform. In one way or another, Spain, France, and England all developed these principles, though England retained an important difference: she never abandoned her representative institutions. The Spanish Cortes gradually died, so that Philip II could complete*

*the structure of a bureaucratic royal absolutism; France first for-
got her Estates and then, in the civil war of the later sixteenth
century, learned to dread all rivals to royal power; in England,
on the other hand, the crown deliberately augmented the power
of the Parliament in order to rest royal government on the safe
basis of national cooperation. At least the Tudors did so; the
Stuarts, unable to operate the delicate mechanism, found Parliament too well established to destroy, and were instead themselves
destroyed in the civil wars of 1642–9. Thus there survived in England a peculiar amalgam of medieval liberties with modern organization, out of which modern political liberty was to grow.*

*The consolidation of these states—the creation of monarchic
power approximating to absolutism, the elimination of rival authorities like the Church, assemblies of estates, free cities, priv-
ileged places and persons—proceeded everywhere because it
benefited not only princes but also the bulk of the people, by securing internal peace. But the powers of princes also raised many
questions, and, from Marsiglio in 1324 (No. 2) to the outburst of
political speculation in civil-war England, this was a period of
vigorous thinking and writing on politics and on law. Law was
still, to everyone except Machiavelli, the fundamental entity of
political life; even Bodin, who laid the stress on sovereignty, saw
this as the power to make law and wished to limit it by fundamental laws. Spain, France, and the German principalities came
under the influence of the civil law ultimately derived from the
law of ancient Rome. England preserved and transformed her
common law, which in course of time was to exercise an even
more world-wide influence than Rome itself. But despite the pre-
vailing belief that political power must adhere to the principles
of natural law—those rules of behavior which God has decreed
for the natural creation and which man can find in his conscience
—Machiavelli's analysis of power came nearer to reality and was
ultimately more fruitful.[1]*

---

[1] For extracts on politics and political thought in other sections, see Nos. 2, 60B,
65, 68, 71, 80, 81.

# 28 / CHARLES IV
# (1316-1378): THE GOLDEN
# BULL (1356)

*The Emperor Charles IV (elected in 1346), the outstand-
ing member of the House of Luxemburg, which dominated central-
European politics for about a hundred years, came to recognize
that no reality attached any longer to the imperial title and that
its holder could hope to exercise authority only on the basis of a
personal territorial power. He built up his own power around the
kingdom of Bohemia, whose capital, Prague, owed its elevation to
major-city status to him. The Golden Bull, mainly an edict settling
the manner in which elections to the imperial crown should be
conducted, accepted in effect the collapse of imperial unity and
the dominance of the territorial princes; it attempted to bring
order into the resultant confusion by providing for the ascendancy
of those seven who as Electors (Kurfürsten) were meant to constitute a superior caucus. Despite the many political and dynastic
changes of the following centuries, the document remained the
foundation of the imperial constitution until the abolition of the
Holy Roman Empire by Napoleon in 1806.[2]*

In the Name of the Holy and Undivided Trinity, amen. Charles IV,
by the mercy of God Roman emperor, ever augmentor of the realm, and
king of Bohemia, for the permanent record of the matter.

A kingdom divided against itself suffers ruin. The princes of the
realm have become the companions of thieves, for which reason the
Lord has sent the spirit of confusion into their midst, so that they grope
about at noontide as if in darkness. He has taken away their candle-
sticks, so that they are become blind and the leaders of blind men.
Those who walk in darkness do evil, and blind men commit crimes in
their thoughts: all of which tends to disunity. Speak, Pride: could you
ever have come to rule Lucifer without the help of disunity? Speak,
hateful Satan: could you have ejected Adam from Paradise without
first separating him from obedience? Speak, Lechery: could you have
destroyed Troy without first dividing Helen from her husband? Speak,

2 Translated from *Aurea Bulla Caroli Quarti Romanorum Imperatoris et Regis
Bohemiae &c* (Mainz, 1549).

Wrath: could you have put down the Republic of Rome unless, with the raging swords of disunity, you had first incited Pompey and Julius even to civil war? And you, Envy: that Christian empire erected by God in the image of the Holy and Undivided Trinity and buttressed with faith, hope and charity (the cardinal virtues), whose foundation stands joyously upon the most Christian kingship—[have you not attacked it] with an ancient poison which like the serpent you have spewed criminally upon the tender shoots of the empire and its adjacent parts, so that, the pillars gone, you may reduce the whole edifice to ruin? Frequent disunity have you sown among the seven lamps which, shining sevenfold in the unity of Spirit, should give light to the Holy Empire.—By virtue of our office, we must feel obliged to do what we can by our imperial dignity to prevent the future perils of disunity and disagreement among the Electors of whose number we, as king of Bohemia, are one. . . .

*Chapter One.* We order and decree by this present imperial edict, of our certain knowledge and in the fullness of our imperial power, that howsoever often and whenever in future the need or occasion arises for the election of a king of the Romans to the imperial dignity, and the Electors have cause to proceed to an election according to the ancient and laudable custom thereof, that then every Elector (if and when required) shall allow safe transit to any other Elector or their envoys sent to the election through his lands, territories and possessions, and also beyond, and offer them safe-conduct to the city where the election is to take place as well as for the return journey: on pain of perjury and of losing his vote for that occasion. . . . Into which penalties we decree that all those automatically fall who in the matter of such conduct show themselves rebellious or negligent. . . .

# 29 / FRANCESCO SFORZA (1401-1466)

*Although he came relatively late in the day, Sforza may be taken as the type of the Italian condottiere, or mercenary captain, who carved out a principality for himself. He inherited claims in the south, which he lost to the Aragonese kings of Naples; he built up a power in the March, east of the Apennine, which in due course disappeared as the papacy extended its hold there; but he made good by inheriting through his wife the Visconti duchy of Milan (1450). The following account is from the pen of Enea Silvio (see p. 20) and was written halfway through Sforza's career; it is therefore a contemporary piece of journalism and gives a vivid impression of the extraordinary confusion and wild uncertainty which made up Italian politics in the fifteenth century.*[3]

On the death of his father, Francesco Sforza, son of the elder Sforza and certainly assisted with money by Filippo [Maria], the young duke of Milan, assembled his troops. Determined to talk them round, he had his mother bring along the books in which nearly all the soldiers were recorded as owing considerable debts to his father, and then addressed them thus: "Fellow soldiers, you know my father is dead; you owed a good deal to him, but I am his heir and what you owed to my father you now owe to me. However, I now free you from money debts and every bond by which you were bound to my father. You are therefore free, and it is up to you whom you want to serve. If you want to stay with me, I shall gladly take you into my service. I shall not fear to entrust my life to those who guarded my father's; but as for my fortune I trust entirely in you and shall follow the leadership of men like you who have long served honorably under my father." Seduced by this speech and liberality, the troops shouted that they would suffer no man to be their general except him for whose father they had girded on the sword; by public acclamation he was put in command of the army and took from it an oath of renewed service. After this Francesco served Pope Martin. He was sent against Braccio [4] and won a victory at Aquila, holding his father's possessions in the kingdom of Naples . . . until King Alphonso [5] deprived him of them during his conquest of that realm. Francesco then moved off into Lombardy where Duke Filippo did him great honor, bestowed on him the title of his house and the arms of the Visconti, and also promised him the hand of his only and illegitimate daughter Bianca, a hope of which he later often disappointed him. Francesco performed a good many famous deeds of arms in Lombardy. He carried Filippo's banners against the duke of Savoy and routed the Savoyards; he expelled the marquess of Montferrat, who had an understanding with Venice, from his dominions; in many places he covered himself with military glory. There was much rivalry between him

---

[3] Translated from Enea Silvio, *De Viris Illustribus* (Stuttgart, 1842), Vol. I, pp. 13 ff.

[4] Braccio da Montone (1368–1424), Italian *condottiere* and enemy of the Sforzas, who died at Aquila, soon after his defeat there

[5] Alphonso V of Aragon (1416–58), who established the Aragonese hold over the kingdoms of Sicily and Naples

and Niccolò Piccinino; although Niccolò was [Milanese] commander-in-chief, Francesco, as the prince's prospective son-in-law, did not think himself inferior. The old hatred between the families of Sforza and Braccio was not yet dead: Sforzeschi and Bracceschi still existed, and Francesco led the former, Niccolò (succeeded by Francesco Piccinino) the latter. Francesco was more popular in Lombardy than Niccolò who was reckoned a Tuscan, while Francesco, coming from the Romagna, was thought half-Lombard. Also the prospect of the succession attracted popular favour to Francesco. After this, when Francesco was sent into the March against Pope Eugenius IV to occupy the province in the name of the [General] Council, he published his political claims; for he had left the duke in no state of amity, even saying that if he had lost an eye in Milan he would not go back for it. There was much discord between him and Niccolò, but it never came to war. He left the duke with all his forces and joined the Venetians and Florentines from whom he received a very large annual subsidy. He was made standard-bearer [6] of the Church; afterwards created also Venetian generalissimo, he did not disdain to threaten war against Filippo. Piccinino was therefore called from [the province of] Tuscia, and both sides prepared large forces; everywhere the land was devastated. In the end, while they were preparing for war, the duke of Milan, about to incur the suspicions of Venice, sought to treat for peace and chose Francesco to arbitrate in their differences. Perhaps he did not expect Venice to accept this; and he promised him his daughter, now of marriageable age, with the city of Cremona for dowry. Venice, however, in view of Francesco's [dubious] loyalty to them, at the same time accepted Florence and Genoa as arbitrators, which was not done without loss to the duke since he was deprived of a large part of his dominions. Francesco accepted both wife and Cremona where he celebrated his marriage to Bianca, and now began to enjoy respect with the princes of Italy, though it was not his prowess but his wife's birth which made him respectable. Next he moved to the March, where, engaged with the king of Aragon, he alternately lost and won; he lost his brother with many men after a rebellion; however, he is still a power in the March.

During a spell in the neighbourhood of Bologna he was practised upon, for Baldassare Aufidio, the commander of Bologna and general to the pope, tried to capture him by a ruse and called upon Niccolò Piccinino for help. So far from coming in on this, Piccinino warned Francesco. Thus that deplorable character Aufidio fell into the trap he had set; captured in Butrino he was killed in a dungeon in Firmano, despite all his entreaties. Since we have occasion to mention Baldassare, it is not off the point to relate one of his worst crimes. Antonio

[6] (properly) vicar

dei Bentivogli, a knight, a trained lawyer, and a nobleman by birth, was for about fourteen years leader of the exiled Bolognese faction; for during Martin V's pontificate he could never go home but was maintained on a pension at Rome. When Bologna was recovered by Eugenius IV, he too wanted to return. The citizens therefore agreed to invite him home, to send gifts, and to follow wherever he led. Fearing that Antonio would take over the city, Baldassare asked him to call at his headquarters under the pretext of a consultation. Antonio arrived, and as he stood outside the chapel in the palace he was seized by attendants, dragged along the stairs, and prevented from saying anything; and incontinently, without confession, communion, or a moment given for repentance, was beheaded inside the palace near the outer gate. He had barely time to gasp, "Help me, Mother of God." This deed greatly annoyed the city: that so noble and learned and excellent a man should be thus murdered without confession or trial. Shortly after the city rebelled against Eugenius and went over to Piccinino; at which time also Annibale, Antonio's illegitimate son, entered the town, killed many men, and afterwards, having driven out Piccinino, ruled together there with Battista de Cannetulo. However, he did not triumph for long either, for Battista afterwards had him murdered; whereupon the party of the Bentivogli rose in rebellion, killed Battista, disposed of many of his followers, and burned their houses. That is the present state of that city, though, to judge from their habits, it will not be so for long.

# 30 / SIR JOHN FORTESCUE (C. 1385-1479): THE GOVERNANCE OF ENGLAND (C. 1471)

*Fortescue was the leading English judge of the fifteenth century, chief justice of the Court of King's Bench from 1442; but after 1461 he was involved in the downfall of the Lancastrian house, whose fortunes he followed, in the civil wars of the Roses (1450–85). He wrote a number of books on law and politics at a time when this was very unusual; his main argument was the excellence of the English common law and political system with its Parliament. His distinction between a* dominium regale *(absolute rule) and a* dominium politicum et regale *(constitutional govern-*

*ment) was to become a commonplace with English writers; it was none the less valid for that.*[7]

There be two kinds of kingdoms, of the which the one is a lordship called in Latin *dominium regale,* and the other is called *dominium politicum et regale.* And they diverse[8] in that the first king may rule his people by such laws as he makes himself. And therefore he may set upon them tallages and other impositions such as he will himself, without their assent. The second king may not rule his people by other laws than such as they assent unto. And therefore he may set upon them no impositions without their own assent. . . .

And how so be it, the French king reigns upon his people *dominio regali;* yet St. Louis,[9] some time king there, nor any of his progenitors set never tallages or other impositions upon the people of that land without the assent of the three estates which when they be assembled be like to the court of the Parliament in England. And this order kept many of his successors until late days that Englishmen made such war in France that the three estates durst not come together. And then for that cause, and for great necessity which the French king had of good for the defence of that land, he took upon him to set tallages and other impositions upon the commons without the assent of the three estates. But yet he would not set any such charges, nor has set, upon the nobles for fear of rebellion. And because the commons there, though they have grudged, have not rebelled . . . the French kings have yearly since set such charges upon them, and so augmented the same charges, as the same commons be so impoverished and destroyed that they may unneth[10] live. They drink water, they eat apples, with bread right brown, made from rye; they eat no flesh but if it be right seldom a little lard, or of the entrails and heads of beasts slain for the nobles and merchants of the land. They wear no woollen but if it be a poor coat under their outermost garment, made of great canvas and called a frock. Their hose be of like canvas and pass not their knees, wherefore they be gartered and their thighs bare. Their women and children go barefoot; they may in no other wise live. . . . They be arcted[11] by necessity so to watch, labour and grub in the ground for their sustenance that their nature is wasted and the kind of them brought to nought. They go crooked and be feeble, not able

---

[7] From Sir John Fortescue, *The Governance of England,* ed. C. Plummer (Oxford, 1885), Chapters 1 and 3.

[8] differ

[9] Louis IX (1226–70)'

[10] hardly

[11] forced

to fight nor to defend the realm; nor have they weapon, nor money to buy them weapon withal. But verily they live in the most extreme poverty and misery, and yet dwell they in the most fertile realm of the world. Wherefore the French king has not men of his own realm able to defend it, except his nobles which bear no such impositions . . . ; by which cause the said king is compelled to make his armies and retinues for the defence of his land of strangers, as Scots, Spaniards, Aragonese, men of Almain,[12] and of other nations. . . . Lo, this is the fruit of his *ius regale*.

If the realm of England, which is an isle and therefore may not lightly get succour of other lands, were ruled under such a law and under such a prince, it would be a prey to all other nations that would conquer, rob or devour it. . . . But, blessed be God, this land is ruled under a better law; and therefore the people thereof be not in such penury, nor thereby hurt in their persons, but they be wealthy and have all things necessary to the sustenance of nature. Wherefore they be mighty and able to resist the adversaries of this realm, and to beat other realms that do or would do them wrong. Lo, this is the fruit of the *ius politicum et regale*, under which we live.

# 31 / VENICE: THE DEVELOPMENT OF INTERNATIONAL DIPLOMACY

*As is well known, the beginnings of an organized system of diplomatic representation and international relations are found in the city states of Italy where, arising from the needs of merchant republics from the thirteenth century onwards, a professional service involving regularly accredited ambassadors and regular dispatches between them and the home government provided an increasingly efficient exchange of the information needed in the formulation of policy. Venice, especially, led the way here and her "orators" (envoys) retained a preeminent place in European diplomacy. Even this competent service, however, had its weaknesses, as was to be expected in an age of slow and often inter-*

---

[12] Germany

*rupted communications, which frequently compelled ambassadors to act without instructions. As these orders show, even the Venetian government faced difficult problems in disciplining its representatives.*[13]

[23 May 1464]. Whereas it is neither convenient nor honest that our orators and envoys should write to their acquaintances and particular friends about matters pertaining to our Signory and state and the embassy committed to them, from which practice there can ensue inconvenience and bad example:

*Agreed* that by the authority of this Council a message be sent to all our present orators, and that a clause be included in the commissions issued to future ones, to the effect that they shall in no wise write to anybody anything about matters touching and pertaining to their embassy and our Signory, but [shall write] solely to this Signory, because if they do otherwise, they shall realize that they have done wrong and shall be proceeded against by the Council of Ten.

[13 July 1478]. An exceedingly bad and harmful custom has been introduced into our affairs by our orators who not only fail to report what they hear from the princes and potentates to whom they are sent (the foremost duty of a true and faithful orator) but also presume to take up matters not in their commissions and to speak and reply beyond the limits of their charge; what is even worse, in their total irreverence they do not hesitate to wish to appear wiser than their elders and betters. And inasmuch as this error needs correction, *it is agreed* that henceforth every one of our orators shall neither dare nor presume to discuss with the princes and potentates to whom he is accredited anything that is not included in his instructions and in the dispatches sent to him from time to time. In particular, no one is to open any matter that has not been expressly specified in his commission. In making reply, none shall say anything on his own initiative, except in accordance with our express instructions to him. But whatever they shall hear or is said to them, that they shall faithfully report and notify, on pain of exclusion from all embassies as well as all offices and promotions within this Signory for a term of five years. In addition, breakers of this our decree are from this moment understood to have been committed to the Advocates of the Commune who, if they wish, shall by advice impose harsher penalties. And of this our resolution all our orators at present on embassy or in future so going shall be given notice.

[13] Translated from Donald E. Queller, "Early Venetian Legislation on Ambassadors," *Travaux d'humanisme et Renaissance*, LXXXVIII (Geneva, 1966). By permission of Libraire Droz, Geneva.

# 32 / OLIVIER DE LA MARCHE (1426-1502): THE RISE OF BURGUNDY

*A French nobleman, La Marche served the dukes of Burgundy from Philip the Good (1419–67) through Charles the Bold (1467–77) to the Habsburg Duke Philip the Fair (1482–1506). A knight rather than a legist, he held an office as master of the household which involved the life of a courtier but the duties of a civil servant. His Memoirs, first published in 1562, cover the history of Burgundy from 1435 to 1492, describing the height of power reached by Philip the Good and its collapse in Charles the Bold's struggle with France and the Swiss. The following extracts show first Duke Philip's activities and person (he was in fact a high-class crook) and second, a characteristic scene of personal government and courtly splendor in the personal court of appeal held by Duke Charles.[14]*

Duke Philip of Burgundy . . . was the one called the good Duke Philip, and he had two names bestowed and given. The first was Philip the Assured; but after a long continued experience of his behavior and virtues he was called the good Duke Philip in name and title, and this title stayed with him; and surely he deserved to be so called, for such he was. It was he who, to avenge the outrage done to the person of Duke John, his father,[15] maintained for sixteen years a war against King Charles of France, the seventh of that name, who was the dauphin in whose presence the duke of Burgundy had been killed. And this Philip allied himself with the king of England, him whom they called Henry the Conqueror,[16] and between them they did much evil to the realm of France. This Duke Philip in his young days fought the French at Saint-Riquier[17] and there was knighted. The better to prove himself and gain his knighthood and his golden spurs, he dressed in simple clothes like a common man-at-arms;

---

[14] Translated from Olivier De La Marche, *Mémoires*, ed. H. Beaune and J. D'Arbaumont (Paris, 1883–8), Vol. 1, pp. 88 ff., 56 f.; Vol. 4, pp. 4 ff.

[15] John the Fearless, assassinated in 1419 at the bridge of Montereau during an interview with the dauphin of France

[16] Henry V (1414–22)

[17] battle of 1421

and when the line was in danger of being broken against him by the French, he bore the burden with just a small body of men backing him up. . . . The duke personally did such deeds of arms that he was taken for a very fine knight. . . .

To this good Duke Philip the duchies of Brabant and Limburg escheated by the death of Duke Philip, his cousin.[18] . . . Likewise, there came to Duke Philip by true succession the countries of Hainault, Holland and Zealand, and the lordship of Friesland. . . . But this succession, even though it was by hereditary right, he did not achieve without conquest. For the Lady Jacqueline of Bavaria, who succeeded to all the abovesaid countries and lordships, was a woman of a bouncing will and great ambition, and no less clever and subtle in making her will serve her desires. Although the good Duke Philip was her nearest relative, bad advice, wilfulness or whatever else made her forever seek and pursue dangerous alliances, contrary to the duke's interest; intending to pass her territory to another hand, she went to England and sought to ally herself in marriage with the duke of Gloucester, brother to King Henry the Conqueror, who was doing great things in France. So the said duke of Gloucester came to Hainault . . . and prepared an army under Lord Fitzwalter and sent it to Holland. To repel it, the duke [Philip] went in person, crossed the sea . . . and fought and overcame the English. . . . He agreed with the Lady Jacqueline to the effect that she remained nominal ruler of those said lands while he governed them for her. . . . And after the said lady's death (she died without heirs) the said Duke Philip lawfully and peacefully became count of Hainault, Holland and Zealand, and lord of Friesland. . . .

This good Duke Philip waged war against the king of France for sixteen years.[19] He was allied to and assisted by the English, and he and his lands prospered by the war. But in due course, proving how justly that later name of "the good duke" was given him, he let himself be readily persuaded to make peace, inasmuch as by nature he was a true, good and entire Frenchman. . . . And by the mediation of the pope and several princes and advisers (some of them kin and some subjects to the two parties), peace was made at the town of Arras between King Charles of France, seventh of that name, and Duke Philip of Burgundy. The two princes showed themselves so upright in protecting their oaths, words and promises that that peace was never broken by them, nor suffered to be broken or invaded [by others]. . . . From this there came such advantage to the realm of France that the English were by that king driven out of Normandy

---

[18] last representative of a younger line of the House of Burgundy
[19] The text says twenty-two, but the editor draws attention to the error.

and Guienne and never again prospered in France; and the lands of the Duke Philip, both those he held from France and those from the Empire, remained for so long in prosperity and free of war that they became the richest and most powerful realm in the world. . . .

## THE NEWS OF HIS DEATH IS RECEIVED

So changed all their past pleasure to weeping and tears, for there was dead a prince of high virtue. In his life he brought two things to a peak. One was that he died the richest prince of his time, for he left 400,000 gold crowns in cash and 72,000 marks of silver in plate of use, not to mention his rich tapestries, valuable rings, gold plate studded with jewels, his great and splendidly stocked library. In short, he died worth 2 millions of gold in movables alone.[18] And for his second achievement: he died the most generous and liberal duke of his time. He married off his nieces at his own expense; he supported great wars, and that for years; he several times rebuilt at his own cost the church and chapel of Jerusalem; he gave 10,000 crowns to build the Tower of Burgundy which stands in Rhodes; he gave 10,000 crowns to the king of Albania. No man ever left his presence without being well rewarded. He maintained a great state, approaching that of a king. For five years he entertained my lord the dauphin at his court;[21] and he was so renowned a prince that all the world spoke well of him. . . .

When the duke [Charles] is in his territories, he holds public audience to hear and despatch all the petitions brought to him, and especially those of poor and small men who might have complaints to make of the rich and great, but might not be able to come near him. For this purpose he personally holds a public audience twice a week; and we will turn to the ceremonies and pomps of that audience, so that everything may be set out in proper order.

This said audience is held on Monday and Wednesday. The duke, having finished dinner, goes to a hall where the audience is prepared. He is accompanied by the nobility of his household, that is to say, princes, knights, esquires and others, not a man of them daring to be absent. The duke takes his seat in his chair which is richly covered

---

[20] The Flemish crown was worth approximately four to five shillings English. Conversion into modern terms is notoriously difficult, or even impossible; one would have to multiply by at least forty (which would make Philip the Good worth some sixty million dollars in cash and movables), but this sort of figure really means very little.

[21] the later Louis XI of France, an exile at the court of Burgundy before his accession

in stuff and cloth of gold, and the dais, which is large and forms three steps, is entirely covered in rich carpeting. At its foot is a small bench where are placed two masters of requests and the audiencer who read out the petitions to the duke, as well as a secretary to record the decisions; these four are on their knees, and behind the secretary is a clerk who files the petitions on a string as the said secretary throws them to him. Benches are set out in rows, facing the gangway, for seating the princes of the blood, the ambassadors, the knights of the Order,[22] and the grand pensionaries, all in order; and each knows where to go. And behind the chair and the duke's back stand the duke's esquires, that is to say those of his chamber (what in France they call pages of honor) who on that day attend to the duties of cup-bearer, server and carver when the prince is in the privacy of his chamber; but not the esquire of the stable, because that is an office which is served publicly.

To continue the description of the audience: the hall is surrounded by a large railed enclosure, all shut off with benches and balustrades covered in hangings bearing the duke's arms. On the right side stand the duke's esquire servers and cupbearers, and on the left the carvers and esquires of the stable; they stand upright by the balustrades. In front of the rails are benches all round the enclosure where the knights, chamberlains and any strangers present sit, and also the masters of the household.[23] At the far end of the enclosure, opposite to the prince, are the gentlemen of the guard, each with a baton at the ready. . . . At the entrance and at the doors are ushers-at-arms, and by the gang-way two sergeants-at-arms, each bearing a mace with the prince's arms. The ceremony is in the charge of the masters of the household. When all is set, two doors are opened on two sides of the hall; by the one enter those who bring petitions and present them to the duke, and by the other they go out. The petitions are put on the bench in front of those whose task it is to read them, and they are read out one after the other. The duke disposes of the petitions at his pleasure, and according as the case requires; and he deals with them all before he leaves the place. During that time everyone keeps silence and order; and when it is all over, the duke returns to his chamber, and then everybody to their business. . . .

---

[22] the Order of the Golden Fleece, founded by Philip the Good

[23] a body of officers responsible for the running of the ducal court, of whom La Marche was one

# 33 / PHILIPPE DE COMMINES (1447-1511): LOUIS XI (1423-1483; KING FROM 1461)

*A minor nobleman of French birth, Commines came from that class of men who proved the most competent and generally most faithful ministers of those strong kings who were consolidating their power in the late fifteenth century: Ferdinand of Aragon, Edward IV and Henry VII of England, and especially Louis XI of France. Commines' picture of this last king is a highly individual portrait, but it also elucidates in general the qualities which gave these monarchs their success: hard work, care over money, shrewd knowledge of men, and that combination of formal piety with unscrupulous dealings now often called "Machiavellian" but, of course, practiced long before Machiavelli was heard of. Commines served Burgundy until 1472, when he entered the service of Louis XI, rapidly reaching a position of influence, although the picture he liked to paint of himself as a guide and elder statesman owed a lot to vanity. His Memoirs, written in the 1490's but added to for the rest of his life, are not only a source of first importance but a very fine piece of literature in their own right.*[24]

### BOOK 1, CHAPTER 10

I have embarked on this subject because I have seen much treachery in this world, particularly by servants against their masters; proud princes and lords, especially, who will not listen to people are more easily deceived than the humble and accessible. And among all those I have known, the wisest at extricating himself from a bad position in time of adversity was King Louis XI, our master, the most humble in words and manner and one who worked most diligently to gain any man who might serve or harm him. He never gave in if he was rebuffed by any man whom he practised to win but continued further, making large promises and granting him such money and honors as

[24] Translated from Philippe de Commines, *Mémoires*, ed. B. de Mandrot (Paris, 1901–3).

he knew would do him pleasure. And those he had abandoned in times of peace and prosperity, he spent much to recover again for his service when he had need of them; nor did he bear them any grudge for things past. He was by nature a friend to men of the middle sort and an enemy to all great men who might surpass him. No man ever so readily offered an ear to men or so busily inquired concerning all things, for he wished to know everybody. And indeed he knew all men of any authority or weight in England and Spain, in Portugal, in Italy, and in the lordships of the dukes of Burgundy and Brittany, just as he knew his own subjects. And these measures and fashions that he used, as I have shown above, saved his crown from the enemies whom he had made when he came to rule his realm. Above all, his great liberality served him best; yet, while he behaved wisely in adversity, when he thought himself a little escaped from danger (even if it was only a truce) he would busy himself to annoy people by mean little ways which did him little service; and he had the greatest difficulty in putting up with peace. He would speak lightly of people, rather more to their faces than behind their backs, except of those he feared of whom there were many, for he was by nature rather timorous. And when by his speech he had done himself some harm, or supposed he might have done, and wished to repair it, he would say to the person in question: "I know well that my tongue has done me much harm, though at other times it has given me much pleasure; however, it is only reasonable that I should make amends." And he never used these intimate words to anyone without conferring some benefit on him; and never a small one.

God indeed bestows a great blessing on any prince if he causes him to experience both good and ill, especially if the good outweighs the other, as it did with the king, our aforesaid master. To my mind, the troubles of his youth, when he fled from his father and stayed with Duke Philip of Burgundy, where he spent six years, did him a great deal of good; for he was taught to be agreeable to those of whom he had need, which proved of no slight advantage in his troubles. When he found himself great and a crowned king, at first he thought of nothing but vengeance; but he soon recognised the uselessness of this, by and by repented of it, and amended this his folly and error by winning over again those he had injured, as you shall see hereafter. And if his upbringing had been no other than that of the nobles whom I have seen abound in this kingdom, I do not believe that he would ever have saved himself. For they are trained only to show themselves fools in their dress and speech; they have no knowledge of letters; no man of sense is allowed near them; they have stewards with whom one must speak of their business—never to their lordships themselves!—and who run their affairs. There are noblemen who, though they have barely £13 in rents, take pride in telling you to "go and speak to my fellows about that," thinking by such talk to imitate the truly great men. Often enough have I seen their servants take advantage of them, giving them to understand that they are fools. And if by chance any of them recovered themselves and wished to know that which concerned them, they were too late to learn the business. For it must be remarked that anyone who ever was great or did great things started very young; and that was due to upbringing or the grace of God.

## BOOK 2, CHAPTER 6

It is great folly in a prince to put himself in the power of another, especially if they are at war. . . . It is greatly to the advantage of princes to have studied history in their youth, from which they would learn of these traps, great frauds, treacheries and perjuries which from ancient times some men have practised on others, capturing and killing those who put trust in their avowals. Not that everybody has behaved like that, but one example is enough to make many wise and put them on their guard. It seems to me, from what I have seen of the hopes of this world (in which for the space of eighteen years or more I have had plain knowledge of the great and secret matters transacted in this realm of France and in neighbouring countries), that one of the great means to make a man wise is to have read the old histories, and to have learned from them and from the example of our predecessors to handle oneself, be on one's guard, and enterprise wisely. For our life is so short that it does not suffice to provide so much experience. . . .

Again, I cannot forbear blaming ignorant noblemen. Surrounding every lord one naturally finds certain clerks and lawyers, as reason is; and they are very useful if they are good, very dangerous if the other thing. For every point they have some law in their mouths or a precedent, able to turn it any way they please; but a wise man who has done his reading will not be deceived, nor will any of these people have the nerve to tell lies to him. Believe me, God did not institute the office of king or prince to be executed by beasts or by such as take pride in saying, "I am no scholar; I leave all that to my council; I rely on them," and then, without giving any further reason, turn to their amusements. If they had been well brought up in youth their minds would work differently and they would be much concerned to be respected for themselves and their virtues. I do not say that all princes are served by such ill-conditioned people, but the most part of those I have known have never been without them in times of need, though certain wise men among them have known well how to be served by better qualified men and how to pick them without causing complaint. And among all the princes of whom I have knowledge, the king our master was best at this and best knew how to honor and esteem men of virtue and valor. He was not without learning; he liked to ask questions and listen to answers concerning every possible subject; he had excellent natural abilities which is a thing far exceeding all other knowledge that we may learn in this world. All the books ever made serve no purpose except to remind one of matters past, and a man who reads a book in three months will understand affairs better than twenty men living one after the other could do by means of their combined ages and experience. In short, to conclude this point, it seems to me that God can send no worse affliction to a country than a prince of little understanding, for from this proceed all other ills. First there come disunity and war because he commits to another's hand the authority which he ought to safeguard beyond all things. From disunion grow famine and death and all other miseries resulting from war. Thus it appears that a prince's subjects have no little cause to grieve if they see his youth spoiled by lack of education and left in the hands of ill-qualified persons.

### BOOK 6, CHAPTER 12

Little of hope ought poor and mean people to have in this world, when so great a king suffered and labored so much, and afterwards had to leave all and could not find one hour to put off his death, try he never so hard. I knew him and served him in the flower of his youth [25] and in his best prosperity; but I never saw him free of labor and care. Of pleasures he loved hunting and hawking in their seasons, but he took most delight in hounds. As for women, he had nothing to do with them all the time I was with him; for about the time of my arrival, he lost a son to his very deep sorrow and in my presence swore an oath to God that he would touch no woman except the queen his wife. And although he ought to have done so anyway by the law of the Church, it was a great thing and much to his credit that he should have stood by his promise, seeing the queen was not one of those in whom a man could take much pleasure, though a good enough lady. . . .

*[There follows a recital of contemporary royal fortunes—France, England, Burgundy, the Turk, etc.]*

So you have seen the death of so many great men in so short a time who had labored so hard to enlarge their power and gain glory,

[25] from 1468, when Louis XI was forty-five years old

and had suffered so many passions and pains and shortened their lives, and perhaps had endangered their souls. In this I do not speak of the said Turk, for I think without doubt he rests with his ancestors. For our king I have some hope, as I have said, that our Lord may have had mercy on him; and He may have shown it to the rest, too, if it is His will. But to speak plainly, as one who has no great understanding either inborn or acquired but has had a little experience: would it not have been better for them and for all other princes and for men of lower estate . . . to have chosen a middle way in these matters? They might have tried to worry less and labor less and engage themselves less in affairs; and rather have been more careful of offending God, and of persecuting their people and their neighbors in such cruel ways as I have shown before, and have spent more time in peace and honest pleasures. Their lives would have been longer, their infirmities later in coming, their deaths more lamented by more people and less wished for; and they would have had fewer doubts at their passing. Could we wish for better examples to learn how insignificant man is, how miserable and brief his life, and how little difference between the great and the small, than this that as soon as they are gone every man's dead body is a horror and abomination, while the soul as soon as it leaves the body must go to its judgment? And the sentence is rendered according to the works and merits of the body.

# 34 / PHILIPPE POT, SEIGNEUR DE LA ROCHE (FL. 1480-1490): THE FUNCTIONS OF THE ESTATES (1484)

*When the French Estates General met in 1484, they confronted the consequences of the accession to the throne, in the preceding year, of the thirteen-year-old Charles VIII. Arrangements for the government of the realm during his minority had been made by the king's uncles; but against the opinion that these should be accepted without question, de la Roche asserted the rights of the Estates to control government by appointing the*

*regency council themselves. His speech presented a constitution-
alist view of the monarchy and the powers of the people that was
by then a little old-fashioned, though it was to find an echo in
Huguenot thought a century later. In 1484, the Estates lost the
battle: the greater nobility declared the king to be of age and
thus enabled him, nominally, to choose his own council.*[26]

. . . To make the matter plain: history tells us, and I have so received it from my forefathers, that in the beginning kings were made
by the voice of the people, those being most preferred who exceeded
the rest in virtue and ability. Each nation chose its rulers for the use
it would have of them. For princes exist not to gain profit and wealth
from their people, but that—forgetting their own advantage—they
may enrich the commonwealth and lead it to better things. Any that
act differently are assuredly tyrants and evil shepherds who, feeding
on their own sheep, deserve the character and name of wolves rather
than shepherds. The people's main concern is to know what law and
what ruler guides the realm; for if the king is excellent so will their
fortune be, and if he is not the people will be ruined and feeble.
Have you not often read that a commonwealth means the weal of the
commonalty? And if a thing touches a man's cause, how can he neglect
it or fail to take care of it? How can these sycophants ascribe all power
to the prince when he was set up by the people? Were not all the
magistrates of the Romans elected by the people, nor any law there
passed which had not first been submitted to the people and been
approved by them? Even today, many countries follow the old fashion
and elect their kings. But I don't now want to consider a king who,
being of age, rightfully governs his realm. The question before us
amounts only to this: what if a king be prevented from exercising
rule by being under age or for some other cause? And first I would
wish you to agree that the commonwealth is the people's concern, by
them remitted to their kings; and that those who hold, by force or
otherwise, without the people's consent, are to be called tyrants and
usurpers of another's rights. It is accepted that our king cannot by
himself dispose of the realm which must therefore obtain the care
and guidance of others. But in such cases it reverts not to any one
of our princes [of the blood], or to several, or even to all of them
together. It must therefore return to the people, the original donors,
who must resume it as their own, especially because any long vacancy
or bad regency will always result only in disaster to themselves. Not

[26] Translated from Jehan Masselin, *Journal des États Généraux de France tenus
à Tours en 1484*, ed. A. Bernier (Paris: Imprimerie Royale, 1835), pp. 146–56.

that I am of a mind to assert that the forms of rule or the rights of lordship can pass to anyone except the person of the king; but the administration and protection of the realm—not title or ownership—are for the time being transferred in law to the people or to those elected by them. By people I do not mean the multitude or simply the subjects of this kingdom but everyone of what estate soever, so that in my opinion the princes are comprised within the name of estates general, nor is anybody excluded who lives in the realm. No one, I take it, will dispute that the princes come within the definition of the nobility, indeed are the powerful part of it. However, since you know that you yourselves are the representatives and learned proctors of all the estates, and that the common will lies in your hands, why do you fear to conclude that you are specially called to the business of deciding how the commonwealth, in a manner vacant by the king's minority, may be ruled by your counsel? Your very writs of summons spoke of this; in his address, which gained weight by the presence of the king and the princes, the chancellor told you so—far from obscurely. All this clearly refutes those who think that our assembly was called merely for the levying of taxes and for no other task or end. I pass over the fact that many provinces are hardly ever summoned for this purpose. The false opinion is most manifestly contradicted by experience, as well as by the record of our proceedings which makes it plain that we have commonly treated of a good many other things. Perchance someone will object that at the beginning of this new reign the princes set up a council, ordered the realm, and provided for everything, so that there is now no need for our deliberations. To this I would reply that all those things were done, as it were, provisionally, because at that moment it was not possible to convene the estates. And thanks are due to those by whose labour and skill the realm was well and prosperously brought even to the time of this assembly. But now that the estates are come together to whom—let us say so with confidence—the law assigns the authority, things done must be confirmed and things to be done taken thought of. For I hold that nothing done has force until approved by the estates, nor can anything exist safely and solidly that is done against their will or without their counsel, or without obtaining their true or implicit consent.

There is nothing new about an assembly of the estates general. It is nothing extraordinary for them to take over the administration of the realm during a vacancy and to entrust it to a council of worthy men chosen from amongst their number, men of the blood royal being preferred provided they have the necessary qualities. Not to seek too distant a precedent: in the time of Philip de Valois, when he and Edward [III] king of England were fighting for the crown, they finally agreed to abide by the law and did not hesitate to submit so high a matter to the judgment of the estates general; and the sentence which these gave for Philip we accordingly use by way of defence against the English. When the estates had authority in a matter of such outstanding importance, why should one deny them an authority to appoint a council or to do any other lesser thing? And when John, king of France, was by the fortunes of war and the adversity of fate taken prisoner, did not the estates take the government and administration of the realm upon themselves and provide for organisation and delegation? And though the same John's son, Charles V, was already twenty years of age, yet the regency was not entrusted to him in perpetuity: the estates assembled again at Paris two years after their first meeting, and the aforesaid Charles took over the government solely by their consent and decree. But why cite these ancient cases? Under Charles VI, who succeeded his father when only twelve years old, the realm was ordered and governed by the advice of the estates, which fact remains in the memory of many; I tell not what I have heard but what I saw myself. When such precedents testify to the authority of the estates and so many reasons support it, why do you hesitate to give your minds and hands to the business of appointing, organising and naming a council? For doing just this will ensure the strength and condition of the realm, or else [omitting it will cause] its ruin and overthrow. You are here to speak and advise freely what, under the guidance of God and your conscience, you judge to be for the good of the realm; should you then fail to attend to this one thing which is the foundation, the head and origin, of all the rest? If you do not attend to it properly, all your other counsels and petitions will be in vain. Who, I ask you, shall hear and judge your pleas and griefs? Who shall give them cure and provide remedy when that one thing is neglected or not well done? I can see no reason to labor in anything else.

But it may be objected that there are those appointed in the roll to be of the council immediately upon the king's death: are we to judge them unworthy of the office and the honor? Let us not, it will be said, resist the king, resist the will and commands of the princes; for that would seem to be empty work and to labor hard for nothing but displeasure. No no, good sirs, not so, I warrant you; your labor will be neither in vain nor cause displeasure if you will discharge your business staunchly and wisely. . . . But why hesitate? Are we to carry peace-branches? Bow our heads to the ground? The main article of the roll produced before us states plainly that that council is appointed only till the assembly of the estates. Now you are assembled and you hesitate: you seem to dread the matter as beyond your powers, though your ancestors never thought such a thing too high for themselves and by their determination preserved their rights intact. Perhaps the princes stand in the way? But no, far from it: they even help and urge you on. What then is it that prevents you from carrying out so excellent and worthwhile a task? Nothing, so far as I can see, except perhaps your indolence and pussillanimity which affright your spirits and alone render you unworthy of this most worthy office. Sirs, you must take good confidence to yourselves, great hope and excellent virtue. Do not allow negligence to destroy the liberty of the estates which your forefathers made it their chief care to guard. Do not appear smaller or feebler than they, lest posterity damn you for employing your powers wickedly to the peril of the commonwealth; make sure that, in place of the fame which your labors deserve, you do not earn everlasting shame.

# 35 / NICCOLÒ MACHIAVELLI (1469-1527)

*Trained as a diplomatist and civil servant, Machiavelli lost office in 1512 when the exiled Medici returned to power in his native Florence; he spent the rest of his life in writing. This is not the place even to attempt a summary of the life and work of one on whom whole libraries have been written. Machiavelli composed an important* History of Florence, *an interesting treatise on* The Art of War, *an excellent comedy which is still sometimes performed, and a good deal else; but his fame rests rightly on his political works. In these he used what he himself regarded as a new method to answer questions not really asked before. He wanted to solve the problem of power in a state—how it is obtained, preserved, and lost—and he wished to discover this by a dispassionate evaluation of historical and contemporary evidence. Admittedly he was not always so coldly empirical as he claimed; his love for Italy and adoration of ancient Rome tended to interfere. Although his conclusions were rarely very original, they seemed to be so because he expressed them in strikingly direct language, without the comfortable padding of conventional morality which, as he recognised, played so little part in affairs. He liked to shock, and for some four centuries he has had his wish. A comes from his lesser but more coherent work,* The Prince

*(1513), in which he drew effectively on his observation of Italian and foreign politicians, especially Cesare Borgia and Ferdinand of Aragon.*[27] *B is from his much larger but much more poorly organized* Discorsi *(1515–17), a commentary on Livy's* History of Rome—*searching political reflections called forth by his author, but given point by examples from his own time.*[28] *In the* Discorsi, *Machiavelli expresses a clear preference for republics over monarchies, which shows that the* Prince *is to be read as science, not propaganda.*

## A. THE PRINCE

### Chapter 1

All states and all political organisations which have possessed or now possess rule over men have been or are either republics or principalities. Principalities are either hereditary (those in which the line of their ruler has for a long time held sway); or they are new. The new ones are either entirely new, like Francesco Sforza's government in Milan; [29] or they are by way of being members annexed to the hereditary state of the prince who has acquired them, as the kingdom of Naples was acquired by the king of Spain. Territories so acquired are either accustomed to live under a prince or are used to liberty; they are gained either by the military power of others or of the prince himself, or by fortune, or by political skill.

### Chapter 2

I shall omit all discussion of republics because I have discussed them at length in another place. I shall confine myself solely to principalities, adhering in this to the order outlined above, and shall consider how such principalities may be ruled and preserved. I may say at once that in hereditary states accustomed to their princely house there is much less difficulty in preserving rule than in new ones, because there it is enough not to go against the customs of one's ancestors and to deal sensibly with anything that may happen; so that such a prince, if he be of ordinary abilities, will always maintain himself in his state; unless he is deprived by some extraordinary and excessive force; but

[27] Translated from *Il Principe*, ed. G. Lisio (Florence, 1899).

[28] From Niccolò Machiavelli, *The Discourses on the first Decade of Titus Livius,* transl. L. J. Walker (London: Routledge & Kegan Paul Ltd., 1950). Reprinted by permission of the publishers.

[29] See No. 27.

if so deprived, he will secure restoration whenever anything doubtful happens to his supplanter.

We have here in Italy, for example, the duke of Ferrara who could not have resisted the Venetian attacks of 1484 or Pope Julius in 1510 by any means except ancient possession of his dominions. For the natural-born prince has less occasion and less necessity to cause offense; from which it follows that he will be more loved; and unless extraordinary vices make him hated, it is reasonable to expect that he will naturally stand well with his people. And in the antiquity and duration of his rule, the memories and inducements which lead to innovation are lost; for one change always leaves behind the foundations on which another arises.

### Chapter 10

In examining the nature of these principalities, another point must be kept in mind, namely whether the prince's authority is such that he can, if need be, maintain himself independently, or whether he must always rely on the protection of others. And to elaborate this point, I say that I hold those capable of maintaining themselves independently who, relying on a large population or a large treasure, can raise an army sufficient to engage with any possible attacker; and similarly I hold that those always stand in need of others who cannot confront an enemy in the field but are forced to retire behind walls and defend these. Of the first case we have already spoken, though we shall, if occasion offers, recur to it. In the second case one can say nothing except to advise such a prince to fortify and strengthen his territory proper [30] and to forget about the open country. And anyone who has seen to the fortification of his town and has managed the other affairs of his subjects in the manner described above (and further to be described below) will always find his attackers properly respectful; for men are always hostile to enterprises seen to be difficult, and the task of attacking a man who has strengthened his defences and is not hated by his people will be recognised as difficult. . . .

### Chapter 12

I have discussed in detail all the characteristics of such principalities as in the beginning I proposed to consider; I have reviewed in some measure the causes of their being good or bad; and I have shown

---

[30] i.e., the city upon which Italian principalities usually centered

the ways in which numbers of men have tried to acquire and retain dominion. It remains to discuss in general the means of offense and defense which are available to each of the types mentioned. We saw above how necessary it is for a prince to rest his rule on really good foundations; otherwise he will assuredly end in ruin. The principal foundations of all states—whether new, old, or mixed—are good laws and good arms. And since there can be no good laws in the absence of sound armaments, and since the presence of good arms ensures good laws, I shall not bother to consider laws at all but shall confine myself to arms.

I therefore say that the forces with which a prince defends his state are either his own, or they are mercenaries, or auxiliaries, or mixed. Mercenaries and auxiliaries are useless and dangerous; a man who rests his political power on mercenary armies will stand neither firm nor safe; for they are disunited, ambitious, undisciplined, faithless, heroes towards their friends and cravens to their enemies; incapable of fearing God or keeping faith with man; disaster is postponed only so long as the battle is postponed. They despoil one in peace, as the enemy does in war. The reason for this is that they have no other loyalty or motive to keep them under arms than their pittance of pay, which is not enough to make them willing to die for you. They have no objection to serving as your soldiers while you are not at war, but when it comes to war they either run away or go over to the other side. These points would not be difficult to prove, for the ruin of Italy has quite simply been caused by our reliance for so many years on mercenary armies. Though these used to put up quite a show and appeared brave enough among themselves, yet when the foreigner came they showed what sort of men they were. . . .

Mercenary captains are either competent or not. If they are, you cannot trust them because they always seek their own greatness by endangering either you who are their employer, or others contrary to your plans. But if the man is no good, he ruins you in the ordinary way. And if it is alleged that anyone, mercenary or not, with arms in his hands will act in the same way, I reply that armies have to be employed either by a prince or by a republic. The prince should go in person and exercise the commander's office; the republic ought to send out its citizens, recalling any proved incompetent and by law preventing a satisfactory officer from abandoning his command. Experience shows that self-reliant princes and armed republics achieve the best results, while mercenaries do nothing but harm. A republic armed with its own weapons is less easily reduced to obedience by one of its citizens than one armed with foreign weapons. Rome and Sparta stood for centuries, armed and free. The Swiss are today the most completely armed and the freest of nations. . . .

## Chapter 14

A prince should have only one end and idea in mind, take only one subject for study, and that is war, its science and discipline; for it is the only science that deals with the ruler's problems. It is of such power that it not only maintains those born to princedoms but often causes men of private origin to rise to that rank; on the other hand, we have seen princes who think more of amusement than of arms lose their states. The first cause of losing power is neglect of this art; the cause of winning power lies in its mastery. Military greatness lifted Francesco Sforza from his private station to the duchy of Milan; his sons, by avoiding and ignoring the profession of arms, have reverted from dukes to private persons. For among other troubles which being disarmed will bring upon you, it causes contempt: this is one of the ignominies against which a prince must protect himself. . . . For there is no way of comparing an armed man with an unarmed; it is not to be expected that an armed man should voluntarily obey an unarmed one, or that a man without arms should be safe among armed attendants. . . . Quite apart from the other ills already mentioned, a prince who does not understand military matters cannot retain his soldiers' respect or loyalty. . . .

## Chapter 17

Is it better to be loved than feared, or the other way round? The answer is that one should want to be both; but, because it is difficult to combine both in one person, it is a good deal safer to be feared than loved if one of the two has to be dropped. For this can in general be said of mankind: men are ungrateful, fickle, dishonest, cowardly in danger and greedy for gain As long as things go well they are entirely yours. They offer you their blood, goods, life and children while there is no present call; but when the need comes closer they revolt. Any prince who has built his all on their words, to the neglect of other preparations, provokes disaster. For friendship bought for money and not by greatness and nobility of mind has no endurance, however well deserved it may be; when the time comes, it cannot be relied upon. People are less reluctant to offend one who has inspired love than one who has inspired fear; for love is maintained by a bond of obligation which, men being what they are, is broken whenever their own advantage calls for it. Fear, on the other hand, is maintained by the expectation of unfailing punishment. Nevertheless, a prince should inspire fear in such a way that, if he cannot gain love, he will at least escape hatred. For he can well stand being feared provided he is not hated, which will be as long as he keeps his hands off his citizens' and subjects' goods and wives. . . .

### Chapter 18

Everyone agrees how praiseworthy it is in a prince to keep faith and to conduct himself uprightly rather than deviously. Nevertheless, one may see from the experience of our own time that those princes have done great things who have put little store by good faith, have known how by deceitfulness to addle men's brains, and in the end have overcome those who trusted in their honesty.

Thus you should know that there are two ways of conducting any struggle, one way by the law and the other by the use of force. The first is proper to men, the second to beasts; but because the first will many a time be insufficient, one must have recourse also to the second. It follows that a prince must know how best to use both beast and man. This point was taught to princes by the ancient writers in the form of an allegory. They tell how Achilles and many other princes of antiquity were put to school with the centaur Chiron who brought them up under his guidance; which means simply that as they had a tutor half beast and half man, so a prince has need to know how to employ either of those natures. One without the other cannot make for success. Therefore a prince, compelled to know the best use of the beast, should choose from among that sort the fox and the lion; for the lion cannot deal with snares, nor the fox with wolves. It needs a fox to recognise the snares and a lion to put fear into the wolves. Those who rely exclusively on the lion do not know their business. A wise lord, therefore, neither can nor ought to keep faith when such persistence turns to his disadvantage and when the reasons which elicited his promise have ceased to exist. If men were altogether good, this advice would be wrong; but since they are bad and will not keep faith with you, you also need not keep faith with them. Nor will a prince ever be short of legitimate excuses to give color to his breaches of faith. Of this one could give any number of recent examples to show how many treaties and agreements have been rendered null and void by the faithlessness of princes; and he who has best known how to play the fox has come off best. But it is important to know how to disguise this ability, to be a great pretender and dissembler. Men are so simple and so obedient to immediate necessity that anyone intent on deception will always find dupes ready to be deceived.

I must not leave out one recent example. Alexander VI [31] did nothing, thought of nothing, that was not connected with the deception

---

[31] pope from 1492–1503

of others, and he always found someone on whom to practise. There never was a man who displayed greater vigor in affirming a thing and used greater oaths in the process, and who yet observed it less. Nevertheless his lies always worked out to his will because he well knew that aspect of the world. It is therefore unnecessary for a prince actually to possess all the qualities outlined before, but he must appear to have them. I shall even make so bold as to assert that to have them and always observe them is dangerous, while an appearance of their possession is profitable: appear merciful, trustworthy, humane, upright and pious, and by all means be so, but so condition your mind that if necessity requires you not to be so you can readily change to the opposite. And you must grasp that a prince, and especially one newly risen, cannot observe all the points by which men are judged good; for the maintenance of his position he is often forced to act contrary to good faith, to charity, humanity and religion. Therefore he needs to have a mind disposed to veer as the winds and changes of fortune command, and ready (as I have said) not to diverge from morality if this can be done, but to know at a pinch how to act without attention to it.

Thus a prince should take great care that nothing ever escapes his lips that is not full of the abovesaid five qualities—that to those who hear and see him he may always appear all mercy, good faith, humanity, honesty and religion. There is nothing more important for a man to appear to have than this last quality. Men in general judge more by the eye than by the hand: anybody can see you but few can touch you. Everybody sees what you appear to be, few feel what you are; and those few dare not oppose themselves to the views of the many who also have the majesty of the state behind them. All men's actions—and more particularly those of princes, where protests are unwise—are judged by results. . . .

## B. THE DISCOURSES

### Part 1, Chapter 29

With respect to the topic under discussion it seems to me relevant to enquire whether ingratitude is better exemplified by a people or by a prince. The better to discuss this I premise that the vice of ingratitude arises either from avarice or from suspicion. For when a people or a prince has entrusted the command of an important enterprise to one of their generals and he is victorious and so acquires much glory, that prince or that people is under an obligation to reward him for this. Hence if, instead of rewarding him, they are discourteous to him or give him offence, and it be avarice that moves them to it in that it is greed that restrains them from giving effect to their desire to satisfy him, in acting thus they commit an error for which there is no excuse, and which is attended with lasting infamy. Yet there are found many princes who offend in this way. Cornelius Tacitus [32] tells us the cause of this when he says "One is more inclined to repay injuries than benefits; for it is burdensome to grant favours, but revenge is profitable."

But when their motive for not rewarding him, or rather for giving him offence, is not avarice, but suspicion, there is in that case some excuse both for a people and a prince. Of ingratitude arising from this cause numerous examples are to be found in history, for the general who by his valour has extended his lord's dominions, vanquished his enemies, won glory for himself and riches for his troops, must needs acquire such a reputation alike with his troops, with the enemy, and with that prince's own subjects, that the victory may not look so good to the lord under whose orders he acted. And because men are by nature both ambitious and suspicious, and know not how to use moderation where their fortunes are concerned, it is impossible that the suspicion aroused in a prince after the victory of one of his generals should not be increased by any arrogance in manner or speech displayed by the man himself. This being so, the prince cannot but look to his own security, and to this end consider putting him to death or depriving him of the standing he has thus obtained with his army and with his people by industriously pointing out that the victory was not gained by the general's valour, but by luck, in that it was brought about either by the cowardice of the enemy or by the prudence of other officers associated with him in the action.

When Vespasian, [33] then in Judaea, was proclaimed emperor by his army, Antonius Primus, who found himself with another army in Illyria, took Vespasian's part and came to Italy to attack Vitellius, who was ruling in Rome. With the utmost valour he broke two of Vitellius's armies and occupied Rome. Hence Mucianus, Vespasian's deputy, found that through Antonius's valour everything had been acquired and all difficulties overcome. The reward which Antonius got was at once to be deprived of his command of the army by Mucianus, and step by step to be reduced to a position of no authority in Rome. When he went to see Vespasian, who was still in Asia, his reception was such that before long he became just a nobody and died in despair.

History is full of such cases. Everybody at present alive knows how in our time Gonsalvo Ferrante, when fighting against the French in

[32] the Roman historian (A.D. 55–120)
[33] emperor of Rome (A.D. 70–79)

the kingdom of Naples on behalf of Ferdinand, King of Aragon, [34] by his industry and valour conquered and overcome that kingdom; and how the reward he got for his victory was that, when Ferdinand left Aragon and come to Naples, he relieved him of his command of the army in the field, then took from him the fortresses and brought him with him to Spain, where shortly afterwards he died in ignominy. This natural suspicion is therefore in princes so intense that there is no defence against it, and it is impossible for princes to show gratitude to those who by victory have made great conquests under the flag of their prince.

Since a prince cannot help himself in this matter it is not to be marvelled at, nor is it a matter more worthy of remark, if a people cannot help itself. Because a city in which freedom prevails has two ends in view. One is to enlarge its dominions; the other is to keep itself free. In both it can err by excess. . . . The errors made in the cause of liberty are, amongst others, these: giving offence to citizens who should be rewarded, and the suspecting of citizens in whom confidence should be placed. Both lines of conduct in a republic which is already corrupt may occasion great evils and the coming of tyranny is thereby often accelerated, as happened in Rome when Caesar took by force what ingratitude had denied him. Nevertheless in a republic which is not corrupt they are highly beneficial and promote the cause of freedom, for owing to the fear of punishment men improve and become less ambitious.

Of all peoples who have ever had an empire gained by the aforesaid means, Rome was the least ungrateful, for of its ingratitude but one instance can be cited, that of Scipio. [35] For Coriolanus and Camillus [36] were banished on account of the injuries which in each case they had done to the plebs. Moreover, though one of them was not pardoned owing to his having always maintained a hostile attitude towards the populace, the other was not only recalled but during the rest of his life was treated like a prince. The ingratitude with which Scipio was treated, on the other hand, arose from the suspicion which the citizens began to have of him, but which they had not felt towards others. This was due to the greatness of the enemy which Scipio had defeated, to the reputation which he had acquired by his victory after so long and so dangerous a war, to the speed with which he had gained it, and to the favours which his youth, his prudence, and his other remarkable virtues had won for him. . . .

[34] Ferdinand the Catholic (1452–1516), whose marriage with Isabella of Castile united the Spanish kingdoms

[35] the conquerer of Carthage (236–184 B.C.)

[36] Roman generals of the fifth century B.C., whose lives appear to be largely legendary

### Part III, Chapter 9

I have often thought that the reason why men are sometimes unfortunate, sometimes fortunate, depends upon whether their behaviour is in conformity with the times. For one sees that in what they do some men are impetuous, others look about them and are cautious; and that, since in both cases they go to extremes and are unable to go about things in the right way, in both cases they make mistakes. On the other hand, he is likely to make fewer mistakes and to prosper in his fortune when circumstances accord with his conduct, as I have said, even though you act as nature constrains you to do.

Everybody knows how Fabius Maximus [37] when in command of the army, proceeded circumspectly and with a caution far removed from the impetuosity and boldness characteristic of the Roman; and by good luck this sort of thing just fitted the circumstances. For Hannibal had arrived in Italy, a young man flushed with success, and had twice routed the Roman people, so that this republic had lost almost all its best troops and was alarmed. Hence it could not have been more fortunate than to have had a general who by his slowness and his caution held the enemy at bay. Nor could Fabius have met with circumstances more suited to his ways; and it is to this that his fame was due.

That in so doing Fabius behaved naturally and not by choice is shown by the fact that, when Scipio wanted to go to Africa with his armies to bring the war to an end, Fabius was much against this, since he could not get out of his ways and habits; so that, if it had been left to him, Hannibal would still be in Italy, for he did not see that times had changed, and that new methods of warfare were called for. So that, if Fabius had been king of Rome, he might easily have lost this war, since he was incapable of altering his methods according as circumstances changed. Since, however, he was born in a republic where there were diverse citizens and diverse dispositions, it came about that, just as it had a Fabius, who was the best man to keep the war going when circumstances required this, so later it had a Scipio at a time suited to its victorious consummation.

For this reason a republic has a fuller life and enjoys good fortune for a longer time than a principality, since it is better able to adapt itself to diverse circumstances owing to the diversity found amongst its citizens than a prince can do. For a man who is accustomed to act in one particular way, never changes, as we have said. Hence, when times change and no longer suit his ways, he is inevitably ruined.

[37] Roman commander in the war with Hannibal (d. 203 B.C.)

Piero Soderini,[38] whom we have mentioned several times, conducted all his affairs in his good-natured and patient way. So long as circumstances suited the way in which he carried on, both he and his country prospered. But when afterwards there came a time which required him to drop his patience and his humility he could not bring himself to it; so that both he and his country were ruined. Pope Julius II [39] during the whole course of his pontificate acted with impetuosity and dash, and, since the times suited him well, he succeeded in all his undertakings; but had other times come which called for other counsels, he would of necessity have been undone, for he could not have changed his ways or his method of handling affairs.

There are two reasons why we cannot change our ways. First, it is impossible to go against what nature inclines us to. Secondly, having got on well with a certain line of conduct, it is impossible to persuade men that they can get on well by acting otherwise. It thus comes about that a man's fortune changes, for she changes his circumstances but he does not change his ways. The downfall of cities also comes about because institutions in republics do not change with the times, as we have shown at length already, but change very slowly because it is difficult to change them since it is necessary to wait until the whole republic is disposed to make the change; and for this it is not enough that one man should change his own procedure. . . .

# 36 / FRANCESCO GUICCIARDINI (1483-1540): HISTORY OF ITALY

*Guicciardini, a friend of Machiavelli's, represents the culmination of historical writing in the Italian Renaissance. A Florentine aristocrat fairly closely connected with the Medici family, he obtained his practical experience of affairs (both civil and military) in the service of the papacy, but he deserves to be remembered for his* History of Italy—*meaning mainly recent history, his model being Thucydides—written in the four years before his death when he was living in resentful retirement. The work is based on careful and critical research but animated by the bitter-*

[38] head of the Florentine republic 1498–1512
[39] 1503–13

*ness and despair natural to an Italian patriot in that age of decline.
His introduction (A) underlines the political and didactic purposes
for which history was written by the best Renaissance practitioners; his account of the 1527 Sack of Rome (B), an event that
shocked all Europe, suggests something of the concise power and
vivid detail of his narrative.*[40]

### A

Having in hand to write the affairs of Italy, I judged it convenient
to draw into discourse those particularities that most nearly resemble
our time and memory, yea even since the self[same] princes of that
country, calling in the armies of France, gave the first beginnings to
so great innovations. A matter for the variety, greatness and nature of
such things very notable and well worthy of memory, and for the
heavy accidents hateful, bloody and horrible. For that Italy for many
years was travailed with all those sorts of calamities with which the
principalities, countries and mortal men are wont to be afflicted, as
well by the just wrath of God as through the impiety and wickedness
of other nations. The knowledge of those things so great and diverse
may minister many wholesome instructions as well to all men generally
as to every one in particular, considering that by the trial, consent and
demonstration of so many examples all princes, people and patrimonies
may see (as a sea driven with diverse winds) to what inconstancy
human things are ordained, and how harmful are the ill measured counsels of princes, many times prejudicial to themselves but always hurtful
to their people and subjects, specially when they are vainly carried
away either with their singular errors or private covetousness, without
having any impression or remembrance of the ordinary changes of
fortune, whereby, turning to the damage and displeasure of others the
power which is given them for the safety, protection and policy of the
whole, they make themselves, either by want of discretion or too much
ambition, authors of innovations and new troubles.

### B

The person of the pope [41] who expected with great devotion in the
palace of Vatican what would be the issue of the assault, hearing that
the enemies were entered, had also (with the others) his passions of
fear and frailty; and in that timorous contemplation of his own peril

---

[40] From *The Historie of Guicciardin, Conteining the Warres of Italie and other
Partes,* translated by Geoffrey Fenton (London, 1579), pp. 1, 1061–3.
[41] Clement VII

he fled with certain cardinals to the Castle. . . . The Spaniards, neither seeing order nor counsel to defend the quarter beyond Tiber, entered the place without any resistance, and from thence, not finding any impediments to stop their victory, the same evening they entered the city of Rome. . . . The soldiers, being within the city which they knew wanted nothing to make them right glorious and well satisfied of all things appertaining to their desires, they began to omit no time to execute the thing they had so dearly bought: everyone ran to pillage with the same unbridled liberty which in such cases makes soldiers both insolent and impious. There was small care or regard borne either to the name of friends, factions or favourers, and much less was respected the authority of cardinals and prelates, or dignity of temples and monasteries. It is hard to particulate the greatness of the prey, both for the general wealth and riches which the greedy hands of the soldiers had made up in heaps, and for other things more rare and precious drawn out of the storehouses of merchants and courtiers; but the matter which made the spoil infinite in value was the quality and great number of prisoners redeemed with most rich and large ransoms. . . . The general slaughter as well at the assault as in the rage of the sacking was about 4,000 bodies. All the palaces of the cardinals were sacked, except some particulars who, to save the merchants that were retired thither with their goods together with the persons and goods of many others reserved of the general calamity, made promise of great sums of money. . . . Right pitiful were the cryings and lamentations of the women of Rome, and no less worthy of compassion the calamity of nuns and virgins professed whom the soldiers ravished by troops out of their houses to satisfy their lust. . . . The rumour went that the valuation and price of this sack in gold, silver and jewels amounted to more than a million of ducats, but the matter of ransom contained a greater quantity.

# 37 / THOMAS STARKEY (1499?-1538): THE LAWS OF ENGLAND

*An English humanist of the second rank originally associated with Reginald Pole (1500–58)—Henry VIII's cousin who followed a scholar's career in Italy which led him to the cardinalate—Starkey was in sympathy with the revolution of the 1530's when England, under Thomas Cromwell's guidance, broke with*

*Rome (see p. 233). He joined Cromwell's stable of able young planners and propagandists. His most interesting work (written in 1535 but not printed until 1871) was* The Dialogue between Reginald Pole and Thomas Lupset, *an imaginary conversation between his erstwhile friend and an older scholar who had died in 1530. This analyzed the English scene and proposed reforms. Among other points, Starkey put into Pole's mouth a violent attack on the English common law as muddled, barbaric, and out of date; he wanted to copy the elegant civil or Roman law by codifying and simplifying the system.* [42]

This is no doubt but that our law and order thereof is overconfuse. It is infinite, and without order or end. There is no stable ground therein, nor sure stay; but everyone that can colour reason makes a stop to the best law that is before-time devised. The subtlety of the serjeant [43] shall inert and destroy all the judgments of many wise men before-time received. There is no stable ground in our common law to lean unto. The judgments of years be infinite and full of much controversy, and beside that, of small authority. The judges are not bounden, as I understand, to follow them as a rule, but after their own liberty they have authority to judge according as they are instructed by the serjeants, and as the circumstance of the cause does them move. And this makes judgments and process of our law to be without end and infinite; this causes suits to be long in decision.

Therefore, to remedy this matter groundly, [44] it were necessary in our law to use the same remedy that Justinian did in the law of the Romans to bring this infinite process to certain ends—to cut away these long laws and by the wisdom of some politic and wise men institute a few and better laws and ordinances. The statutes of kings, also, be over-many, even as the constitutions of the emperors were. Wherefore I would wish that all these laws should be brought into some small number, and to be written also in our mother tongue, or else put into the Latin, to cause them that study the civil law of our realm first to begin of the Latin tongue, wherein they might also afterward learn many things to help this profession. This is one thing necessary to the education of the nobility, the which only I would should be admitted to the study of this law. Then they might study also the laws of the Romans, where they should see all causes and

---

[42] From Thomas Starkey, *Dialogue between Reginald Pole and Thomas Lupset,* ed. Kathleen M. Burton (London: Chatto and Windus Ltd., 1948), pp. 173–5. Reprinted by permission of Chatto and Windus Ltd.

[43] senior member of the bar

[44] thoroughly

controversies decided by rules more convenient to the order of nature than they be in this barbarous tongue Old French, which now serves to no purpose else. This, Master Lupset, is a great blot in our policy: to see all our law and common discipline written in this barbarous language, which after, when the youth has learned, serves them to no purpose at all.

And beside that, to say the truth, many of the laws themselves be also barbarous and tyrannical, as you have before heard. Wherefore, if we will ever bring in true civility into our country by good policy, I think we must abrogate of those laws very many; the which is the only remedy to cure such faults as we found before. . . . All by this one remedy should be amended and correct, if we might induce the heads of our country to admit the same: that is, to receive the civil law of the Romans, the which is now the common law almost of all Christian nations. . . .

# 38 / CHARLES V (1500-1558): ADVICE TO HIS SON (1555)

*Charles V was the greatest monarch of his age and the last Holy Roman emperor who could without absurdity suppose himself called to universal rule. By birth a Habsburg, by upbringing a Burgundian, he inherited the Spanish crowns in 1516 and was elected emperor in 1519. Thereafter he spent a hardworking reign in trying to govern his enormous but scattered dominions, to overcome the power of France, to stem the Turkish advance in Hungary and the Mediterranean, and to suppress the Lutheran schism in the Church. In none of these tasks was he ever more than temporarily successful, despite his notable abilities, great reserves of power, and unwavering attention to duty. He represents the personal monarchy of his day at its most conscientious and without the disastrous determination to control everything in person, which beset his son, Philip II of Spain. By 1555, worn out and in despair, he resolved to surrender his crowns and retire to die in privacy, and he took the opportunity, not for the first time, to write a political testament addressed to his son, who was to inherit the Spanish, Italian, and Netherlandish parts of his empire.*[45]

[45] Translated from Charles V, *Instructions à Philippe II son Fils* (The Hague, 1788).

I have resolved, my dear son, to remit to your hands the sovereignty of my dominions, having told you several times that I had formed this design. . . . Since the number of princes who have divested themselves of their supreme power in order to invest their successors with it is very small, you shall understand from this how great the love is that I bear to you, how thoroughly I am persuaded of your goodness, and how much I desire your increasing greatness, seeing that rather than remain in possession of the sovereignty over my realms to the end of my life (as do nearly all other princes) I prefer to follow such rare examples and reduce myself from sovereign to the status of a subject. . . .

I will not further stress this point, and I think I need not endeavor to exhort you to imitate the conduct which I have adhered to during the course of my life, nearly all of which I have passed in difficult enterprises and laborious employment, in the defence of the empire, in propagating the holy faith of Jesus Christ, and in preserving my peoples in peace and security. I will only say that at the beginning of your reign the two advantages you have—of being my son and of looking like me—will, if I am not mistaken, win for you the love of your subjects; in addition, you on your side must treat them so well that in due course you will have no need of memories of me to assist you in preserving their affection.

Do not imagine, my very dear son, that the pleasure of ruling so many peoples, and the freedom which flatters the feelings of sovereign princes, are not mixed with some bitterness and linked with some trouble. If one knew what goes on in the hearts of princes one would see that the suspicions and uncertainties which agitate those whose conduct is irregular torment them day and night, while those who govern their realms wisely and sensibly are overwhelmed by various worries which give them no rest. And truly, if you weigh in a fair balance, on the one hand, the prerogatives and preeminences of sovereignty, and on the other the work in which it involves you, you will find it a source of grief rather than of joy and delight. But this truth looks so much like a lie that only experience can make it believable.

You must know that the charge of ruling the realms which today I place upon your shoulders is more trying than the government of Spain which is a kingdom of ancient inheritance, firm and assured; whereas the acquisition of the states of Flanders, Italy, and the other provinces into whose possession you are to enter, is more recent, and they are exposed to more difficulties and upheavals, especially because they have for neighbors powerful and belligerent princes. Furthermore, the great number and vast extent of these states and kingdoms increases the cares and troubles of him who rules them; as the addition of a small piece to a reasonable burden will overwhelm him who carries it, or as superfluous food cannot but cause indigestion in a stomach which has taken sufficient nourishment. . . .

Remember, the prince is like a mirror exposed to the eyes of all his subjects who continually look to him as a pattern on which to model themselves, and who in consequence without much trouble discover his vices and virtues. No prince, however clever and skilful he may be, can hope to hide his actions and proceedings from them. If during his life he can shut their mouths and prevent them from making his irregularities and excesses public, they will after his death convey the memory of them to posterity. Therefore adhere to so just and orderly a conduct towards your peoples that, seeing the trouble you take to govern them well, they will come to rely entirely on your prudence and take comfort from your valor; and in this way there will grow between you and them a reciprocal love and affection. . . .

It is certain that people submit to the rule of their princes more readily of their own free will than when they are kept in strict bondage, and that one can retain their services better by love than by violence. I admit that the power which rests on a sovereign's gentle kindness is less absolute than that which rests only on fear; but one must also agree that it is more solid and enduring. . . .

A prince must preserve his credit with the merchants, which he will easily achieve if he takes precise care to pay them both their capital and the interest arising on it. You should especially act thus with the Genoese because, being involved in your kingdoms through the money they lend, they will be attached to you; without which you would have to garrison their city which they would not suffer without great difficulty. In this way you will make yourself master of Genoa, which is a most important place in Italy, just as the king of France has attached the Florentines to his interests through their trade with Lyons.

And since it is impossible for princes (especially those possessing several realms) to govern all alone, they must be assisted by ministers who will help them to carry so heavy a burden. From which it follows that it is extremely important to have honest and intelligent ones. I will therefore say a little more on this subject.

The three principal qualities called for in a minister are sound sense, love of his prince, and uprightness. Sound sense makes them capable of administration; love ensures that they have their master's interests at heart; and uprightness helps them to discharge their business efficiently. . . . But while it is difficult to find such men, you must do all you can, and spare no trouble, to acquire them when you meet them; for experience shows that all princes who have had this advantage have ruled their peoples with glory and success, al-

though they themselves might be full of faults. . . . Certainly it is
high wisdom in a prince, when by nature he is not sufficiently competent to govern his realms himself, to know how to choose those who
are and to put trust in them. In this way he enjoys the abilities of
several persons joined together, and he will gain much advantage,
more than those who have only their own knowledge to fall back on.
But that prince may be called very unfortunate who has neither the
ability to rule by himself nor the good sense to follow wise counsels.
. . . Do not think that any prince, however wise and able he may be,
can do without good ministers. . . .

In criminal matters, where it is a question of life and other corporal pains, see to it that the judges modify severity with some mildness, and mildness with severity, and that they pay regard to the case,
the persons, the circumstances of place and time, the manner in
which the deed was done, and other like considerations. For those
who govern states ought to accommodate themselves to the occasion
and to the condition of affairs; otherwise they have reason to fear that
they may be accused of having respect of persons. In effect, in order
to follow the rules of sense and justice, one should consider the nature
of cases, and when these are entirely alike one must proceed in the
same manner; for injustice does not consist in judging now severely
and now mildly, but in imposing different sentences in similar circumstances.

True, this would seem in part to contradict what I said before
about laws being inflexible and immutable; but that referred to the
dead law which should always be enforced according to its meaning
and tenor. This is not so in the living law, which is the prince; [46] his
ministers, in executing the dead law, must keep in mind the point of
which we have just spoken, provided that in expounding the law they
do not violate it. For the prince and the judges have a right to interpret law, and they should thoroughly examine all the circumstances
of a case in order to arrive at an equitable decision. . . . Take care
that your courts lean rather to mildness than to severity and cruelty,
except that in particular cases, for the sake of example and to deter
criminals, they should not fail to exact rigorous execution.

Lavish display on special occasions will give you great authority;
ordinary dress, following common usage, will gain you popularity.
Use the same with respect to your table and in other things, taking
care that excess of show do not lead your subjects to dislike you, nor
conformity with their habits and too much familiarity cause them to
despise you. In peace time, you should engage in occupations worthy

[46] The contrast is between the enacted, positive law (dead, i.e., fixed) and the
equitable discretion of the prince.

of a prince, such as doing things useful to your peoples, repairing bridges, improving roads, building houses, beautifying churches, palaces and squares, re-building town-walls, reforming the religious orders, establishing schools, colleges, universities, law courts, and similar things. . . . But I ought to warn you that all this must be done without exacting new taxes from them, for their burdens are already grievous, no matter what purpose you have in mind when imposing them. . . .

*[The rest is mostly a careful discussion of problems of international relations and foreign policy.]*

# 39 / THE OTTOMAN EMPIRE: TREATY WITH VENICE (1540)

*The irruption of the Turkish empire into Europe was one of the major events of fifteenth–sixteenth century history. Having captured Constantinople in 1453 and conquered the Balkans, the Turks were held back for decades by the resistance of the kingdom of Hungary. But this collapsed at the battle of Mohács (1526), and in 1529 the Turks were besieging Vienna, though without success. Thereafter, and especially as long as the great Sultan Suleiman the Magnificent (1520–1566) ruled, the Ottoman threat remained a first preoccupation for European statesmen. The Habsburgs, necessarily (as rulers of Spain and Austria) the champions of Christendom against Islam, reacted with unwavering hostility; others, especially France, found the Turks useful allies against enemies in Europe. However, the first to come to terms with the new rulers of the eastern Mediterranean were the Venetians who, though driven by the Turks from their possessions there, wished to preserve their important trade with those parts. The treaty of 1540 signalled the arrival of the Sultan in the European state system. Its terms also exemplify the arrogance and bigotry of the most powerful military and territorial complex of the day.*[47]

[47] Translated from Wilhelm Lehmann, "Der Friedensvertrag zwischen Venedig und der Türkei vom 2. Oktober 1540," *Bonner Orientalistische Studien* 16 (Stuttgart, 1936).

### ARTICE I

The tenor of the exalted and fame-commanding Edict of the Sultan, and of his glorious world-ruling imperial name, which becomes effective by the hand of God and the grace of the. Almighty, is as follows:

I, now Sultan of Sultans, proof of the imperial race, who distributes crowns to the rulers of the world, Sultan Soliman, son of Sultan Selim.

Whereas the Doge of Venice, Pietro Lando, has accredited Aloise Badoer, one of his able and trustworthy people, as ambassador to my Porte, the place of bliss;

Whereas he has offered submission and devotion to my Supreme Porte, and there exists between us a relationship of friendship and agreement, and he has besought my imperial grace that there may be peace and friendship with my Supreme Porte;

Whereas he has surrendered of the Venetian possessions in the Morea the castles of Nauplia and Monembasia (after the removal of their cannon, bells and other instruments of war) to my world-dominating Porte, on condition that the officers and troops there may go with their possessions whithersoever they will, and that of the inhabitants those who choose to stay may do so, while those who wish to leave with what they own shall be free to go;

Whereas he has undertaken to pay into my treasury the sum of 300,000 florins, of which 100,000 fl. shall be paid now, 50,000 fl. later this year, and the remainder in two annual instalments of 75,000 fl.;

Whereas he most submissively has prayed that I may grant to Venice my imperial treaty;

Therefore I have allowed my excessive imperial mercy to appear, have conceded to the Venetians—subject to the particular conditions to be stated—my high treaty, and have granted them this imperial and fortune-bearing Edict upon which my high treaty rests.

And in order that my imperial treaty may be firm and established, I swear by the Unity of God the Blessed and Divine, who created heaven and earth, that so long as nothing contrary to this treaty is done I too shall do nothing hostile to my high agreement.

.   .   .

### ARTICLE II. FREEDOM AND SAFETY OF TRAFFIC

No man in the provinces and departments of my well-guarded realm, and none of my servants (resplendent as the stars) shall cause harm or damage to any Venetian territories and castles and fortresses and people. And should any of the governors and victory-accustomed soldiers subject to my high and glorious majesty cause harm and damage to their territories and castles and fortresses and people, such harm and damage shall receive compensation by my high edict, and the causers thereof shall be severely punished.

None of the said [Venetian] merchants and people shall travel unannounced in their galleys to the following parts of my well-guarded lands, by sea or land: Istanbul, Galata, Alexandria and Cairo in the regions of Arabia, the narrows below Gallipoli, the narrows of Lepanto and Prevesa, the harbour of Methoni [in Navarino Bay]. They shall first inform the local commander and enter only with permission, unless the wind should reach the level of a storm or they are pursued by the vessels of pirates and freebooters, and there is no other place for them to find refuge, so that they arrive under compulsion: in such cases they may enter. Wherever possible they shall give notice, and if they wish to travel onwards they shall not leave without permission. Any who leave unlicensed or offer resistance shall be punished severely. This shall not be matter of accusation against any Venetian governors. And this clause shall become effective in six months' time, so that the ships of Venice may be informed and nothing contrary to my high treaty may come to pass.

## ARTICLE III. NAVY AND MERCHANT MARINE

When vessels and fleets coming from my well-guarded realm encounter the ships of Venice, they are to express friendship to one another and cause neither harm nor damage. The Venetians, when they encounter any of the fleets or ships sailing under my authority, shall strike their sails and thus demonstrate their friendship and loyalty. If, having struck sail and thus testified to friendship, they then cause damage and harm, such damage is to be made good, provided it is caused to men, materials or animals.

. . .

Should a Venetian vessel happen to encounter a pirate, should this pirate deliberately engage in attack, and should by the will of God the Venetian defeat the pirate, they are on no account to kill any of the survivors (those killed in battle always excepted) but to send them untouched and sound to my Blessed Porte, so that they may be punished severely; and I shall award them such punishment that they shall be a warning and example to all others.

Whenever my fleets sail from my well-guarded realm into other waters, this shall be of no concern to Venice; the fleets of Venice, quietly and in friendship, shall remain at their moorings, shall make no move, shall not set sail and shall aid no one, and shall be no cause of harm or damage to my fleet. They shall not join the ships of anyone involved in hostilities with myself, shall not aid them or victual them.

Any Venetian captains contravening this my command shall be severely punished by the government of Venice, in that place in which they have offended. And this shall be a warning and example to the rest.

.   .   .

### ARTICLE IV. FUGITIVE DEBTORS

If anyone comes to Venice to trade in my well-guarded realm and before paying all that is due by trickery flees and escapes, [the courts of Venice] shall, if the man is found and if a request based on my high judgment is received, award his goods to their owner.[48] On the other hand, if anyone from my well-guarded realm trades with a man of Venice and, not having paid all that is due, flees and arrives back here, [the Venetian defrauded] shall have justice in so far as the case is proved. If anyone from my well-guarded realm incurs debts or in some other way becomes liable, and then disappears, no innocent party shall be arrested in his place. The rulers of Venice shall be charged with no liability, except in the case that the guilty man arrives in their territory and settles there. And we shall act likewise.

[The remaining twenty-two articles deal in similar fashion with prisoners taken into slavery, shipwreck, immunity against privateers, extradition, the privileges of Venetian factors, protection in the courts, free traffic at sea, the tribute payable by Cyprus, and so on.]

# 40 / SIR THOMAS SMITH (1513-1577): ON THE ENGLISH PARLIAMENT (1565)

*Educated in the humanist Cambridge of his youth, Smith became one of the more notable intellectuals of the Tudor age: professor of Roman Law at Cambridge, social planner, diplomatist, and from 1572 second secretary of state. However, his gifts, marred by an impatient and outspoken temper, never took him into the top ranks of government. Of his various writings, the best-known is an outline of England and its constitution written for*

---

[48] i.e., the defrauded vendor

*some French acquaintances while he was on embassy in France.
His remarks on Parliament in effect amount to saying that in England sovereignty was vested in a mixed body of king, lords, and
commons, though there were many things which the law assigned
to the exclusive action of the monarch. The passage underlines
the constitutionalism of Tudor England, so different from contemporary developments in France and Spain.*[49]

The most high and absolute power of the realm of England consists in the Parliament. For as in war, where the king himself in person, the nobility, the rest of the gentility and the yeomanry are, is
the force and power of England: so in peace and consultation where
the prince is to give life and the last and highest commandment, the
barony for the nobility and higher, the knights, esquires, gentlemen
and commons for the lower part of the commonwealth, consult and
show what is good and necessary for the commonwealth, and to consult together and upon mature deliberation (every bill or law being
thrice read and disputed upon in either House) the other two parts
—first each part and after the prince himself in presence of both the
parts—does consent unto and allows. That is the prince's and whole
realm's deed; whereupon justly no man can complain but must accommodate himself to find it good and obey it. That which is done by this
consent is called firm, stable and *sanctum,* and is taken for law. The
Parliament abrogates old laws, makes new, gives orders for things past
and for things hereafter to be followed, changes rights and possessions
of private men, legitimates bastards, establishes forms of religion,
alters weights and measures, gives forms of succession to the Crown,
defines of doubtful rights whereof is no law already made, appoints
subsidies, tallies, taxes and impositions, gives most free pardons and
absolutions, restores in blood and name as the highest court, con-
demns or absolves them whom the prince will put to that trial. . . .
The Parliament of England . . . has the power of the whole realm,
both the head and the body. For every Englishman is intended to be
there present, either in person or by procuration and attorneys, of
what preeminence, state, dignity or quality soever he be, from the
prince (be he king or queen) to the lowest person in England. And
the consent of the Parliament is taken to be every man's consent. . . .

[49] From Thomas Smith, *De Republica Anglorum,* ed. L. Alston (Cambridge,
1906), pp. 48–9.

# 41 / JEAN BODIN (1530-1596): ON SOVEREIGNTY (1576)

*Bodin, a lawyer who held several not very important government posts during the upheavals of the French Wars of Religion, was distinguished by his ability to think straight to the heart of a problem. Thus in his work on prices (1574) he for the first time gave the correct interpretation of the inflation, mostly caused by the influx of American silver, which so troubled sixteenth-century Europe; and in his political treatise he seized upon sovereignty as the essential feature of a state, thereby providing the theoretical analysis of the sort of national states which had by then grown out of the agglomeration of interests that had marked medieval society. Since sovereignty was to him indivisible, he could find it only in the single ruler, the monarch; but he refused to admit that it need involve despotism, because he believed in the existence of fundamental laws which even the sovereign cannot touch.*[50]

Sovereignty is that absolute and perpetual power vested in a commonwealth which in Latin is termed *Majestas*. . . . One can give absolute power to a person or group of persons for a period of time, but that time expired they become subjects once more. Therefore even while they enjoy power, they cannot properly be regarded as sovereign rulers, but only as the lieutenants and agents of the sovereign ruler, till the moment comes when it pleases the prince or the people to revoke the gift. The true sovereign remains always seized of his power. . . . Consider the force of the word absolute. The people or the magnates of a commonwealth can bestow simply and unconditionally upon someone of their choice a sovereign and perpetual power to dispose of their property and persons, to govern the state as he thinks fit, and to order the succession, in the same way that any proprietor, out of his liberality, can freely and unconditionally make a gift of his property to another. Such a gift, not being qualified in any way, is the only true gift, being at once unconditional and irrevocable. Gifts burdened with obligations and hedged with conditions are not true gifts. Similarly sovereign power given to a prince charged with

[50] From Jean Bodin, *Six Books of the Commonwealth*, trans. Marion J. Tooley (Oxford: Basil Blackwell, n.d.), pp. 25–8, 197–8. Reprinted by permission of Basil Blackwell & Mott Ltd.

conditions is neither properly sovereign nor absolute, unless the conditions of appointment are only such as are inherent in the laws of God and nature. . . . If we insist, however, that sovereign power means exemption from all law whatsoever, there is no prince who can be regarded as sovereign, since all the princes of the earth are subject to the laws of God and of nature, and even to certain human laws common to all nations. . . . It is the distinguishing mark of the sovereign that he cannot in any way be subject to the commands of another, for it is he who makes law for the subject, abrogates laws already made, and amends obsolete law. No one who is subject either to the law or to some other person can do this. . . .

The principal mark of a commonwealth, that is to say the existence of a sovereign power, can hardly be established except in a monarchy. There can only be one sovereign in the commonwealth. If there are two, three or more, not one of them is sovereign, since none of them can either impose a law on his companions or submit to one at their instance. Though one can imagine a collective sovereign power, vested in a ruling class, or a whole people, there is no true subject nor true protector if there is not some head of the state in whom sovereign power is vested, who can unite all the rest. A simple magistrate, not endowed with sovereign authority, cannot perform this function. Moreover if the ruling class, or the people, are, as often happens, divided, the dispute can only be settled by force, and by one taking up arms against another. Even when the majority is agreed, it can easily happen with a people that the minority have considerable resources, and choose a leader whom they force upon the majority, and so carry all before them. . . . It is impossible for a people or an aristocracy themselves to issue sovereign commands, or give effect to any project which requires a single person to undertake it, such as the command of an army and such like matters. They have to appoint magistrates or commissaries to this end, and these have neither the sovereign power, the authority, nor the majesty of a king. Whatever powers they have in virtue of their sovereignty, when popular or aristocratic states find themselves engaged in a perilous war either with a foreign enemy, or with one another, or in difficulty in bringing some overmighty subject to justice, in securing public order in times of calamity, in instituting magistrates, or undertaking any other weighty matter, they set up a dictator as sovereign ruler. They thereby recognise that monarchy is the sacred anchor on which of necessity, all must in the last instance rely. . . .

# 42 / ROBERT BEALE (1541-1601): DUTIES OF A SECRETARY OF STATE (1592)

*Beale was not only a successful English civil servant (he served as a diplomatist and as chief assistant to Sir Francis Walsingham, secretary of state, 1572–90) but also a member of Parliament with Puritan leanings, not afraid to criticize the government he served. In 1592 he drew up a set of very detailed notes for the guidance of an incoming secretary of state. These underline three points relevant to the internal administration of these consolidated monarchies: the personal importance of the monarch with whom all business had in the last resort to be discussed and agreed, the use of councils of confidential officeholders to administer the realm, and the key position of the secretary of state, an office which came to prominence in sixteenth-century Europe as the chief executive agency of government.*[51]

My meaning is not to speak anything of such qualities as are fit to be in one that should be a prince's secretary or councillor. That argument has been handled by others, and whom Her Majesty [52] shall call to that place my simple judgment must think sufficiently qualified. Wherefore my intention shall be only to note such things as belong unto the practice or the place of a secretary, which consists partly in dealing with Her Majesty, and partly with the rest of Her Highness' most honourable Privy Council.

Touching matters to be handled before the Council, to avoid the number and trouble of many unnecessary suits it were convenient to have at the first entrance the order renewed and observed which has been many times made by the Lords of the Council: for them to attend unto matters of state either at home or abroad, to refer private suits to the masters of requests or other ordinary courts of

[51] Robert Beale, "Instructions for a Principal Secretary," in C. Read, *Mr. Secretary Walsingham and the Policy of Queen Elizabeth* (Oxford: Clarendon Press, 1925), Vol. 1, pp. 423 ff. Reprinted by permission of Clarendon Press.

[52] Queen Elizabeth I (1558–1603)

justice. . . . And yet, where there is great cause, I would not have Her Majesty's Council wholly abridged of that prerogative, for in times past they did deal in such causes, as appears by the first book or register of the Court of Requests and many other precedents of great moment.

Of such things as the secretary is to proffer to the Council, let him first have in a several [53] paper a memorial or docket of those which he minds to propound and have dispatched at every sitting. He is to proffer the public before the private and discern of things which require speedy answer before such as may tarry longer leisure. Especially let not such messengers long stay which come either from beyond the seas or other parts and must have allowances for their journeys and attendances.

When the Council meets, have a care that the time be not spent in matters of small moment, but to dispatch such things as shall be propounded unto them, for you shall find that they will not meet so often as you would desire, sometimes for sickness and sometimes for other employments. . . .

If there be any occasion of treaties, obligations or contracts with foreign princes or states in Latin, besides former precedents and your own learning you shall do well to use the help of the doctors of the civil law and some discreet and well-experimented notaries, which were more used in former times than of late years. Remember the saying of Lord Hastings, lord chamberlain to King Edward IV [54] (in Commines): that the Englishmen have been more overtaken by the French in their treaties than in their wars. . . .

A secretary must have a special cabinet, whereof he is himself to keep the key, for his signets, ciphers and secret intelligences, distinguishing the boxes or tills rather by letters than by the names of the countries or places, keeping that only unto himself, for the names may inflame a desire to come by such things. . . .

It is convenient for a secretary to seek to understand the state of the whole realm, to have Sir Thomas Smith's book, [55] although there be many defects which by progress of time and experience he shall be able to spy and amend. Then to have a book or notice of all the noblemen, their pedigrees and alliances among themselves and with other gentlemen. A secretary must likewise have the book of Ortelius' maps, [56] a book of the maps of England with a particular note of the divisions of the shires . . . and what noblemen, gentlemen and other

[53] separate

[54] 1461–83

[55] See No. 40.

[56] Abraham Ortelius of Antwerp (1527–98), a map maker who from 1570 published a world atlas which he kept revising and improving

be residing in every one of them; what cities, boroughs, market towns, villages; and also a good description of the realm of Ireland. . . .

Touching foreign service, I would wish that you did, as soon as you can, inform yourself of such things as have passed between this realm and other states, at the least for the space of one year before, to the intent you may join your service with that which went before.

It is a secretary's duty beforehand to consider of the state of the realm and the rest of the princes' states with whom there have been and are any doings, and what dangers may happen and how they may be remedied. Security has always been the bane of all kingdoms and states; and it has been in the end seen that when counsels are daily taken and varied according to the uncertainty of affairs, either at home or abroad, upon sudden events, the wisest men have been often overtaken and put to hard shifts and have not known what counsel to give or take. . . . Wherefore, if occasion serve, no opportunity is to be omitted to compound all discontents with neighbours abroad, so as the same may be with the honour of God and benefit of the realm, and to procure as much friendship as may be; lest, by suffering things to run on carelessly at random, our enemies prevent us of the means and they cannot be recovered when we would wish it. . . .

Things to be done with Her Majesty. Have in a little paper a note of such things as you are to propound to Her Majesty and divide it into the titles of public and private suits. . . .

Learn before your access Her Majesty's dispositions by some of her privy chamber with whom you must keep credit, for that will stand you in much stead; and yet yield not too much to their importunity for suits, for so may you be blamed; nevertheless, pleasure them when conveniently you may.

Show yourself willing to pleasure any of Her Majesty's kin, for although perhaps nothing be obtained yet it will be well taken, as though you did it in respect they appertain unto her. . . .

When Her Highness is angry or not well disposed, trouble her not with any matter which you desire to have done, unless extreme necessity urge it.

When Her Highness signs, it shall be good to entertain her with some relation or speech, whereat she may take some pleasure. . . .

# 43 / WILLIAM CECIL LORD BURGHLEY (1520-1598): ADVICE TO HIS SON (C. 1590)

*Burghley was Queen Elizabeth's chief minister for forty years and one of the great European statesmen of his age. The counsel he gave to his second son Robert, designed to be his successor in office, illustrates well both his own personal character, marked by a kind of sober and half-cynical prudence, and the peculiar spirit of these "new men" who really made the sixteenth-century monarchies work. The extract may also explain why many are convinced that Burghley was the model for Shakespeare's Polonius.*[57]

1. When it shall please God to bring thee to man's estate, use great providence and circumspection in choosing thy wife. For from thence will spring all thy future good and evil. And it is an action of life, like unto a stratagem of war, wherein a man can err but once. If thy estate be good, match near home and at leisure; if weak, far off and quickly. . . . Let her not be poor how generous [well born] so ever, for a man can buy nothing in the market with gentility. Nor choose a base and uncomely creature altogether for wealth, for it will cause contempt in others and loathing in thee. Neither make choice of a dwarf or a fool; for by the one thou shalt beget a race of pygmies, the other will be thy continual disgrace and it will irk thee to hear her talk. For thou shalt find to thy great grief that there is nothing more fulsome than a she-fool.

And touching the guiding of thy house, let thy hospitality be moderate, and (according to the means of thy estate) rather plentiful than sparing, but not costly. . . . Banish swinish drunkards out of thine house, which is a vice impairing health, consuming much, and makes no show. I never heard praise ascribed to the drunkard but for the well-bearing of his drink, which is a better commendation for a brewer's horse or a drayman than for either a gentleman or a servingman. Beware thou spend not above three or four parts of thy revenues, nor

[57] From Francis Peck, ed., *Desiderata Curiosa* (London, 1779), i.47–9.

above a third of that in thy house. For the other two parts will do
no more than defray thy extraordinaries which always. surmount the
ordinary by much; otherwise thou shalt live, like a rich beggar, in
continual want. And the needy man can never live happily or con-
tentedly, for every disaster makes him ready to mortgage or sell.
And that gentleman who sells an acre of land sells an ounce of credit.
For gentility is nothing else but ancient riches. . . .

2. Bring thy children up in learning and obedience, yet without
outward austerity. Praise them openly, reprehend them secretly. . . .
I am persuaded that the foolish cockering of some parents and the
over-stern carriage of others causeth more men and women to take ill
courses than their own vicious inclinations. Marry thy daughters in,
time, lest they marry themselves. And suffer not thy sons to pass the
Alps, for they shall learn nothing there but pride, blasphemy and
atheism. And if by travel they get a few broken languages, that shall
profit them nothing more than to have one meat served in divers
dishes. Neither, by my consent, shalt thou train them up in wars.
For he that sets up his rest to live by that profession can hardly be
an honest man or a good Christian. Besides, it is a science no longer
in request than in use. For soldiers in peace are like chimneys in summer.

3. Live not in the country without corn and cattle about thee . . .
and what provision thou shalt want, learn to buy it at the best hand.
For there is one penny saved in four betwixt buying in thy need and
when the markets and seasons serve fittest for it. . . .

4. Let thy kindred and allies be welcome to thy house and table.
Grace them with thy countenance and further them in all honest
actions. For by this means thou shalt so double the band of nature
as thou shalt find them so many advocates to plead an apology for
thee behind thy back. But shake off those glowworms, I mean parasites
and sycophants, who will feed and fawn upon thee in the summer
of prosperity, but in an adverse storm will shelter thee no more than
an arbor in winter.

5. Beware of suretyship for thy best friends. He that payeth another man's debts, seeketh his own decay. But if thou canst not otherwise choose, rather lend thy money thyself upon good bonds, although
thou borrow it. So shalt thou secure thyself and pleasure thy friend.
Neither borrow money of a neighbour or a friend, but of a stranger,
where, paying for it, thou shalt hear no more of it. Otherwise thou
shalt eclipse thy credit, lose thy freedom, and yet pay as dear as to
another. But in borrowing of money be precious of thy word. For he
that hath care of keeping days of payment is lord of another man's
purse.

6. Undertake no suit against a poor man with[out] receiving much

wrong; . . . it is a base conquest to triumph where there is small resistance. Neither attempt law against any man before thou be fully resolved that thou hast right on thy side; and then spare not for either money or pains. For a cause or two so followed and obtained will free thee from suits a great part of thy life.

7. Be sure to keep some great man thy friend, but trouble him not for trifles. Compliment him often with many, yet small, gifts, and of little charge. And if thou hast cause to bestow any great gratuity, let it be something which may be daily in sight. Otherwise, in this ambitious age, thou shalt remain like a hop without a pole: live in obscurity and be made a football for every insulting companion to spurn at.

8. Towards thy superiors be humble yet generous. With thine equals, familiar yet respective. Towards thine inferiors show much humanity and some familiarity, as to bow the body, stretch forth the hand, and to uncover the head. . . . The first prepares thy way to advancement. The second makes thee known for a man well bred. The third gains a good report which, once got, is easily kept. For right humanity takes such deep root in the minds of the multitude as they are easilier gained by unprofitable courtesies than by churlish benefits. Yet I advise thee not to affect or neglect popularity too much. Seek not to be Essex; shun to be Raleigh.

9. Trust not any man with thy life, credit or estate. For it is mere folly for a man to enthral himself to his friend, as though, occasion being offered, he should not dare to become the enemy.

10. Be not scurrilous in conversation, nor satirical in thy jests. The one will make thee unwelcome to all company, the other pull on quarrels and get thee hated of thy best friends. For suspicious jests (when any of them savour of truth) leave a bitterness in the minds of those which are touched. And . . . I think it necessary to leave it to thee as a special caution because I have seen many so prone to quip and gird as they would rather leave their friend than their jest. And if perchance their boiling brain yield a quaint scoff, they will travail to be delivered of it as a woman with child. These nimble fancies are but the froth of wit.

# 44 / ELIZABETH I (1533-1603): THE GOLDEN SPEECH (1601)

*The great queen who ruled England from 1558, during the formative years when a small offshore state first began to expand into what was to be the most extensive empire ever known, demonstrated what personal monarchy could be at its best: a rule not despotic in any sense, but definitely paternal. Throughout her reign Elizabeth found Parliament loyal but ready to be difficult. This speech of 1601 was addressed to it after a particularly stormy session; there had been violent protests at the oppressive monopolies granted by the Queen for the sale and manufacture of various commodities, and Elizabeth had had to retreat. While the speech was, of course, designed to bring back peace in the particular circumstances, it was also a sincere expression of the true relationship between her and her people.*[58]

I do assure you there is no prince that loves his subjects better, or whose love can countervail our love. There is no jewel, be it of never so rich a price, which I set before this jewel: I mean your love. For I do esteem it more than any treasure or riches; for that we know how to prize, but love and thanks I count unvaluable.[59] And, though God has raised me high, yet this I count the glory of my crown, that I have reigned with your loves. This makes me that I do not so much rejoice that God has made me to be a Queen, as to be a Queen over so thankful a people. Therefore, I have cause to wish nothing more than to content the subject; and that is a duty which I owe. Neither do I desire to live longer days than I may see your prosperity; and that is my only desire. And as I am that person that still yet under God has delivered you, so I trust, by the almighty power of God, that I shall be His instrument to preserve you from every peril, dishonour, shame, tyranny and oppression. . . .

Of myself I must say this: I never was any greedy, scraping grasper, nor a strait, fast-holding Prince, nor yet a waster. My heart was never set on any worldly goods, but only for my subjects' good. What you

---

[58] From J. E. Neale, *Elizabeth I and Her Parliaments,* Vol. 2 (London, Jonathan Cape Ltd.; New York, St. Martin's Press, Inc., 1957), pp. 389–91. Reprinted by permission of the publishers.

[59] impossible to estimate

bestow on me, I will not hoard it up, but receive it to bestow on you again. Yea, mine own properties I account yours, to be expended for your good. . . .

I have ever used to set the Last-Judgment Day before mine eyes, and so to rule as I shall be judged to answer before a higher Judge, to whose judgment seat I do appeal, that never thought was cherished in my heart that tended not unto my people's good. And now, if my kingly bounties have been abused, and my grants turned to the hurt of my people, contrary to my will and meaning, and if any in authority under me have neglected or perverted what I have committed to them, I hope God will not lay their culps [60] and offences to my charge; who, though there were danger in repealing our grants, yet what danger would I not rather incur for your good, than I would suffer them still to continue?

I know the title of King is a glorious title; but assure yourself that the shining glory of princely authority has not so dazzled the eyes of our understanding, but that we well know and remember that we also are to yield an account of our actions before the great Judge. To be a King and wear a crown is a thing more glorious to them that see it, than it is pleasant to them that bear it. For myself, I was never so much enticed with the glorious name of a King or royal authority of a Queen, as delighted that God had made me His instrument to maintain His truth and glory, and to defend this Kingdom (as I said) from peril, dishonour, tyranny and oppression.

There will never Queen sit in my seat with more zeal to my country, care for my subjects, and that will sooner with willingness venture her life for your good and safety, than myself. For it is my desire to live nor reign no longer than my life and reign shall be for your good. And though you have had and may have many princes more mighty and wise sitting in this seat, yet you never had nor shall have any that will be more careful and loving. . . .

[60] crimes

# 45 / HUGO GROTIUS (1583-1645): THE LAW OF NATIONS (1625)

*The great Dutch scholar, statesman, and jurist spent an adventurous life (including a long exile from his native land) in the service of scholarship and diplomacy. Though not the first to study the problems involved in the relations of sovereign powers, he wrote in his* De Iure Belli et Pacis *the first treatise giving a systematic account of national laws relevant to international relations and of the laws operating between individual states. His intention was to describe rather than prescribe. His most famous work, the foundation of all later study and development of international law, formed only a small part of his enormous output of history, law, theology, philosophy and poetry.*[61]

## INTRODUCTION

Many have endeavored to write explanatory commentaries or concise surveys of the municipal law, for instance, of Rome or of a man's own country. Few, however, have attempted the law which applies to the relations of several nations or of their rulers, whether it be derived from nature itself or instituted by custom or tacit contract, and no one so far has treated of it completely and systematically. Yet mankind has a concern that this be done. Cicero was right to ascribe the greatest importance to the study of the alliances, treaties and agreements of peoples, kings and national states, in short of all the law of war and peace. Euripides even preferred such learning to a knowledge of things divine and human, for he has Theoclymenes addressed thus:

> Ill were it if a man like you,
> Who knows the affairs of men and God,
> The present and the future, knew not what's just.

The present work is the more necessary because men are not lacking now, nor have they been in the past, who despise this branch of

[61] Translated from Hugo Grotius, *De Iure Belli et Pacis Libri Tres* (Paris, 1626).

legal studies to the point of holding that it exists only in an empty name. Most people can quote Thucydides, to the effect that nothing is unjust to a king or a state having power. Other *obiter dicta* maintain that at the top of the tree equity equals strength, or that politics cannot be conducted without wrong being done. Moreover, the conflicts that arise among peoples and kings usually end in the arbitrament of Mars. Not only the vulgar think that war is farthest from justice; even men of learning and sense often drop remarks tending that way. No pair of opposites is more commonly found in literature than "law and arms". . . . A passage from Tertullian may stand for the lot: "Deceit, cruelty and injustice are the proper aspect of the wars." . . .

However, since the discussion of a law is futile if the law itself does not exist, it will help to commend the work and to guard in advance against criticism if this very serious error is briefly refuted. And, not to get involved with a crowd, let me appoint counsel for the prosecution. Who better than Carneades [62] who reached the absolute height of his calling—that is to say, could employ the powers of his eloquence as readily in the service of falsehood as of truth? Thus when he undertook to argue against justice, especially of the kind with which we are here concerned, he found no argument stronger than this: man-made law, established for utility's sake, differs as men's customs differ and in the same community is often changed in the change of time; there is no such thing as a law of nature, for all men and other living creatures are drawn by nature to seek their own advantage; for which reason there either is no justice, or if it exists it equals the height of stupidity since in allowing for the concerns of others a man harms himself.

But there is no need at all to accept this philosophical view, incidentally supported by Horace with his "By nature none can tell what's right from wrong." True, man is an animal, but of a very superior kind, a great deal more removed from the others than their species differ one from another; many activities peculiar to the human race show this. Among the special characteristics of mankind is a desire for society, that is for a life in common lived not anyhow but in tranquillity and (to satisfy one's intellect) arranged with men of one's own kind. So the supposition that every animal naturally seeks only its own advantage is true of other animals, but of man only before he has achieved the employment of his peculiarly human qualities. However, even in the case of other animals this exception must be added

[62] Greek philosopher (214–128 B.C.) who on a diplomatic mission to Rome delivered two speeches, one in praise of justice and one against it, in order to demonstrate his lack of dogmatic belief

that they somewhat modify the search for individual advantage by a regard for their offspring and for others of their species. In them, we believe this to spring from some externally imposed instinct because in other acts no more difficult than these no equal intelligence becomes apparent. Since men, however, act thus also in similar situations, it is clear that they possess an intrinsic intelligence to which character-istics not belonging to all animals correspond. That preference for society agreeable to man's intellect, of which I have already spoken, is the source of *ius* properly so called [Natural Law]. It involves absten-tion from another's property, its restitution to him if we do happen to possess it, as well as of any gain made from it, the obligation to fulfill promises, reparation of damage done by fault, and an admission that punishment may be applied among men.

From this meaning of the word flows another and larger. For man surpasses other animals not only in the social impulse of which I have spoken, but also in his judgment of what is profitable and what harm-ful, and not only of that which profits and harms now but also what may do so in the future, and of what may conduce to either. There-fore we may suppose that it accords with the nature of the human intellect to follow in such matters a judgment truly formed, seduced by neither fear nor the attraction of immediate pleasure, nor carried away by rash impulses; and whatever is plainly adverse to such judg-ment may be held contrary to the law of nature, that is human nature. . . .

It is quite wrong to suppose, as some imagine, that in war all laws ceàse to apply; indeed, war should never be engaged in except to obtain lawful ends, nor once engaged in should it be waged except within the bounds of law and good faith. Demosthenes was right to argue that war is an action directed against those who cannot be constrained by process of law. For such process works against those who recognise their relative weakness; those who establish or think themselves equal must be dealt with by wars. But to be acceptable, those wars must follow the rules as carefully as is usual in legal process. By all means, therefore, "let the laws fall silent in the clash of arms," that is to say, laws civil, judicial, proper to peace, but not those others which are permanent and apply at all times. . . .

Holding it thus firmly established that there exists among nations a common law with force for and in wars, I had many and weighty reasons for writing a book about it. Throughout Christendom I saw a readiness to make war of which even barbarians might be ashamed. Men take up arms for light causes or none at all, and once at war they discard all respect for the laws of God and men, just as though that one step had sanctioned all violence and crime. The sight of such atrocities has induced a good many truly reputable writers to forbid Christian men all recourse to arms since it is their special duty to love all men. . . . The idea seems to be that things bent out of true one way are best bent right over the other, so as to make them straight again. However, such attempts at overcorrection tend to defeat their own purpose, for the exaggeration is easily recognised and detracts from the authority of what truth there may be in the argument. A remedy must be provided against both the extremes—that nothing is permitted, and that everything is. . . .

### BOOK I, CHAPTER 5

As in other things, so in the actions of the will there are commonly three efficient causes: the principal, the auxiliary, and the instrumental. The principal efficient cause in war is usually the party concerned, in private war a private person, in public war a public person, especially a sovereign power. Whether another may make war on behalf of inactive parties we shall consider elsewhere. Meanwhile we hold to this, that each man is by nature the champion of his own rights. That is why we have been given hands.

But to assist another to the best of our power is not only permitted but creditable. Those who have written on obligation rightly stress that nothing is so useful to one man as another man. There are various links between men which encourage mutual aid. Blood-relations combine to help one another; one may call on neighbors or fellow-citizens. . . . Aristotle maintained that everyone should fight for himself if injured, or to assist his kin, or for his patrons and allies if they have suffered injury. Solon taught that in a successful polity each man will make other men's troubles his own. However, to pass over other ties, a shared humanity is enough. "Nothing human is alien to man. . . ."

By "instrumentals" we do not here mean weapons or similar things but voluntary agents whose will derives from another's. Such an instrument is a son to his father, being obviously part of him by nature, or a servant [to his master], part of him, so to speak, by law. . . . As the servant in the household, so is the subject in the commonwealth, and therefore he is an instrument of the ruler.

There is no doubt that by the law of nature all subjects may be drafted for war, though some may be excluded by a particular law, as slaves were in Rome or as the clergy are generally now. Such a law, however, as all of that kind, must be ready to carry an exception concerning extreme necessity.

### BOOK III, CHAPTER 1

The means which lead to an end in a moral matter acquire an intrinsic value from that end. Therefore, whatever is necessary for the attaining of a lawful end (necessity being interpreted not in terms of physical precision but morally) we are thereby entitled to use. By entitlement I mean that which is strictly so called and signifies an ability to act solely with respect to society. For if I cannot save my life any other way, I may restrain the attacker with any force whatsoever, even though he be quite free from any fault at law: this right properly rises not from a fault in another but from the title granted to me by nature on my own behalf. I may intrude upon another's property from which certain danger threatens me, without consideration of that other man's guilt; however, I cannot obtain possession, a step not directed towards the particular end, but may occupy only till my security is sufficiently provided for. . . . Thus natural law permits me to take from another man any thing of mine that he detains, or if that were too difficult some equivalent; and I have the same right for the recovery of a debt. In such cases, ownership also arises, since the damaged equilibrium cannot otherwise be restored. Thus where punishment is lawful, all such force without which punishment cannot be applied is also lawful; and so is whatever is part of the punishment, as the destruction of property by burning or otherwise, within just limits answering the offence. . . .

### BOOK III, CHAPTER 4

Our next point, the liberty to cause injury, extends first of all to persons. . . . This right is very broad, for firstly it comprehends not only those who in actual deed bear arms or are subjects of the power engaged in war, but also all those found within the hostile territory, as is plain from the formula found in Livy, "Let him be declared an enemy and all those in his protection." This is so because they, too, may occasion fear of harm, and in a continuous and general war this suffices to create the right of which we speak. The case differs from that of sureties which, as has been said, was modelled on the example of burdens imposed to pay the debts of a state, so that it is no wonder to find Baldus [63] assert that war involves much greater licence than that permitted by the law of pledges. Nor can it be doubted that this also applies to foreigners who enter enemy territory after war is known to have been declared. Those who enter before the outbreak of war appear by the law of nations to be regarded as enemies only after a reasonable time has been allowed for departure. . . .

Touching those who are truly enemy subjects, that is from a permanent condition, the law of nations permits them to be injured, as to their persons, in any place. When war is declared against anyone it is simultaneously declared against the men of his people. . . . We

---

[63] Baldus de Ubaldis (1327–1400), one of the great medieval legists

may therefore lawfully kill them on our own soil, on enemy soil, or on soil belonging to no one, or on the high seas. It is not permitted to kill them on [neutral] territory remaining at peace: but this law is derived from the rights of that territory's ruler, not from the personal rights of enemies. . . . How widely this liberty extends may be seen from the fact that the killing even of children and women is held to be lawful and included in this law of war. . . . Not even prisoners are exempt . . . nor is the power to kill such slaves (i.e., prisoners of war) limited in time, as far as the law of nations is concerned, although some municipal laws restrict it in varying degrees. . . .

The violation of women is variously regarded as permitted or not. Those who allow it consider only the injury done to the person, which they hold it agreeable to the law of arms to inflict on anything belonging to the enemy. The other opinion is better: it takes into account not only the injury but also the act of unbridled lust and concludes that something pertaining to neither safety nor punishment should be no more lawful in war than in peace. This latter view is not the law of all nations, but it is the law of the more respectable ones. . . .

# 46 / SIR EDWARD COKE (1552-1634): THE ENGLISH COMMON LAW (1628)

*Coke was and remains a giant among common lawyers. Attorney general in several famous state trials, chief justice successively of the courts of Common Pleas (1606–13) and King's Bench (1613–16), he quarrelled with King James I and was dismissed, only to continue his struggle for the law and against absolute monarchy in the parliamentary battles of 1621–28. Influential enough as a judge, he did even more for the law as a writer, especially in the four volumes of the* Institutes of the Laws of England, *the first of which discusses the law of real property. Here he set out to assemble a systematic description of England's law and legal system, rather in the manner demanded by Starkey a century before (No. 37). The importance of the common law lay in great part in its stubborn protection of existing rights. While this could make social reform difficult, it also helped to protect England against political innovation and Stuart despotism.*[64]

When I had finished this work of the first part of the Institutes and looked back and considered the multitude of the conclusions in law, the manifold diversities between cases and points of learning, the variety almost infinite of authorities (ancient, constant, and modern), and withal their amiable and admirable consent in so many successions of ages, the many changes and alterations of the common law and additions to the same . . . by many acts of Parliament; and that the like work of Institutes had not been attempted by any of our profession whom I might imitate; I thought it safe for me . . . not to take upon me or presume that the reader should think that all that I have said herein to be law. Yet this I may safely affirm, that there is nothing herein but may either open some windows of the law, to let in more light to the student by diligent search to see the secrets of the law; or to make him to doubt, and withal to enable him to enquire and learn of the sages, what the law together with the true reason thereof in these cases is; or lastly upon consideration had of our old books, laws and records (which are full of venerable dignity and antiquity) to find out whereof any alteration has been, upon what ground the law has since been changed; knowing for certain that the law is unknown to him that knows not the reason thereof, and that the known certainty of the law is the safety of all. . . .

# 47 / THE COMMON LAW IN ACTION

*Coke might wish to treat the English common law as an object of philosophical admiration; its practice was more mundane and sufficiently arcane. The following opinion of one of the judges in the case of* Willion v. Berkeley *(1563) shows something of the technicality of the law but also illustrates the powers of reasoned analysis and common sense that it demanded. The main preoccupation of the law was with disputes over landed property, and this case is no exception. Lord Berkeley had granted some lands to King Henry VII and his heirs male, with remainder to his own*

---

[64] From *The First Part of the Institutes of the Laws of England* (London, 1628), Epilogue, p. 395.

*heirs: that is to say, if the male heirs of Henry VII ran out, the lands were to revert to whatever Berkeley descendant was then the grantor's direct heir. He thus created what is known as an estate tail (taillé, cut off: the grantee's interest is limited). However, Henry VIII, inheriting quite properly from his father, had granted the property to his last wife, Catherine Parr, from whom it had further descended. With the death of Edward VI in 1553, the male line of Henry VII came to an end. The dispute was therefore between those who claimed as heirs to Catherine Parr (relying on Henry VIII's grant) and those who claimed as Lord Berkeley's heirs (relying on the terms of the original grant). It was held that Henry VIII had had no right to grant away an estate tail and thus to deprive the remainder-men of their rights; the lands reverted to Berkeley's heirs. Among other things, therefore, the case demonstrates the ascendancy of the common law even over actions of the royal prerogative which was here adjudged to have done a wrong remediable by the courts.[65]*

ANTHONY BROWN, JUSTICE: I am of opinion to the contrary. And first, where the remainder is limited to King Henry VII by the name of King Henry VII, it seems to me well limited by such name. For the king naturally, properly and fully cannot purchase by any other name than by the name of king, for the name of king has drowned his surname, and in the name of king his surname and proper name also are included. And this name of king cannot be omitted in his purchases, or in his patents or writs, for it is his name and by it he is known and commonly called. And so in this statute it is said, "The lord the king perceiving etc. has ordained etc.", signifying by the name of "the lord the king" King Edward I. So we say "nullum tempus occurrit regi" [limitations do not affect the king's rights], and a man shall forfeit to "the lord the king," and "the lord the king sent his writ in these words," without expressing his name of baptism. So that the name of "the lord the king" contains the king in certain, viz. the king which then is, or the king spoken of. And although it is usual at this day to say King Henry VIII or King Edward III or King Edward IV, this is but for distinction's sake, to know what king we mean, for several of them had one same name as Henry or Edward, and the addition of a number, as first, second or third, shows which of them we mean that have reigned heretofore; and it is to no other purpose. For the word "king" is a name of substance by itself without the name of baptism, and this politic name of king includes the king's natural name, as the names of

[65] From *The Commentaries or Reports of Edmund Plowden* (ed. Dublin, 1792), pp. 244-5.

duke of Norfolk or earl of Arundel include their natural names. And if land is given to Edward VI or Henry VIII, omitting the word king, they shall take nothing. But *e contra*, if a patent is made by King Henry VIII by the words, "the king has granted," omitting Henry, or by the present queen by the words "the queen has granted," omitting Elizabeth, the gift is good. And so a gift to the king or queen, omitting their name of baptism, is good, for the natural name is included in the politic name of king or queen. But, sir, the majesty and name of the king, when they are conjoined with the natural person, alter the quality and degree of the natural person in the eye of the law, so that if he was within age [66] before he shall then be adjudged of full age to all purposes; and if his body natural was attainted [67] before (as Henry VII was), *eo instante* that when the dignity royal comes to it the disability is gone; for the greater removes the imperfection of the lesser, and the body politic has the preeminence over the body natural. So that if land is given to the king by the name of baptism, and by the name of king also, as to Henry the king, and to his heirs, this shall go in succession as the crown shall go. And if a man that is king by descent on the part of his mother purchases land to him and to his heirs, and in the purchase he is called by the name of baptism and by the name of king also, if he dies without issue the heir on the part of his mother, who has the dignity royal, shall have the land; for the name of the king being greater than the name of baptism, which signifies only the natural body, shall have the greater preeminence in the purchase and shall draw the land with it. So, if land is given to Edward king of England and to his heirs, if he dies without issue his brother of the half blood, being king, shall have it, *causa qua supra*. And, sir, although such is the nature of the king's person, yet it seems to me that the estate here limited to King Henry VII vested in his body natural, and in that capacity he took it. For although it was limited to him by the name of King Henry VII, so that there is as well the politic name of king as his name of baptism, yet the body natural may be signified by this name of king, as it has been said, for it includes the body natural, and the donor is at liberty to give the land to the one body or to the other. And here he has given it to him and to his heirs male of his body, which is a limitation to the natural body that may beget issues, for the body politic cannot beget issues. And by this limitation none shall have the land after the death of Henry VII but those who were begotten of his body. And if it had so happened that after the death of Henry VII another had been king who was not issue of the body of Henry VII, it would not have been reasonable that he should have had the land, for the

---

[66] a minor
[67] deprived of all legal existence by act of parliament

donor did not appoint it to him but directed his gift to those who should issue of the body of Henry VII; for which reason it cannot vest in the body politic and go in succession to him that shall be king, whosoever he is, for such is not the limitation of the donor. And if the donor intended to give it to the body natural, he could not have used more proper words, for they are such as he ought to have used to a stranger if he had given it to a stranger in his body natural. And therefore it is limited merely to the body natural, and in that body it vested because to that body the donor was pleased to give it.

# 48 / CHARLES I: THE ENGLISH CONSTITUTION (1642)

*On the eve of the English Civil War, King Charles I, replying to the Nineteen Propositions of the House of Commons (which, if accepted, would have terminated the independent power of the crown), offered a description of the government of England that was highly constitutional and entirely in line with the doctrine developed and practiced in the sixteenth century, but more fully worked out so as to become the basis of all conventional thinking on the subject until the rise of democratic doctrines in the nineteenth century. The document was in fact drafted by some of Charles's moderate adherents—men who had supported parliamentary opposition to him so long as it confined itself to removing "abuses" but refused to follow it into invasions of the King's time-hallowed prerogatives. Others of Charles's followers regarded the document as too conciliatory and as giving away too much; nor is there any reason to think that, if he had won the war, the King would have observed its very proper constitutionalism.[68]*

. . .

We supposed these demands by this time to appear such as the demanders cannot be supposed to have any such real fear of us as has been long pretended: they are too much in the style not only of equals but of conquerors. . . . As if, there being differences and suits between two persons whereof one would have from the other several

[68] From *Historical Collections*, ed. J. Rushworth, III/1 (London, 1691), pp. 730–2.

parcels of ancient land, he should propose to him, by way of accommodation, that he would quit to him all those in question, with the rest of his estate, as the most necessary and effectual means to remove all those suits and differences. But we call God to witness that for our subjects' sake these rights are vested in us, so for their sakes, as well as for our own, we are resolved not to quit them, nor to subvert (though in a parliamentary way) the ancient equal, happy, well-poised and never enough commended constitution of the government of this kingdom—not to make ourself, of a king of England, a duke of Venice, and this of a kingdom a republic.

There being three kinds of government among men: absolute monarchy, aristocracy, and democracy, and all of these having their particular conveniences and inconveniences. The experience and wisdom of our ancestors has so moulded this out of a mixture of these as to give to this kingdom (as far as human prudence can provide) the conveniences of all three without the inconveniences of any one, so long as the balance hangs even between the three estates and they run jointly on their proper channel (begetting verdure and fertility in the meadows on both sides) and the overflowing of either on either side raise no deluge or inundation. The ill of absolute monarchy is tyranny; the ill of aristocracy is faction and division; the ills of democracy are tumults, violence and licentiousness. The good of monarchy is the uniting the nation under one head, to resist invasion from abroad and insurrection at home; the good of aristocracy is the conjunction of counsel in the ablest persons of a state for the public benefit; the good of democracy is liberty and the courage and industry which liberty begets.

In this kingdom, the laws are jointly made by a king, by a house of peers and by a house of commons chosen by the people, all having free votes and particular privileges. The government according to these laws is trusted to the king; power of treaties of war and peace, of making peers, of choosing officers and councillors of state, judges for law, commanders for forts and castles; giving commissions for raising men; to make war abroad, or to prevent or provide against invasions or insurrections at home; benefit of confiscations, power of pardoning, and some more of the like kind are placed in the king. And this kind of regulated monarchy, having this power to preserve the laws in their force and the subjects in their liberties and properties, is intended to draw to him such a respect and relation from the great ones as may hinder the ills of division and faction; and such a fear and reverence from the people as may hinder tumults, violence and licentiousness.

Again, that the prince may not make use of this high and perpetual power to the hurt of those for whose good he has it, and make use of the name of public necessity for the gain of his private favourites and followers, to the detriment of the people, the house of commons (an excellent conserver of liberty, but never intended for any share in government or the choosing of them that should govern) is solely entrusted with the first propositions concerning the levies of monies (which is the sinews as well of peace as of war) and the impeaching of those who for their own ends, though countenanced by any surreptitiously gotten command of the king, have violated the law which he is bound (when he knows it) to protect, and to the prosecution of which they were bound to advise him, at least not to serve him to the contrary. And the lords, being trusted with a judiciary power, are an excellent screen and bank between the prince and the people, to assist each against any incroachments of the other; and by just judgments to preserve that law which ought to be the rule of every one of the three. For the better enabling them in this, beyond the examples of any of our ancestors, we were willingly contented to oblige ourself both to call a parliament every three years and not to dissolve in fifty days, and for the present exigent, the better to raise money and to avoid the pressure (no less grievous to us than to them) our people must have suffered by longer continuance of so vast a charge as two great armies, and for their greater certainty of having sufficient time to remedy the inconveniences arises during so long an absence of parliaments, and for the punishment of the causers and ministers of them, we yielded up our right of dissolving parliament,[69] expecting an extraordinary moderation from it in gratitude for so unexampled a grace and little looking that any malignant party should be encouraged or enabled to have persuaded them first to countenance the injustices and indignities we have endured, and then by a new way of satisfaction for what was taken from us at once to confirm what was so taken and to give up almost all the rest. . . .

---

[69] The reference is to the two acts of 1641 compelling the summons of a parliament three years after the dissolution of its predecessor, and barring the dissolution of the Long Parliament without its own consent. The "two great armies" are the Scottish one which invaded north England in 1640 and the notional one which Charles had raised against it; he was paying for both.

# 49 / JEAN ARMAND, CARDINAL RICHELIEU (1585-1642): POLITICAL TESTAMENT

*As the younger son of a noble French family, Richelieu was put into the Church; he was a bishop at twenty-one. His real talents, however, lay in politics, and after a difficult eight years' struggle he became Louis XIII's (1610–43) chief minister in 1624. He spent his life in a double task. First, he brought to fruition the absolute monarchy which had been intermittently building in France since Philip IV. The work of Francis I (1515–47) and Henry II (1547–59) had been undermined by the Wars of Religion, that of Henry IV (1589–1610) arrested by his assassination; now Richelieu completed the process of subjecting all France and every section of society to the unquestioned authority of an irresponsible crown. Second, he destroyed the Habsburg domination of Europe and substituted the ascendancy of France, an achievement made possible by the Thirty Years' War (1618–48). The great minister, an austere and formidable man who frightened his own king, was not, however, the most brilliant of writers. Nevertheless, his review of his work and reflections on the nature of political rule, addressed to Louis XIII by way of justification and exhortation, help both to understand his success and to explain the nature of the French monarchy.[70]*

## PART 1, CHAPTER 1

When Your Majesty decided to give to me at the same time a place on your Council and a high place of trust in the conduct of your affairs, I can say truthfully that the Huguenots shared the state with you, that the great men behaved as though they were not subjects, and the most powerful provincial governors acted as though they were sovereigns in their regions.

I can say that the bad example of both these last was so prejudicial

---

[70] Translated from Cardinal Richelieu, *Testament Politique*, ed. L. André (Paris: Robert Laffont, 1947). By permission of Robert Laffont.

to this realm that the best-ordered institutions began to feel a lack of order and in certain cases infringed your legitimate authority as much as they managed to maintain their own beyond all reason.

I can say that everybody measured his merit by his effrontery, so that instead of valuing the benefits received from Your Majesty at their proper worth, they esteemed them only in proportion to their misruled fancy; and the most daring were held to be the most worthy and wise, and often ended by being the most fortunate.

I can say that foreign alliances were ignored, particular interests preferred to the general interest, and in a word the dignity of the king's majesty was by the default of those who then had the principal charge of your affairs so much lowered and made so different from what it should have been that it was almost impossible to recognise it. It was possible neither to continue the methods of those to whom your majesty had entrusted the helm of the state, nor on the other hand to change them at a stroke without doing violence to the dictates of prudence which will not let one swing from one extreme to the other without some middle way. . . .

*[There follows the story of the reign, to demonstrate the improvements produced by the cardinal's administration.]*

## CHAPTER 5

Having spoken in turn of the various orders which compose the state, nothing in effect remains for me to say, except perhaps that, even as a whole only exists in the union of its parts in their natural order and place, so also this great kingdom cannot flourish if Your Majesty does not see to it that the orders of which it is composed are in their proper hierarchy— the Church holding the first place, the nobility the second, and the officers who march at the head of the people the third. . . .

## CHAPTER 8

It is no small problem in politics whether a prince who governs his state out of his own head is preferable to one who, not trusting his own abilities, defers a great deal to his Council and does nothing without their advice. One could fill whole volumes with arguments on one side or the other. However, confining myself to the particular case, I must say that I prefer the prince who acts more through his Council than on his own, rather than him who prefers his own head to those of all his councillors. I cannot help saying that, just as the worst government is that which has no resources beyond the single head of a prince who, though incompetent, is presumptuous enough to pay no attention to his Council, so the best of all is that in which the prime mover is the mind of a sovereign who, though quite able to act by himself, has sufficient modesty and judgment to do nothing without good advice, based on the principle that one eye cannot see as clearly as several. Apart from the fact that reason supports the validity of this view, truth compels me to say that my experience bears it out so well that I should not know how to remain silent without doing violence to myself.

A capable prince is a great treasure to the state. A skilled and proper Council is so no less. But the cooperation of the two is beyond compare, and it is on this that the fortunes of states depend.

It is certain that the happiest states are those whose princes and councillors are the wisest.

It is also certain that there are few princes who by themselves could govern their states, and, moreover, even if there were many it would not be right to allow them to do so.

The almighty power of God, His infinite wisdom and His providence, do not prevent Him from using the services of a minister of second causes, in matters where if He wished He could act alone. Thus kings, whose perfection (so far from being infinite) has its limits, would commit a notable fault if they did not follow His example.

However, since it is not in their power, as it is in God's, to make good the errors of their servants, they must be extremely careful to choose the most perfect and accomplished that they possibly can. Many qualities are required to make a perfect councillor. They may nevertheless be reduced to four, namely ability, loyalty, courage and industry. . . .

## PART 2, CHAPTER 2

The light of nature teaches us that man, having been created reasonable, should never act except by reason, for otherwise he would go against his nature and therefore against Him who is his creator. By the same token, the greater and more distinguished a man is, the more he values this rule and the less should he abuse his intelligence, which is his essence; for the superiority which he has over others compels him to take care of that which is his nature. . . . As one should wish for nothing that is not reasonable and just, so one should not will anything that will not be done, or where the order is not followed by obedience; otherwise reason does not reign supreme. . . .

Authority constrains to obedience, but reason persuades to it. It is distinctly more sensible to govern men by means which insensibly win over their wills rather than by those which, as a rule, drive them to action instead of leading them on. . . . It is true that subjects will always be religiously careful to obey when princes are determined and persistent in commanding. From this it follows that in disordered states rulers are the more to blame inasmuch as it is certain that their indifference and weakness are the cause of the trouble. . . .

## CHAPTER 9

Power being one of the most necessary things for the greatness of kings and the good fortune of their rule, those who hold the principal places in a state are especially obliged to overlook nothing that can help to make their master so strong that, by this means, he gains the respect of all the world. As kindness is the object of love, so power is the cause of fear. It is certain that among all the principles capable of ruling a state, fear based on respect and reverence is the strongest, for it is this which engages the interests of all in whom it in turn shows an interest. If the principle is so effective in the internal government of states, it has no less relevance to external relations; subjects and foreigners look with the same eyes upon a redoubtable power, and both refrain from offending a prince whom they know to be capable of doing harm to them, should he be so inclined.

I remarked in passing that the basis of that power of which I speak should be esteem and respect. I would now add that this point is essential: if power rests on some other principle it is most dangerous, inasmuch as instead of being the cause of a reasonable fear it makes princes hated, and princes can be in no worse position than when they find themselves the object of general aversion. That power which makes princes respected and feared has several different aspects. It is a tree with various branches which draw their food and substance from one root. The prince should be powerful by reputation; by having a reasonable number of troops permanently under arms; by a revenue sufficient for the payment of his ordinary expenses, and by a sizable money reserve in his coffers for emergencies arising when least thought of; lastly, by possessing the hearts of his subjects. . . .

## CHAPTER 10

To end this work on a happy note, it only remains for me to show Your Majesty that kings, being obliged to do many more things as sovereigns than as private persons, cannot however little neglect their duties without doing wrong by omission in ways which a private person would not know how to do by commission. . . .

In a word, if princes do not do all they can to set in order the various estates of their realm; if they are careless about choosing a good Council; if they ignore salutary advice; if they do not take special trouble so to behave that their example may be a "speaking law"; if they are slow to establish the rule of God, compounded of reason and justice; if they fail to protect the innocent, to reward signal services rendered to the public, and to chastise disobedience and crime which disturb the good order of the state; if they do not endeavour to the full extent of their duty to foresee and forestall any ills that may come, and by careful labors to turn away storms whose clouds often come from farther off than one thinks; if they let favors hinder them from choosing well those whom they will honor with the great offices and principal duties of the realm; if they do not use every endeavor to maintain the state in a necessary condition of power; if on every occasion they do not prefer the public to the private interest, in short, live good lives in every respect—

Then they will be more guilty than those who actually transgress the laws and commandments of God, it being certain that to omit what one must do and to commit what one should not do are one and the same thing. . . .

I pray Your Majesty, even from this hour, to think of things of which so great a prince perhaps will not think till the hour of his death; and in order to buttress my advice as much by example as by reason, I promise you that there shall be no day of my life on which I shall cease to concentrate in the proper spirit of duty, to the day of my death, on such affairs of state as it shall please you to commit to my care.

# 50 / COMMENT: GARRETT MATTINGLY (1900-1962) ON DYNASTIC POWER POLITICS

*Professor Mattingly, from 1948 professor of European History at Columbia University, concentrated on the history of sixteenth-century Europe. This passage is taken from his* Renaissance Diplomacy.[71]

National interest was still too vague a concept to guide or even to excuse the policies of the monarchies. When the spokesman for the Estates General of 1506 besought Louis XII not to marry his daughter, the heiress of Brittany, to any but the natural heir to France, when an independent member of Parliament grumbled that the last English war across the Channel had cost more than twenty such ungracious dog-holes as its conquest, Therouanne, would be worth, when the Cortes of Castile besought their king to think less about Milan and Burgundy and more about reducing taxes and clearing the seas of Moorish pirates, perhaps these citizens were fumbling towards what the nineteenth century would have regarded as a valid idea of national interest. But their notions were still unformed. Mostly the third estates just wanted peace and lower taxes, and their infrequent mutterings were dismissed by their betters as the petty and shortsighted views of tradesmen unfit to meddle with the affairs of princes.

The sixteenth-century struggle for power had a dynastic, not a national orientation. The kingdom of Naples and the duchy of Milan were wealthy and famous provinces; the conquest of either would increase the apparent strength of the prince who could effect it, and indubitably increase, for a time, the benefits he would be able to bestow on his captains and counsellors. Whether such conquests would be worth to his people the blood and treasure they would cost was an irrelevant, absurd question. Nobody expected that they would.

[71] Garrett Mattingly, *Renaissance Diplomacy* (London: Jonathan Cape Ltd.; Boston: Houghton Mifflin Co., 1955), pp. 162–6. Reprinted by permission of the publishers.

Historians have been able to discover one general principle in sixteenth-century diplomacy related to the idea of national interest, the principle of the balance of power. There are, indeed, episodes in the period 1494 to 1559 when it looks as if that principle was really being applied, especially when it was a question of the combination of two or more strong states against a weak one. Here the principle requires such a partition of the victim's territories as not to change decisively the strength of any victor in relation to his partners. In the arrangements for cutting up the Milanese between France and Venice, or Naples between France and Spain, or the Venetian territories among the allies of the League of Cambrai, the principle was more or less consciously observed. But since it really means little more than that the biggest dog gets the meatiest bone, and others help themselves in the order of size, it is hard to be sure that the sixteenth century appreciated the full beauty of a balanced system. It is harder because none of the arrangements lasted, and because each was upset (two of them before they had begun to be carried out) with the full sanction of the chief Italian power, the papacy, which had presided over them in its role as the special custodian of the idea of balance.

The Holy League of 1495 and the League of Cognac of 1526 illustrate another aspect of what is taken for balance-of-power diplomacy, the combination of a group of powers against an apparent victor. In the sixteenth century, however, what the allies always hoped was not just to balance the strongest power, but to outweigh it. A real balance of power requires at least two groups, so evenly matched that neither can easily defeat the other, with a third holding the balance between them. This classic English conception is usually supposed to have been invented by Cardinal Wolsey, somewhere in the reign of the first two Tudors. But, though Wolsey may have had more in mind than he told his master, on the evidence, what Henry VIII wanted, and what Wolsey persuaded him each time he would get, was not just to preserve the status quo but to be on the winning side so as to share the spoils. None of Henry VIII's fellow sovereigns was any more altruistic than he. . . .

If considerations of national interest had small part in forming the policies of the dynasts, it is easy to believe that regard for public morality or zeal for religion had as little. Of course, such sentiments were frequently invoked. "For the preservation of peace among Christians," "for the welfare of the Christian Republic," "for maintaining the freedom and authority of Holy Church," "for the defence of Christendom against the infidels," these phrases never fail in the preambles of treaties. Major agreements usually show them all, and elaborate one or more with pious fervour. Ambassadors' formal orations, powers for extraordinary embassies, proclamations of popes and princes were commonly stuffed with them. And, on occasion, there was also big diplomatic talk of "ending intolerable scandals in the papacy," "reforming the Church in its head and members," and similar echoes of the militant conciliar movement. But kings generally talked about reforming the Church when they wanted to put pressure on a pope for a political end. When they talked about "preserving the peace of the Christian Republic" they were seeking a breathing spell after an exhausting war and gathering their forces to begin a fresh one. And when they named the crusade, "the defence of Christendom against the Turks," they were the most dangerous of all. . . .

And yet, a dismissal of the moral tags in the treaties as always mere hypocrisy may be too easy an attitude. In the days when Frenchmen and Spaniards, Germans and Swiss were fighting over the bleeding body of Italy there was still a European public conscience, just as there were still, in every part of Europe, masses of people—and not just the simple and humble—to whom religion was more than a mask or a catchword. It is not certain that Erasmus and Contarini, Luis Vives and Thomas More were any less typical of their era than Ferdinand of Aragon or Niccolò Machiavelli. It is not even certain which of the cynical realists of the new politics were as single-minded as we take them to be. The ironies of Machiavelli get their bite from the bitterness of disillusioned idealism, of idealism perhaps not completely disillusioned. . . . The heart of man may not have been more prone to evil in the sixteenth century than at other periods, and professions of good intentions may not always have been hollow, even though they were not followed by good results. When we find treaty after treaty full of noble phrases but with consequences squalid or null, the simplest judgment is that the phrases were all hypocritical to begin with. Yet, unless these diplomats and statesmen were capable of completely sustained hypocrisy in their daily behaviour and their most confidential writing, some of them—in fact, a good many of them—did believe in the substance of their professions. One is driven to conclude that some of them at least did actually want peace and the welfare and unity of Christendom, and were at times sickened and bewildered by the elusiveness of ends so simply stated. One sees them again and again roused to an unjust fury of suspicion against those with whom they dealt, each side finding malice and deceit where (sometimes, at least) there were only blunder and bewilderment. . . .

# V / THE REFORMATION

It is the less necessary to attempt a brief survey of the Reformation here because such a survey by the present writer is included as No. 64. A word, therefore, only on the main content of the extracts printed. The Reformation naturally took place in a setting of social, political, and economic circumstances which were in part responsible for its outbreak, development, and fate, and which it in turn profoundly affected. But in itself it was a religious movement, concerned with the overriding problem of man's soul, of salvation and the future life. It therefore expressed itself in theological terms. Luther wrote about the iniquities of the papacy, Müntzer attacked the oppressors of the poor, Calvin contemplated the nature of civil government. But all this, and more, was seen against the challenge of the Bible and Christ's message; enveloping all other problems and subsuming them was the question of how a man shall be saved.

The great reformers did not want to found churches; they wanted to reform the one and only Church. Even the sects usually believed themselves called to convert the world to their own particular thinking. They all started and continued in total dissatisfaction with the particular papal Church confronting them, but they meant to cleanse and transform it. That instead of this they produced multiple schism and spreading disunity was in part due to the inherent problems of a movement which relied exclusively on Scripture, so easily interpreted in so many ways, and in part to the almost unexpected tenacity of the papacy. In the outcome, therefore, the Reformation brought diversity of religious opinion and, after the failure of attempts to restore unity by force, also toleration.

# 51 / MARTIN LUTHER (1483-1546)

*Luther's enormous literary activity covered many fields, but for his fundamental teaching it is best to go to the great treatises which he published as early as 1520. Two of them are included here. A, "On the Liberty of a Christian Man," explains the revolutionary doctrines of justification by faith alone and the priesthood of all believers; B, "To the Christian Nobility of the German Nation Concerning the Better Ordering of the Christian Commonwealth," is an appeal to the lay powers (who are told that they also are priests) to assist in the battle against Rome by calling a reforming council. These works were issued after Luther's rebellion had gone beyond hope of retreat but before he was outlawed by the Imperial Diet of Worms (1521); that is, he was writing in hopes of finding a universal, or at least a generally German, response.[1] Extract C records a conversation between Luther and one of his disciples, held in April 1532; it shows something of Luther's pastoral methods and illumines the nature of his personal faith.[2]*

## A. THE LIBERTY OF A CHRISTIAN MAN

An easy thing has Christian faith seemed to many, and not a few have counted it simply as one of the Christian virtues; which they do because they have never proved it by experiment nor ever tasted the power of its virtue. For to write well about it or fully to understand what has rightly been written of it is impossible for those who have never tasted its spirit when oppressed by tribulations. Once, however, a man has tasted of it no matter how little, he can never have enough of writing, speaking, thinking and hearing about it. For it is a living "well of water springing up into everlasting life," as Christ calls it (John 4.14). But I, though I cannot boast of an abundance of faith and know how small my supply is, yet hope to have attained to some drop of it, assailed as I have been by many and various temptations; and I think I can speak of it with more substance, if not more elegance,

---

[1] Translated from the Weimar Edition of Luther's *Werke*, Vol. 7 (1897), pp. 49 ff.; Vol. 6 (1888), pp. 404 ff.

[2] Translated from *Tischreden Luthers aus den Jahren 1531 und 1532*, ed. W. Preger (Leipzig, 1888), pp. 76–7.

than have earlier discourses by some men of letters and remarkably subtle disputants who cannot even understand their own writings.

In order to open an easier road for the unlearned (whom alone I serve), I shall begin with the following two propositions about the liberty and servitude of the spirit.

> A Christian man is the most entirely free lord of all, subject to none.
> A Christian man is the most entirely dutiful servant of all, subject to everybody.

Although these sentences may seem to be in conflict, yet if they were to be found in agreement they would serve our purpose fairly. They are both sayings of Paul himself: "For though I be free from all men, yet have I made myself servant unto all" (1 Cor. 9.19), and "Owe no man anything, but to love one another" (Rom. 13.8). Love by its nature is ready to serve and obey him who is loved. So Christ, too, though lord of all, was born of woman, was born under the law, at once free and slave, at the same time "in the form of God" and "in the form of a servant" (Phil. 2.6–7).

Let us start further back and more simply. Man has a twofold nature, spiritual and corporal. After the spiritual, called the soul, he is termed spiritual, inner or new man; after the corporal, called the flesh, he is termed carnal, outward or old man. . . . It is because of this diversity that Scripture says contradictory things of the same men; for these two men struggle inside the same man as long as "the flesh lusteth against the Spirit and the Spirit against the flesh" (Gal. 5.17).

First we consider the inner man: in what manner does a man become just, free and truly Christian—that is, spiritual, new and inner? It is clear that no external thing, by whatever name it may be called, can in any way conduce to Christian righteousness or liberty, any more than it can lead the way to unrighteousness or bondage. This can be shown by a simple argument. What can it profit the soul if the body is well, free and active, if it eats, drinks and does as it likes, since in these respects even the most impious slaves of vice may stand very well? On the other hand, what harm can the soul take from illness, imprisonment, hunger, thirst, or any external discomfort, since in these respects even the most godly men—free men in the purity of their conscience—may be afflicted? None of these things touches the liberty or servitude of the soul. Thus it will profit nothing if the body be adorned with holy garments in the manner of priests, or live in holy places, or occupy itself with holy offices, or pray, fast, abstain from certain foods, and do whatever labor can be done by the body and in the body. A far other thing is needed for the righteousness and liberty of the soul, since the works I have rehearsed might be observed by any sinner, and their pursuit produces nothing but hypocrites. By the same token, it will not harm the soul if the body be dressed plainly, live in unconsecrated places, eat and drink as others do, do not pray aloud, and leave out everything which, as I have said, can be done by hypocrites.

To clear the ground completely: even contemplation, meditation, and everything the soul can do are of no avail. One thing, and one thing only, is necessary for the Christian life, righteousness and liberty. It is the most Holy Word of God, the gospel of Christ, as He says (John 11.25): "I am the resurrection and the life: he that believeth in me, though he were dead, yet shall he live"; or again (John 8.36): "if the Son therefore shall make you free, ye shall be free indeed"; and (Matt. 4.4): "Man shall not live by bread alone, but by every word which proceedeth out of the mouth of God." Therefore let us accept it as certain and firmly established that the soul may lack all things except the Word of God, without which, in turn, there is no help for it at all. Having the Word it is rich, lacks nothing; for it is the word of life, truth, light, peace, righteousness, salvation, joy, liberty, wisdom, power, grace, glory and every inestimable blessing. That is why the prophet, in the 119th Psalm and many other places, yearns and calls for the Word of God with so many sighs and in so many expressions. God can send no worse plague of his wrath than a famine of hearing His Word, as Amos says (8.11); nor is there a greater mercy than when He sends forth His Word, as it says in Psalm 107.20—"He sent his Word, and healed them, and delivered them from their destructions." Nor was Christ sent for any other office than that of the Word, and the apostolical, episcopal and entire order of the clergy has been called and instituted solely for the ministry of the Word.

You may ask, "What then is the Word of God, and how shall it be used, since there are so many words of God?" I answer: the apostle explains in Rom. 1 that it is the gospel of God concerning His Son who was made flesh, suffered, rose again from the dead, and was glorified through the spirit that sanctifies. To have preached Christ is to have fed the soul, to have made it righteous and free, to have saved it—provided the soul believed in the preaching. For faith alone is the saving and efficacious use of the Word of God: "If thou shalt confess the Lord Jesus with thy mouth, and shalt believe in thine heart that God hath raised him from the dead, thou shalt be saved" (Rom. 10.9). . . . Nor can the Word of God be received and cherished by any works whatsoever but only by faith alone. Therefore it is clear that as the soul needs only the Word to live and be just, so it will be justified by faith alone and not by any works. For if it could be justified by anything else, it would not need the Word, nor in consequence would need faith. . . .

Now how comes it that faith alone justifies and provides, without works, such a treasure of blessings, although so many works, ceremonies and laws are prescribed in Scripture? In answer to this, remember above all what has already been said: faith alone, without works, justifies, frees and saves, a point which will be further clarified below. For the moment it must be pointed out that the whole Scripture of God is divided into two parts, commandments and promises. The commandments teach certain good things, but their teachings are not at once carried into reality; they show us what we ought to do, but do not confer the power of action; they are ordained so that man may know himself, whereby he may come to recognise his impotence to live righteously and despair of his own strength. They are therefore called what indeed they are, the Old Testament. For example, "Thou shalt not covet" is a commandment which convinces us all that we are sinners, since no man, in spite of all endeavor, can be free of covetousness. In order, therefore, to be not covetous and thus to fulfill the commandment, a man is forced to despair of himself and to seek elsewhere and through another the help which he does not find in himself. . . . And as for this one commandment, so for the rest; for all of them are equally impossible to us.

Now when a man is taught his powerlessness by the commandments and is in trouble to know by what effort he may satisfy the law—since the law must be satisfied so that no jot or tittle of it be lost; otherwise he will without any hope be damned—then, truly humble and reduced to nothing in his own eyes, he cannot find in himself the means of justification and salvation. Here the second part of Scripture comes to the rescue, namely God's promises which declare the glory of God and say: "If you want to fulfill the law and avoid covetousness as the law demands, believe in Christ in whom are promised you grace, righteousness, peace, freedom and all things. If you believe, you shall have; if you do not, you shall lack." For what you find impossible to do by all the works of the law, which are many and in a manner useless, you will achieve with easy speed by faith. Because God the father has made all things depend on faith, so that whosoever has faith shall have all things, he who has none shall have nothing. . . .

All this makes it easy to understand the source from which faith gets such power, and the reason why any or all good works cannot equal it. No work can cleave to the Word of God or live in the soul, which is ruled by faith alone and the Word. The Word transmutes the soul to its own quality, just as hot iron glows like fire because it has become united with fire. To say it plainly: a Christian man finds his faith suffi-

cient for all purposes and has no need of works to be justified; if he
has no need of works, he has none of the law; if he does not need the
law, assuredly he is free of the law and it is true that "the law is not
made for a righteous man" (1 Tim. 1.9). Therefore this is that Christian liberty: our faith, which does not lead us to idleness or wickedness but frees man from the need of the law and of works for his
justification and salvation. . . .

Not only are we the freest kings of all, but we are also priests for
all time, which is much better than any kingship. Our priesthood fits
us to appear before God, to pray for others, and to teach one another
the things that are God's. This constitutes priesthood, and these functions cannot be granted to any unbeliever. If we believe in Him, Christ
has thus made us not only His brethren, co-heirs, and fellow kings,
but also His fellow priests, ready in the spirit of faith to come boldly
before God and to cry, "Abba, Father," to pray for one another, and
to do all things which we see represented by the visible and corporeal
office of priests. . . .

The question arises, "If all who are in the Church are priests, by
what name are those whom now we call priests distinguished from
laymen?" To this I answer that an injury was done to those words—
priest, cleric, spiritual person, ecclesiastic—when they were transferred
from the totality of Christians to those few who are now by false usage
called churchmen. For Holy Scripture makes no such distinction, except that it gives the names of ministers, servants or stewards to those
who now boast the names of popes, bishops and lords, and who in the
ministry of the Word should serve the rest by teaching them the faith
of Christ and the freedom of believers. For while it is true that we are
all equally priests, yet we cannot all—nor, if we could, should we—
minister and teach in public. . . .

Now let us turn to the other part, the outer man. Here I shall
answer all those who, shocked by the word "faith" and all I have said,
ask: "If faith does all things and by itself is enough for salvation, why
then are good works commanded? We will rest at leisure and do no
works, being content with faith." To which I reply: not so, you wicked
men, not so. The argument would be true if we were entirely and
perfectly inner and spiritual men; but that we shall be only at the last
day when the dead shall rise. While we live in the flesh, we can only
make a beginning and take a few steps towards that which in the
future life shall be perfect. . . . Although (as I have said) the inner
man is abundantly and fully justified by faith, through the Spirit, having all he should have, except that this faith and these riches must
grow from day to day until the life to come; yet in this mortal life he
remains on earth where he necessarily must control his body and have
dealings with men. This is where the works come in: here there is

no idling, here he must certainly take care to exercise the flesh by fastings, vigils, labors and other moderate disciplines, and so subject it to the Spirit that it will obey and conform to the inner man and faith —not rebelling against this latter or hinder that former, as is its nature when not constrained. . . .

But no one must think that these works are done to achieve justification before God: faith, which alone is righteousness before God, will not suffer such false doctrine. They are done to reduce the body to servitude and purify it from its evil lusts; all efforts must concentrate on driving out lusts. For since the soul by faith is purified and brought to the love of God, it wants everything else to be equally pure— especially its own body—so that all things may join it in loving and praising God. In consequence man, because of the pressing needs of his body, cannot be idle and is forced to perform many good works to reduce it to servitude. But the works themselves are not that which justifies him before God; rather does he do them out of spontaneous love, in the service of God, seeking nothing but God's approval whom he would most particularly obey in all things. . . .

### B. TO THE CHRISTIAN NOBILITY OF THE GERMAN NATION

The Romanists have with great skill built three walls around themselves, with which till now they have protected themselves so that no one has been able to reform them; whereby all Christendom has suffered woefully. In the first place, when attacked by the temporal power they have laid it down that temporal power has no authority over them, but that on the contrary the spiritual power is superior to the temporal. Secondly, when Scripture was cited for their correction, they have objected that no one may interpret Holy Writ except the pope. Thirdly, when threatened with a General Council, they have invented the notion that only the pope may call one. Thus privily robbing us of three rods, they have escaped punishment; they have sat behind the safe fortification of these three walls and practised all the villainy and wickedness which now we see. Even when compelled to convene a Council, they have beforehand deprived it of its sting by first putting the princes under oath to leave things as they were. Also they have given the pope full power over the business of the Council, so that it has been no matter whether there are many Councils or none; they have deceived us with mockeries and shadow-fights. So fearfully do they guard their skins against a truly free Council and have put kings and princes in doubt, till these believe it to be against God not to obey them in all these villainous and cunning little games.

Now may God help us and give us one of the trumpets which overthrew the walls of Jericho, that we may blow down these straw and paper walls, set free the Christian rods of correction, and bring to daylight the devil's tricks and cheats, so that through penitence we may be reformed and recover His favor.

The first wall attacked.

They have invented a distinction of calling the pope, the bishops, the priests and the cloistered sort the estate spiritual, while princes, lords, artificers and peasantry are called temporal. Which is a pretty comment and gloss, though no one need take fright at it, for this reason: all Christians are in truth the spiritual estate, and there is no distinction among them except of office. As Paul says (1 Cor. 12.12): we are all one body, but every member has his own proper function in serving the others. All that matters is that we share one baptism, one gospel, one faith, and are equally Christians; for baptism, gospel and faith alone make spiritual and Christian people. Unction by pope or bishop, tonsure, ordination, consecration, clothes different from a layman's—all these may make a hypocrite or painted idol but can never make a Christian or a spiritual man. In truth we are all consecrated as priests by baptism, as St. Peter says (1 Pet. 2.9) "you are . . . a royal priesthood, a holy nation," and again (Rev. 5.9–10) "by thy blood . . . [thou] hast made us . . . kings and priests." For if we had no higher consecration than pope or bishops can give, a pope's or bishop's hands could never make a priest, nor could anyone say mass or preach or grant absolution.

Thus the bishop's act of ordination does this only: acting for the whole congregation, he takes one man from the crowd (all of whom have the same authority) and orders him to exercise this authority for the rest. It is a case like that of ten brothers, children and co-heirs to a king, who choose one among themselves to rule their inheritance for them: they are equally kings and of equal authority, and yet one is told off to rule. To put it more plainly still: suppose a little group of true Christian laymen are captured and left in a desert, having among them no priest ordained by a bishop; and suppose they then agree to elect one among themselves, be he married or not, and convey to him the office of baptising, saying mass, absolving and preaching, that man will be as truly a priest as though all popes and bishops had ordained him. This is why in an emergency anybody may administer baptism and absolution, which would be impossible if we were not all priests. This great grace and power contained in baptism and the Christian's estate they have with their canon law nearly destroyed and kept us ignorant of. . . .

Thus it follows that there is no real difference among laymen, priests, princes, bishops, and—as the phrase goes—spiritual and temporal, except on grounds of office or occupation; certainly none of estate.

For they are all of the estate spiritual—are truly priests, bishops and popes—but differ in their work, even as not all priests and monks do the same work. . . . Christ has not two bodies or two kinds of body, one secular and one spiritual. He is one head and has one body.

Therefore those now called spiritual—priests or bishops or pope—differ from other Christians to no greater or more important degree than that they shall administer the Word of God and the sacraments. That is their work and office. The temporal power holds the sword and the rod to punish evildoers and protect the pious. The cobbler, the smith, the ploughman have each their proper function and work, and yet are all equally ordained to be priests and bishops; and each in his function or work shall be useful and serve the rest, so that the work of many shall contribute in common to the welfare of body and soul, as the members of the body all serve one another.

Now see in how Christian a manner they maintain and say that the temporal arm is not superior to the spiritual and cannot control it. That is to say, the hand shall do nothing even though the eye be in serious trouble. Is it not unnatural, let alone unchristian, for one member not to help another and protect it against disaster? The more noble the member, the more the rest ought to help it. Therefore I say, because the temporal arm is ordained by God for the punishment of evildoers and the protection of the pious, its exercise is to be left free and unhindered throughout the whole body of Christendom, not respecting any persons, be they pope, bishop, parsons, monks, nuns, or whoever else. If to limit the secular arm it were enough to say that among Christian offices it is inferior to the functions of the preacher and confessor, or the estate of the spirituality, it would follow that tailors, cobblers, masons, carpenters, cooks, household servants, peasants and all temporal labourers should be stopped from providing shoes, clothes, houses, food or drink for the pope, the bishops, priests and monks—or from paying them taxes. . . .

So I think the first paper wall is down. The temporal power has been shown to be a member of the Body Christian and to be of the estate spiritual, even though its occupation is in matters temporal. Therefore its operation shall extend freely and without hindrance to all members of the whole body; it shall punish and constrain where guilt merits it or need demands, without favor to pope and bishop and priest, however much they may fulminate and excommunicate. That is why guilty priests, when handed over to the secular law, are first deprived of their priesthood; which would not be right if by God's ordinance the temporal sword did not before this possess power over them. It is also intolerable that in the spiritual law the freedom, persons and goods of the clergy should be accorded such special respect, as though the laity were not as good spiritual Christians as the clergy, or as much part of the Church. Why should your body, life, goods and honor be exempt, and not mine, seeing that we are equally Christians and share one baptism, faith, spirit and all things? Kill a priest, and the land falls under an interdict; why not also when a peasant is killed? Whence come these great distinctions among equal Christian men? Solely from man's laws and inventions. . . .

The second wall is less solid and resistant. The Romanists claim to be sole masters of Scripture, even though all their lives they may never have learned a word of it. They arrogate authority to themselves and juggle with impudent words, saying the pope, bad or good, cannot err in matters of faith, though they cannot quote so much as a letter in support. This is why the canon law contains so much heretical and unchristian, aye, even unnatural law; though this is not the place to speak of that. Thinking that the Holy Spirit will not desert them however unlearned and wicked they may be, they make bold to lay down what they please. If this were so, what need or purpose were there in Holy Scripture? Let us burn their law and be content to contemplate the unlearned gentlemen at Rome who have the Holy Spirit "within themselves," that Holy Spirit which in truth inhabits only pious hearts. Had I not read it, I should have thought it incredible that the devil should pretend such clumsy things at Rome and find support for them. . . . It is a wicked lie and fable, for which they can bring never a letter to prove it, that the pope alone can interpret Scripture or give authority to its interpretation. They took that power to themselves. And where they pretend that the authority was granted to St. Peter when he received the keys: it is manifest enough that the keys were not given to St. Peter alone, but to the whole community. Moreover, the keys were ordained not for doctrine or government, but only for the power to bind and loose. . . .

The third wall falls by itself when the first two are thrown down; for where the pope acts contrary to Scripture it is incumbent upon us to stand by Scripture and punish him. . . . Also they have no ground in Scripture for maintaining that only the pope has the right to summon or sanction a General Council; that is only part of their own law which has validity only as long as it does no harm to Christendom and the laws of God. When the pope does wrong, such laws cease, because it would be harmful to Christendom not to punish him by means of a Council. . . . Therefore, where necessity commands and the pope causes an offense in Christendom, whosoever can first do so as a true member of the whole body shall see to the calling of a really free Council. This no one is so well able to achieve as the temporal arm, especially because it is composed of fellow Christians, fellow priests, fellow spirituals, fellows in all capacities, who ought to exercise their office and place by which God has placed them over everyone, without restraint, wherever necessity and advantage call. Would it not be an unnatural proceeding, when a fire breaks out in a city, if everyone had to stand aside, allowing anything that can to burn on and on, solely because the fire started at the mayor's house? In such a case, is not every citizen bound to stir up and call upon the rest? How much more should this happen in Christ's spiritual city when a fire of offense breaks out, let it be in the pope's government or anywhere else. . . .

Therefore let us firmly maintain that Christian authority can do nothing contrary to Christ, as St. Paul says (2 Cor. 13.8), "For we can do nothing against the truth, but for the truth." If it labors contrary to Christ, then it is the authority of Antichrist and the devil, even though it may rain and hail miracles and plagues. Miracles and plagues prove nothing, especially in these latter days of evil for which false miracles are prophesied in all Scripture. Therefore we must with a firm faith hold to the Word of God; and the devil, I warrant you, will leave off his miracles.

Herewith, I hope, the false and lying terrors, with which for a long time the Romanists have made us fearful and of a feeble conscience, shall lie destroyed. Together with all the rest, the Romanists are subject to the sword, have no right to interpret Scripture by mere assertive power and without adequate learning, and have no authority either to prevent a Council or to pledge it, prejudge it, or rob it of its liberty. When they do such things they are in truth the congregation of Antichrist and the devil, having of Christ nothing but the name.

*[There follows a detailed program for a reforming Council, embodying attacks on the worldliness of the papacy, on the cardinals, and on the general burden of papal administration and abuses; with twenty-eight proposals for reform.]*

### C. SPIRITUAL COUNSEL

So [Luther] said to me: "Why so low? Cheer up." I replied, "Ah, dear doctor, I should be glad to, but I can't, I'm hindered by so many and grave temptations." He asked, "What sort of temptations?" I answered: "Sorry, I cannot express how I feel them." To which Doctor Martin: "Your temptations, and those of all men and mine, come by way of a sign. We may be tried in the first article: I believe in God the Father. Either you don't believe that the Father is your creator, or you don't believe that he is your father; or thirdly, you don't believe that he is well inclined to us. The second article: I believe in Jesus Christ, etc. If I believe that Jesus is the Son of God, given for me, who suffered and rose again, what shall I lack? The third article: I believe in the Holy Spirit, the Holy Catholic Church, the remission of sins—it's in this that I feel the lack most and am enemy to myself. In which article do we find your temptation? Is it the one with which Satan attacks us: ye shall be as the sons of God? That is my temptation," said the doctor.

Another time I said to him: "Whenever I think of God and Christ, it comes into my mind thus: you are a sinner, therefore God is angry, therefore your prayer avails nothing." The doctor answered: "Must I not pray until I believe—when then should I pray? If the Devil suggests to you that you are a sinner and that God does not listen to sinners, you turn round bravely and say: I pray just because I am a sinner, and I know that the prayers of the afflicted are efficacious with God. We [men] want to gain peace of mind not through grace but by our own efforts. Why should God give us grace if we do not feel and know the sin? When the real troubles appear, then God says— this is where I can help. So be glad and rejoice." "Master Doctor," I answered, "I cannot believe that all depression comes from the Devil. The law oppresses the conscience, but the law of God is good; if the law, which causes depression and fear, comes from God, that depression is not the work of the Devil." He replied: "Here I'm content with Paul: the law is given for transgression's sake. People will not be pious, and so God says, I must send the Devil after them to plague them with the law. It's like our emperor who has the sword in his hand or his power but gives it to the hangman and makes him cut off heads when it pleases him to punish evildoers; but whenever he likes, he takes it back into his own hand. So God does with the law. In short: that we are so plagued, vexed and troubled, that is a sign of Doomsday, not only for the pope but for all the world. The Devil feels his rule is near its end: that is why he kicks up such a fuss. So take comfort, hold by the Word of God, let us pray and call on God that we may remain in and with dear Jesus Christ; and we shall soon meet cheerfully on the Day of Judgment."

# 52 / PHILIP MELANCHTHON (1497-1560): LOCI COMMUNES (1521)

*A humanist scholar and infant prodigy, Melanchthon came to Wittenberg in 1518 to teach Greek. From 1519 he was Luther's devoted follower, being just the man to provide the systematic theological thinking and drafting of which the new movement stood in need, and which Luther, an inspired rather than an orderly thinker, could not himself supply. Melanchthon's* Loci Communes *(Commonplaces) were in fact a kind of Lutheran theological dictionary. The first version (1521) stood most under Luther's personal influence; later editions include modifications reflecting their author's gentler, more accommodating mind.*[3]

## OF GRACE

As the law [4] embodies the knowledge of sin, so the gospel embodies the promise of grace and righteousness. . . . However, is there anyone qualified to dispose effectively of the scholastics who have so foully abused that sacrosanct word "grace" by falsely employing it to express the quality that is in the souls of the saints? Most stupid of all are the Thomists who find the quality of grace inherent in the nature of the soul; faith, hope and charity are in the powers of the soul. And how feebly and stupidly they battle over these powers of the soul! However, these impious men might as well decay in total filth; let these despisers of the gospel suffer pains for their frivolities. You, my reader, should pray that the Spirit of God might reveal the gospel to our hearts. For the word of the Spirit is such that it can be taught only by the Spirit, as Isaiah (54.13) says, all are "taught of the Lord."

In the books of the New Testament the word "grace" is generally used for a Hebrew word rendered *charis* by the translators of the Greek Septuagint; as in Exodus 33.12, "Thou hast also found grace in my sight," etc., and in many other places. Here it clearly has the meaning of the Latin *favor.* I wish the translators had in fact used *favor* rather than *gratia;* for then the sophisters would not have had occasion for much nonsense in their comments on the point. As the teachers of grammar may say that "Julius favors Curio"—meaning that in Julius there is a favor within which he encloses Curio—so in Scripture grace means favor, this grace or favor being in God, and being the quality with which He encloses the saints.[5] Away with Aristotelian figments about qualities! For grace, to describe it more precisely, is nothing but God's good will towards us, or the will of God taking pity on us. Therefore the word grace does not describe any quality within ourselves, but rather the very will of God or God's good will towards us.

Paul in Rom. 5.15 distinguishes the gift from grace: "For if through the offense of one many be dead, much more the grace of God, and

---

[3] Translated from *Melanchthons Werke in Auswahl* (Gütersloh: C. Bertelsmann Verlag, 1952), Vol. 2, pp. 85 ff. By permission of C. Bertelsmann Verlag.

[4] i.e., the Old Testament

[5] "Saints" here means all those saved by the grace of God.

the gift of grace, which is by one man, Jesus Christ, has abounded unto many." Grace he calls that favor of God with which he has enclosed Christ, and therefore in Christ and for Christ's sake all the saints. Thus because he shows favor, God cannot help but pour out his gifts on those on whom he has taken pity. In this way men advance the cause of those they favor and share their goods with them. The gift of God is that very Holy Spirit which God pours into the heart of all he chooses. John 20.22: "He breathed on them and saith, Receive ye the Holy Ghost." And Rom. 8.15: "Ye have received the Spirit of adoption, whereby we cry, Abba, Father." Again, according to Gal. 5.22, the works of the Holy Spirit in the hearts of the saints are faith, peace, glory, charity, etc. . . .

In sum, grace is nothing but the forgiveness or remission of sin. The gift is the Holy Spirit, regenerating and sanctifying the heart. . . . The gospel promises both grace and gift. . . .

## OF JUSTIFICATION AND FAITH

We are therefore justified when, mortified by the law, we are raised up by the grace promised in Christ, or by the gospel which forgives sin; and when we cling to Christ in faith, nothing doubting that Christ's righteousness is our righteousness, that Christ's satisfaction is our expiation, that Christ's resurrection is ours. In short, if we nothing doubt that our sins are forgiven and God has bestowed His favor and benevolence on us. Therefore no work of ours, however good it may seem or be, constitutes righteousness; but faith alone, through the mercy and grace of God in Jesus Christ, makes righteous. . . .

Faith, therefore, is nothing but trust in God's mercy promised in Christ, and therefore trust in any sign whatever. This trust in the benevolence or mercy of God first pacifies the heart; thereafter it incites us to give thanks to God for his mercy, so that we perform the law freely and joyfully. On the other hand, in so far as we have not faith, there is no inner sense of God's mercy. Where there is no sense of God's mercy, there is contempt and hatred of God. Wherefore all great works of the law that are done without faith are sin. . . .

## OF MAGISTRATES

I have thought it particularly desirable to include a discussion of magistrates, and first, for pedagogic reasons, I shall follow the usual classification. Magistrates are held to be divided into civil and ecclesiastical. A civil magistrate is he who possesses the sword and preserves the civil peace (see Paul in Rom. 13). Under the "sword" are comprehended these categories: civil laws, civil ordinances constituting judicial tribunals, and the punishment of criminals. The right of the sword involves the administration of laws against killing, revenge, etc. Therefore a magistrate's administration of the sword is consonant with piety. The same goes for lawyers when they give an opinion about the law or protect the oppressed; though litigation as such is a very serious sin. Concerning the exercise of this power of the sword I hold as follows:

One, if princes command anything contrary to God this is not to be obeyed. . . .

Two, if they command anything arising out of the public interest this must be obeyed. . . .

Lastly, if any of their commands are tyrannical, here too the magistrate is to be suffered for charity's sake in all cases where change is impossible without public commotion or sedition. . . . But if you can get out of it without scandal or public commotion, do so: for instance, supposing you are innocently thrown in jail and can escape without a public disturbance, nothing stands in the way of escape. . . .

My views of ecclesiastical magistrates are these: in the first place bishops are ministers,[6] not potentates or rulers. Next, they have no right to make laws, having but a mandate to preach the Word of God. . . .

First, therefore, if ecclesiastical magistrates teach Scripture they are to be heard like Christ, according to Luke 10.16: "He that heareth you, heareth me." This refers to. Scripture and not to human traditions.

Second, if they teach anything contrary to Scripture they must not be heard. . . . At the time of writing, the pope has issued a decree contrary to the law divine in his bull condemning Luther: in this he is emphatically not to be heard.

Third, if they order anything outside Scripture intended to fetter consciences they are not to be heard. For nothing binds the conscience except the law of God. . . .

Fourth, if one is prepared to regard episcopal law not as a burden on the conscience but to see in it an outward burden only (which accords with the practice of spiritual men and recognises that the conscience cannot be fettered by any human law), one will treat episcopal law in the same way as the tyranny of a civil magistrate. For whatever bishops command beyond Scripture is tyranny; they have no right to command it. One should bear these burdens for charity's sake. . . . However, if without scandal one can do otherwise, then there is no prohibition. . . . Christ dispensed from the traditions of the Pharisees (Matt. 8 and 11); but from the civil law he did not dispense. . . . The administration of all human laws involves faith and charity and also

[6] i.e., servants

necessity. This frees us from all traditions in every instance in which either the soul or the life of the body may by a tradition be brought into peril.

# 53 / THOMAS MÜNTZER (1489-1525): SERMON BEFORE THE PRINCES (1524)

*Müntzer, a parish priest at Zwickau and later at Allstedt in Saxony, at first followed Luther, but very soon broke with him when he realized that Luther was determined to avoid extremism and social revolution. These were just Müntzer's desires. An enthusiast fascinated by apocalyptic visions, a rebel against all authority, a passionate partisan of the lower orders, he began to preach that the Second Coming was near and that the saints (those who accepted his gospel) were to achieve it by violence. The world was to be cleansed in the blood of the wicked. Müntzer found even Scripture of insufficient authority: only the "inner spirit"—God speaking to the individual—counted. Examples of his kind of mystical exaltation boiling over into violent action are found throughout the history of Christianity. He ultimately ended up in the Peasants' War of 1525 and was executed after its collapse. In 1524 he preached a sermon before two Saxon princes on that classic passage of apocalyptic imaginings, Daniel's dream of the great statue of gold, silver, brass, and iron, with feet of clay, destroyed by the stone that grows to a mountain (Daniel, 2).*[7]

You shall know that poor, miserable and divided Christendom can get neither counsel nor help, unless the diligent and undiscouraged servants of God daily follow Scripture with singing, reading and preaching. But for this the heads of the delicate priestlings will all the time have to suffer great knocks, or else the work will be neglected. But

[7] Translated from Thomas Müntzer, *Politische Schriften*, ed. C. Hinrichs (Tübingen: Max Niemeyer Verlag, 1950), pp. 5–28. The many scriptural citations are omitted. By permission of Max Niemeyer Verlag.

how could one do otherwise to them while Christendom is being so pitifully devastated by ravening wolves? For, as in the days of the dear prophets Isaiah, Jeremiah and Ezekiel the whole congregation of God's elect had so entirely drifted into ways of idolatry that even God would no longer help them but let them be led away into captivity and so long tormented among the heathen till once again they recognised His holy name; so no less in our fathers' and our own day poor Christendom has been growing still more rotten, though it bears the unspeakable semblance of a godly generation with which the devil and his minions prettily adorn themselves. Yea, so prettily that God's true friends are thereby deluded and despite the most assiduous diligence can barely discern their error. All this is accomplished by pretended holiness and by the time-serving absolution of the godless enemies of God, who say that the Church of Christ cannot err, even though, to avoid error, it ought to be constantly edified and preserved from error by the Word of God—yea, should recognise the sin of its own ignorance. But this, I suppose, is true: Christ, the Son of God, and his apostles, and even before him the holy prophets, did in the beginning found a true and pure Christianity. They sowed the pure wheat in the field; that is to say, planted the precious Word of God in the hearts of the elect. However, the idle and negligent ministers of this same Church have not troubled to perfect and maintain it by a busy vigil, but have followed their own concerns instead of those of Jesus Christ. . . .

You are to know this opinion that God is so entirely well disposed to his elect that as He can give them warning in the least little thing so He could in the highest matters, if they would only receive it in their great unbelief. Here this text from Daniel agrees with St. Paul (1 Cor. 2.9–10), which is taken from Isaiah (64.4), where it says that eye has not seen nor ear heard, nor is that come to any man's heart, which God has prepared for those who love Him. But to us God has revealed it through His Spirit, for the Spirit searches all things, even the deep things of God, etc. Therefore in short this is what we earnestly hold: we must have personal revelation, and not just airily believe, what in the things given to us comes from God, or from the devil, or from nature. For our natural understanding of these things must be captured for the service of the faith; it must achieve the ultimate degree possible to its comprehension. But man can never achieve an ultimate comprehension well grounded in conscience without the revelation of God. He will plainly discover that he cannot get to Heaven on his head alone and that first he must become altogether an inward fool. Oh what a strange wind blows there for the clever, carnal, lustful world! There soon follow the pains as of a woman in labor. There Daniel finds, and every pious man with him, that to him as to other ordinary folk all things are by such [natural] means impossible to discover from God. That is the meaning of the Preacher when he indicates (Eccl. 3.11) that whoever would seek out the glory of God will be overwhelmed by His splendor. For the more the natural man reaches out after God, the more the working of the Holy Spirit is alienated from him. If only man could grasp how presumptuous is the light of nature, he would undoubtedly cease to bolster himself up with stolen goods from Scripture, as some scholars do with a scrap or two; he would quickly feel the effect of God's Word well from out of his own heart. . . . The Word is not far from thee: behold, it is in thy heart (see Deut. 30.14). You ask, how does it enter the heart? I answer, it comes down from God on high in a terrifying revelation. . . .

It is true, and I know it to be so, that the Spirit of God has in our day revealed to many pious and chosen people how very necessary an excellent, invincible future reformation now is, and that it must be brought about, no matter how men may resist it. The prophecy of Daniel remains unaffected even though no one will believe in it. The text is clear as the sun, and the work of ending the fifth monarchy of the world is even now in full swing. The first of them, represented by the golden head, was the empire of Babylon. The second—the silver breast and arms—was that of the Medes and Persians. The third was the empire of the Greeks, resounding with intelligence, as is indicated by the sounding brass. The fourth was the empire of Rome, won by the sword, a government of force. But the fifth is that which we have before our eyes. It too is of iron and would like to use force, but it is stuck together with muddy clay, as we see before our sensible eyes— vain pretences of that hypocrisy which writhes and wriggles all over the earth. For those who [nowadays] cannot practise deceit must be weak in the head. You can see that handsome sight of eels and vipers all fornicating in a heap. The priests and all evil clergy are the vipers, as John the Baptist calls them (Matt. 3.7); and the temporal lords and rulers are the eels, as it is represented in Lev. 11.10–12 under the simile of the fishes, etc. The kingdoms of the devil have smeared themselves with clay. Ah, my dear lords, how prettily the Lord will go smashing among the clay pots with his rod of iron. Therefore, you most dear and beloved princes, learn your lesson straight from the mouth of God and do not be deceived by your hypocritical parsons, nor held back by a false notion of patience and mercy.[8] For the stone that was without hands torn from the mountain has grown great: the poor laity and commons see it much more clearly than you. God be praised, it has grown so great that if other lords or neighbors would persecute you

---

[8] an allusion to Luther and to the doctrine of justification by faith which, Müntzer alleges, holds his hearers back from revolution

for the gospel's sake they would be driven out by their own people; that I know full well. Yea, the stone is great: the silly world has long dreaded it. It fell upon the world when it was yet small; how shall we do now that it has become so great and powerful? Now that it has struck the great statue so strongly and irresistibly and has shattered it down to the old bits of clay? Therefore, you dear princes of Saxony, step bravely on the stone as did St. Peter and seek true steadfastness in the will of God. . . .

# 54 / THE BREAK WITH HUMANISM (1524)

*At first, Luther's supporters found themselves agreeably at one with the pre-Reformation critics of the Church, especially Erasmus; but it soon became apparent that the two sides had too little in common to remain allies. Luther's attacks on man's free will, as well as his revolutionary stance vis-à-vis the papacy, quickly alienated Erasmus and his followers. The pamphlet from which this extract is taken exemplifies the resentful reactions of the reformers to what they regarded as a betrayal resulting from worldly greed. Written in German by an anonymous author, this dialogue between a peasant (who represents the true people's support of the Reformation), a devil, Erasmus, and John Fabri (a conservative theologian and pamphleteer) was meant to rouse popular feeling against the contemptible flight from the truth of which Erasmus was accused by men who had first welcomed him as a harbinger of the great reform. The attack had some grounds: Erasmus and his friends had certainly undermined the authority of the Church and drew back only when they saw where such views could lead to in less academic settings. At the same time, they had a good case for not following Luther's apocalyptic vision and his relentless rush into schism, a case which naturally is not recognized in this piece of propaganda.*[9]

PEASANT: How marvellous are the works of God! He grants his spirit and grace to humble hearts that put their trust, hope, consolation and

---

[9] Translated from "Gesprächbüchlein von einem Bauern, Belial, Erasmo Roterodam und Doctor Johann Fabri (1524)," in *Flugschriften aus den ersten Jahren der Reformation*, ed. Otto Clemen (Halle, 1906–11), vol. 1, pp. 313–36.

faith in him, and he withdraws them from those who trust in their own reason, human fancy and wit.

ERASMUS: What's that peasant mumbling about? Does he suppose we do not know that where God giveth there he also taketh away?

PEASANT: And has he not highly and generously endowed Erasmus of Rotterdam with all the skills of human understanding? Was not the same equipped by God with so high a knack of pretty writing that not only many scholars but even almost all the world stand in amazement?

BELIAL: Aye, fellow, that's what I, as governor of the infernal regions, have long since relied upon. Never have I ceased from seducing men, with all possible diligence, from God's teaching: and I have succeeded. And I haven't persuaded only a number of mean, miserable and wicked men to deny the truth, but have also won over this master of delicate Latin, so that now he no longer sees nor understands what before this he has said, written and published abroad. . . .

ERASMUS: But haven't I, by means of my art, persuaded the whole world, and especially the German nation, to think me a marvel and a portent?

PEASANT: Quite so, dear fellow: undoubtedly you are thought a marvel—you who can no longer comprehend yourself. Years ago, by the grace of God, you were a sensible Christian man, but now—in defiance of the plain and open truth, of your own conscience and the true confession—you have become a great flatterer of popes and a shameless blasphemer.

BELIAL: I have no doubt, now that my friend Erasmus has deserted that truth which sentenced me and my fellows to eternal pains, he will make us good cheer; for I know well there are many so enamoured of his pretty writings and his false and flattering judgment that they will greatly prefer them to the Word of God.

PEASANT: Silence, Belial, silence. You fail in this and lose your hopes, for the truth is so strong and powerful and undefeatable that not only Erasmus, for all his pretty worldly wit and art, cannot hinder it, but even you, Belial, with all your tricks and forces of hell, cannot overcome it. The truth stands for all time.

ERASMUS: Nevertheless I am quite certain that with my publications I have won more favour with the pope's holiness, all the cardinals and bishops, and also other princes, than ever did Luther and all his company who have called down upon themselves envy, hatred and persecution—afflictions which all my life I have managed to avoid.

PEASANT: My dear Erasmus, we are well aware that you are careful not to tangle with foxes. The truth, which has its own effect and which respects neither small nor great, high estate or low, has never found much thanks among the hierarchies and powers. It has always attracted persecution and envy, and upon its followers it has always inflicted that cross that you don't much like. Your nature and quality drive you rather to worship Antichrist than have to live on herbs. . . .

FABRI: What, you Lutheran heretic, still here? When will you recant? What moves you to destroy your soul by following Luther? You are not content with seducing yourself: you must teach your neighbours disobedience too. By my troth, it will not go well with you.

PEASANT: We have the Word of God, the holy gospel—in that we believe and not in the chatter that comes from your idol in Rome. For we have now learned that that is nothing but lies, deceit, trickery, robbery and usury—just to get our money.

FABRI: Think you, if the holy fathers, the popes and the Councils were to do an injustice, that so many holy fathers would have applauded and approved? Moreover, your forefathers have for hundreds of years believed those things which you and your Lutheran rabble now profess to despise in your disobedience to the See of Rome. You'd do better to follow the example of your parents.

PEASANT: That I deny, for take a case: if your father was hanged and your mother died of a stabbing, would you then follow their example? Not me; but if your inclinations lie that way, good luck to you. My faith stands not upon my parents but upon the Word of God, on the consolation and promise of Christ announced in the holy gospel. While I build upon that, I stand upon unmoving, solid ground and am sure that I cannot err.

FABRI: You vile louts, you all want to be Lutheran now, you need whipping.

PEASANT: Don't you know that the hairs on our heads are counted? Truly, you and your merchants of grace cannot pull out the least one of them without the Lord allows it.

FABRI: You German rogues, you never do good unless a foreign nation be brought in to teach you the faith and also how to prove obedient to the See of Rome.

PEASANT: Ah, Faber, away with you. All this pulling of cruel faces. We peasants no longer fear you and your Antichrist at Rome. We know whence you come. The rulers of this world, being pious, will not compel us to leave off the Word of God upon which depends our salvation, the greatest treasure we have. But if, for lack of understanding or from mischievous knavery, they were to try, we will first, in all humility, ask them to allow us the Word. And thereafter, with the power and grace of the Lord God, we shall be strong enough to be more obedient to him than to you apostate blasphemers. And we shall let no one take the holy Word of the gospel away from us, and upon that we wager our lives and all we have.

FABRI: Fellow, the point is noted. We'll punish you so cruelly that thousands upon thousands shall learn the lesson. Or do you think that I wouldn't do it to you?

PEASANT: Faber, I truly believe you do no more than the will of God.

FABRI: Then it will be his will that I punish you.

PEASANT: Aye, and it may be his will that you get my fist in your teeth.

FABRI: Hold hard. I am councillor and servant to the emperor's deputy and well acquainted with the members of the government. You ought to be thrown into a dungeon and secretly drowned, so that your neighbours won't know what has become of you.

PEASANT: You may have me drowned, but that won't enable you to get hold of everybody. . . . I warn you and tell you that it would be easier and better possible for you and your bishops to pull down the sky than to suppress the truth. Push it down in one place—it will only rise elsewhere a hundredfold higher; and it shall see to it that it will go hard with you and your bishops.

FABRI: Now, fellow, I hear well what your mind is: you seek rebellion and insurrection.

PEASANT: Not so, not so: all we ask is that you rob us not of God's Word. . . .

# 55 / ANABAPTISM

*The Reformation quickly produced many truly extreme movements, and since most of them made adult baptism the center of their creed, they came all to be called by the comprehensive name of Anabaptists—re-baptizers. The large number of sects which developed had many tenets in common; all of them suffered violent persecution because they were both disruptive of religious uniformity and opposed to civil obedience. No distinction was made between those who held that God's cause demanded violence and the much larger number who believed in meekness and suffering. An early victim was Michael Sattler (1490?–1527) from southern Germany; an ex-monk of a genuinely spiritual piety, he was converted to Anabaptism at Zürich in 1525, presided over the conference at Schleitheim (1527) which agreed on a basic set of articles acceptable to the sects, and was in the same year tried and burned for heresy at Rothenburg on the Neckar. The articles alleged against him and his answers give some idea both of Anabaptist views and of popular reaction to them.*[10]

Here follow the articles:

1. That he and his fellows have acted against the imperial command.

2. He taught, held and believed that the body and blood of Christ are not in the sacrament.

3. He taught and believed that infant baptism does not help to salvation.

4. They have rejected the sacrament of unction.

5. Have despised and blasphemed the Mother of God and the saints.

6. He said that one should take no oath to obey authority.

7. Began a new and unheard-of custom in the Lord's Supper: they put wine and bread in one bowl and ate it.

8. He left his order and took a woman to wife.

9. He said: if the Turk came, he should not be resisted, and if war were justified he would rather fight against Christians than against Turks; which is a great matter, to draw upon us the greatest enemy of our holy faith. . . .

Then [Sattler] spoke and answered without fear.

To the first: that we have acted against the imperial command we do not admit; for that says that one should not adhere to Luther's doctrine and delusion but only to the gospel and the Word of God; and so have we done. For I do not know that I have acted contrary to the gospel or the Word of God; let this be proved by the word of Christ.

To the second: that the sacrament does not contain the real body of our Lord Jesus Christ, that we admit; for the Scripture says thus: Christ ascended into heaven and sits on the right hand of his heavenly father where he will judge the quick and the dead. It follows that if he be in heaven and not in the bread, he cannot be eaten corporeally.

To the third: concerning baptism we say: infant baptism is not useful for salvation, for it is written that we live by faith alone. Also he who believes and is baptised shall be saved. . . .

To the fourth: we have not rejected the oil of unction, for it is a creature of God. What God has made is good and may not be rejected. But as for the pope, bishops, monks and priests pretending to make better of it, that we hold for nothing, for the pope has never done any good. That of which the Epistle of James [5.14] speaks is not the pope's oil.

---

[10] Translated from *Glaubenszeugnisse oberdeutscher Taufgesinnter,* ed. Lydia Müller (Leipzig, 1938), pp. 38–40.

To the fifth: we have not blasphemed the Mother of God and the saints. Christ's mother is to be praised above all women, for she received the favor of giving birth to the Savior of all the world. But that she should be an intermediary and advocate, of that the Scripture knows nothing; for she must with us await the judgment day. . . . Concerning the saints, we say that we who live and believe are the saints, which I will prove from Paul's epistles to Romans, Corinthians, Ephesians and elsewhere, where he always writes "to the beloved saints." Therefore we who believe are the saints. Those who have died in the faith we called the blessed.

To the sixth: we hold that we are not to take an oath to the authorities, for the Lord says (Matt. 5.34–7) "Swear not at all . . . but let your communication be Yea, Yea, Nay, Nay."

To the seventh: when God called me to testify to his Word and I read Paul, and when I considered the unchristian and perilous state in which I was, seeing all the pomp, pride, usury and great whoredom of monks and priests, then I went and according to God's command took unto me a wife; for Paul well prophesied of this when he says (1 Tim. 4) that in the last days it shall happen that men shall forbid marriage and the grateful eating of the food which God has created.

To the eighth: if the Turk comes he shall not be resisted, for it is written, Thou shalt not kill. We are not to defend ourselves against the Turk and other persecutors, but are to pray heartily to God that He be our protection and defence. That I said that if war were right I would rather fight against the supposed Christians who persecute, hunt and kill true Christians than against the Turk, was for this reason. The Turk is a true Turk and knows nothing of the Christian faith; he is a Turk in the flesh. So you would be Christians and boast of Christ, but persecute Christ's true witnesses and are Turks in the spirit. . . .

# 56 / HANS HUT (D. 1527): ON THE MYSTERY OF BAPTISM (C. 1525-1526)

*Hut was a bookbinder and traveling bookseller from central Germany, that is, a small master craftsman neither really poor nor particularly well off. It was from this aspiring and dissatisfied layer of society that most of the Anabaptist preachers and teachers came. Hut experienced conversion in about 1524 and came under the influence of Müntzer. Lucky enough to escape the aftermath of the Peasants' War, he is next found as a wandering preacher in Austria and in 1526 in Moravia, where the Swiss Brethren, led by Balthazar Hubmaier, had made many converts. As against Hubmaier's moderation and willingness to accept some civil government, Hut was an extremist who refused the "sword" (civil authority) any rights over the sects and preached the use of violence. He was captured and tortured; before he could be executed, he died in a fire which mysteriously destroyed his prison. This mystical treatise on the nature and efficacy of baptism—the regeneration of sinful men in Christ, Anabaptism's central tenet —is with some confidence ascribed to him.* [11]

Now we will turn to the baptism of regeneration which is no outward sign to show Christ, but a bath to wash and cleanse the soul of all lusts and desires of the heart. It is a killing and extinguishing of all the lusts and rebellions which are and move within men against God. In the time of Noah God did thus to the old world when with his Flood he washed all wickedness from the earth; and thus happened to Pharaoh and his Egyptians in the baptism of the Red Sea as they sank to the bottom like lead. The whole world, with Noah and with Pharaoh and his men, together with all Israel, stands in the baptismal flood together; but their fate is not the same, they do not profit alike. The wicked go in, but they do not come out again; for they with delight sink down among created things, reject election for themselves and for the creatures, and would gladly live for ever in lust and the love of creation. Therefore they persecute the chosen who do not cleave to the world as they do but endeavor to swim out of it and, like Peter, unremittingly struggle towards the bank or the jetty, endeavoring to reach the safe land from the uncertain sea of this world and from the waters of misery and reprobation, because they see God's hand stretched forth to help them. This is the baptism of those who walk in a regenerated life: not a drenching and drowning, but a joyful escape from the eddies and waves, the stirrings of our own desires. . . . Oh, the path of life grows narrow where we must walk through the death of the old Adam to a new way of life in God: and that is what regeneration in baptism means. Man is overcome by terrible anguish, trembling and dread, like to the fear of a woman in labor. When God pours such waters through the soul it needs patience till

[11] Translated from *Glaubenszeugnisse oberdeutscher Taufgesinnter*, ed. Lydia Müller (Leipzig, 1938), pp. 12–15.

understanding and knowledge are acquired and peace on earth is born out of the prick of the flesh. Thus through the ages of life, by suffering the work of God's hand, men become a finished and ready seat and habitation for God. And as the troubled waters grow clear, the bitter sweet, the tempestuous quiet and peaceful, so the sun of God appears on the waters, stretches out its hand, and testifies to Him in the whirlpools. . . . The waters which enter the soul are tempta-tion, sorrow, trembling and misery: baptism is suffering. So Christ trembles in his baptism until he is perfected in the death of life. True baptism is nothing but a struggle against sin all life long. . . . John's baptism in water is incomplete and cannot free from sin, for it is only an image, preparation and foreshadowing of the true baptism in Christ. . . . Thus all that dies in Adam lives in Christ; but whosoever will not have this baptism remains in the dead Adam. . . .

# 57 / HULDREICH ZWINGLI (1484-1531): AN EXPOSITION OF THE FAITH (1531)

*Zwingli's sway extended much more widely than his re-stricted area of operations, the Swiss city state of Zürich, would seem to make likely. He owed much to his humanist training, which provided him with far-ranging contacts among the reform-ing pastors of Switzerland, southern Germany, and England. More important, however, were a certain logic and clarity in his teaching, especially on the eucharist, his views on which led to the break between him and Luther. Zwingli's doctrine that Holy Communion was purely a commemorative service of Christ's sacri-fice was much simpler and more easily accepted than Luther's tortuous attempt to preserve a species of the real presence in the elements of bread and wine while discarding the Catholic doc-trine of transubstantiation, which depends on special miracle-working powers in the priest. At the same time, Zwingli's teaching proved in the long run a little too cool and rational; Calvin's modification (maintaining a spiritual, but not a corporal, presence in the sacrament) satisfied more people because it avoided mak-*

*ing the central act of Christian worship into a mere social gathering.*[12]

To eat the body of Christ spiritually is equivalent to trusting with heart and soul upon the mercy and goodness of God through Christ, that is, to have assurance of an unbroken faith that God will give us the forgiveness of sins and the joy of eternal salvation for the sake of his Son. . . . You eat the body of Christ spiritually, but not sacramentally, every time your soul puts the anxious question: "How are you to be saved? We sin every day, and every day we draw nearer to death. After this life there is another, for if we have a soul and it is concerned about the future, how can it be destroyed with this present life? How can so much light and knowledge be turned into darkness and oblivion? Therefore if the soul has eternal life, what sort of life will be the portion of my poor soul? A life of joy or a life of anguish? I will examine my life and consider whether it deserves joy or anguish."

But when you think of all the things which we men habitually do either in passion or desire, you will be terrified, and so far as your own righteousness is concerned, in your own judgment you will declare yourself undeserving of eternal salvation and will completely despair of it. But then you assure your anxious spirit: "God is good: and he who is good must necessarily be righteous and merciful and kind. . . . If God is just, his justice demands atonement for my sins. But because he is merciful, I cannot despair of pardon. Of both these things I have an infallible pledge, his only begotten Son our Lord Jesus Christ." . . . So then, when you come to the Lord's Supper to feed spiritually upon Christ, and when you thank the Lord for his great favour, for the redemption whereby you are delivered from despair, and for the pledge whereby you are assured of eternal salvation, when you join with your brethren in partaking of the bread and wine which are the tokens of the body of Christ, then in the true inward sense of the word you eat him sacramentally. You do inwardly that which you represent outwardly, your soul being strengthened by the faith which you attest in the tokens. . . .

Now for some time there has been bitter contention amongst us as to what the sacraments or signs themselves either do or can do in the Supper. Our adversaries allege that the sacraments give faith, mediate the natural body of Christ, and enable us to eat as substantially present. But we have good cause to think otherwise.

12 From *Zwingli and Bullinger*, Vol. XXIV, pp. 258 ff., Library of Christian Classics. Tr. G. W. Bromiley. Published 1953, The Westminster Press. By permission.

First, because no external things but only the Holy Spirit can give that faith which is trust in God. All sacraments do give faith, but only historical faith. All celebrations, monuments and statutes give historical faith, that is, they remind us of some event, refreshing the memory. . . . Now the Lord's Supper, too, does create faith in this way, that is, it bears sure witness to the birth and passion of Christ. But to whom does it bear witness? To believers and unbelievers alike. For whether they receive it or not, it testifies to all that which is the power of the sacrament, the fact that Christ suffered. But only to the faithful and pious does it testify that he suffered for us. For it is only those who have been taught inwardly by the Spirit to know the mystery of the divine goodness who can know and believe that Christ suffered for us: it is they alone who receive Christ. For no one comes to Christ except the Father draw him. And Paul settles the whole dispute with a single word when he says: "Let a man examine himself and so let him eat of the bread and drink of that cup." Therefore if we are to examine ourselves before we come, it is quite impossible that the Supper should give faith: for faith must be present already before we come. . . .

# 58 / MARTIN BUCER (1491-1551): ON AUTHORITY

*Bucer, one of the younger generation of humanists who early followed the call of the Reformation, became the movement's classic peace-maker. For nearly a quarter of a century (1524–48) he presided over the reform at Strassburg, a city open to every sort of influence and exceptionally well placed to provide a bridge between the two centers of the Reformation, Luther's Saxony and Zwingli's Switzerland. His chief contribution in theology was the development of the notion af adiaphora (things indifferent)—the notion that there were parts and points of religion on which conformity, while desirable, was not necessary to salvation. This concept permitted the existence of agreed differences within one church. Because it came to form the main distinguishing characteristic of the Anglican form of Protestantism, it was appropriate that Bucer should spend his last three years in England, assisting in the making of the Edwardian Reformation. He was also the outstanding Protestant representative at the last serious attempt to bring the rival faiths into accord—the Colloquy of Regensburg in 1541. Earlier he had written this book, in German and therefore for the general reader, in which, among other things, he tried to confront one of the reformers' crucial problems—the problem of obedience to constituted authority. Taught by their devotion to Scripture and especially St. Paul that "all powers that be are of God" (Romans, 13), they had to explain why they should reject the pope's exercise of a power sufficiently well established to claim that same authority. Bucer tried to do this here, with less than perfect success. The contributors to his dialogue bear meaningful names: Peaceful (Friedlieb), Hardy (Hartmut), and Thoughtful (Sinnprecht).[13]*

[The Sixth Dialogue]

FRIEDLIEB: First let us consider together whether the rulers *qua* rulers should concern themselves with religion and the service of God; secondly, to what extent; and thirdly whether this applies to all rulers including such as have further higher authorities above them.

HARTMUT: That seems a reasonable order of debate, but I suggest that we must first discuss what we mean by rulers and authorities.

SINNPRECHT: I agree. We have settled what we mean by religion and the service of God, namely the true faith with all its fruits, and especially liturgical worship ordained for the promotion of the faith and therefore of all the virtues which assuredly flow from faith, and which must be so used. Therefore we must, I think, first investigate what we mean by the word and name of "authorities."

F: Suits me.

H: Right, Friedlieb— you are in trade. You tell us what we should understand by rulers and magistracy.

F: In the first place it means no more than people put in authority over others—those who have the power to instruct and to judge the others as their subjects.

S: That makes for a lot of what you might call "rulers." Husbands are placed over their wives, fathers over their children, masters over their servants, schoolmasters over their pupils, gildmasters over their gilds, mayors and councils over their cities, captains over their soldiers, princes and lords over their territories, emperors and kings over their realms.

F: Yes, all these have authority, and to the extent of its range they

---

[13] Translated from Martin Bucer, *Dialogi oder Gesprech von der gemeinsame vnnd den Kirchenübungen der Christen* (Augsburg, 1535).

must use it fully to serve God from whom all power and all virtue flow. They must promote religion to the best of their ability—everywhere, of course, but particularly among those who are specially committed to their care. Above all the true and sincere faith and everything that pertains to such faith and depends on it, and especially to take care of the holy worship of the Church which guides all good order and manners and whatever may stand well and be right.

H: The problem, you know, is this: who should be responsible for the reform of the outward observances of the Church, for the appointment and dismissal of preachers, and for amending other religious practices.

S: Yes, Friedlieb, that's what we two were debating before you joined us.

F: If we are to discuss especially what authorities should be active in the general conduct and economy of the Church, should remove things objectionable and promote better things, and should undertake a general public reformation and edification, we shall have to interpret "authorities" to mean those whom the Apostles call "powers" (Rom. 13; Tit. 3; 1 Peter 2). That is to say, those who bear the sword, exercise capital jurisdiction and issue general statutes and ordinances.

S: You mean, those who possess *imperium merum*—total power as defined by Ulpian: [14] power of the sword, power to punish transgressors, a power also called *potestas,* or εξωσια by St. Paul.

H: As you know, in Germany authorities come in all shapes and sizes. You can find one which can issue orders and prohibitions to its subjects and enjoys their full service and obedience, yet lacks the sword and the right to capital jurisdiction. On the other, there are magistrates there possessed of that jurisdiction who can't command or prohibit anything nor look after the peace. We must allow the existence of magistrates whose powers to command and forbid are not general but confined to particular things. In many principalities, for instance, certain appointed councillors are responsible for arresting and judging criminals and yet have no other power to make general laws.

F: As you say, Hartmut, our German authorities fall into all sorts of categories. But religion and public worship are the things which give meaning to men's lives and lead them in the right way: and therefore in this discussion we'll stick to those authorities who themselves have power, without reference to higher authority, to decree general laws and statutes, to issue orders and prohibitions. Since it is their office to make sure that people live justly and rightly, it follows that their first task is to take care of that on which all life depends—namely religion. That is why all the famous legislators and planners of right polities—

[14] leading Roman jurist; died A.D. 223

Plato, Xenophon, Aristotle, Cicero and others—consider the settlement of religion the most important aspect of the work and lay down rules for it.

H: Christian emperors have laboured for it, too; in their legislation they give pride of place to religion—just look at the *Codex* and the *Autentica*.[15]

s: Those whom we now call the spiritualty have the power touching religion. As St Paul teaches us, when speaking of the powers of rulers, we should consider how far any power extends. For he says: The powers that be are of God. It follows that the range of all power is set by the order of God.

H: I wonder if it is not really necessary to leave to God the definition of all power and authority. For if people decided to dispute whence and in what form a ruler derives his power, or uses it, or how far he might rightfully exercise power when he has made a promise and confirmed it by oath, and if people then wished to measure their obedience by comparing that power to what is just, there would be little obedience or peace.

F: Therefore attend solely to the will of God, the law of all laws. All power is of God: he gives to each man at all times as much as pleases him; no man can have an inch more of power than God gives him. Thus: no matter what power a man may have, whether he got it by fair means or foul, whether he uses it too narrowly or too generously, well or badly—for us it should always be sufficient grounds for sincere obedience that power and authority are present there. That fact should serve for seal and parchment and all paraphernalia, no matter in what fashion the situation came about. The deed proclaims God's will which in itself is always just and good, irrespective of what evil yoke human beings may hang onto it. Emperors and kings have held sway who had murdered their own masters and kings, and who had thus acquired their power entirely without a right to it. But so long as God apportions the power to them, obedience is due to them for as long as God in his power will suffer them.

s: From this it follows that the spiritualty should be left in possession of their power and obedience which now they have, and for a long time have had, in the Church. And not just touching the order of the Church or over members of their own estate—those ordained into it—but over all who call themselves Christians—over emperor and kings and all powers on earth. This power they manage to get confirmed under oath by the highest authorities and it is exercised in practice.

F: All this comes from God; he knows to whom he will grant power

[15] the basic texts of the Roman law

over us. It is the order of God, which cannot be wrong, no matter what sort of people may be exercising the power.

H: You mean we should obey pope and priests?

F: The Apostle says that he who resists authority resists God's holy decree. For "all power everywhere is commanded by God" (Rom. 13). There is no getting away from that. It's the Word of God.

S: Yes, I agree.

H: Well, well. If we obey the shavelings, we'll have to do without reform of ceremonies and without proper preaching. Indeed, we shall have to worship idolatry and protect it with all we have.

F: How do you mean?

H: Those people, you say, have power over such matters; and they use it to maintain idolatry and to suppress and destroy all true Christian doctrine and ceremonies.

F: We have agreed on what power is and its abuse, and how it is to be obeyed and its abuse to be suffered. Ask the defenders of the pope's power what powers the pope and the spiritualty might have.

H: Power? I'm to ask *them?* They'll say that the pope has power in heaven, on earth and under the earth, over angels, men and devils, the living and the dead, emperor and king, over all matters spiritual and temporal, over men's goods, honour, body and soul.

S: Oh come, Hartmut, you are laying it on.

H: My dear fellow, ask the pope's canonists and see whether they do not teach precisely that. You remember how Alexander VI undertook in his jubilee [16] to issue orders to angels and devils: he instructed the angels to guide all pilgrims safely to Rome, and the devils he stopped from hindering them. He claims to have the keys of St Peter and to decide for whom he will open or close the gates of heaven, whom to damn into hell and whom to loose into heaven. . . . He claims the right to appoint and depose kings and emperors, and to do as he wills with any man's goods and honour and body and soul; and anyone who fails to obey him he makes into a heretic rejected and condemned of God. And even though he so misuses his power that he leads innumerable people into hell, yet no one shall punish or judge him.

F: True, alas. All this the popes themselves admit, while their flatterers—canonists and schoolmen—confirm it. . . . But if you ask the canonists how the popes got all that power they point to our Lord's saying to St Peter: "pasture my sheep." In saying this, the Lord commanded one thing, namely that the sheep should be governed for their own salvation and be taught (ordered and prevented) according to his will. For he himself remains the arch-shepherd, as the popes them-

---

[16] the papal bull of 1500, offering special rewards to those who by pilgrimage increased Rome's income from tourism

selves concede. In short, there can be no power except for edification.
. . . Therefore let us freely grant the popes and the bishops that power
which they claim for themselves and can ever use.

H: Careful, don't concede too much.

F: Look: the pope himself says that all his power amounts to pas-
turing the sheep of Christ, which is to say to protect and rule them in
all good virtue—so to instruct them and to give them such orders and
prohibitions that they will do well according to the will of God.
Wouldn't you gladly have him exercise such power over you and anybody else as best he may? Wouldn't you gladly obey him in such a
cause? After all, there is nothing more salutary than to do what is right
and pleasing to Christ.

H: The pope doesn't use his powers in that way.

F: Well, if he fails to instruct you, if he neither commands nor for-
bids anything, you obviously can't follow or obey him.

H: Oh, he commands me: I am to hold to his unchristian doctrine
and worship, to avoid challenging his abuses, not support those he
punishes, not read Christian books, and so on, and so on—things that
I cannot do and stay with God!

F: No one can order you to do what you "cannot do and stay with
God." No one has power and authority to that purpose. The pope himself admits this: he teaches that one must humbly resist authority when
it orders evil deeds.

H: What if he orders me to do things which are not contrary to God
but which he has no business to command? For instance, when without
good right he demands my money, or orders me to fight against the
infidel, or to travel to Rome, and such like?

F: You have your ordinary rulers to whom you are subject in such
matters and whom in such affairs you should obey. They will admit or
deny such unsuitable papal claims. If they deny them and allow that
you are in the right, the pope clearly has no power over you. . . . On
the other hand, if your ordinary rulers support the pope's command
to you, it becomes the command of your ordinary rulers who have
lawful power over you. . . .

# 59 / GUSTAVUS I VASA (1496?-1560): THE SWEDISH REFORMATION

*The first king of the House of Vasa (crowned in 1523) obtained the throne by rebellion against Sweden's Danish rulers; he devoted his reign to the successful creation of an independent nation and a strong monarchy. In this task he found the Lutheran Reformation, with its acceptance of princely rule in the Church, of massive assistance. With the help of a few German-trained theologians, he introduced the Reformation by stages that were not complete until the Diet of Västeras of 1544 (B). The king emphasized throughout his sovereign control over all that went on and could even write very sharply to such a leading supporter as his archbishop of Uppsala when he thought that the clergy were showing too much independence (A). The brothers Petri (Peterson) were Sweden's foremost reformers, but the elder, Olavus (1493–1552), fell into disgrace by opposing the king's autocracy, whereas Laurentius (1499–1573) accepted all rebukes and practiced obedience.*[17]

## A

### Gustavus I to Laurentius Petri, archbishop of Uppsala, 24 April 1539

Our special favour, etc. Although, Bishop Laurentius, the replies contained in your letters to us, which refer to the exhortations we sent you in our earlier missive, are very suitable and in no sense to be despised: yet we understand from the article then following that you are in part grieved at our demanding of you greater conformity in your see of Uppsala with respect to preaching and reformation. It were well that all might be done conformably. Our intentions were of the best, for you know well that our people are rude and have little understand-

---

[17] Translated from P.E. Thyselius, "Beiträge zu Schwedens Reformations= und Kirchengeschichte unter König Gustav I.," *Zeitschrift für historische Theologie*, 1847, pp. 232–5, 247–8.

ing of such things; and this causes inconveniences. You yourself know well, if you will take example from Scripture (which you, after all, read more often than we do), that there you find Christ and the Apostles preaching before anyone celebrated mass; yet you wish to have masses and weddings etc., but no sermons. And thus there arise inconveniences and uproar, the people not being instructed before reform is in hand; and all is done in our name, for which we suffer sufficient obloquy. Would to God that there had been more conformity; there was need of it. And therefore it is advisable that you should first appoint good and Christian preachers who will teach the simple commons the faith and its fruits; that is the first necessity, and after that one may introduce reforms touching masses and the rest, as need requires. And where you advise us that the lack of good preachers is not your fault, as though we had stood in the way of finding such persons: we are not conscious of having done so. The whole problem can surely not be linked with the single person who came to us from thence. Furthermore [you state] that you are not able to maintain so many persons, twenty or thirty: to this we cannot answer. You have taken small counsel with us in this matter or in anything else touching the gospel. Yet we hope that you have well understood our meaning, namely that we have always favoured the promotion of the clear and pure Word of God. And if we had not done more than you have, we do not know that matters would have come to the pass in which now they stand. You touch upon canons' prebends, cathedral scholars, and so forth: we do not know why there should be any need of so many scholars since those who attend the school [also] mostly sing in the cathedral choir. However, that is not the import of your saying. We understand your purpose well, namely that you would like to shear the sheep and keep the wool; but how to guard the flock, that you do not know. True, we have some canonries in our gift, but we trust that those upon whom they are bestowed will contribute to the common good as much as you can. You complain that you lack the means. There is no need for this: if the will were good and greed less, there would be enough for everything. We note well the game you play, against which Christ has commanded. There shall be a preaching clergy, but no lords; you are (if you will confess the truth) not overlooked in your office in doing justice. You must not think that we shall ever again permit the bishops to wield the sword.[18] Further you say that you know how to preach other things at Uppsala than of the Swedish mass, of marriage, of the eating of flesh, etc.; and if you thereby mean penitence and edification, a true Christian faith, brotherly love, a pious and righteous life, patience in adversity, etc., we shall indeed not punish such preaching.

---

[18] i.e. to exercise secular rule and jurisdiction

But even if such things are preached at Uppsala it does not follow that they are heard throughout the realm. Not Uppsala alone calls for pastoral care, but the whole diocese and all the realm; and it is not too much to ask that you should take your share in the work.

Also you say and demand from us an open letter to the people which would teach the right way to the common man. God knows, we would gladly do this. But we do not know what occasion we might have for it, because for some years now we have been much attacked on these very grounds from the pulpits here in Stockholm, and also perhaps elsewhere, though sometimes in covert ways. There is nothing heard but cries of "tyranny, tyranny and unkind rule." Therefore we do not know what to write in such matters, since well we know how it will be taken. Christ and St Paul teach submission and obedience, of which least is here heard but (as we have said) nothing but "tyranny" and cries for mercy. Nor do we know what or how we might write in this respect, inasmuch as we have no help either from you or from others who in these matters ought to offer strong assistance to the magistrate. On the contrary, the common people hear the preaching of disobedience, as it was clearly expressed in the lately published writing touching swearing, as though the ruler were responsible for all the oaths which (would that God provided a remedy) are in common use, as well as for all the other evils that, alas, prevail. All this [the clergy] ascribe to the magistrate, even though (God be praised) you will never be able to offer just proof of it. And we think such preaching and printing more a cause of uproar and disorder than of Christian doctrine. There Christ and St Paul teach very differently, namely that the preacher should first instruct and exhort [evildoers] three or four times to do better, not make their failings public at once, as you have done. And even if in this you had had good reason, you should not have cried out upon the magistrate before the Christian congregation, as you have done. And therefore be assured that from this day we will not have any reform undertaken except that we have first approved and authorised it. Also, for the reasons stated, no writing is to appear in print but that we have first perused and allowed it. This you will do as instructed. And to conclude: if in future we see and learn that you and those of counsel with you do not proclaim God's Word in a more Christian manner and on better grounds than now we see you do, we do not know what our mind shall be, and we may, as God gives us grace, look differently upon it.

P.S. Nor, Bishop Laurentius, do we want you in future to send preachers among the common people except such as you know to be right and proper for the purpose and well instructed in what they are to teach and preach. We would rather that the older men already beneficed should do it, than that young men of little understanding should be ordered to the task who in their preaching cause perhaps more inconvenience and disorder than would those others. Therefore you will take wise order in this respect. And we want you to make no changes among the clergy except in the presence of our commissioners, so that it may be done with our and their agreement.

## B

### *The Ordinance of Västeras, 1544*

First, that the Word of God and Holy Scripture shall generally be used in the Christian congregation here in Sweden. 2. It is forbidden to worship or pray to departed saints. 3. Pilgrimages, holy water, salt, wax, incense and roods are forbidden. 4. The days of a few holy men and holy women, as listed in the new calendar, shall be observed. 5. The common people shall attend in church during the hours of worship. 6. Gilds and societies are abolished; so are masses for the dead, year's masses, votive masses and mortuary masses; yet mortuary fees of 5 pence are lawful upon order of his majesty. 7. Parsons shall be ever ready to visit the sick, without delay. 8. There shall be no sacring of corpses, either at the church-door or at home. 9. Our gracious lord the king, the Council of the whole realm, the nobility, bishops, prelates, municipalities and commons have taken oath that they will never depart from the doctrine now established. 10. Our gracious lord has exhorted the common people that God's tithe be fairly paid on everything obtained by land as well as by sea, upon pain. 11. The common people are warned to go frequently to God's table.[19] 12. His grace has commanded, with the assent of his Council, that the common people shall send their sons to school and shall assist scholars with alms. 13. The king's son, Duke Eric, has been chosen, approved and elected by the commons to be the future king of the realm of Sweden, and his descendants after him, one after another. 14. His grace has pardoned the unfaithful behaviour of those of Småland and other his subjects. 15. His grace has sworn never to seek anything but the good, the profit and the well-being of Sweden. 16. His grace has proclaimed peace within the realm and outside it. 17. The whole realm have promised that if treason be discovered in the kingdom they will themselves punish and suppress it. 18. The commons have sworn fealty, submission, loyalty and service in war to our gracious lord. 19. His grace has announced that he does not mean to maintain his rule by means of beams and stones,[20] and the commons are absolved from payments. 20. Fornicators, murderers, perjurers and other evildoers shall obtain absolution from the clergy, or they shall be whipped and excluded from the Church. 21. Strong oaths and drunkenness are forbidden, on pain of punishment and correction by his

[19] i.e. take holy communion

[20] i.e. by building castles

majesty. 22. Any person keeping dancing or banqueting establishments shall pay a fine of three marks to the king. 23. Offertory boxes shall be taken away from this day forward, until their abuses are remedied. 24. Our gracious lord and the commons of the realm have agreed that anyone contravening this ordinance and thereof convicted by two witnesses shall be outlawed and held to be an heretic and infidel.

# 60 / JEAN CALVIN (1509-1564)

*Calvin contributed two main pillars to Protestantism. His theology centered on a complete and logical exposition of the doctrine of predestination; but this is here left to another author to expound (No. 62). Secondly, he extracted from Scripture a form of Church government, usually called presbyterian, which not only did away altogether with the government from above embodied in pope, bishops, and Church courts, but also operated somewhat against the powers of lay rulers over their territorial churches. Though Calvin was not fully in control at Geneva until 1555, the* Ecclesiastical Ordinance of 1541 *(A) already shows what he believed to be the correct government of the Church.*[21] *However, Calvin's preference for forms of election and lay elders did not mean that he himself denied or even seriously limited the authority of civil government ("the magistrate"). His views on this (B) form the last chapter of his great work,* The Institutes of the Christian Religion *(first published in 1536, final edition 1559), a systematic exposition of theology and ecclesiology. They agree in general with Luther and with the prevalent trend among secular writers in demanding obedience to princes and denouncing rebellion. Despite certain reservations, these authoritarian views became troublesome when spreading Calvinism encountered repression by governments and had to find theoretical justification for resistance (see No. 80).*[22]

[21] From *Calvin: Theological Treatises*, Vol. XXII, pp. 58 ff., Library of Christian Classics. Tr. J. K. S. Reid. Published 1954, The Westminster Press. By permission.

[22] Translated from the 1559 edition of the *Institutes in Corpus Reformatorum*, Vol. 30, ed. W. Baum, E. Cunitz, E. Reuss (Brunswick, 1864), Book 4, Chapter 20.

## A. ECCLESIASTICAL ORDINANCE

There are four orders of office instituted by our Lord for the govern-ment of his Church.

First, pastors; then doctors; next elders; and fourth, deacons.

Hence if we will have a Church well ordered and maintained we ought to observe this form of government.

As to pastors, whom Scripture also sometimes calls elders and ministers, their office is to proclaim the Word of God, instruct, admonish, exhort and censure, both in public and private, to administer the sacraments and to enjoin brotherly corrections along with the elders and colleagues. . . .

### *There follows, to whom it belongs to institute Pastors*

It will be good in this connection to follow the order of the ancient Church, for it is the only practice which is shown to us in Scripture. The order is that ministers first elect such as ought to hold office; afterwards that he be presented to the Council [of the city]; and if he is found worthy the Council receive and accept him, giving him certification to produce finally to the people when he preaches, in order that he be received by the common consent of the company of the faithful. . . .

As to the manner of introducing him, it is good to use the imposition of hands, which ceremony was observed by the apostles and then in the ancient Church, providing that it take place without superstition and without offence. But because there has been much superstition in the past and scandal might result, it is better to abstain from it because of the infirmity of the times. . . .

Now as it is necessary to examine the ministers well when they are to be elected, so also it is necessary to have good supervision to maintain them in their duty.

First it will be expedient that all the ministers, for conserving purity and concord of doctrine among themselves, meet together one certain day each week, for discussion of the Scriptures; and none are to be exempt from this without legitimate excuse. . . .

If there appear difference of doctrine, let the ministers come together to discuss the matter. Afterwards, if need be, let them call the elders to assist in composing the contention. Finally, if they are unable to come to a friendly agreement because of the obstinacy of one of the parties, let the case be referred to the magistrate to be put in order. . . .

### Concerning the second order, which we have called Doctors

The office proper to doctors is the instruction of the faithful in true doctrine, in order that the purity of the Gospel be not corrupted either by ignorance or by evil opinions. As things are disposed today, we always include under this title aids and instructions for maintaining the doctrine of God and defending the Church from injury by the fault of pastors and ministers. So to use a more intelligible word, we will call this the order of the schools. . . . Let no one be received if he is not approved by the Ministers on their testimony, for fear of impropriety.

### Concerning the third order, which is that of Elders

Their office is to have oversight of the life of everyone, to admonish amicably those whom they see to be erring or to be living a disordered life, and, where it is required, to enjoin fraternal corrections themselves and along with others. . . . [They are to be elected by the city.] It is inexpedient that they be changed often without cause, so long as they discharge their duties faithfully.

### The fourth order of ecclesiastical government, that is, the Deacons

There were always two kinds in the ancient Church, the one deputed to receive, dispense and hold goods for the poor, not only daily alms, but also possessions, rents and pensions; the other to tend and care for the sick and administer allowances to the poor. This custom we follow again now for we have procurators and hospitallers. . . . The election of both . . . is to take place like that of elders; and in electing them the rule proposed by Paul for deacons is to be followed [I Tim. 3; Tit. 1] . . .

The elders, as already said, are to assemble once a week with the ministers . . . to see that there be no disorder in the Church and to discuss together remedies as they are required. . . .

Secret vices are to be secretly admonished; no one is to bring his neighbour before the Church to accuse him of faults that are not in the least notorious or scandalous, unless after having found him contumacious.

For the rest, those who despise particular admonitions by their neighbour are to be admonished anew by the Church; and if they will not at all come to reason or acknowledge their fault when convicted of it, they will be informed that they must abstain from the Supper until such time as they return in a better frame of mind.

As for vices notorious and public which the Church cannot dissimulate, if they are faults that merit admonition only, the duty of the elders will be to summon those who are implicated to make friendly remonstrance to them in order that they make correction, and, if amendment is evident, to do them no harm. If they persevere in doing wrong, they are to be admonished repeatedly; and if even then there is no result, they are to be informed that, as despisers of God, they must abstain from the Supper until a change of life is seen in them.

As for crimes which merit not merely remonstrance in words but correction by chastisement, should any fall into them, according to the needs of the case, he must be warned that he abstain for some time from the Supper, to humble himself before God and to acknowledge his fault the better.

If any in contumacy or rebellion wish to intrude against the prohibition, the duty of the minister is to turn him back, since it is not permissible for him to be received at the Communion. . . .

## B. THE AUTHORITY OF CIVIL GOVERNMENT

I have already stated that man is subjected to two kinds of government, and have elsewhere discussed at sufficient length one of the two, namely that placed in the soul or inner man which concerns eternal life. Now, in this place, I must say a little of the second kind: that which relates to the institution of civil and outward jurisdiction over behavior. Although this discussion may seem alien to the spiritual doctrine of faith which I undertook to analyse, the sequel will show that I am right to include it; indeed, that I am necessarily compelled to do so. In particular, on the one hand, there are certain insane barbarians who try to subvert this divinely sanctioned order by violence,[23] while on the other worshippers of princes, immoderately extolling their power, go so far as to set it up over against even God's authority. Unless both these aberrations are resisted, the pure faith will die. In addition it is of no small importance to know how well God has provided for mankind in this matter, so that the pious zeal to testify to our gratitude may grow stronger in us.

First, before approaching the subject itself, we must stress again the distinction made above, lest—as too often happens—we find ourselves confusing these two things whose natures are altogether different. For the first sort just mentioned hear in the gospel the promise of a freedom which recognises no king among men and no magistrate, but looks to Christ alone; and so they conclude that they cannot enjoy the fruits of their freedom as long as they see any power established

[23] a reference to Anabaptism

over them. In consequence they imagine that nothing will go well unless the whole world be radically reformed by the abolition of courts, laws and authorities, or anything of that sort which they regard as hostile to their liberty. However, anyone who can distinguish between body and soul, between this present transitory life and future eternity, will have no difficulty in understanding that the spiritual kingdom of Christ and civil rule are two quite separate things. . . .

Yet this distinction does not mean that we should treat the state as sinful and of no relevance to Christian men. . . . While, as I have just pointed out, the nature of this rule differs from the spiritual and inward kingdom of Christ, it must be stressed that they are in no kind of conflict with each other. . . . Earthly government is decreed for our life among men: it is to promote and cherish the worship of God, to protect the sound doctrine of religion and the position of the Church, to accommodate our lives to the society of men, shape our behavior in accord with civil justice, maintain concord among individuals, guarantee a general peace and tranquillity. All this, I admit, would be superfluous if the kingdom of God, as it now exists within us, were to put an end to the temporal life. If therefore it is the will of God that during our journey to the one true country we shall be pilgrims on earth, and if that pilgrimage needs such crutches, he who deprives man of them takes from him this humanity. . . .

Let no one be disturbed because I now commit the charge of maintaining true religion to the human state, after I may earlier on have seemed to put it beyond human authority. No more than before do I here allow men to legislate concerning religion and divine worship; I only accept state action designed to prevent the violation and defilement, by open public blasphemies, of the true religion contained in the law of God. A more systematic treatment will make my meaning clear; it will assist the reader to understand better what should be held concerning the whole business of civil rule if I take its parts in turn. These are three: the magistrate, who is the guardian and keeper of the law; the laws by which he governs; and the people, ruled by the laws and obedient to the magistrate. . . .

*[Scripture ordains obedience to magistrates.]*

Those who are not moved by so many proofs of Scripture but still dare to impugn this sacred ministry as a thing abhorrent to religion and Christian piety, surely insult God himself whose dishonor must of necessity be involved in any abuse directed at His ministers. . . . Moreover, although there are various forms of magistracy, yet there is no distinction among them in this respect that by God's decree they all are to be accepted. Paul (Rom. 13.1) comprehensively asserts that there is no power but from God. That form of it which has always found least favor—I mean the rule of one man—is especially commended. Because this form involves universal servitude except for the one man to whose will everything is subject, it has always been deprecated by heroic and distinguished minds; yet Scripture, opposing these unjust views, expressly affirms that kings reign by the providence of God's wisdom and orders us specifically to "honor the king" (Prov. 8.15; 1 Pet. 2.17).

Now to say something of the nature of magistracy, as described in the Word of God, and of the particular duties comprised in the office. If Scripture did not teach that [civil rule] extends to both the tables of the law,[24] one would learn this from the secular writers. For every treatise on the office of magistrates, on legislation and on the state opens with a discussion of religion and worship. And so they all agree, that no state can be happily constituted unless its first care is to promote piety, and that laws which, ignoring the law of God, concern themselves with man only, are absurd. Since, therefore, religion holds pride of place for all the philosophers, and since this has always been supported by the universal consent of all nations, Christian princes and magistrates should be ashamed of their indolence if they neglect this duty. We have already seen that God has particularly committed these matters to them . . . and pious kings receive their chief praise in Scripture because they restored the worship of God when that had become corrupt or lost, or because they so well looked after religion that under their rule it flourished pure and safe. Indeed, sacred history considered it one of the evils of anarchy that there was no king in Israel and every man therefore did as he pleased (Judges 21.25). All this demonstrates the folly of those who would wish magistrates to concentrate solely on doing justice among men, to the exclusion of matters of religion. As though God would create officers in His name to decide temporal disputes, but would omit a matter of vastly greater moment, namely the pure worship of Himself according to the order of His law. . .

From this follows another thing: with their minds inclined to proper respect, subjects must prove the fact of their obedience by obeying orders, paying taxes, undertaking public duties and burdens necessary for the defence of the community, and carrying out all other commands. . . .

So far I have discussed a magistrate who truly answers his description: the father of his country, shepherd (as the poet calls him) of his people, keeper of the peace, guardian of justice, protector of innocence. Only a madman would disapprove of such a government. But

[24] i.e., both the temporal and the spiritual duties of men

just about every age has provided examples of princes who, careless of everything on which they should have bestowed their care, give themselves up to pleasure in idle disregard of every problem. Others again, absorbed in their own interests, prostitute all laws, privileges, rights and decrees for money; or rob the people of wealth which they then pour out in insane abandon; or commit plain outrages by pillaging houses, violating virgins and matrons, murdering infants. A good many people cannot believe that such men should be recognised as princes whose rule they should obey as far as possible. . . . Indeed, the minds of men have always been naturally inclined to execrate tyrants no less than they love and venerate legitimate kings. However, if we turn back to the Word of God it will take us much further: we are subject not only to the rule of princes who discharge their duty to us honestly and with due trust, but also to that of all who in any way have authority, even though nothing may be further from their minds than a proper performance of all the duties of a prince. For though the Lord testified that the magistrate is a supreme gift of His munificence, intended to preserve human welfare, and though He defines their office Himself, He yet at the same time declares that, no matter what sort they may be, they hold power from Him alone. Those who govern for the common weal are true examples and specimens of His beneficence; those, however, who lord it unjustly and despotically He has raised up to punish the people's sins. All are equally endowed with that sacred majesty with which He has invested legitimate authority. . . .

However men's acts may be judged, the Lord exercised His work upon them equally when He broke the bloodstained sceptre of insolent kings and overthrew unbearable dominions. Let princes hear and fear. But we meanwhile must take the greatest care that we do not spurn or violate the majestically venerable authority of magistrates which God has instituted by His most solemn decrees, even though it may be held by quite unworthy men who, as far as they may, befoul it with their inquity. For if the punishment of tyrants belongs to the vengeance of God, we must in no way come to think that it is committed to us: we have received no other command than to obey and be patient. I am throughout speaking of private persons. For if at the present time there exist any people's officers responsible for controlling the wilfulness of kings—like the ephors who were once set over against the kings of Sparta, or the tribunes against the consuls of Rome, or the demarchs against the senate of Athens; or perhaps, to take a modern example, any bodies with the powers now enjoyed in particular realms by the three estates assembled in full session—I am so far from forbidding them to intervene by virtue of their office against the raging licentiousness of kings that in my view any failure of theirs to prevent kings from violently oppressing and molesting their people amounts to wicked perfidy. They thus betray the people's liberty which, as they know, they have been appointed by God to safeguard.

However, to that obedience which I have shown to be due to the authority of rulers there is always one exception, and that a fundamental one. It must not seduce us from obedience to Him to whose will the desires of kings must be subject, to whose decrees their laws must give precedence, to whose majesty their symbols of power must bow. It would be absurd if in an endeavor to do right by man one found oneself doing wrong by Him for whose sake men ought to be done right by. The Lord is the king of kings . . . and if they command anything against Him, the matter is void. . . . Let us console ourselves with the thought that we truly display that obedience which God demands of us when we suffer anything rather than be turned away from righteousness. And that our purpose may not weaken, Paul offers yet another thought in aid (1 Cor. 7.23): that Christ has redeemed us at the great cost of His redemption so that we may not be servants to the corrupt desires of men, much less slaves of impiety.

# 61 / JOHN KNOX (1505-1572): THE REFORMATION IN SCOTLAND

*If Knox did not reform Scotland single-handed, he still stands out head and shoulders among the ministers and the self-seeking nobility who assisted him. In addition, in his* History of the Reformation in Scotland *(first published in 1584) he told the story, although modern scholarship is beginning to introduce some modifications. He began preaching the Reformation in 1547 (A), but for thirteen years, some of which he spent as a prisoner on the French galleys and some an exile in England and Geneva, the situation in Scotland was not propitious. Then, in 1558, Knox returned, and in two years of passionate preaching all over Scotland he broke the hold of the old Church. In 1560, assisted by English intervention and a party among the robber-barons who composed the Scottish aristocracy, he got the Parliament at Edinburgh to pass various measures introducing the Reformation (B). A good deal remained to be done; in particular, the presbyterian Church order, with which the Church of Scotland was to be so*

*generally identified, was not established without fierce struggles
with the monarchy.*[25]

## A. THE BEGINNINGS OF THE SCOTTISH REFORMATION

And so the next Sunday was appointed to the said John to express his mind in the public preaching place. Which day approaching, the said John took the text written in Daniel, the seventh chapter, beginning thus: "And another king shall rise after them, and he shall be unlike onto the first, and he shall subdue three kings, and shall speak words against the Most High, and think that he may change times and laws, and they shall be given into his hands, until a time, and times, and dividing of times."

1. In the beginning of his sermon, he showed the great love of God towards his Church, whom it pleaseth to forewarn of dangers to come so many years before they come to pass. 2. He briefly entreated[26] the estate of the Israelites, who then were in bondage in Babylon, for the most part; and made a short discourse of the four Empires, the Babylonian, the Persian, that of the Greeks, and the fourth of the Romans; in the destruction whereof, rose up that last Beast, which he affirmed to be the Roman Church: for to none other power that ever has yet been, do all the notes [of the Beast] that God has shown to the Prophet appertain, that such as are not more than blind, may clearly see them. 3. But before he began to open the corruptions of the Papistry, he defined the true Kirk, showed the true notes of it, whereupon it was built, why it was the pillar of verity, and why it could not err, to wit "Because it heard the voice of its own pastor, Jesus Christ, would not hear a stranger, neither yet would be carried about with every kind of doctrine."

Every one of these heads sufficiently declared, he entered to the contrary; and upon the notes given in his text, he showed that the Spirit of God in the New Testament gave to this king other names, to wit, "the Man of Sin," "the Antichrist," "the Whore of Babylon." He showed that this man of sin, or Antichrist, was not to be restrained to the person of any one man only, no more than by the fourth beast was to be understood the person of any one Emperor. But by such names the Spirit of God would forewarn his chosen of a body and a multitude, having a wicked head, which should not only be sinful himself, but

---

[25] Taken from John Knox, *History of the Reformation in Scotland,* ed. W. Croft Dickinson (Edinburgh: Thomas Nelson & Sons Ltd., 1949), Vol. 1, pp. 84–6, 338–9.

[26] treated of

that also should be occasion of sin to all that should be subject unto him (as Christ Jesus is cause of justice to all the members of his body); and is called the Antichrist, that is to say, one contrary to Christ, because that he is contrary to him in life, doctrine, laws, and subjects. And then began to decipher [27] the lives of divers Popes, and the lives of all the shavelings for the most part; their doctrine and laws he plainly proved to repugn directly to the doctrine and laws of God the Father, and of Christ Jesus His Son. This he proved by conferring [28] the doctrine of justification, expressed in the Scriptures, which teach that man is "justified by faith only"; "that the blood of Jesus Christ purges us from all our sins"; and the doctrine of the Papists which attributes justification to the works of the law, yea, to the works of man's invention, as pilgrimage, pardons, and other such baggage. That the papistical law repugned to the laws of the Evangel, he proved by the laws made of observation of days, abstaining from meats, and from marriage, which Christ Jesus made free; and the forbidding whereof, Saint Paul called "the doctrine of devils." In handling the notes of that Beast given in the text, he willed men to consider if these notes "There shall one arise unlike to the other, having a mouth speaking great things and blasphemous" could be applied to any other but to the Pope and his kingdom. For "if these (said he) be not great words and blasphemous: 'the Successor of Peter,' 'the Vicar of Christ,' 'the Head of the Kirk,' 'most holy,' 'most blessed,' 'that cannot err,' that 'may make right of wrong,' and wrong of right,' that 'of nothing, may make somewhat,' and that 'hath all verity in the shrine of his breast,' yea, 'that has power of all, and none power of him,' nay, 'not to say that he does wrong, although he draw ten thousand million of souls with himself to hell'; if these (said he) and many other, able to be shown in his own Canon Law, be not great and blasphemous words, and such as never mortal man spake before, let the world judge. And yet (said he) is there one most evident of all, to wit, John, in his Revelation, says, 'That the merchandise of that Babylonian harlot, amongst other things, shall be the bodies and souls of men.' Now, let the very Papist themselves judge, if ever any before them took upon them power to relax the pains of them that were in Purgatory, as they affirm to the people that daily they do, by the merits of their Mass, and of their other trifles." In the end he said, "If any here (and there were present Master John Mair, the University, the Subprior, and many Canons, with some friars of both the orders), that will say, That I have alleged Scripture, doctor, or history, otherwise than it is written, let them come unto me with sufficient witness, and by con-

[27] analyse
[28] comparing

ference I shall let them see, not only the original where my testimonies are written, but I shall prove that the writers meant as I have spoken."

Of this sermon, which was the first that ever John Knox made in public, were divers bruits.[29] Some said, "Others sned [30] the branches of the Papistry, but he strikes at the root, to destroy the whole." Others said, "If the doctors, and *Magistri nostri*, defend not now the Pope and his authority, which in their own presence is so manifestly impugned, the Devil have my part of him, and of his laws both." Others said, "Master George Wishart [31] spake never so plainly, and yet he was burnt: even so will he be." In the end, other said, "The tyranny of the Cardinal [32] made not his cause the better, neither yet the suffering of God's servant made his cause the worse. And therefore we would counsel you and them, to provide better defences than fire and sword; for it may be that else ye will be disappointed; men now have other eyes than they had then." . . .

## B. THE TRIUMPH OF PROTESTANTISM IN SCOTLAND

Our Confession was publicly read, first in audience of the Lords of Articles, and after in audience of the whole Parliament; where were present, not only such as professed Christ Jesus, but also a great number of the adversaries of our religion, such as the forenamed Bishops, and some others of the Temporal Estate, who were commanded in God's name to object, if they could, any thing against that doctrine. Some of our Ministers were present, standing upon their feet, ready to have answered, in case any would have defended the Papistry, and impugned our affirmatives: but while that no objection was made, there was a day appointed to voting in that and other heads. Our Confession was read, every article by itself, over again, as they were written in order, and the votes of every man were required accordingly. Of the Temporal Estate, only voted in the contrary the Earl of Atholl, the Lords Somerville and Borthwick; and yet for their dissenting they produced no better reason, but, "We will believe as our fathers believed." The Bishops (papistical, we mean) spake nothing. The rest of the whole three Estates by their public votes affirmed the doctrine; and many, the rather, would nor durst say nothing in the contrary; for this was the vote of the Earl Marischal—"It is long since I have had some favour unto the truth, and since that I have had a

[29] rumours
[30] lopped
[31] Scottish reformer and martyr (1514–46)
[32] Cardinal Beaton, regent of Scotland, murdered in 1546

suspicion of the Papistical religion; but, I praise my God, this day has fully resolved me in the one and the other. For seeing that my Lords Bishops who, for their learning can, and for the zeal that they bear to the verity would, as I suppose, gainsay anything that directly repugns to the verity of God; seeing, I say, my Lords Bishops here present speak nothing in the contrary of the doctrine proponed, I cannot but hold it the very truth of God, and the contrary to the deceivable doctrine. And therefore, as far as in me lies, I approve the one and damn the other: And do further ask of God that not only I, but also all my posterity, may enjoy the comfort of the doctrine that this day our ears have heard. And yet more, I must vote, as it were, by way of protestation, that if any persons ecclesiastical shall after this oppose themselves to this our Confession, that they have no place nor credit, considering that they, having long advisement [33] and full knowledge of this our Confession, none is now found in lawful, free, and quiet Parliament to oppose themselves to that which we profess: And therefore, if any of this generation pretend to do it after this, I protest he be reputed rather one that loves his own commodity and the glory of the world than the truth of God and the salvation of men's souls."

After the voting and ratification of this our Confession by the whole body of the Parliament, there were also pronounced two Acts, the one against the Mass and the abuse of the Sacrament, and the other against the Supremacy of the Pope. . . .

# 62 / WILLIAM PERKINS (1558-1602): ON PREDESTINATION

*A fellow of Christ's College, Cambridge, Perkins enjoyed in his lifetime, and for long after, a great reputation as a theologian, teacher, and preacher. He was one of the strongest influences of his day on students at the university, a shining light among the powerful Cambridge Puritans. An uncompromising Calvinist, he gave a clear-cut and lucid account of the doctrine of predestination as it was generally held among Calvin's sixteenth- and seventeenth-century followers in his* A Golden Chain, or Description of

---

[33] notice

Theology *(1590), a book which found many readers and general approval also outside England.*[34]

God's decree inasmuch as it concerns man is called predestination: which is the decree of God by which he has ordained all men to a certain and everlasting estate, either to salvation or condemnation, for His own glory. . . . The means of accomplishing God's predestination are twofold: the creation and the fall.

The creation is that by which God made all things very good, of nothing, that is of no matter which was before the creation. . . .

Adam's fall was his willing revolting to disobedience by eating the forbidden fruit. . . . Without constraint, they willingly fell from their integrity, God upon just causes leaving them to themselves and freely suffering them to fall. For we must not think that man's fall was either by chance, or God not knowing it, or barely winking at it, or by his bare permission, or against his will; but rather miraculously, not without the will of God but yet without all approbation of it. . . . Out of this corrupt estate of our first parents arose the estate of infidelity or unbelief whereby God has included all men under' sin that He might manifest His mercy in the salvation of some and His justice in the condemnation of others. . . .

Predestination has two parts: election and reprobation. . . . Election is God's decree whereby on His own free will He has ordained certain men to salvation. . . . There appertain three things to the execution of this decree. First the foundation, secondly the means, thirdly the degrees.

The foundation is Christ Jesus, called of His Father from all eternity to perform the office of the mediator that in Him all those which should be saved might be chosen. . . .

After the foundation . . . it follows that we should treat of the outward means of the same. The means are God's covenant and the seals thereof. God's covenant is His contract with man concerning life eternal, upon certain conditions. This covenant consists of two parts: God's promise to man, man's promise to God. God's promise to man is that whereby He binds Himself to man to be his God, if he break not the condition. Man's promise to God is that whereby he vows his allegiance unto his Lord and to perform the condition between them. Again, there are two kinds of this covenant: the covenant of works and the covenant of grace. . . . The covenant of works . . . is expressed in the moral law. . . . The covenant of grace is that whereby

---

[34] From Perkins' *Works* (Cambridge, 1600), pp. 10 ff. The many scriptural citations are omitted.

God, freely promising Christ and his benefits, exacts again from man that he would by faith receive Christ and repent of his sins. . . .

The declaration of God's love in those of years of discretion has especially four degrees.

The first degree is an effectual calling whereby a sinner, being severed from the world, is entertained into God's family. Of this there be two parts. The first is election which is a separation of a sinner from the cursed estate of all mankind. The second is the reciprocal donation or free gift of God the Father whereby He bestows the sinful man to be saved upon Christ, and Christ again actually and most effectually upon that sinful man, so that he may boldly say this thing, namely "Christ, both God and man, is mine, and I, for my benefit and use, enjoy the same." . . .

The second degree is justification, whereby such as believe are accounted just before God, through the obedience of Christ Jesus. . . .

The third degree is sanctification, whereby such as believe, being delivered from the tyranny of sin, are by little and little renewed in holiness and righteousness. . . . Sanctification has two parts, mortification and vivification. The mortification of sin is the first part of sanctification, whereby the power of sin is abated and crucified in the faithful. The means that works mortification is the death and burial of Christ. . . . Vivification is the second part of sanctification whereby inherent holiness, being begun, is still augmented and enlarged. . . . The preservative of vivification is a virtue derived from Christ's resurrection to those that are quickened, which makes them to rise up to newness of life. . . .

The fourth degree of the declaration of God's love is glorification. Glorification is the perfect transforming of the saints into the image of the Son of God. . . . The beginning of glorification is in death, but it is not accomplished and made perfect before the last day of judgment. The death of the elect is but a sleep in Christ, whereby the body and soul is severed. The body that after corruption it may rise to greater glory; the soul that it, being fully sanctified, may immediately after departure from the body be transported into the kingdom of heaven. . . .

Thus much shall suffice for the decree of election; now follows the decree of reprobation. The decree of reprobation is that part of predestination whereby God, according to the most free and just purpose of His will has determined to reject certain men unto eternal destruction and misery, and that to the praise of His justice. . . .

In the executing of this decree there is to be considered the foundation or beginning, and the degrees proceeding thereof. The foundation of executing the decree of reprobation is the fall of Adam. . . . Whom

God rejects to condemnation, those He hates; this hatred of God is whereby he detests and abhors the reprobate when he is fallen into sin, for the same sin. . . .

Reprobates are of two sorts: they that are called (namely, by an ineffectual calling), and they that are not called.

In the reprobates which are called, the execution of the decree of reprobation has three degrees, to wit, an acknowledgment of God's calling, a falling away again, and condemnation.

The acknowledgment of God's calling is whereby the reprobates for a time do subject themselves to the calling of God, which calling is wrought by the preaching of the Word. And of this calling there are five other degrees. The first is enlightening of their minds whereby they are instructed of the Holy Ghost to the understanding and knowledge of the Word. The second is a certain penitence. . . . The third degree is a temporary faith whereby the reprobate does confusedly believe the promises of God made in Christ; I say confusedly, because he believes that some shall be saved but he believes not that he himself particularly shall be saved. . . . neither does he so much as conceive any purpose, desire, or endeavour to apply the same or any wrestling or striving against security or carelessness or distrust. . . . The fourth is a tasting of heavenly gifts, as of justification, and sanctification, and of the virtues of the world to come. . . . The fifth degree is the outward holiness of life for a time, under which is comprehended a zeal in the profession of religion, a reverence and fear towards God's ministers, and amendments of life in many things. . . .

The second degree of the execution of God's counsel of reprobation . . . is a falling away again. . . . First the reprobate is deceived by some sin. Secondly his heart is hardened by the same sin. Thirdly, his heart being hardened, it becomes wicked and perverse. Fourthly, then follows his incredulity and unbelief. . . . Fifthly, an apostasy or falling away from faith in Christ does immediately follow this unbelief. . . .

The third degree is damnation whereby the reprobates are delivered up to eternal punishment. The execution of damnation begins in death and is finished in the last judgment.

The execution of the degree of reprobation in infidels which are not called is this: First, they have by nature ignorance and vanity of mind. After that follows hardness of heart whereby they become void of all sorrow for their sins. Then comes a reprobate sense which is when the natural light of reason, and of the judgment of good and evil, is extinguished. Afterward, when the heart ceases to sorrow there arises a committing of sin with greediness. Then comes pollution, which is the fullness of sin. Lastly, a just reward is given to all these, to wit, fearful condemnation. . . .

# 63 / COMMENT:
# HEINRICH BOEHMER
# (1869-1927) ON LUTHER

*Heinrich Boehmer, a German Protestant theologian and Church historian, devoted himself to an oddly assorted pair of subjects—Luther and Loyola—on both of whom he wrote dispassionate history.*[35]

It is still commonly asserted that his outward and inward isolation, growing steadily through the years, naturally resulted from the reformer's unmeasured violence and his polemical excesses. But his generation was not so sensitively constructed. It did not feel the wounds struck by Dr. Martin's "pig-spear" nearly so much as the "pin and bodkin pricks" of Master Philip [Melanchthon], or the poisonous irony of Erasmus, or the mocking superiority of Erasmus' pupil, Zwingli. The cause lies deeper, not in the reformer's passions but in his obstinacy and in the crippling influence which medieval moods and ideas in some measure continued to exercise on his thought even after he broke with the old Church. How much that influence could at times obscure his clear insight into what was right, how that quality in him could seduce him into obstinately adhering to false views, is apparent in the story of Philip of Hesse's matrimonial involvements. Even more clearly it shows up in his behavior during the quarrel over the eucharist. It is often said that he was never greater than in that hour of decision in Marburg Castle when he refused Zwingli's proffered hand. And this is true. At hardly any other moment of his life does the foremost strength of his soul, the ultimate cause of his historic success, become so manifest: I mean that unconditional surrender to truth and conscience which made it simply impossible for him ever to do anything contrary to conscience for the sake of political or other surface advantages. But no other moment also so clearly demonstrates the fatal weakness which inwardly alienated from him precisely the ablest and most intelligent of his spiritual sons. That weakness did not lie in the difficulty he had in entering the mind of Zwingli, or any alien mind for that matter. For, as he rightly felt, Zwingli's "spirit" really was different. He was willing to make pretended concessions in

---

[35] This passage translated from Heinrich Boehmer, *Luther im Lichte der neueren Forschung* (*Luther in the Light of Recent Research*), 4th ed. (Leipzig, 1917), pp. 203–5, 227.

matters of doctrine in order to gain political advantage. . . . It is quite true that the disagreement over the Lord's Supper hid a profound difference in religious attitudes of which both Luther and Zwingli were equally aware. Zwingli's Christianity bore a markedly moralistic and intellectual stamp; with Luther, religion predominated. Like all the great Christians . . . he felt the inner need to realise personal communion with his Lord and Master not only with his mind, but truly to live it, and to live it in the sacrament. Zwingli simply did not understand this need. Calvin (as Luther immediately recognised) not only understood it, but felt it himself and tried to provide for it in a new way by his teaching on the eucharist. Luther chose another way. He developed no new doctrine, but in order to resist the sacramentarians and anabaptists he went back to the old scholastic theories; in the heat of the battle, he so stubbornly dug himself in among those antiquated doctrines, which entirely failed to fit his new fundamental religious views, that his theology acquired a genuinely medieval air, a touch of the old naturalistic conception of the nature of grace as efficacious in the performance of certain material acts. His refusal to see or admit this error was fateful for himself and for the future of his life's work, for thereby he repelled the boldest, freest, and most pious spirits of his time. . . .

The recognition that religion is a state of mind which can be called forth and nourished only by spiritually operating means, that is Luther's most fruitful discovery. For all his other later discoveries— the abolition of "other-worldly asceticism," the destruction of the Catholic doctrine of the sacraments, etc.—follow logically from that first and fundamental principle. Three of these consequences had particular importance for the future. Firstly, the recognition that there is only one way to knowledge of God and communion with God, the way of faith. This invalidated the whole traditional complex of theology; at the same time, the neoplatonic mysticism which had hitherto played so large a role also in private devotion was deprived of its reason for existence. Secondly, the recognition that there is only one manner of worshipping God, namely faith; faith seen on the one hand as trust in God's merciful love for sinners, on the other as a living and bold confidence in the gracious guidance and providence of God which makes all things work together for man's good. This destroys the value of the whole traditional system of divine worship with its enormous sacramental and hierarchical apparatus. What remains of divine service is not worship in the technical sense, but only a kind of instructive performance for the edification and education of the congregation. Thirdly, since religion is an attitude of the heart which can be at work at any time and in any condition of life, it is vain to believe that man should flee and withdraw from the world. Rather, God has put man in the world so that he may overcome the world in the world, in that station to which providence has assigned him. Not the cloister, therefore, but the ordinary occupation or calling is the usual place for proving faith and love of one's neighbor. Of course, a mere devotion to one's calling does not by itself fulfil the moral ideal. It does so only if it springs from obedience to the will of God, revealed in the natural order of society, and if the calling is treated as a means of serving one's neighbor in self-denying love. . . .

# 64 / COMMENT:
# G. R. ELTON (B. 1921)
# ON THE REFORMATION [36]

The "age" of the Reformation should be defined as that period during which the new Churches were on the offensive. It therefore begins properly (and traditionally) with the date of Luther's ninety-five theses (1517) and extends in general to the later 1550's. . . . In those forty years the Reformation achieved an extraordinary spread, both rapid and wide. No part of western Christendom remained altogether unaffected by it, even though Spain, and Italy to a smaller degree, managed a measure of aloofness. Elsewhere Protestantism in one of its forms grew overnight from the fervour of a few preachers into a wide and popular movement. What gave it so general an appeal remains up to a point uncertain: no one today would be willing to list "the causes" of the Reformation. So complex a phenomenon sprang from so many things that only a general analysis of some hundred years of history comes near to answering the question. There existed a widespread dislike of the clergy, which played its part; often it went with hostility to Rome and with fervent nationalism. Greed and envy no doubt entered into it, as did policy. But that the reformers' message answered a savage spiritual thirst, which the official Church (not for the first time in its history) was failing to satisfy, cannot be denied; nor can the fact that the stages reached by the Reformation itself did not always content all those who had looked to it for nourishment, so that extremist groups soon began to develop by the side of the more acceptable revolutionaries. The preachers of the Reformation did not

[36] From the Introduction to *The New Cambridge Modern History*, Vol. 2, *The Reformation*, ed. G. R. Elton (Cambridge: Cambridge University Press, 1958), pp. 2–6. By permission of Cambridge University Press.

need political support to attract followers wherever they went, however necessary such support may have proved in the consolidation which followed the first prophetic onrush. It must never be forgotten that in its beginning and in much of its essence the Reformation was a movement of the spirit with a religious message.

On the other hand—and this should be stressed—the Reformation was not a movement for liberty, except in a very specialised sense. Protestantism in all its forms came to reject one particular authority— that of the Church and the popes—but nearly all its forms substituted some other authority and avoided the thoroughgoing individualism which has at times been associated with the movement. The Bible formed the overriding authority, its interpretation carried out by attention to the text itself without the intervention of the mediating Church. The results were naturally very mixed, ranging from a genuine recovery of the Christian message to all the absurdities associated with a rigorous and uncomprehending fundamentalism. In politics, the leading reformers tended to support the secular arm; though Luther was not the subservient tool of princes and enemy of the people that he is sometimes made out to be (with quotations from his writings against the peasants), he, like most Protestants, had a healthy respect for the magistrate provided he was godly. Perhaps the last liberty to be promoted by the Reformation in the sixteenth century was that of the mind. Movements of missionary passion are not given to tolerance and scepticism, nor do they provoke such reaction in those they attack; among the first victims of this new age of religious controversy were the spirit of free enquiry and the patience extended to the nonconformist. Luther could be highly obscurantist at the expense of intellectuals of Erasmus's type; the fate of the so-called Catholic reformers of Italy shows how under the pressure of the great heresies toleration of reasonable diversity changed into fierce hostility; Thomas More developed from the speculative humanist of *Utopia* (1516) into the persecuting lord chancellor of 1530.

The age was passionate, partisan and narrow. In trying to assess its achievements fairly it does not help that the passions of a time of conflict tend to baffle understanding when the content of the conflict has gone. It is sometimes argued that the twentieth century, familiar with ideological struggles and persecution, should—and does—comprehend the sixteenth century from a fullness of knowledge. It is, however, fatal to overlook the differences between secular ideologies and transcendental religion, concentrating only on their likenesses; the result (seen too often) is to read the twentieth century into the sixteenth. In some ways the Reformation is more remote from the present day than the century or so that had preceded it. The fundamental intellectual attitude of the Reformation involved the doctrine of a decline from an ideal in the past and a devoted attachment to theology and ecclesiology at the expense of other studies; neither of these is a characteristic element in Western thought after 1700. Admittedly it will be well to remember that besides the stream directly issuing from the Reformation there flowed a sizeable river of writings concerned with secular things and increasingly "scientific" in its methods of analysis and interpretation. As one might expect, there are both traces of established modes of thinking and faint hints of great changes to come. Substantially, however, the Reformation was conservative—even backward-looking—in thought: since it was avowedly intent on restoring a lost condition, it could hardly be anything else.

The desire for spiritual nourishment was great in many parts of Europe, and movements of thought which gave intellectual content to what was in many ways an inchoate search for God have their own dignity. Neither of these, however, comes first in explaining why the Reformation took root here and vanished there—why, in fact, this complex of anti-papal "heresies" led to a permanent division within the Church that had looked to Rome. This particular place is occupied by politics and the play of secular ambitions. In short, the Reformation maintained itself wherever the lay power (prince or magistrates) favoured it; it could not survive where the authorities decided to suppress it. Scandinavia, the German principalities, Geneva, in its own peculiar way also England, demonstrate the first; Spain, Italy, the Habsburg lands in the east, and also (though not as yet conclusively) France, the second. The famous phrase behind the settlement of 1555—*cuius regio eius religio*—was a practical commonplace long before anyone put it into words. For this was the age of uniformity, an age which held at all times and everywhere that one political unit could not comprehend within itself two forms of belief or worship.

The tenet rested on simple fact: as long as membership of a secular polity involved membership of an ecclesiastical organisation, religious dissent stood equal to political disaffection and even treason. Hence governments enforced uniformity, and hence the religion of the ruler was that of his country. England provided the extreme example of this doctrine in action, with its rapid official switches from Henrician Catholicism without the pope, through Edwardian Protestantism on the Swiss model and Marian papalism, to Elizabethan Protestantism of a more specifically English brand. But other countries fared similarly. Nor need this cause distress or annoyed disbelief. Princes and governments, no more than the governed, do not act from unmixed motives, and to ignore the spiritual factor in the conversion of at least some princes is as false as to see nothing but purity in the desires of the populace. The Reformation was successful beyond the dreams of earlier, potentially similar, movements not so much because (as the phrase goes) the time was ripe for it, but rather because it found favour with the secular arm. Desire for Church lands, resistance to imperial and papal claims, the ambition to create self-contained and independent states, all played their part in this, but so quite often did a genuine attachment to the teachings of the reformers.

There was, however, one aspect of the Reformation which owed nothing to princes and little to the great reformers, a truly popular and very widespread movement to which it became customary to attach the name of Anabaptism. The so-called Anabaptists turn up in many places and guises, a convenient term covering a motley collection of beliefs which range from mad millenarianism to pietism, from the reckless use of force to pacifism, from the extremes of personal egotism to humble piety and devotion. All these men and women have one thing in common: they do not fit in with any of the established religions and thus offend the principle of uniformity wherever they go. But the persecution which they so regularly encountered arose from yet another shared quality: the movement spread among the lower orders. It contained strong elements of social protest and (or so it was thought) danger of revolution. . . . We shall not go far wrong if we see in the protean spread of Anabaptist and similar doctrines a sign of the age-old, usually obscure, social antagonism to the powers that be, an antagonism to which the Reformation, by producing an upheaval in the higher reaches of the social order, gave a chance of coming into the open. . . .

# VI / ENGLAND AND THE CHURCH OF ENGLAND

*The English Reformation started and progressed in a manner all its own. Its inception lay in politics—in Henry VIII's (1509–47) matrimonial difficulties and the political solution propounded and carried through (1529–36) by Thomas Cromwell. This left a national church, subject to the king as supreme head in the pope's place, but otherwise essentially unaltered in constitution or doctrine.*

*However, this revolution harbored the elements of two further changes. One lay in the fact that although the king seemed absolute in the church, he was limited in the state by Parliament and the law. Since the Church of England embodied a concept of state and church as simply two different manifestations of the same society and people (see No. 7), such a situation could not endure. By 1558 the royal supremacy had admitted Parliament to a form of partnership. Elizabeth's personal use of her monarchic powers and the absolute ambitions of the early Stuarts allowed the development of a constitutional conflict over the place and powers of Parliament, and this was one of the two main issues in the civil war which broke out in 1642 and led to the temporary abolition of the monarchy (1649–60).*

*The second problem raised by the Henrician Reformation was whether an antipapal church could remain Catholic in dogma. The reign of Edward VI (1547–53) replied by introducing the Protestant Reformation, and, despite an attempted reaction back to Rome under Mary I (1553–8), that answer was confirmed by the Elizabethan Settlement of 1559. However, the church then set up was insufficiently reformed in the opinion of the growing number of English Puritans, so called because they wished to purify it of popish practices. These dissidents, both clergy and laity, represented various degrees of extremism, some objecting only to details, some (presbyterians) wanting to abolish government by bishops, some (sectarian separatists) denying the need for a national church altogether. The fortunes of Puritanism went up and down, until the violent repression by Archbishop William Laud in the 1630's sealed the long-standing alliance between Puritan and Parliamentary oppositions. Puritan hostility to the established church was the second main issue in the civil war.*

*Thus, without debating the vexed question of what social and economic stresses (if any) underlay the civil war, one can see how its chief issues developed naturally enough from the history of the English Reformation. The war itself released a spate of political and religious speculation, with many democratic and sectarian notions current but never triumphant. The Church of England always meant to be comprehensive and tolerant of minor differences; it got into serious danger only when either of its wings— the high, ritualistic, Catholic stream, or the low, evangelical, Calvinist groups—tried to capture the whole structure for itself. After the civil war and Puritan domination (1640–60), internal tolerance was gradually augmented by permitting nonconformist bodies to exist outside the church.*

# 65 / THOMAS CROMWELL (1485?-1540): A NATIONAL CHURCH

*Cromwell, a man of low origin who reached high office by the use of a superb intelligence and great executive gifts, entered Henry VIII's service in 1530 after the fall of his previous master, Cardinal Wolsey. From 1532 until his own fall and execution in 1540, he dominated the King's government and policy. It is reasonably certain that he introduced the ideas which underlay the establishment of the royal supremacy and expulsion of the pope from England, and that he proved to Henry VIII the advantages to be gained from cooperating with the nation represented in Parliament. Thus the reformed English state retained*

*the medieval constitutionalism (adapted to new ways) which was
in full retreat in the continental monarchies. Cromwell was no
writer, but his ideas emerge from the preambles of the parliamentary statutes which he drafted. The preambles of the 1533
Act Against Appeals to Rome (A) and the 1534 Dispensations Act
(B) show something of what he thought about the nature of
church and state and about the sovereignty of Parliament.[1] One
of his many addresses to the bishops of the Church (a circular
letter enclosing a formal royal directive) shows something of his
mind touching Church and state—his search for the "middle way"
in religion, and his interpretation of the duties of his office.[2]*

## A. ACT AGAINST APPEALS TO ROME

Where by divers sundry old authentic histories and chronicles it
is manifestly declared and expressed that this realm of England is an
Empire, and so has been accepted in the world, governed by one
supreme head and king having the dignity and royal estate of the
imperial crown of the same, unto whom a body politic, compact of all
sorts and degrees of people divided in terms and by names of spiritualty and temporality, be bound and owe to bear next to God a
natural and humble obedience; he being also institute and furnished by
the goodness and sufferance of Almighty God with plenary, whole and
entire power, preeminence, authority, prerogative and jurisdiction to
render and yield justice and final determination to all manner of folk
residents or subjects within this realm, in all causes, matters, debates
and contentions happening to occur, insurge or begin within the limits
thereof, without restraint or provocation [3] to any foreign princes or
potentates of the world; the body spiritual whereof having power
when any cause of the law divine happened to come into question
or of spiritual learning, then it was declared, interpreted and showed
by that part of the said body politic called the spiritualty, now being
usually called the English Church, which always has been reputed
and also found of that sort that both for knowledge, integrity and
sufficiency of number, it has been always thought and is also at this
hour sufficient and meet of itself, without the intermeddling of any
exterior person or persons, to declare and determine all such doubts
and to administer all such offices and duties as to their rooms spiritual
does appertain. For the due administration whereof and to keep them

---

[1] From *Statutes of the Realm* (London, 1810–28), Vol. 3, pp. 427, 464.

[2] From R. B. Merriman, *The Life and Letters of Thomas Cromwell* (Oxford, 1902), pp. ii, 111–13.

[3] appeal to another court, or calling up of a case into that court

from corruption and sinister affection, the king's most noble progenitors, and the antecessors of the nobles of this realm, have sufficiently endowed the said Church both with honour and possession. And the laws temporal for trial of property of lands and goods, and for the conservation of the people of this realm in unity and peace without ravin or spoil, was and yet is administered, judged and executed by sundry judges and administrators of the other part of the said body politic called the temporalty, and both their authorities and jurisdictions do conjoin together in the due administration of justice, the one to help the other. . . .

## B. DISPENSATIONS ACT

Most humbly beseech your most royal majesty your obedient and faithful subjects, the Commons of this your present Parliament assembled . . . that where your subjects of this your realm . . . by many years past have been and yet be greatly decayed and impoverished by such intolerable exactions of great sums of money as have been claimed and taken and yet continually be claimed to be taken out of this your realm . . . by the bishop of Rome, called the pope . . . in pensions, censes,[4] Peter's Pence [etc.] . . . and also for dispensations, licences [etc.] . . . which matter has been usurped and practised by him and his predecessors by many years in great derogation of your imperial crown and authority royal, contrary to right and conscience. For where this your grace's realm, recognising no superior under God but only your grace, has been and is free from subjection to any man's laws but only to such as have been devised, made and ordained within this realm . . . or to such other as by sufferance of your grace and your progenitors the people of this your realm have taken at their free liberty by their own consent to be used amongst them, and have bound themselves by long use and custom to the observance of the same . . . it stands therefore with natural equity and good reason that in all and every such laws human, made within this realm or induced into this realm by the said sufferance, consents and customs, your royal majesty and your Lords spiritual and temporal and Commons, representing the whole state of your realm in this your most high court of Parliament, have full power and authority not only to dispense but also to authorise some elect person or persons to dispense with those and all other human laws of this your realm and with every one of them . . . ; and also the said laws and every of them to abrogate, annul, amplify or diminish. . . .

[4] taxes

## C. CIRCULAR TO BISHOPS (1536)

After my right hearty commendations to your lordship. Ye shall herewith receive the king's highness' letters addressed unto you, to put you in remembrance of his highness' travails and your duty touching order to be taken for preaching, to the intent the people may be taught the truth and yet not charged at the beginning with over many novelties, the publication whereof, unless the same be tempered with much wisdom, do rather breed contention, division and contrariety in opinion in the unlearned multitude than either edify, or remove from them and out of their hearts such abuses as by the corrupt and unsavoury teaching of the bishop of Rome and his disciples have crept in the same. The effect of which letters, albeit I doubt not but as well for the honesty of the matter as for your own discharge ye will so consider and put in execution as shall be to his grace's satisfaction in that behalf, yet forasmuch as it has pleased his majesty to appoint and constitute me in the room and place of his supreme and principal minister in all matters that may touch any thing his clergy or their doings, I thought it also my part for the exoneration of my duty towards his highness, and the rather to answer to his grace's expectation, opinion and trust conceived in me and in that (amongst other) committed to my fidelity, to desire and pray you in such substantial sort and manner to travail in the execution of the contents of his grace's said letters: namely for avoiding of contrariety in preaching of the pronunciation of novelties without wise and discreet qualification, and the repression of the temerity of those that either privily or apertly,[5] directly or indirectly, would advance the pretended authority of the bishop of Rome. As I be not for my discharge both enforced to complain further and to declare what I have now written unto you for that purpose, and so to charge you with your own fault and to devise such remedy for the same as shall appertain. Desiring your lordship to accept my meaning herein tending only to an honest, friendly and Christian reformation for avoiding of further inconvenience, and to think no unkindness though in this matter, wherein it is almost more than time to speak, I write frankly— compelled and enforced thereunto both in respect of my private duty, and otherwise for my discharge, forasmuch as it pleaseth his majesty to use me in the lieu [6] of a councillor, whose office is as an eye to the prince, to foresee and in time to provide remedy for such abuses, enormities and inconveniences as might else, with a little sufferance,

[5] secretly or openly
[6] place

engender more evil in his public weal than could after be redubbed [7] with much labour, study, diligence and travail. And thus most heartily fare you well.

# 66 / HENRY VIII (1491-1547): SPEECH TO THE PARLIAMENT OF 1545

*The Henrician Reformation, contrary to the King's conservative instincts and cautious desire for peace in the realm, naturally and under continental influences unleashed plenty of theological debate. Though Henry tried to avoid change, he steered in fact a somewhat erratic course between the parties. His real desire was for an end to disputes which he ascribed to wilfulness, as in this speech to his last Parliament. The mixture of fatherly cajolery and reproof with majestic threats was very typical of the man, and the concern for peace and unity totally typical of Tudor governments. Appeals for concord continued throughout the upheavals produced by the Reformation.* [8]

Although my chancellor for the time being has before this used very eloquently and substantially to make answer to such orations as has been set forth in this high court of Parliament, yet is he not so able to open and set forth my mind and meaning and the secrets of my heart, in so plain and ample manner as I myself am and can do. Wherefore I, taking upon me to answer your eloquent oration, Master Speaker, say that where you, in the name of our well beloved Commons have both praised and extolled me, for the notable qualities that you have conceived to be in me, I most heartily thank you all that you have put me in remembrance of my duty: which is to endeavour myself to obtain and get such excellent qualities and necessary virtues as a prince or governor should or ought to have. Of which gifts I recognise myself both bare and barren. But of such small qualities as God has endued me withal, I render to His goodness my most humble thanks, intending with all my wit and diligence to get and acquire to

[7] recovered from
[8] From Edward Hall, *Chronicle*, first published 1548 (London, 1809), pp. 864–6.

me such notable virtues and princely qualities as you have alleged to be incorporate in my person.

These thanks for your loving admonition and good counsel first remembered, I . . . thank you again because that you, considering our great charges (not for our pleasure but for your defence, not for our gain but to our great cost) which we have lately sustained . . . have freely of your own mind granted to us a certain subsidy,[9] here in an act specified, which verily we take in good part, regarding more your kindness than the profit thereof, as he that sets more by your loving hearts than by your substance. Beside this hearty kindness, I cannot a little rejoice when I consider the perfect trust and sure confidence which you have put in me, as men having undoubted hope and unfeigned belief in my doings and just proceedings, for you (without my desire or request) have committed to my order and disposition all chantries,[10] colleges, hospitals and other places specified in a certain act, firmly trusting that I will order them to the glory of God and the profit of the commonwealth. . . .

Now since I find such kindness on your part towards me, I cannot choose but love and favour you, affirming that no prince in the world more favours his subjects than I do, nor no subjects or commons more love and obey their sovereign lord than I perceive you do me; for whose defence my treasure shall not be hidden, nor if necessity requires my person shall not be unadventured. Yet although I with you, and you with me, be in this perfect love and concord, this friendly amity cannot continue except both you, my lords temporal, and you my lords spiritual, and you, my loving subjects, study and take pain to amend one thing which surely is amiss and far out of order, to the which I most heartily require you; which is that charity and concord is not amongst you, but discord and dissension bears rule in every place. St. Paul says to the Corinthians, in the thirteenth chapter, "Charity is gentle, Charity is not envious, Charity is not proud," and so forth in the said chapter. Behold then what love and charity is amongst you when the one calls the other heretic and anabaptist, and he calls him again[11] papist, hypocrite and pharisee. Be these tokens of charity amongst you? Are these the signs of fraternal love between you? No, no, I assure you that this lack of charity amongst yourselves will be the hindrance and assuaging[12] of the fervent love between us, as I said before, except this would be saved and clear made whole. I

[9] a direct tax, which could only be levied by consent of Parliament

[10] small religious foundations. The institutions mentioned were dissolved by statute in this session of Parliament and their lands transferred to the Crown.

[11] in return

[12] lessening

must needs judge the fault and occasion of this discord to be partly by negligence of you, the fathers and preachers of the spiritualty. For if I know a man which lives in adultery, I must judge him a lecherous and a carnal person; if I see a man boast and brag himself, I cannot but deem him a proud man. I see and hear daily that you of the clergy preach one against another, each one contrary to another, inveigh one against another without charity or discretion. Some be too stiff in their old *mumpsimus;* others be too busy and curious in their new *sumpsimus.*[13] Thus all men almost be in variety and discord, and few or none preach truly and sincerely the word of God, according as they ought to do. Shall I now judge you charitable persons doing this? No, no, I cannot so do. Alas, how can the poor souls live in concord when you preachers sow amongst them in your sermons debate and discord! Of you they look for light, and you bring them darkness. Amend these crimes, I exhort you, and set forth God's word, both by true preaching and good example-giving, or else I, whom God has appointed his vicar and high minister here, will see these divisions extinct and these enormities corrected, according to my very duty; or else I am an unprofitable servant and untrue officer.

Although, as I say, the spiritual men be in some fault that charity is not kept amongst you, yet you of the temporalty be not clean and unspotted of malice and envy. For you rail on bishops, speak slanderously of priests, and rebuke and taunt preachers, both contrary to good order and Christian fraternity. If you know surely that a bishop or preacher errs or teaches perverse doctrine, come and declare it to some of our Council or to us to whom is committed by God the high authority to reform and order such causes and behaviours; and be not judges yourselves of your own fantastical opinions and vain expositions; for in such high causes you may lightly err. And although you be permitted to read Holy Scripture and to have the Word of God in your mother-tongue, you must understand that it is licensed you so to do only to inform your own conscience and to instruct your children and family, and not to dispute and make Scripture a railing and a taunting stock against priests and preachers, as many light persons do. I am very sorry to know and hear how unreverently that most precious jewel, the Word of God, is disputed, rhymed, sung and jangled in every alehouse and tavern, contrary to the true meaning and doctrine of the same. And yet I am even as much sorry that the readers of the same follow it in doing so faintly and coldly; for of this I am sure that charity was never so faint amongst you, and virtuous and godly living was never less used, nor God himself amongst Chris-

---

[13] cant terms for adherents to the conservative and reformist lines in religion

tians was never less reverenced, honoured or served. Therefore, as I said before, be in charity one with another like brother and brother; love, dread and serve God, to the which I as your supreme head and sovereign lord exhort and require you; and then I doubt not but that love and league that I spoke of in the beginning shall never be dissolved or broken between us. . . .

# 67 / RICHARD BANCROFT (1544-1610): THE OPINIONS AND DEALINGS OF THE PRECISIANS (C. 1584)

*A Cambridge scholar and career ecclesiastic, Bancroft came to prominence as an opponent of the Puritans (also sometimes called precisians) in the Church of England; when more energetic repression began with the appointment of Archbishop John Whitgift (1583–1604), Bancroft became his chief assistant in enforcing uniformity. Bishop of London from 1597, he eventually succeeded Whitgift at Canterbury. Unlike the strictly Calvinist Whitgift, Bancroft leant to a less austere theology and represented the first revival of "high" views which was to culminate with William Laud. This document belongs to his anti-Puritan campaign; it summarizes a wide variety of Puritan objections to the Church in a typical mixture of the trivial and fundamental.*[14]

Imprimis, that in matters touching ceremonies, discipline, and government it is not sufficient the laws be not contrary to the Word of God, but they must have direct and particular proof of the same.

2. Item, that those which are not preachers are no ministers,

[14] From *Tracts ascribed to Richard Bancroft*, ed. A. Peel (Cambridge: Cambridge University Press, 1953), pp. 10–12. By permission of Cambridge University Press.

though they be allowed of the Church; and the sacraments ministered by them are no sacraments. . . .

3. Item, they refuse the order set down in the Communion Book both touching baptism and marriage. As in baptism, they condemn the cross, godfathers and the vows; in marriage, the ring, the words used in the delivery thereof, and the giving of the woman.

4. Item, they utterly condemn all holy days as superstitious, such as the prince may not command.

5. Item, they condemn the prescribed form of prayer, and the most of them think there ought to be no prescribed form at all.

6. Item, they condemn the prescribed form of apparel appointed for ministers, as superstitious and unlawful to be used.

7. Item, they hold it to be lawful for every minister without any licence or allowance thereunto by the bishop or otherwise to preach where and when soever it pleases him; contrary to that which they have sometimes maintained, viz. that it is not lawful for one to preach in another's cure.

8. Item, they condemn the authority of bishops and ecclesiastical officers as wicked, unlawful, and not agreeable to God's word.

9. Item, they condemn all censures of the Church now used in England, as suspensions, interdictions and excommunications, as superstitious, popish and unlawful.

10. Item, they condemn the usual manner of kneeling at the communion as idolatrous, superstitious and unlawful.

11. Item, they condemn the white veil accustomably used by women in their giving of thanks as a whorish attire.

12. Item, they condemn private baptism in all respects as unlawful; yet they allow preaching in private places, as their common practice in gentlemen's houses does testify.

13. Item, they condemn all fasting days appointed by the laws of the realm as popish and superstitious. . . .

14. Item, they think it not lawful to receive the communion, or to have their children baptised, in their own parishes unless their minister be a preacher and do preach immediately before the ministration; and therefore in such cases they carry their children to other parishes. . . .

15. Item, though they dwell a hundred miles asunder and one never saw the other, yet they know of another's doings and their opinions that they hold. . . .

17. Item, they generally condemn all bishops, deans and archdeacons, and desire to have certain elders or superintendents (as they call them) to be placed in their rooms, and therefore they refuse to pray for them. Some also refuse to pray for the queen as supreme governor in all causes ecclesiastical.

18. Item, they condemn all others for papists, not holding their opinions; some of them refuse to salute any that they know to be of contrary judgment to them. . . .

# 68 / RICHARD HOOKER (1544?-1600): THE LAWS OF ECCLESIASTICAL POLITY (C. 1595)

*Hooker's classic defense of the Church of England was in form a controversial treatise against the Puritans, but it was also a major contribution to political thought. The author, a country parson and scholar with no ambitions in the world, rested his argument on two main propositions: the good ordering of God's creation is embodied in the law of nature, and the Church's development in history is as much a revelation of God's purpose as is its foundation in Scripture. Thus Hooker adapted the inheritance of the Middle Ages to the needs of Protestant England and justified the preservation of continuity. The qualities which distinguished him as a controversialist were reason and charity.*[11][15]

The like power in causes ecclesiastical is by the laws of this realm annexed to the crown. And there are [those] which imagine that kings, being mere lay persons, do by this means exceed the lawful bounds of their calling. Which thing to the end that they may persuade, they first make a necessary separation perpetual and personal between the Church and the commonwealth. Secondly, they so tie all kind of power ecclesiastical unto the Church, as if it were in every degree their only right which are by proper spiritual function termed Church governors, and might not unto Christian princes in any wise appertain.

To lurk under shifting ambiguities and equivocations of words in matters of principal weight is childish. A Church and a commonwealth

[15] Richard Hooker, *Laws of Ecclesiastical Polity*, ed. J. Keble (Oxford, 1888), Vol. 3, pp. 328–30, 340.

we grant are things in nature the one distinguished from the other. A commonwealth is one, and a Church another way, defined. In their opinion the Church and the commonwealth are corporations, not distinguished only in nature and definition, but in substance perpetually severed; so that they which are of the one can neither appoint nor execute, in whole nor in part, the duties which belong unto them which are of the other, without open breach of the law of God, which hath divided them, and does require that being so divided they should distinctly and severally work, as depending both upon God, and not hanging one upon the other's approbation for that which either has to do.

We say that the care of religion being common unto all societies politic, such societies as do embrace the true religion have the name of Church given unto every of them for distinction from the rest; so that every body politic has some religion, but the Church that religion which is only true. Truth of religion is that proper difference whereby a Church is distinguished from other politic societies of men. We here mean true religion in gross, and not according to every particular: for they which in some particular points of religion do swerve from the truth, may nevertheless most truly, if we compare them to men of a heathenish religion, be said to hold and profess that religion which is true. . . . With us therefore the name of a Church imports only a society of men, first united into some public form of regiment, [6] and secondly distinguished from other societies by the exercise of Christian religion. With them on the other side the name of the Church in this present question imports not only a multitude of men so united and so distinguished, but also further the same divided necessarily and perpetually from the body of the commonwealth: so that even in such a politic society as consists of none but Christians, yet the Church of Christ and the commonwealth are two corporations, independently each subsisting by itself.

We hold, that, seeing there is not any man of the Church of England but the same man is also a member of the commonwealth; nor any man a member of the commonwealth, which is not also of the Church of England . . . so, albeit properties and actions of one kind do cause the name of a commonwealth, qualities and functions of another sort the name of a Church to be given unto a multitude, yet one and the selfsame multitude may in such sort be both, and is so with us, that no person appertaining to the one can be denied to be also of the other. . . . Wherefore to end this point, I conclude: First, that under dominion of infidels, the Church of Christ, and their com-

[6] ordered government

monwealth, were two societies independent. Secondly, that in those commonwealths where the bishop of Rome bears sway, one society is both the Church and the commonwealth; but the bishop of Rome does divide the body into two diverse bodies, and does not suffer the Church to depend upon the power of any civil prince or potentate. Thirdly, that within this realm of England the case is neither as in the one, nor as in the other of the former two: but from the state of pagans we differ in that with us one society is both the Church and the commonwealth, which with them it was not; as also from the state of those nations which subject themselves to the bishop of Rome, in that our Church has dependency upon the chief in our commonwealth, which it has not under him. In a word, our estate is according to the pattern of God's own ancient elect people, which people was not part of them the commonwealth, and part of them the Church of God, but the selfsame people whole and entire were both under one chief Governor, on whose supreme authority they did all depend. . . .

# 69 / THE TROUBLED CONSCIENCE

*The spiritual writings of the Elizabethan and Jacobean clergy include a sizable number of autobiographical heart-searchings—somewhat standard accounts of worldly lives misspent in youth and then rescued by God's direct intervention in the soul. This was, in fact, one of the really essential experiences of the true Puritan, the experience of personal conversion in which (as he thought) he was newly made over in one sudden flash of divine grace. The autobiography here extracted, by an otherwise quite obscure parson (William Langley, born in Lancashire and beneficed from the 1630's into the 1660's, except during his deprivation by the Puritan victors of the Civil War, as rector of Lichfield in Staffordshire) differs in one important respect: he remained a loyal Anglican and good royalist all his life. This also accounts for the rather less hysterical or exalted tone of his remarks. Nevertheless he shared with the Puritans a guilt-ridden sense of sin derived from ordinary indispositions and a pervasive feeling that he was not using his talents in the manner that God demanded; his absurd preoccupation with the trivial is also characteristic. Because he lacked the fervor that made most men who felt as he did into*

*Puritans, his notes are useful in reminding us that similar experiences could lead to very varying results.*[17]

I was born at Prestwich Anno Christi 1596, my father, Mr Langley, being at that time curate to his cousin who was the parson there. I was brought up there in my youth and went to the grammar school at Manchester where I received good instruction in grammar learning before I was entered at Brasenose College, Oxford, my father being wrought upon . . . to send me thither. I was from my youth given to industry and was seasoned well with pure religion and letters, so that after I commenced master of arts I was chosen to read the humanity lecture.

When I was a child I did as the apostle says children do, I was tempted with lust and after that was frequently troubled with fits of incontinence and many times with heaviness of heart, great fear in the night when I was alone, and sometimes in the day, which did so deject me and trouble my spirit that I was very desirous to get rid of it, but neither knew what I feared nor what was the cause of my fear. My parents had not been negligent of me, as they feared God and trained their child in the path of godliness, and divine exercises were daily observed. My tutors also were pleased with my progress in learning, but . . . even the fear of falling away and not reaching the goal before me often disturbed my boyhood's peace. My father lamented my weakness and sought to settle my fears by pointing out to me that my body was overwrought by much study and not corrupted by sloth and that my gloom was part of the *lex peccati;* [18] so he bid me seek [the Lord] in prayer and to avoid all little sins. . . .

I learned that our natures at the first are very sensible of the grievance of lust, though they apprehend not that lust is the cause of this grievance; for as a heavy weight it oppresses and dulls the powers. . . . Being taken and sore chastised for this fault, fear to commit was hereby grafted in a tender heart that long after, being tempted at Manchester when I was of riper years, I abhorred and shunned all those allurements; yet sometimes fits of incontinence did trouble me and seemed to grow. . . . And at that time our Church dissensions did oppress me, and I saw no bough in the cloud, and all was dark, especially when I came into the country from Oxford. Then I met with the frowns of my once friends, but now friends no more, who did not see evil in contention nor good in the Church whose orders and laws they openly broke and incontinently made wide rents and ugly schisms, but as for

[17] From *The Autobiography of Mr Langley of Prestwich,* ed. F. R. Raines (Manchester, Chetham Society, 1878).

[18] law of sin

peace and holiness, they left them to the world where they never yet were found. Once when speaking of these dissensions, when at Middleton in the presence of some of my elders, a good preacher . . . said to me, "In quibus, nec vitia nostra pati possumus nec remedia," [19] and the saying was well directed. . . . Sometimes I did eat things at Oldham which I feared were more pleasant than wholesome; sometimes I took too much of what was not wholesome as oppressed my stomach and bred pain therein; but while I was at school I did abstain from all strong drinks and had no such thing offered me. Once at Middleton in the alehouse I drank a little ale which did forthwith so dull and amaze my brain that I told [a friend] I would never do so more; and at Manchester I yielded once to . . . drink strong beer, but I drank little and my heart was unquiet and troubled with fear while I was there. And all this time I was generally studious and industrious and had pleasure in my books, nor did any impurity issue from me. . . . Nor did I ever before I went to Oxford drink a health, but at Oxford I quickly began to drink healths and with so doing I was twice extreme sick upon my first waking. The second time, upon my waking, finding my stomach sore oppressed, I did arise about three o'clock and went into the fellows' garden, for it was summer, when I sat down and was so vehemently oppressed with pain that I thought I should have died instantly. Whereupon I vehemently lifted up my heart to God that he would pardon me and preserve me at this time, and I would never do so again. Whereupon I instantly vomited up apples which I had eaten amongst our cups, which had been so parched and dried in the stomach that there was no juice or moisture remaining in them; and presently after I was rid of pain and felt well again. Yet did I not keep my purpose thus solemnly made, thus graciously and instantly remanded; I soon forgot it and after yielded to like excess again.

. . . When I had thus weakly yielded to small temptations of my companions or inferiors I was tempted afterwards by men of learning and account and greatly my superiors, after I was master of arts. One time, however, being sent for of my tutor and well knowing for what purpose, I reasoned the matter with myself whether I should go, and I feared exceedingly both present and after harm if I went and was very loath to go, yet I went. Thus when we have yielded, against the checks of conscience and something better, to such temptations as we might easily withstand, we shall have greater when we are less able to withstand than we were at the beginning; for the oftener we yield the more frail we are to yield again. After I had thus committed wilful sins several times, my heart was oppressed with heaviness and a great burden which I knew not how to get rid of. I was now truly wretched.

[19] "We can bear neither our errors nor their remedies."

I felt that I lived for nothing and was without hope for a time, *sine re, sine spe*.[20] I carried fair in College and had friends who lived more free and who knew not of my checks and temptations, but there were wise undergraduates who in my heart I envied. . . .

I was now at a stand and confounded in my studies, full of doubts and fears and led on with vain fancies and imaginations. In College I could dispute on no error or false appearance, nor set my heart to search after truth, and if by chance I apprehended any material truth it vanished and I could make no impression on my wandering and unsettled spirit, nor could I teach others. Sisyphus-like, I resumed my vain fancies again and again and was led in a round. When I came to an end, I was even to begin. My memory and intellectuals quite failed me, so that I misquoted passages, and doted and mistook in ordinary talk, and quite forgot many things I was to do. I could not at that time be in company or society without shame and trouble. I seemed to myself to be had in reproach, and when I was to go amongst my betters my heart was full of fear and disquieted with care, with to say and do and how to behave myself. And when I was amongst mixed society I knew not how to look: my heart was grieved within me, my countenance sour, though once smiling, my behaviour silly, though once grave; so that it was a grief to me to think I was to leave my chamber and to go any whither. When I had to write or translate or invent anything, or had any other business, it was a burden and a grief to me. I could not induce myself to set to it. I was advised to leave Oxford and go into the country amongst my friends, but when I got to Manchester I could not conceal myself. I soon met with hot disputants who loved neither the Church nor Oxford, and who essayed to draw one into controversy about episcopacy and Church order and our ancient liturgy, but I was often so dull and heavy that I could not argue as I ought to have done, although I knew that my cause was good and theirs rotten, and that mine in other hands would have been easily defended beyond all gainsaying: so that I had to comfort myself with St Augustine—"tu ratiocinari, ego miror; disputa tu, ego credam." [21]

While I was in the country I had some respite and ease by physic and recreation and the care of my friends; but soon after, when new and greater temptations arose I yielded to intemperance, though my rheum, coughs, and inwards stoppings and burnings, drowsiness and intermission of my wonted alacrity and activeness, did testify my body to be corrupt. At last my speech was taken away with distillations, and I laid aside all study and never opened a book, and this I did by the

---

[20] restless and hopeless

[21] "By all means use your reason: I shall stand in wonder; argue, if you will, I shall believe."

advice of Mr Mynshull, the surgeon who attended me. Four months and more being past, my voice was restored; four or five months after that I stayed still at home and then went to Oxford again; but I fell soon into great languishment. . . . I got strength again to go into the country where when I was settled and freed from a busy mind I found ease by bodily exertion and pleasure, and it was very welcome to my thirsty, weary and worn out spirit. Wherefore I thought that I had hitherto refrained myself too much from pleasure and that now I would enjoy the pleasure of my youth, not keep select and choice company, give myself to mirth and revive my spirits with pleasant meats and drinks. But alas, all my former troubles were nothing to those which this course soon bred in me. Before this my sicknesses were kindly. I was neither troubled with doubts nor fears of mind on solemn subjects, nor with distempered hunger and thirst, nor with much impatience, nor with sullen discontent. But now I was troubled with many longings; my food would not please me; I would have had many things which I had not; many things otherwise ordered than they were. I was dissatisfied, and nothing would please me. In my sickness I was afraid to eat, not knowing a mean. I did not so much accuse myself by eating so much when indeed I did, as I did at other times when I had eaten so little. . . . I became such a slave to my appetite that when my heart told me that instead of fasting I ate shamefully too much, and when my stomach was already sore oppressed, I could not refrain till I had stretched my belly and trounced it with the pain of the rack, and my meat became a heavy burden to me all the day long. Lust grew raging within me, and in the church of God, and at the times wherein I received the holy communion, I was not free from the grievous provoking thereof. But this is most to be wondered at: I was strangely led or driven with a vain imagination when first I was disabled from my ordinary studies and employments. Forthwith I did nothing but think and tumble vain conceits to and fro in my uneasy mind all the day long. . . . Yet did it always take me in the time of prayers, of divine service, and when I heard sermons of God's Holy Word read unto me, for then was my mind exceedingly busied with lustful or other vain and proud imaginations, and my ears wholly stopped from attending to the business in hand. It is true that I very often did sore afflict myself with much fasting, bodily labour, hard study and thoughtfulness how to redress these matters. But I did it in a muddled and distracted mind, apt even then to be deluded with many foolish suggestions, not able to examine anything properly nor to discover either the right way or the wrong. At last deliverance came and the grace of God was sufficient for me. I resisted the enemy on my knees, at thy Cross, blessed Jesus, and I felt that "restitisse vicisse est." [22]

22 "To have resisted is to have triumphed."

# 70 / JOHN MILTON (1608-1674): AREOPAGITICA (1644)

*The great poet John Milton was also a fervent Puritan and powerful political pamphleteer. Since the invention of printing, the problem of controlling opinion had exercised all European governments. From Henry VIII's day the government of England had operated a system of licensing and censorship. When, after the outbreak of civil war, part of England came under the rule of a rebellious Parliament, it might have been supposed that these weapons of authoritarian government might lapse. However, in 1643 the Parliament issued its own ordinance for the control of the press, and the next year Milton published this protest. The classical plea for freedom of the press, it is also significant of the way in which the war was releasing libertarian thought. In form it is addressed to the two Houses of Parliament as the responsible government.*[23]

I deny not but that it is of greatest concernment in the Church and commonwealth to have a vigilant eye how books demean themselves as well as men; and thereafter to confine, imprison, and do sharpest justice on them as malefactors. For books are not absolutely dead things but do contain a potency of life in them to be as active as that soul was whose progeny they are; nay, they do preserve as in a vial the purest efficacy and extraction of that living intellect that bred them. I know they are as lively and as vigorously productive as those fabulous dragon's teeth; and, being sown up and down, may chance to spring up armed men. And yet, on the other hand, unless wariness be used, as good almost kill a man as kill a good book; who kills a man, kills a reasonable creature, God's image; but he who destroys a good book kills reason itself, kills the image of God (as it were) in the eye. Many a man lives a burden to the earth; but a good book is the precious life-blood of a master spirit, embalmed and treasured up on purpose to a life beyond life. . . . We should be wary, therefore, what persecution we raise against the living labours of public men, how we spill that seasonal life of man preserved and stored up in books; since we see a kind of homicide may be thus

[23] From John Milton, *Areopagitica: For the Liberty of Unlicensed Printing*, ed. J. W. Hales (Oxford, 1898).

committed, sometimes a martyrdom, and—if it extend to the whole impression—a kind of massacre whereof the execution ends not in the slaying of an elemental life but strikes at that ethereal and fifth essence, the breath of reason itself—slays an immortality rather than a life. . . .

Another reason whereby to make plain that this order will miss the end it seeks, consider the quality which ought to be in every licenser. It cannot be denied but that he who is made a judge to sit upon the birth or death of books, whether they may be wafted into this world or not, had need to be a man above the common measure both studious, learned and judicious. . . . If he be of such worth as behoves him, there cannot be a more tedious and unpleasing journey-work, a greater loss of time, levied upon his head, than to be made the perpetual reader of unchosen books or pamphlets, ofttimes huge volumes. There is no book that is acceptable unless at certain seasons; but to be enjoined the reading of that at all times, and in a hand scarce legible, whereof three pages would not down at any time in the fairest print, is an imposition which I cannot believe how he that values time and his own studies, or is but of a sensible nostril, should be able to endure. In this one thing I crave leave of the present licensers to be pardoned for so thinking, who doubtless took this office up, looking on it through their obedience to the Parliament whose command perhaps made all things seem easy and unlaborious to them; but that this short trial has wearied them out already, their own expressions and excuses to them who make so many journeys to solicit their licence are testimony enough. Seeing therefore those who now possess the employment by all evident signs wish themselves well rid of it, and that no man of worth, none that is not a plain unthrift of his own hours, is ever likely to succeed them, except he mean to put himself to the salary of a press-corrector, we may easily foresee what kind of licensers we are to expect hereafter: either ignorant, imperious and remiss, or basely pecuniary. . . .

I lastly proceed from the no good it can do to the manifest hurt it causes, in being first the greatest discouragement and affront that can be offered to learning and to learned men. . . . If therefore ye be loath to dishearten utterly and discontent, not the mercenary crew of false pretenders to learning, but the free and ingenuous sort of such as evidently were born to study and love learning for itself, not for lucre or any other end but the service of God and of truth, and perhaps that lasting fame and perpetuity of praise which God and good men have consented shall be the reward of those whose published labours advance the good of mankind; then know that so far to distrust the judgment and the honesty of one who has never yet offended as not to count him fit to print his mind without a tutor and examiner . . . is the greatest displeasure and indignity to a free and knowing spirit that can be put upon him. . . .

And as it is a particular disesteem of every knowing person alive, and most injurious to the written labours or monuments of the dead, so to me it seems an undervaluing and vilifying of the whole nation. I cannot set so light by all the invention, the art, the wit, the grave and solid judgment which is in England, as that it can be comprehended in any twenty capacities, how good so ever. . . . Truth and understanding are not such wares as to be monopolised and traded in by ticket and statutes and standards. We must not think to make a staple commodity of all the knowledge in the land, to mark and license it like our broadcloth and our woolpacks. What is it but a servitude like that imposed by the Philistines not to be allowed the sharpening of our own axes and coulters, but we must repair from all quarters to twenty licensing forges? . . . Debtors and delinquents may walk abroad without a keeper, but inoffensive books must not stir forth without a visible jailer in their title. Nor is it to the common people less than a reproach; for if we [are] so jealous over them as that we dare not trust them with an English pamphlet, what do we but censure them for a giddy, vicious and ungrounded people, in such a sick and weak state of faith and discretion as to be able to take nothing down but through the pipe of a licenser? That this is care or love of them we cannot pretend, when in those popish places where the laity are most hated and despised the same strictness is used over them. . . .

Lords and Commons of England, consider what nation it is whereof ye are, and whereof ye are the governors: a nation not slow and dull, but of a quick, ingenious and piercing spirit, acute to invent, subtle and sinewy to discourse, not beneath the reach of any point the highest that human capacity can soar to. . . . Behold now this vast city: a city of refuge, the mansion house of liberty, encompassed and surrounded with His protection. The shop of war has not there more anvils and hammers waking, to fashion out the plates and instruments of armed Justice in defence of beleaguered Truth, than there be pens and heads there, sitting by their studious lamps, musing, searching, revolving new notions and ideas. . . . ; others as fast reading, trying all things, assenting to the force of reason and convincement. What could a man require more from a nation so pliant and so prone to seek after knowledge? What wants there to such a towardly and pregnant soil but wise and faithful labourers, to make a knowing people, a nation of prophets, of sages and of worthies? . . . What should ye do then, should ye suppress all this flowery crop of knowledge and new light sprung up and yet springing daily in this city? Should ye set an oligarchy of twenty engrossers [24] over it, to bring a famine upon our minds again when we shall know nothing but what is measured to us by their bushel? . . . If it be desired to know the immediate cause of all this free writing and free speaking, there cannot be assigned a truer than your own mild and free and humane government. It is the liberty, Lords and Commons, which your own valorous and happy counsels have purchased us, liberty which is the nurse of all great wits; this is that which has rarified and enlightened our spirits like the influence of heaven; this is that which has enfranchised, enlarged and lifted up our apprehensions degrees above themselves. Ye cannot make us now less capable, less knowing, less eagerly pursuing of the truth, unless ye first make yourselves (that made us so) less the lovers, less the founders of our true liberty. We can grow ignorant again, brutish, formal and slavish, as ye found us; but you then must first become that which ye cannot be—oppressive, arbitrary and tyrannous, as they were from whom ye have freed us. . . . Give me the liberty to know, to utter, and to argue freely, above all liberties. . . .

. . . For who knows not that Truth is strong next to the Almighty? She needs no policies, no stratagems, nor licensings to make her victorious; those are the shifts and the defences that error uses against her power. Give her but room and do not bind her when she sleeps, for then she speaks not true. . . . Yet it is not impossible that she may have more shapes than one. What else is all that rank of things indifferent wherein Truth may be on this side or the other without being unlike herself? . . . How many other things might be tolerated in peace and left to conscience, had we but charity and were it not the chief stronghold of our hypocrisy to be ever judging one another. . . . If it come to prohibiting, there is not aught more likely to be prohibited than Truth itself, whose first appearance to our eyes, bleared and dimmed with prejudice and custom, is more unsightly and unplausible than many errors. . . .

---

[24] monopolists; usually used of businessmen who cornered wheat in a time of scarcity

# 71 / THE AGREEMENT
# OF THE PEOPLE (1647)

*The English civil war did not start as a political or social revolution, but the collapse of the traditional structure soon released demands for both. The so-called Levellers put forward a democratic political program based on the concept of the sovereignty of the people. In 1647 they embodied it in this draft constitution. Strong in the rank and file of Oliver Cromwell's victorious army, they looked for a time likely to succeed; but they were suppressed by Cromwell and their ideas discarded. However, these doctrines were not forgotten; they survived underneath the aristocratic constitution of the seventeenth and eighteenth centuries and reappeared in the prehistory of both the American War of Independence and the constitutional reforms which in the nineteenth century made Great Britain a democracy.*[25]

Having by our late labours and hazards made it appear to the world at how high a rate we value our just freedom, and God having so far owned our cause as to deliver the enemies thereof into our hands, we do now hold ourselves bound in mutual duty to each other to take the best care we can for the future to avoid both the danger of returning into a slavish condition and the chargeable remedy of another war; for, as it cannot be imagined that so many of our countrymen would have opposed us in this quarrel if they had understood their own good, so may we safely promise to ourselves that, when our common rights and liberties shall be cleared, their endeavours will be disappointed that seek to make themselves our masters. Since, therefore, our former oppressions and scarce-yet-ended troubles have been occasioned, either by want of frequent national meetings in Council, or by rendering those meetings ineffectual, we are fully agreed and resolved to provide that hereafter our representatives be neither left to an uncertainty for the time nor made useless to the ends for which they are intended. In order whereunto we declare:

I. That the people of England, being at this day very unequally distributed by Counties, Cities, and Boroughs for the election of their

[25] From *Constitutional Documents of the Puritan Revolution*, ed. S. R. Gardiner, 3rd ed. (Oxford, 1906), pp. 333–5.

deputies in Parliament, ought to be more indifferently proportioned according to the number of the inhabitants. . . .

II. That, to prevent the many inconveniences apparently arising from the long continuance of the same persons in authority, this present Parliament be dissolved upon the last day of September which shall be in the year of our Lord 1648.

III. That the people do, of course,[26] choose themselves a Parliament once in two years. . . .

IV. That the power of this, and all future Representatives of this Nation, is inferior only to theirs who choose them, and does extend, without the consent or concurrence of any other person or persons, to the enacting, altering, and repealing of laws, to the erecting and abolishing of officers and courts, to the appointing, removing, and calling to account magistrates and officers of all degrees, to the making of war and peace, to the treating with foreign states, and, generally, to whatsoever is not expressly or impliedly reserved by the represented to themselves:

## Which are as follows.

1. That matters of religion and the ways of God's worship are not at all entrusted by us to any human power, because therein we cannot remit or exceed a tittle of what our consciences dictate to be the mind of God without wilful sin: nevertheless the public way of instructing the nation (so it be not compulsive) is referred to their discretion.

2. That the matter of impresting and constraining any of us to serve in the wars is against our freedom; and therefore we do not allow it in our Representatives. . . .

3. That after the dissolution of the present Parliament, no person be at any time questioned for anything said or done in reference to the late public differences. . . .

4. That in all laws made or to be made every person may be bound alike, and that no tenure, estate, charter, degree, birth, or place do confer any exemption from the ordinary course of legal proceedings whereunto others are subjected.

5. That as the laws ought to be equal, so they must be good, and not evidently destructive to the safety and well-being of the people.

These things we declare to be our native rights, and therefore are agreed and resolved to maintain them with our utmost possibilities against all opposition whatsoever. . . .

---

[26] as a matter of course; regularly

# 72 / THE LEVELLERS:
# A SELF-DEFENCE

*The Leveller movement, seeking something like a political democracy and the abolition of all privilege of birth, reached its height in 1647–1648 when it found much support in the victorious parliamentary army and among the middling and lower ranks of society in southeast England. However, among those who resisted it were not only the propertied classes who were afraid of the implications of communism in the Levellers' teaching, but also (more important) the commanders of the army, especially Oliver Cromwell, who in 1649 took steps against the agitators and mutineers undermining the efficiency of the only instrument now capable of preserving peace and order in the country. Several leading Levellers found themselves in the Tower, but their confinement was not so rigorous as to stop them from issuing this pamphlet (poorly printed), in which they defended themselves against the more extreme suspicions entertained with respect to their opinions. Though in measure disingenuous—they were neither so moderate nor so conciliatory as they here make themselves out to be—they had a good case when they rebutted charges of anarchism and atheism.[27]*

. . . We are necessitated to open our breast and show the world our insides, for removing of those scandals which lie upon us. . . .

First, then, it will be requisite that we express ourselves concerning Levelling, for which we suppose is commonly meant an equalling of men's estates and taking away the proper right and title that every man has to what is his own. This as we have formerly declared against . . . so do we again profess that to attempt an inducing the same is most injurious, unless there did precede an universal assent thereunto from all and every one of the People. Nor do we, under favour, judge it within the power of a Representative [28] itself, because their power is supreme yet it is but deputative and of trust and consequently must be restrained expressly or tacitly to some particulars

[27] From *A Manifestation from Lt. Col. John Lilburn, Mr. William Walwyn, Mr. Thomas Price, and Mr. Richard Overton (now prisoners in the Tower) and others, commonly (though unjustly) styled Levellers* (1649).
[28] Representative assembly (parliament)

essential as well to the People's safety and freedom as to the present government.

The community amongst the primitive Christians was *voluntary*, not *coactive;* they brought their goods and laid them at the Apostles' feet; they were not enjoined to bring them; it was the effect of their charity and heavenly mindedness which the blessed Apostles begat in them, and not the injunctions of any constitution. . . . It was not esteemed a duty but reckoned a voluntary act occasioned by the abundant measure of faith that was in these Christians and Apostles.

We profess that we never had it in our thoughts to level men's estates, it being the utmost of our aims that the commonwealth be reduced to such pass that every man may with as much security as may be enjoy his property.

We know very well that in all ages those men that engage themselves against tyranny, unjust and arbitrary proceedings in magistrates, have suffered under such appellations, the People being purposely frighted from that which is good by insinuation of imaginary evil.

But be it so: we must notwithstanding discharge our duties which being performed the success is in God's hands to whose pleasure we must leave the clearing of men's spirits, our only certainty being tranquility of mind and peace of conscience.

For distinction of orders and dignities, we think them so far needful as they are animosities [29] of virtue or requisite for the maintenance of the magistracy and government; we think they were never intended for the nourishment of ambition or subjugation of the People, but only to preserve the due respect and obedience in the People which is necessary for the better execution of the laws.

That we are for government and against popular confusion we conceive all our actions declare when rightly considered, our aim having been all along to reduce it as near as might be to perfection; and certainly we know very well the pravity and corruption of man's heart is such that there could be no living without it; and that though tyranny is so excessively bad, yet of the two extremes confusion is the worst. 'Tis somewhat strange consequence to infer that because we have laboured so earnestly for a good government, therefore we would have none at all: because we would have the dead and exorbitant branches pruned and better scions grafted, therefore we would pluck the tree up by the roots.

Yet thus have we been misconceived and misrepresented to the world, under which we must suffer till God sees it fitting in his good

---

[29] animators

time to clear such harsh mistakes, by which many, even good, men keep a distance from us.

. . .

Whereas it is said, we are atheists and antiscripturalists, we profess that we believe there is one eternal and omnipotent God, the author and preserver of all things in the world. To whose will and directions, written first in our hearts and afterwards in his blessed Word, we ought to square our actions and conversations. And though we are not so strict upon the formal and ceremonial part of his service, the method, manner and personal injunction being not so clearly made out unto us, nor the necessary requisites which his officers and ministers ought to be furnished withal as yet appearing to us in any that pretend thereunto; yet for the manifestation of God's love in Christ, it is clearly assented unto by us as being, in our apprehensions, the most eminent and the most excellent in the world and as proceeding from no other but that God who is goodness itself. . . .

# 73 / COMMENT: A. G. DICKENS (B. 1910) ON THE ENGLISH REFORMATION

*Mr. Dickens, now Director of the Institute of Historical Research in the University of London, has established himself as one of the leading authorities on the history of the sixteenth-century Church. This passage is from the concluding chapter of his* The English Reformation.[30]

In the field of religion many weaknesses of the late medieval Church were plainly apparent to intelligent but orthodox contemporaries. Though we should beware of exaggerating their importance in ordinary custom-ridden minds, we find heavy support from the sources when we refuse to see them through the pre-Raphaelite spectacles of our grandfathers. Scholastic religion, having overestimated its powers, had ended in disharmony, irrelevance and discredit. Beliefs of mar-

---

[30] A. G. Dickens, *The English Reformation* (London: B. T. Batsford Ltd., 1964), pp. 326–36. By permission of B. T. Batsford Ltd.

ginal authenticity, especially those relating to purgatory and saint-worship, had been suffered in everyday practice to occupy central places in the Christian life. The professional education of parish priests was criticised as quite inadequate by numerous writers of unquestioned Catholic orthodoxy, and its character was reflected in the paucity of direct religious teaching outside the larger towns. With certain notable exceptions monasticism was uninspired; it shed little spiritual light into the world outside the cloister and its amassing of appropriated benefices hampered the didactic functions of the Church. Again, when ordination was so little selective, a small fringe of disreputable clerics was bound to accumulate and to taint the moral reputation of the priesthood. The authority of the latter had come to depend in too great a degree upon its sacramental functions, too little upon the moral and intellectual pre-eminence of clergymen in society. The finest aspects of late medieval religious life, mysticism and the related *devotio moderna* tended to be too demanding and esoteric for ordinary people, whereas the popular cult-religion . . . seemed to the sophisticated both childish and unduly directed to the raising of money.

At least by the year 1500 the fostering of a sound middle way of devotion between these two extremes should have become the chief aim of the Church, yet in England more than in most countries such a development was inhibited by the old anti-Lollard suspicions against religious literature in the vernacular and especially against biblical translation. Our bishops, in these matters among the most cautious and unimaginative in Europe, were mostly civil servants, often educated in the Roman law and always busied by secular duties; they tended to think of the Church in terms of jurisdiction rather than in terms of religious education. Even the more intelligent and spiritually-minded, like John Fisher, failed to perceive that a shifting lay outlook demanded new methods, and they tended merely to be shocked when, to put the matter crudely in our modern terms, they found the gentry and merchants of the Renaissance age less docile than the illiterate barons and villeins of a former world.

In the atmosphere of the sixteenth century it had become more difficult to soothe lay curiosity by an ecclesiastically-processed version of the Faith. Nevertheless, in the first instance it was a group of intellectual clerics, some of them friars, who discovered Luther and introduced his concepts into both English universities. This movement soon found lay supporters, both in the international world of the merchants and among members of the former Lollard groups of London and southeastern England. A new and incomparably powerful weapon came to hand in Tyndale's New Testament, itself made possible through the protection afforded to Tyndale (and to subsequent translators) by an astute confederacy of businessmen in London and Antwerp. The force of this new appeal to the laity resided less in Luther's doctrine of the priesthood of all believers than in the fact that Lutheranism, enormously aided by the printers, placed the primary evidences of the Christian Faith in the hands of laymen. The gulf so revealed between the Church of St. Paul and that of Cardinal Wolsey supplied the clinching argument for radical revisions both of theology and of institutions. Neither in England nor elsewhere was the existing establishment organised to guide, control and survive a general study of the Primitive Church. By the same token many who felt called to study it were unqualified to do so intelligently. There followed an unpleasant clash between the Reformers, too often arrogant in their new-found knowledge, and the bishops, who showed too little enthusiasm for common-sense reforms but placed only a half-hearted reliance on the faggot and the dungeon. The State was left as *deus ex machina*.

To critical people in search of positive beliefs Lutheranism offered a seductive solution. It streamlined the teaching of the New Testament around the doctrine of Justification by Faith Alone, a belief which abruptly demolished the need for the cult-religion and for a whole mass of hoary observances. Anglican and Catholic writers have seldom given full weight to the intrinsic attractiveness of these ideas to many minds of that century; however much repetition and overstatement may since have staled them, they lacked nothing in freshness and vitality for many of our best Tudor minds. Whatever its merits and demerits, the rise of Protestantism was based upon a positive evangel; we deceive ourselves if we describe the process in terms of drab negation or attribute its success merely to the shortcomings of contemporary Catholicism.

Meanwhile, Henry VIII carried the great conservative bulk of the nation with him in his dual action—the severance of England from the Roman jurisdiction and the curtailment of the wealth and privileges enjoyed by the English Church. Having initiated these processes he found himself confronted by the unwelcome demand for a third revolution, embracing Lutheran doctrine and based upon the presentation of the Bible in Protestant dress by Tyndale and Tyndale's followers. Despite his strong character and doctrinal conservatism Henry opposed these developments neither so passionately nor so consistently as historians have often supposed. His new Archbishop had strong sympathies with the Lutherans. In Thomas Cromwell the King found an administrative virtuoso capable of executing the immense technical tasks involved in the subjugation of the Church, yet he also allowed Cromwell scope to develop ideas more radical than his own. The minister organised the first great barrage of press-propaganda in English history, and his publicists not only defended the royal policy but anticipated several of the basic concepts of the Anglican *via media*. Still more important, Cromwell took the lead in making the English Bible public property in further versions by Coverdale and other English Protestants. The sale of Bibles, and free access to them in the churches, proved an event of primary importance in the history of the Reformation; it was just as irreversible as the dispersal of the monastic lands, and in the long run more revolutionary in its implications. . . .

The Edwardian years display a rough poetic justice. The seizure of chantries and church goods marred the public image of the Reformation in the eyes of many people. The fund of social idealism amongst the Reformers, deeply impressive on paper and in the pupilt, availed little at this stage to check the profiteering which it so vociferously denounced. On the other side, Cranmer's accomplished liturgical work survived persecution to afford a solid basis for Elizabeth's resumption of the Edwardian experiment. More than any other factor this work gave a distinctive and unique flavour to the national Church. Cranmer bequeathed to the latter a liturgy too politically and devotionally attractive to be displaced by Calvinist or other continental models; he also preserved some Catholic elements, which half a century later attained a new importance when Anglicanism sought to broaden its scope.

While Cranmer and Ridley showed that Englishmen could read the Bible and the Fathers and then do some theological thinking on their own account, Hooper used his longer continental associations to found a Puritan tradition with its roots in Zürich and Geneva. So far as foreign influences are concerned—and the most patriotic English churchman could not deny their immense importance—the reign of Edward VI saw a major reorientation. Before its close the direct influence of Wittenberg had decisively waned and in the main the foreign pressures were coming from Swiss sources and increasingly from Calvin's Geneva. In the event they came in two waves. Protestant scholars and refugees from the severities of Charles V- who at this point made his second great contribution to the English Reformation—flooded into Edwardian England. Some were welcomed to key-positions in the universities, while others provided a public exhibition of Reformed religion in the heart of London. Amongst these men the close disciples of Luther were a negligible element. The second wave arrived a decade later with the return to England of the Marian exiles, who had been repulsed by Lutheran Germany but welcomed at Geneva, Zürich, Strassburg, Frankfurt and other centres where consubstantiation and prince-worship were not regarded as passports to respectability. In these foreign backgrounds Ponet, Knox and Goodman evolved anti-monarchical theories of politics more advanced then those about to emanate from the Huguenots. The immensely important change from prince-worship to 'civil courage', the change which made the Puritan attitude to authority so very different from that of Henry VIII's subjects, had begun both among the martyrs at home and among the English exiles on the continent. . . .

Its reputation badly compromised by Northumberland, the Reformation derived unexpected support from the blunders of Queen Mary. At first she incurred hatred through her Spanish marriage, but in the end the fires of Smithfield did not fail to damn her cause, at all events in London and the south-east, where for the most part the drama was enacted and where public opinion had to be respected by any successful English government. Equally important, the conduct of the eminent clerical martyrs raised the sagging moral status of the Protestant cause. Public opinion cannot, however, be regarded as homogeneous throughout mid-Tudor England, and we should be wise to abandon simplifying statements as to what 'the Englishman' thought concerning all these vicissitudes. During this long crisis there were slow-moving areas and swift-moving areas, yet whereas Protestantism appealed to the latter, Mary failed to enlist the positive enthusiasm of the former. Our new knowledge of the Marian North gives no hint that she aroused its still conservative society from the torpor into which the failure of its previous reactions and its lack of spiritual leaders had plunged it. And even in these remoter provinces there is clear evidence both of an advancing Protestantism and of a proletarian heresy still owing something to the old Lollard tradition. . . .

The critical events which followed Elizabeth's accession sprang chiefly from the political acumen of these returning exiles, yet the nature of the Settlement and of the early Anglican Church was deeply affected by certain background factors, to which as yet we have had little chance to refer. While at this time Protestantism inspired only a minority of the nation, so did Catholicism. A fair amount of evidence shows the existence of a third factor comprised of secularism, relative indifference to religion, weariness of doctrinal contentions, obsession with peace and security. It is hard to resist the impression that this third force exerted at least as much weight as all the religious impulses in sanctioning the Elizabethan Settlement and in guaranteeing its stability against pressures from enthusiasts on the left and on the right. This mundane phenomenon should not be too roughly criticised by historians of religion. To some extent it represented the nation's instinct for material self-preservation, yet it was not wholly a negative reaction against the perils of religious fanaticism. Something more creative than mere disillusion. or self-interest was also coming to birth in English society. The later acts of the drama we have described were enacted upon a shifting platform of European and of national culture. The Copernican enlargement of the universe, the transoceanic discovery of non-Christian civilisations, the increasing dominance of society by its former middle orders with the resultant substitution of the family-man for chivalric and monastic models, these and many other forces were now swiftly reshaping the mental contours of educated society throughout the West.

The belief that English humanism declined after the execution of Thomas More has lately been revealed as fictitious. . . . But the label 'humanism' with its classical, Italian and Erasmian connotations seems quite inadequate to express the whole of this tidal movement, the direction and depth of which can best be ascertained by examining the intellectual interests, not of great or even eminent minds, but of ordinary readers and writers in Tudor England. Provincial surveys undertaken by the present author suggest a striking mental development among such people around the mid-century. Before about 1550–1560 the interests of these literate provincial Englishmen relate overwhelmingly to religion and to the Church; lay writers remain relatively few and the whole scene is still dominated by the professional interests of clergymen. Thereafter a dramatic broadening and diversification becomes apparent. Both laymen and clerics are now concerned with science, medicine, natural history, poetry, genealogy, history, the law, social and economic problems. Religious writing and publication do not necessarily decline in bulk, but they occupy a far smaller share of an enormously swelling output. In England as elsewhere, this powerful upgrowth of lay interests and lay writers occurred for reasons largely independent of the Reformation. Puritan zeal failed to retard it and it developed apace around and even within the Puritan mind. While it cooled the atmosphere, it also complicated the intellectual and spiritual situation of the educated man. In Sir Thomas Browne's famous metaphor he had now become an Amphibian, able to swim in more than one distinct element. This new situation may well be regarded as marking the end of the Middle Ages, yet in time it also caused the teachings of Luther and even Calvin to seem less than complete answers to the questioning of humanity. . . .

Confusion has usually resulted from attempts to denounce or to justify essentially religious movements by reference to the non-religious phenomena accompanying them. When the Reformation is being debated in terms of religious and ethical values, its political, economic and social background, which sprang in large part from a pre-existent order, should be introduced into the debate with restraint and discrimination. When, for example, French historians deplore the supposed impoverishment inflicted by the English Reformation upon the peasantry, it is legitimate to ask them whether the lot of the French peasantry was more equitable under Louis XIV than that of its English counterpart under Queen Anne. The worlds of religion and economics were never closely geared together. It is certain that Catholic principles did not prevent the subjects of Henry VIII from buying monastic lands, and it is questionable whether at any stage the practices or codes of Protestant landlords and businessmen can be distinguished ethically from those of their Catholic counterparts. Again, it would be less than rational to impugn the religious opinions of Cranmer or Hooper because they failed to control the desperate financial policies of Northumberland. With an equal lack of good sense one might blame the horrors of the Fourth Crusade upon Innocent III or condemn the Counter-Reformation by reference to the cruel persecutions of Louis XIV. In short, the Reformation has been too often distorted, its worldly effects misrepresented, by all sorts of doctrinaires, anachronists and wishful thinkers, both sacred and profane by inspiration.

# VII / THE COUNTER-REFORMATION AND THE WARS OF RELIGION

*The recovery of the papacy and the Church of Rome is usually called the Counter-Reformation, a name which suggests that it took place in reaction against the Reformation rather than spontaneously. Despite some debate about this, the view seems to be essentially correct. It is perfectly true that movements for reform existed in the Church long before Luther; by the early sixteenth century they centered on the enlightened views of Erasmus and were supported by a good many sober, decent, and civilized men in the hierarchy itself. The trail runs past Luther into the 1530's (No. 74), but there it disappears. It is also true that many of the old religious orders in this century produced reformed and reinvigorated offspring, and that the doctrines categorically established at the Council of Trent are in the main to be found in the pre-Reformation Church. Nevertheless, the whole temper and character of the Roman Church changed in the years between 1540 and 1565. The most significant event in the history of the orders was not the new life in old bottles, often enough characteristically different itself (note the greater stress on teaching and missionary, as against devotional, activities), but the foundation of a totally new and original order in the Society of Jesus. Trent not only reaffirmed doctrine; it discarded much pre-Reformation dispute and variety. The papacy itself changed in the hands of zealous but narrow men: it dropped territorial ambitions, but seriously revived militant universal claims. The late-medieval Church had been predominantly Italian and French;*

*the post-Tridentine Church was hispanized. This reformed Church, an armed attacking force, can only be understood in relation to the new schismatic churches; and, of necessity, it itself was also very largely new.*

*The existence of two aggressive Christian faiths, both determined to conquer the Christian world, set characteristic features on the political history of the nearly one hundred years between the conclusion of Trent (1563) and the Treaty of Westphalia (1648). The problems of politics and society were, as usual, difficult and violent; international rivalry was as certain to lead to war then as at any other time. The revolt of the Netherlands (1560) sprang from social, economic, and personal causes. The French civil wars between 1560 and 1589 arose directly enough out of a contest between powerful noble factions for the enfeebled crown. Philip II's struggle with England took place against the backcloth of English expansion in the Americas. The terrible conflict in Central Europe which we call the Thirty Years' War (1618–48) involved a great variety of nonreligious problems— from Bohemia's national resistance to Austrian rule and Sweden's dynamic expansion in the Baltic, to the French ambition to destroy the Habsburg stranglehold. These and other points must certainly not be overlooked. But it was religion that provided both the distinguishing and the unifying factors in the story. Whatever else they were, these struggles also formed part of the battle between Reformation and Counter-Reformation. Religion supplied the cause and the passion without which wars do not last; religion either created or modified the respective battle lines; contemporaries, however mistakenly at times, thought they were fighting for religion. The religious issue was at its most obvious while Philip II (1556–98) dominated the Catholic camp; when Catholic France, in alliance with Swedish and German Protestants, established her ascendancy in the 1630's and 1640's, it was clear that the age of religious wars had come to an end.*

# 74 / CATHOLIC REFORM: ADVICE ON THE REFORM OF THE CHURCH (1537)

*During the early years of Paul III's pontificate (1534–49), the moderate, "Erasmian" reformers obtained some influence. In 1536 nine leading churchmen, including the humanist cardinals Giacomo Sadoleto (1477–1547), Gasparo Contarini (1483–1542) and Reginald Pole (1500–58), as well as the more fanatical Gian Pietro Caraffa (1476–1559, later Pope Paul IV), were commissioned to investigate the ills of the Church and propose reforms. Their report, rendered in the following year, unhesitatingly placed the burden of guilt where it belonged—on the papacy. But in its specific proposals, all concerned with administrative details, it revealed the weakness of these reformers: there was no recognition at all of what a truly spiritual revival would have to achieve. Small wonder that this sort of reforming activity led nowhere and was soon superseded by more impassioned ideas.[1]*

Most blessed father, we are very far from able to express in words what thanks Christendom ought to give to Almighty God for that he has made you pope at this time and shepherd of his flock, and has given you the mind you have. . . . For the Spirit of God, by which the heavens are held up (as says the prophet), has decreed that Christ's Church, falling and indeed almost collapsed, should be restored by you and that your hand should save it from ruin; and that you should re-erect it in its earlier glory and return it to its pristine splendour. We have had clearest proof of this divine decree—we whom your holiness has ordered to inform you, without respect to your interests or any-one else's, of those abuses, not to say most serious diseases, of which God's Church and especially this court of Rome are suffering. . . . And your holiness . . . knows well that the origin of all these evils arose from the fact that several popes, your predecessors, . . . collected expert [opinions] according to their desires, not in order to learn from them what they should do, but to find by their zeal and craft a reason to justify their wills. Thus . . . there at once appeared certain doctors

[1] Translated from *Quellen zur Geschichte des Papsttums und des römischen Katholizismus*, ed. C. Mirbt, 4th ed. (Tübingen: J. C. B. Mohr (Paul Siebeck), 1924), pp. 267–70. By permission of the publisher.

to teach that the pope is lord of all benefices: and that therefore, since a lord can rightly sell his own, it necessarily follows that the pope cannot be guilty of simony. So that the pope's will, whatever its character, should be the rule governing his proceedings and doings. From which it followed without doubt that whatever he likes is lawful. From this spring, holy father, as from the Trojan horse, burst forth into God's Church so many abuses and such grave ills, under which we now see her to have labored almost to despair of salvation; and the fame of these things has spread even to the infidels who for that particular reason deride the Christian religion, so that Christ's name is by us—by us, we say—blasphemed among the nations. . . .

Concerning the institution of ministers by means of whom, as by instruments, the worship of God is to be well administered and Christ's people are to be well instructed and guided in the Christian life, the first abuse here is the ordination of the clergy, and especially of priests, in which no care is taken or diligence displayed. Whoever they might be—totally unlearned, of the vilest origins and appalling morals, or under age—they are regularly admitted to holy orders, and particularly to priesthood, that condition ·which most notably expresses Christ. Hence innumerable scandals, hence contempt for the clerical estate, hence the respect for the divine services not so much diminished as vitually extinct. . . .

Concerning the government of the Christian people . . . a great and intolerable abuse, by which all Christian people are scandalized, lies in the impediments put in the way of bishops ruling their flocks, especially as to the punishment and correction of crime. For in the first place many evil-doers, especially among the clergy, are in many ways exempt from the jurisdiction of their ordinary;[2] furthermore, if not exempt, they at once take refuge with the penitentiary or the datary[3] where they rapidly find the road to impunity—a road, what is more, opened for money. This scandal, most blessed father, so seriously troubles the Christian people that it cannot be expressed in words. . . . A great and dangerous abuse exists in the public schools especially in Italy, where many professors of philosophy teach heterodoxy. Even in some churches most impious debates take place; and even if they happen to be orthodox, still, matters of religion are very irreverently discussed there before the people. . . .

Abuses in dispensations granted by your holiness. . . . Another abuse is absolution from simony. Alas, how this pestilent vice reigns in God's Church, so much so that people are no longer afraid of committing simony; they at once seek absolution from the penalty and

---

[2] their diocesan superior
[3] papal officials charged with the sale of dispensations

even purchase it; and so retain the benefice which they have acquired for money. . . .

Concerning the bishop of Rome. This city and church of Rome are the mother and teacher of other churches. Therefore the worship of God and honesty of manners should flourish here above all; and therefore, most blessed father, all foreigners are scandalized when they enter St. Peter's where certain low priests, ignorant men and dressed in garments and vestments which it would not be right to wear in a hovel, celebrate mass; this is a great scandal to everybody. In this city whores perambulate the town like matrons, or ride on mule-back, with whom certain noblemen, the familiar friends of cardinals and clerics, consort in broad daylight. . . . There are hospitals here, there are orphans, there are widows: their care is very much incumbent upon the bishop and ruler. . . .

# 75 / SOCIETY OF JESUS: FOUNDATION CHARTER (AUGUST, 1539)

*The Jesuit Order, the work of St. Ignatius Loyola (1491–1556) and his small group of friends, encountered difficulties from the jealousy and disapproval of older orders both in its inception and during its existence. This document is the draft charter which, with difficulty promoted at Rome by Cardinal Contarini, was formally embodied by Paul III in his Bull* Regimini Militantis Ecclesiae *of September, 1540.*[4]

First: All those who want to fight under the banner of God in our Society, which we wish to designate with the name of Jesus, and who are willing to serve solely God and his vicar on earth, shall after a solemn vow of chastity resolve their minds as follows. They will be part of a community instituted for this supreme purpose; they will employ themselves principally in the propagation of the faith by the ministry of the Word, by spiritual exercises, and by works of charity, and more specifically in teaching Christianity to children and the un-

[4] Translated from *Monumenta Ignatiana*, Vol. I, pp. 14–16 (*Monumenta Historica Societatis Jesu*, Vol. 63) (Rome, 1934). By permission of the Instituto Storico della Compagnia di Gesù.

educated; and they will endeavor to have always before their eyes first of all God and secondly the reason of this their membership (which is a way to God), and to attain with all their power to the end set them by God. Each man, that is to say, according to the grace granted him by the Holy Spirit and the proper degree of his vocation (so that no one shall use [excessive] zeal), but not according to human understanding. The assessment of their individual degree [of vocation] and the allocation and distribution of offices shall be entirely in the hands of a provost or prelate to be elected by us, so that a decent order, necessary to a community well designed in all things, may be observed. . . . [The provost shall be assisted by a Council.]

Second: All members shall be aware—and that not only at the time of their first profession but as long as they live, and shall daily keep it in mind—that this entire Society and its members serve as soldiers in faithful obedience to the most holy lord Paul III and his successors. We are subject to the rule and divinely instituted authority of Christ's vicar to such a degree that we not only obey him according to the general duty owed by all the clergy but are so tied to him by the bond of an oath that whatever His Holiness may ordain for the profit of souls and the propagation of the faith we are bound to carry out instantly, as far as in us lies, without any evasion or excuse: whether he send us to the Turks, or into the New World, or to the Lutherans, or into any other realms of infidels or believers. . . .

Third: All individuals shall swear to be obedient to the provost of the Society in all matters concerning the observation of our Rule. He in his turn shall order such things as he shall see are necessary for the construction of the purpose put before him by God and the Society; in his leadership he shall always remember Christ's benignity, gentleness and love, as well as the injunctions of Peter and Paul. Both he and the Council shall pay special attention to this rule; they shall take particular care over the instruction of children and the unlearned in the Christian doctrine of the Ten Commandments and other like rudiments, so far as they think suitable, allowing for the condition of persons, places and times. . . .

# 76 / COUNCIL OF TRENT (1545-1563)

*The much-discussed reforming Council, originally demanded by Charles V for the restoration of unity in the Church, met abortively at the north Italian town of Trent in 1545–7 and*

*1550–5. Its third assembly (1562–3) was conclusive, but also very different from what had been envisaged. The Protestants of all kinds were absent; the pope, not the emperor, controlled the Council; its deliberations were dominated by a reformed medieval scholasticism, mostly in Dominican hands, which ensured the triumph of the teaching of St. Thomas Aquinas (1225–74) over the late-medieval innovations (e.g., Nominalism), out of which so much of Luther, for instance, had come. Politically the Council was no more than a body preparing the consolidated doctrine.of one of the several Christian churches, a General Council only in name. Its canon on the Sacrament of the Altar typifies its method: by denouncing as heretical a variety of views (Lutheran, Zwinglian, and so forth), it left none of the doubt about doctrine which fourteenth- and fifteenth-century speculation had induced.[5]*

On the most holy sacrament of the eucharist.

If anyone denies that, in the sacrament of the most holy eucharist, are contained truly, really and substantially, the body and blood together with the soul and divinity of our Lord Jesus Christ, and consequently the whole Christ; but says that He is only therein as in a sign, or in figure, or virtue; let him be anathema.

If anyone says that, in the sacred and holy sacrament of the eucharist, the substance of the bread and wine remains conjointly with the body and blood of our Lord Jesus Christ, and denies that wonderful and singular conversion of the whole substance of the bread into the Body, and of the whole substance of the wine into Blood—the species only of the bread and wine remaining—which conversion indeed the Catholic Church most aptly calls Transubstantiation; let him be anathema. . . .

If anyone says that, after the consecration is completed, the body and blood of our Lord Jesus Christ are not in the admirable sacrament of the eucharist, but are there during the use, whilst it is being taken, and not either before or after . . . ; let him be anathema. . . .

If anyone says that Christ, given in the eucharist, is eaten spiritually only, and not also sacramentally and really; let him be anathema. . . .

If anyone says that faith alone is sufficient preparation for receiving the sacrament of the most holy eucharist; let him be anathema. And for fear lest so great a sacrament may be received unworthily, and so unto death and condemnation, this holy Synod ordains and declares

[5] From *The Canons and Decrees of the Council of Trent*, trans. J. Waterworth (London, 1848), pp. 82–4.

that sacramental confession, when a confessor may be had, is of necessity to be made beforehand by those whose conscience is burdened with mortal sin, how contrite even so ever they may think themselves. But if any one shall presume to teach, preach or obstinately to assert, or even in public disputation to defend the contrary, he shall be thereupon excommunicated.

# 77 / PIUS IV (1559-1565): CONFIRMATION OF THE COUNCIL OF TRENT (1564)

*Pius IV stood on the watershed between the Renaissance and Counter-Reformation popes. He had grown up in the bright atmosphere of humanist reason, but fitted in well with the more somber temper produced by the call of battle. He managed to get the Council to conclude its business and to prevent it from infringing papal authority. The Council debated and defined; but the pope made sure that its decrees should have no force until ratified by him in this Bull,* Benedictus Deus, *which also reserved to the papacy full control over interpretation and execution. In fact, the Reformation did not, as the popes had feared, lead to a revival of conciliarist views, but assisted the papacy, within the now more restricted territory of the Roman Church, to a greater autocracy.*[6]

To extirpate very many and most pernicious heresies, to correct manners, and to restore ecclesiastical discipline, to procure the peace and concord of the Christian people, an oecumenical and general Council had been, a long time previously, indicated by our predecessor, Paul III, of pious memory, and had been begun by holding several sessions. Having been, by his successor, recalled to the same city, the Council . . . could not be even then brought to a conclusion: it was, therefore, for a long time interrupted . . . whilst the Church daily more and more implored that remedy. But we, upon having entered upon the government of the Apostolic See, undertook to accomplish

[6] From *The Canons and Decrees of the Council of Trent*, trans. J. Waterworth (London, 1848), pp. 285–9.

so necessary and salutary a work . . . ; trusting in the Divine Mercy, and aided by the pious zeal of our most beloved son in Christ, Ferdinand, emperor elect of the Romans,[7] and by that of other Christian kings, republics, and princes, we have at length attained to that which we have not ceased to labour after by daily and nightly watchfulness. . . . For whereas a most numerous assembly of bishops and of other distinguished prelates . . . had, upon being convoked by our letters, and impelled also by their own piety, been gathered together from all sides out of the nations of Christendom, at the said city; together with whom were very many other persons of piety, preeminent for skill in sacred letters, and knowledge of divine and human law; the legates of the Apostolic See presiding in the said Synod; ourselves so favourable to the liberty of the Council, as even to have . . . voluntarily left the said Council free to determine concerning matters properly reserved to the Apostolic See; such things as remained to be treated of, defined and ordained, touching the sacraments and other matters, which seemed to be necessary for confuting heresies, removing abuses, and amending morals, were by the holy Synod . . . defined, explained and ordained, which being completed, the Council was brought to a close with so great unanimity on the part of all who assisted thereat, that it was plain that such agreement was the Lord's doing. . . .

And whereas the said holy Synod, in its reverence towards the Apostolic See, and following also in the traces of the ancient Councils, has, in a decree made thereon in public session, requested of us the confirmation of all its decrees . . . we, being made acquainted with the request of the said Synod, . . . after mature deliberation had thereon with our venerable brethren the cardinals of the Holy Roman Church, and above all having invoked the assistance of the Holy Spirit; after that we had ascertained that all those decrees were Catholic, and useful and salutary to the Christian people, . . . have this day, in our secret consistory, confirmed by Apostolic authority all and singular those decrees, and have ordained that the same be received and observed by all the faithful of Christ. . . .

Furthermore, in order to avoid the perversion and confusion which might arise, if each one were allowed, as he might think fit, to publish his own commentaries and interpretations on the decrees of the Council; we, by apostolic authority, forbid all men, as well ecclesiastics . . . as also laymen . . . to presume, without our authority, to publish, in any form, any commentaries, glosses, annotations, scholia, or any kind of interpretation whatsoever of the decrees of the said Council; or to settle anything in regard thereof, under any plea whatsoever, even under pretext of greater corroboration of the decrees, or the more

[7] Ferdinand I (1558–64)

perfect execution thereof, or under any other colour whatsoever. But if anything therein shall seem to anyone to have been expressed and ordained in an obscure manner, and it shall appear to stand in need on that account of an interpretation or decision, let him "Go up to the place which the Lord has chosen" (Deut. 17.8); to wit, to the Apostolic See, the mistress of all the faithful, whose authority the holy Synod also has so reverently acknowledged. For, if any difficulties and controversies shall arise in regard of the said decrees, we reserve them to be by us cleared up and decided, even as the holy Synod has itself in like manner decreed; being prepared, as that Synod has justly expressed its confidence in regard of us, to provide for the necessities of all the provinces, in such manner as shall seem to us most suitable; declaring that whatsoever may be attempted to the contrary in this matter, whether wittingly or unwittingly, by any one, by what authority so ever, is, notwithstanding, null and void. . . .

# 78 / THE ROMAN CATECHISM (1566)

*Issued by Pope Pius V (1566–72), an austere Dominican who, though not able to avoid politics, at least did not allow them to influence his always principled, often foolhardy, acts, the Catechism of 1566 was intended to provide that simple definition of the faith which the reformed Church of Rome badly needed for its missionary activities among both heretics and heathens. It exemplifies the unwavering adherence of the post-Tridentine Church to the supremacy of Rome and the exclusive claims of the papacy.*[8]

### FAITH

Because in theology the word faith has many meanings, we will speak of it here. By virtue of it we entirely assent to all traditions derived from God. No one shall rightly doubt that [faith] is necessary for the attainment of salvation, especially as it is written "Without faith it is impossible to please God" (Hebr. 11.6). For since the goal insti-

[8] Translated from *Quellen zur Geschichte des Papsttums und des römischen Katholizismus*, ed. C. Mirbt 4th ed. (Tübingen: J. C. B. Mohr (Paul Siebeck), 1924), pp. 342–7. By permission of the publisher.

tuted to render men blessed is higher than man's intellect can comprehend, it was necessary for him to receive knowledge of it from God. This knowledge is nothing but the faith which effects that we believe that to be certain which the authority of Holy Mother Church approves as handed down from God. . . .

## THE NATURE OF THE CHURCH

By the common custom of Holy Scripture this term (Church) is reserved to signify the Christian community and the gathering of only the faithful; those, that is, who are called by faith to the light of truth and knowledge of God, so that, having rejected the darkness of ignorance and errors, they worship in piety and sanctity the true and living God and serve him with all their hearts; and (to end this matter in one word), the Church is, as St. Augustine says, the faithful people dispersed throughout the whole world. . . .

The Church especially consists of two parts of which one is called triumphant and the other militant. The triumphant is the most splendid and happy gathering of blessed spirits and of those who have overcome the world, the flesh and the devil, and who, being free and secure from the cares of this world, enjoy eternal bliss. The Church militant, on the other hand, is the gathering of all the faithful who still live on earth, which is called militant because they have to wage eternal war with the ever-present enemies—the world, the flesh and the devil. . . . It embraces not only the good but also the wicked. . . .

The qualities of this Church are to be expounded to the faithful. . . . Its first quality is described under the sign of the Father, that it is *one.* The second quality is that it is *holy.* . . . No one need be surprised that the Church is called holy although it contains many sinners. The faithful are called holy who have become the people of God and who have consecrated themselves to Christ by faith and the reception of baptism. The Church is to be called holy because, as a body having its sacred head in the Lord Christ, it is linked with the whole fountain of holiness from which pour forth the gifts of the Holy Spirit and the riches of God's mercy. Moreover, the Church alone possesses the legitimate cult of sacrifice and the salutary use of the sacraments. . . . The third quality is that it is called *catholic,* or universal. . . . For the Church is not, as are men's political arrangements or the congregations of heretics, confined to the borders of one kingdom or to one sort of men; but in the bosom of its charity it embraces all men, be they barbarians or Scythians, bond or free, male or female. . . . It is called universal because all who want to attain to eternal life must adhere to and embrace it. . . .

Inasmuch as the one Church cannot err in matters of faith and morals, since it is ruled by the Holy Spirit, so all others who arrogate the name of Church to themselves, being led by the devil, must of necessity live in the most pernicious errors of doctrine and morals. . . .

### THE BISHOP OF ROME

The ruler and governor of the Church is one; of the invisible [Church] it is Christ . . . but of the visible he who occupies the cathedral-church of Rome as the legitimate successor of Peter, the first of the Apostles. . . . .

# 79 / ST. TERESA (1515-1582): LETTERS

*The Counter-Reformation was by no means only a theological and administrative movement; for many it represented mainly a spiritual and ethical revival within the doctrinal orthodoxy of Rome. In particular the Spanish mystics proved that personal religion was no Protestant prerogative. Teresa of Avila, a Carmelite nun canonized in 1622, was both a leader of reform and a personal mystic, experiencing trances and visions of the living Christ, as well as a noted spiritual instructress. Within her own order she promoted the movement of the Descalzos (the shoeless), a return to primitive austerity which involved her in a prolonged struggle with the authorities both because the official Church always distrusted the kind of zeal which might be only self-advertisement (St. Teresa appreciated these doubts) and because she interfered with the self-interest of others. Her letters tell of her spiritual experiences as well as of the administration of her reformed order; her main influence was exercised in her spiritual teaching and writing, developed further by her foremost disciple, the great poet and mystic. St. John of the Cross (1542–91).*[9]

Toledo, 9 Sept., 1576: To Mother Mary of St. Joseph, prioress of Seville.[10]

. . . In regard to the cousins of Garci Alvarez, I do not know

[9] From *St. Teresa's Letters*, translated by the Benedictines of Stanbrook (London, 1921), Vol. 2. By permission of the Benedictines of Stanbrook.

[10] Letter no. 112, pp. 39 ff.

whether you remember my being told that one of them had such a severe attack of melancholia as to lose her reason. I do not think it was Dona Constanza. Speak plainly about the matter. I know nothing of his niece; but anyone connected with him would have a special claim on us if she were suitable. Make careful enquiries and if you are satisfied, write to our Father [11] for permission. . . . As for the postulants, I told you that the one with the fine voice never returned. There is another whom Nicolas very much wishes to enter, and she would do much for your house, Father Mariano tells me. She would bring a trousseau and rather over four hundred ducats to be given at once, which is what I want. You could then discharge the rent and would be free from anxiety; you might even pay off part of the duties as we agreed. I am sorry the affair was not settled before that person died; however, perhaps it is all for the best.

Remember this: in all cases an agreement is best: never forget that. Our Father wrote telling me that a very learned man at court had informed him that the right was not on our side. But even if it had been, "lawsuits are bad things".: recollect that. . . . I repeat once more that I do not wish to sell the sisters' annuity. Seek some other means, or we shall be left with a heavy debt which we could not pay off with Pablo's money. It would be a relief to you to be freed from it. . . .

I am glad to hear that your house at Seville is cool: I willingly bear the heat of Toledo in payment for it. For charity's sake send me nothing more, for the cost exceeds the value. Some of the quinces (but very few) arrived in good condition; the dogfish were fresh. The tunny remained at Malagon, and a good thing too. . . .

Toledo, 17 Jan. 1577. To Don Lorenzo de Cepeda.[12]

. . . For more than a week I have been in a spiritual state which, if it continues, may cause me ill success with my many business affairs. Before I last wrote, my ecstasies had returned, which distressed me as they sometimes occurred in public and during Matins. Resistance is useless and they cannot be concealed. I felt so utterly ashamed that I wanted to hide myself no matter where. I have prayed earnestly that I may no longer have raptures in public; will you pray about it, for there are many disadvantages and it does not seem to me a higher form of prayer.

During the last few days I have appeared to be half intoxicated: at least it is evident that the soul is well off, but the powers being bound, it finds it difficult to attend to anything except Him Whom it loves. During the preceding week I was often incapable of a single good thought, being in a state of complete aridity. In fact, in one way

[11] Father Gracian, a friar in spiritual charge of the reformed Carmelite nuns
[12] Letter no. 166, pp. 214 ff.

I was rather glad of it, as I had been in my present state for several days, and it is a joy to realise how little we can do ourselves. Blessed be He Who can do all things! Amen. I have told you much: the rest cannot be written or even spoken about. . . .

I have passed through this state of prayer after which, as a rule, the soul enjoys peace and sometimes wishes to perform penance, especially if the impulse of love has been very strong. The soul then seems as though it could not endure doing nothing for God, for this is a touch which transforms the soul into love, and if it increases you will understand what was mysterious to you in the verses, for it is keen pain and sorrow, yet most delicious, coming from we know not whence. In fact, the love of God wounds the soul which cannot tell where the wound comes from, nor how it came, nor whether it is wounded, or what is taking place, yet feels a delicious anguish. . . . When this love of God actually touches the soul, it finds no trouble in withdrawing from the love of creatures. . . . When God takes possession of a soul He gives it, by degrees, the empire over all created things even when He withholds the realisation of His presence and His consolations, which is what you complain about. Although these disappear as though they had never been, as far as regards the sensitive faculties to which God was pleased to impart some of the joy of the soul, He does not quit the soul itself nor fail to leave it rich in graces, as is proved by the after effects. . . .

# 80 / PHILIPPE DUPLESSIS-MORNAY (1549-1623): AN ATTACK ON TYRANTS (1579)

*The Wars of Religion raised in acute form one of the fundamental problems of political thought: that of obedience and resistance to constituted authority, especially whether a ruler can demand obedience in matters in which he seems to go counter to the individual conscience. Monarchic doctrine, supported by Luther and Calvin (see No. 60B), permitted the individual at most a right of passive resistance, but the conflicts of the later sixteenth century made this seem insufficient to many. Jesuit teaching was to allow even tyrannicide (the assassination of heretical rulers).*

*On the Protestant side, it was the French Calvinists (Huguenots) who developed theories of active resistance, based on anti-monarchic doctrines which made the king merely an appointed official of the people. The clearest exposition of this view appeared in this work, probably produced in collaboration by Duplessis-Mornay, a Huguenot nobleman and lawyer who from 1573 was chief adviser to the Protestant leader Henry of Navarre (the later Henry IV), and Hubert Languet (1518–81).*[13]

*Question Three:* Whether and how far it is lawful to resist a prince who either oppresses or ruins the state; also to whom, in what manner, and by what right it is permitted to do so.

Because we must here touch on the legitimate authority of a prince, I have no doubt that the question will be hateful to tyrants and bad princes. For they think their own will justifies all their actions; small wonder that they cannot by any means bear to listen to the voice of reason and law. However, I hope good princes at least will take pleasure in this; they know that any magistrate, no matter how great his authority, is only the law come to life. . . . Therefore, what is here said against tyrants is very far from infringing the rights of kings; on the contrary, the more the former are attacked, the more the latter are exalted; the first cannot be denounced without this bringing praise to the second. . . .

We have shown before this that it is God who institutes kingship, gives kingdoms to kings, chooses kings. Now we say that the people make kings, confer the right to rule, approve their election by their voices. God wanted this to be done in this manner in order that kings should acknowledge that they all owe all their authority and power, next to Himself, to the people. Therefore they are to concentrate all their care, thought and diligence on the needs of the people. They are not to think themselves superior to other men by dint of some natural excellence, even as men are to sheep and cattle. They must remember that they are born to exactly the same fate as the rest, that the voices and (as it were) the shoulders of the people have lifted them from the ground to their station in order that thereafter the burden of the state might in great part rest on their shoulders. . . . In short, all kings were in the beginning elected. And those who today would seem to succeed to the crown by inheritance must first be confirmed by the people. Finally, although the people may commonly in certain places choose their kings from a particular line, on account of some notable distinction, yet it is the line they choose and not any particular branch

---

[13] Translated from *Vindiciae contra Tyrannos* (Hanover, 1595), pp. 73 ff.

of it, nor does that choice prevent them from choosing another if the first degenerates. For the members of the line, even those nearest to it, are kings made and not born; they are held to be not kings but candidates for the crown.

Since kings are made by the people, it is entirely manifest that the whole people is above the king. For it is quite obvious that one who is created by another is considered below him; one who receives his authority from another is inferior to his authoriser. . . . It is certain that kings were appointed for the sake of the people. Surely it is less probable that all mankind should have been created for the use of a hundred manikins more or less, who as a rule are less worthy and admirable than the rest, than the other way round. . . . Innumerable peoples manage to survive without kings, but one cannot even conceive of a king without a people. . . . Take the people away from the king, and however good his sight and hearing, however well set-up and healthy he seemed before, he will at once be blind, deaf and decrepit; however high his state, at once everyone will treat him as nothing. . . .

Now what we have said of the whole people applies also . . . to those who legitimately represent the whole people in a kingdom or a city. These are properly to be described as the officers of the realm, not of the king. The king's officers are appointed and dismissed at the king's mere will. When he dies, they cease to have authority and are in a manner reckoned dead. The officers of the realm, on the other hand, receive their authority from the people in public assembly—or at least at one time used so to receive it—and cannot be dismissed without the people's verdict. The former depend on the king, the latter on the realm; the former on the highest officer of the realm, that is the king, the latter on the sovereign rule of the people on which the king himself, no different from them, should depend. The king's officers are charged with looking after the king; the realm's with seeing that no harm comes to the realm. The ones, like the domestic servants of any master, must attend on and serve the king; the others must guard the rights and privileges of the people and energetically provide that not even the prince himself endangers the nation by what he either does or fails to do. In short, the ones are the king's attendants, servants, domestics, appointed simply to do service; the others, however, are in a manner the king's associates in doing justice, sharers of the royal power, to the intent that they no less than the king shall concern themselves with the government of the state. The king is, so to speak, their president; he has but the first place among them. And as the whole people is superior to the king, so these [officers], though individually below him, must yet as a group be held superior. . . .

# 81 / JAMES I (1566-1625): THE TREW LAW OF FREE MONARCHIES (1598)

*Antimonarchic doctrine produced its reaction in the fully developed theory of the divine right of kings, and from no one more so than that scholar-king, James VI of Scotland (son of Mary, Queen of Scots), who in 1603, as James I of England, brought the Stuart dynasty to the English throne. The theory itself was, of course, very much older; that kingship was instituted by God Himself for the civil government of His people was the main basis of Western monarchy from at least Charlemagne onward. At the same time, it had always coexisted with aspects of monarchy derived from popular approval (the primitive Germanic kingship) and feudal control (the king as the first among relatively equal rulers); only in the sixteenth century were the absolutist doctrines inherent in a kingship imposed by God allowed to emerge untrammeled. James I gave much system to the view that kings, appointed by God alone, are also responsible to God alone and must not be resisted or disobeyed by any of their subjects. England offered a stony soil for such theories, but they were to stand embodied in the monarchy of Louis XIV of France and to exercise widespread influence in the seventeenth and eighteenth centuries.[14]*

Since I have so clearly proved then out of the fundamental laws and practice of this country what right and power a king has over his subjects, it is easy to be understood what allegiance and obedience his lieges owe unto him. . . . If it be not lawful to any particular lords, tenants or vassals, upon whatsoever pretext, to control and displace their master and overlord (as is clearer nor the sun by all laws of the world), how much less may the subjects and vassals of the great overlord, the king, control or displace him? And since in all inferior judgments in the land, the people may not upon any respect displace their magistrates, although but subaltern: for the people of a borough can-

[14] From *The Political Works of James I*, ed. C. H. McIlwain (Cambridge, Mass.: Harvard University Press, 1918), pp. 64–6. By permission of Harvard University Press.

not displace their provost before the time of their election, nor in ecclesiastical policy the flock can upon any pretence displace the pastor nor judge of him, yea even the poor schoolmaster cannot be displaced by his scholars: if these, I say . . . cannot be displaced for any occasion or pretext by them that are ruled of them, how much less is it lawful upon any pretext to displace or control the great provost and great schoolmaster of the whole land, except by inverting the order of all law and reason. . . .

The king towards his people is rightly compared to a father of his children, and to a head of a body composed of divers members. For as fathers the good princes and magistrates of the people of God acknowledged themselves to their subjects. And for all other well-ruled commonwealths, the style of *pater patriae* was ever and is commonly used to kings. And the proper office of a king towards his subjects agrees very well with the office of the head towards the body and all members thereof. For from the head, being the seat of judgment, proceeds the care and foresight of guiding and preventing every evil that may come to the body or any part thereof. The head cares for the body; so does the king for his people. As the discourse and direction flows from the head, and the execution thereunto belongs to the rest of the members, everyone according to their office, so it is betwixt a wise prince and his people. . . .

It is cast up by divers that employ their pens upon apologies for rebellions and treasons that every man is born to carry such a natural zeal and duty to his commonwealth as to his mother; that seeing it so rent and deadly wounded, as whiles it will be by wicked and tyrannous kings, good citizens will be forced, for the natural zeal and duty they owe their own native country, to put their hand to work for freeing their commonwealth from such a pest.

Whereunto I give two answers. First, it is a sure axiom in theology that evil should not be done that good may come of it. The wickedness, therefore, of the king can never make them that are ordained to be judged by him to become his judges. And if it be not lawful to a private man to revenge his private injury upon his private adversary (since God has only given the sword to the magistrate), how much less is it lawful to the people, or any part of them (who are all private men, the authority being always with the magistrate, as I have already proved) to take upon them the use of the sword, whom to it belongs not, against the public magistrate whom to only it belongs. Next, in place of relieving the commonwealth out of distress (which is their only excuse and color), they shall heap double distress and desolation upon it; and so their rebellion shall procure the contrary effects that they pretend it for. For a king cannot be imagined to be so unruly and tyrannous but the commonwealth will be kept in better order, notwithstanding thereof, by him than it can be by his away-taking. . . . All sudden mutations are perilous in commonwealths, hope being thereby given to all bare men to set up themselves and fly with other men's feathers, the reins being loosed to all the insolencies that disordered people can commit by hope of impunity, because of the looseness of all things. And next it is certain that a king can never be so monstrously vicious but he will generally favor justice and maintain some order, except in the particulars wherein his inordinate lusts and passions carry him away; where by the contrary, no king being, nothing is unlawful to none. . . .

# 82 / COMMENT: FERNAND BRAUDEL (B. 1902) ON PHILIP II

*Professor Braudel, director of the* Centre de Recherches Historiques *in Paris, is well known as the leader of a school of historical writing which uses the analysis of economic and environmental circumstances to produce a structural description of society and politics.*[15]

The essential characteristic of Philip II's empire was, assuredly, its Spanishness, or more properly its Castilianism. This truth did not escape contemporaries, whether friends or enemies of the Prudent King: they saw him like a spider in the middle of his immense web, to all intents immobile. But if Philip, after September, 1559, and his return from Flanders, never again left the peninsula, was his reason only sentiment on his part, a decided preference for Spain? Was it not also, and in the main, necessity? We have shown how the states of Charles V's empire, one after the other and without a word being said, refused to support and pay the costs of his policy. All these budgetary deficits made Sicily, Naples, Milan, in the end even the Netherlands, unsuitable for the monarch to dwell in. To live there meant to the king death from financial consumption. Philip II had personal experience of this in the Netherlands between 1555 and 1559, when far too often

---

[15] Translated from Fernand Braudel, *La Méditerranée et le monde méditerranéen à l'époque de Philippe II* (Paris: Librairie Armand Colin, 1949), pp. 523–5. By permission of the author and publisher.

he managed to live only thanks to the supply of silver coming from Spain, or in hopes of its arrival. Now that he had succeeded to the crown it became difficult to obtain these supplies unless he settled in the place where they were organised. Was not Philip II's retreat to Spain a necessary retreat to the silver of America? His mistake, if mistake there was, lay in not going as far as possible to meet that silver— to the Atlantic itself, to Seville or later to Lisbon. Was it the attraction of Europe, the necessity of knowing better and more swiftly what was going on in that buzzing beehive, that kept the king in the geometrical centre of the peninsula, in that Castilian Thebes which he also instinctively liked?

The fact that the centre of his web was fixed in Spain brought a good many automatic consequences. First of all an increasing, a blind affection in the Spanish masses for a king dwelling in their midst. Philip II was quite as much loved by the Castilians as his father had been by the good people of the Netherlands. Furthermore, did there not result a logical predominance of the people, the interests and the desires of the peninsula? Of those hard and haughty men, that intransigeant nobility, who made up Castile and whom Philip II employed abroad —even if at home, in the execution of policy and in bureaucratic business, he showed a marked preference for lesser men. In an empire broken up into diverse countries, Charles V perforce became a vagrant; he had to circumambulate a hostile France in order to bestow upon all his realms in turn the warmth of his presence. Philip II's immobility encouraged the lumpishness of a sedentary administration whose luggage is never reduced by the needs of travel. The tide of paper rolled more massively and more slowly than ever. The different parts of the empire imperceptibly slipped into the position of second-rank countries, while Spain became metropolitan, a development seen most clearly in the Italian provinces. Everywhere, hatred of Spain grew a little stronger. It was a sign of the times.

That Philip II had no lively sense of these changes, that he believed himself to be the eager continuator of Charles V's policy—his disciple—is true enough; and indeed the disciple proved to have learned his lessons too well and to have a mind too fully aware of the prehistory of the situations he was supposed to deal with. In this he was assisted by those who laboured around him, by the duke of Alva or Cardinal Granvelle, that remarkable catalogue, that living record of a defunct imperial policy. Undoubtedly, Philip II often found himself in situations similar to, or apparently similar to, those which had confronted the emperor. Thus, being, like Charles V, master of the Netherlands, why should he not be on terms with England, indispensable as she was to the safety of those crossroads of the north? Again, ruling his states as his father had done, why should he not live in that image, cautious and temporising, engaged in orchestrating their widely separated and never well articulated histories?

Nevertheless, circumstances dictated radical changes. All that remained of the past was its trappings. At the beginning of Philip II's reign, indeed even before the peace of 1559, the grand—the excessively grand—policy of Charles V surely stood condemned and brutally liquidated by the financial disaster of 1557. The situation demanded repair and reconstruction, a slow restarting of everything. In his breathless career, Charles V had never known such sudden checks; the determined return to peace in the first years of Philip II's reign is a small hint of a novel weakness. A grand policy was to reappear only much later, and then less as the product of the monarch's desires than under the pressure of circumstances. Bit by bit and spreading steadily, that powerful movement of Catholic reform which we misleadingly call the Counter-Reformation came to the fore. Born of a whole series of efforts and tentative beginnings, vigorous from the 1560's onwards and at that time already capable of affecting the policy of the Prudent King, it exploded violently in the face of the Protestant north in the 1580's. It was this movement which drove Spain into the great struggles of the end of Philip II's reign, and which made that monarch the champion of Catholicism and defender of the faith. He was borne up by religious passions much more in this than in the crusade against the Turks, that mediterranean war entered into so much against his will in which Lepanto seems to have been little more than an accident.

Another factor in this grand policy: in the years after 1580, the flood of precious metals from the new world attained an hitherto unknown volume. Now Granvelle could win over the court of Spain: the hour was singularly propitious to him. However, we admit that the imperialism of the end of the reign was not created solely by him. The great war of the 1580's and after was in truth undertaken for the control of the Atlantic Ocean, now the center of the earth. The question was whether that ocean should belong to the Reformation or to Spain, to the people of the north or to the Iberians; for it was certainly the Atlantic that was now the issue. The Spanish empire swung round to the west, towards that enormous theater of war, with all its money, its arms, its ships, its resources, and its political notions. At the same moment, the Ottomans turned their backs decisively on the inner sea in order to involve themselves in struggles in Asia. This alone would remind us, if a reminder were necessary, that the two great mediterranean empires lived in an identical rhythm, and that at least in the last twenty years of the century the inner sea ceased to be central to their ambitions and aspirations. Does not here, in the Mediterranean, sooner than elsewhere, the hour strike for the retreat of empires, or rather of outsize states?

# 83 / COMMENT: PIETER GEYL (1887-1966) ON THE DIVISION OF THE NETHERLANDS

*The Dutch historian, who was one of the most reasonable and devastating critics of Arnold Toynbee's schematic interpretation of history, made his name with a revision of Netherlands history in the age of Philip II. He demonstrated that neither the origin nor the ultimate outcome of the war of independence owed much to religious factors, that it was an almost national revolt, and that the split which resulted was due to geographical facts governing a military situation.[16]*

Next to the geographical configuration of their country, it was to their superiority at sea and on the rivers that the Northerners owed their independence. Under the provisions of the Truce,[17] which left to the States the most part of the river-courses in the Netherlands, as well as all the estuaries and sea arms, and which, moreover, did not prevent their navigation to the Indies, that superiority could be fully developed —and always with the help of the trading resources in men and capital that had been wilfully expelled from the South. In the next generation or two the Republic was thus to rise to undreamt-of heights of prosperity and power, but it must be added that the international constellation created, during most of that time, exceptionally favourable circumstances.

Yet these could not but be temporary. As soon as they began to fail the Republic, it became apparent that she, with all her advantages of situation and of trade, was a small-sized state, very small indeed in the midst of the Great Powers of Europe. North Netherlands historians have often praised the fate by which the forces of the whole of the Netherlands people were drawn together on that small territory north of the rivers, since as a consequence this narrow strip of land became the scene of an incomparable splendour of political, economic, and intellectual life. This view betrays a sad lack of imagination. Those

[16] From Pieter Geyl, *The Revolt of the Netherlands*, 2nd ed. (London: Ernest Benn Ltd., 1958), pp. 256–9. By permission of Ernest Benn Ltd.
[17] between Spain and the United Provinces (1609)

whom it satisfies must turn a blind eye to the political, economic, and intellectual misery which that concentration was to bring to the southern half of the Netherlands people. We shall in our last chapter see something of the contrast that was provided during the last decades of our period by the buoyant intellectual activity in the North and the desolation in the South. It would be difficult indeed to look upon that unnatural spectacle and rejoice.

It is true that at the time the North seemed so much the darling of fortune that not even the emigrant Flemings and Brabanders could fully realize that the split was a disaster to the Netherlands people as a whole. As a matter of fact the consequences to the South were without comparison heavier. Brabant and Flanders, only a generation earlier the heart of the Netherlands people, the rich source out of which had been drawn so many of the best forces now helping to build up the young state in the North, were lying overpowered and disheartened, under the cloak of a national Government subjected more helplessly than ever to a foreign ruler and destined only to serve his policy. No doubt the Catholic spirit, which owed to the conqueror its triumphant return, again possessed spiritual creativeness now that it had been rejuvenated by the Counter-Reformation. As soon as the worst war misery had subsided, during the Truce, a cultural life of marked character grew up in the South, Antwerp and Leuven being the centres. But circumstances were really too unpropitious. The deadness of economic life, the lack of independence paralysing political life, the renewed conjunction with the Walloon provinces under a foreign court, the gallicized nobility possessing greater influence than ever, and this at a time when the war and the difference of religion were raising obstacles in the intellectual intercourse with the suddenly emancipated North—all these factors could not but weigh heavily, to the detriment of the entire Dutch-speaking community, on the civilization of Dutch-speaking Flanders and Brabant.

In addition to this the unnatural restriction of its territory involved dangers for the North and its state and society. Exhaustion soon followed upon the overstrain of "the golden age"; that splendour was short-lived. Speaking politically, the weakness of the Southern Netherlands was very far from being an unmixed benefit to the Dutch Republic. That unhappy country was but a fragment of the Burgundian state which fate had overtaken in its rise, a fragment with indefensible frontiers, which, as it were, offered a standing invitation to invaders. Had the Archdukes been able to pursue a truly South Netherlandish policy, they would have sought the friendship of the North in order to be covered on one side at least. Since they were but the agents of Spain, the war with the Republic was resumed after the Truce, and the menace of France, reinvigorated under Richelieu, held therefore the greater danger. Long before the peace of Münster, the northward expansion of France at the expense of the Southern Netherlands began to rouse uneasiness at The Hague. No more proof can be required that the split of the Netherlands had not merely weakened the powers of resistance of the Southern provinces, but that it had compromised the safety of the whole of the Netherlands race, which in the Middle Ages already had found in Flanders a bulwark against the French advance.

After the account given . . . it is unnecessary to subject to a set criticism the view, which has long been current, and according to which the split was determined by some inherent divergence within the Netherlands people. A Protestant North (not without numerous Catholics however) and a Catholic South were not predetermined by the natures of the populations. Those two great cultural currents of Catholicism and Protestantism originally mingled their courses in both North and South. It was only the outcome of strife, of war with the foreign ruler, which brought about that fatal redistribution of forces which was to estrange the two regions for so long. That outcome was not determined by any greater courage possessed by the North, or even by Holland and Zealand alone (for the conventional view conveniently overlooks the fact that the Eastern provinces had to be reconquered for the Republic by force). That outcome was determined by the great rivers. Brabant and Flanders lay open for the enemy, and soon therefore their Protestants went to strengthen those in the impregnable river area. Gelderland, Overysel, and Groningen, much less affected by Protestantism than Flanders and Brabant, could not be held for the Catholic Church because the swords of Parma and Spinola [18] lost their striking-force when stretched precariously beyond the rivers.

North Netherlands historians have been slow to see these matters in their true colours, because the dazzling brilliance of the Dutch seventeenth century prevented them, as it had prevented contemporaries, from discerning failure in the course of events. National and Protestant self-consciousness, moreover, seemed to require the carrying through of a contrast as against "Belgians" and Catholics. Certain Belgian historians, on their side, wanting to give a respectable historical background to present-day Belgium, which they look upon as the natural state organism for both Walloons and Flemings, cannot but welcome the emergence of the Southern Netherlands, which I pictured as an indefensible and subjected fragment, but in which present-day Belgium can for the first time be unmistakably recognized. To them this must be an inevitable development—nay, a fulfilment.

---

[18] Alexander Farnese, duke of Parma, and Ambrosio Spinola, Spanish governor and commander-in-chief in the later stages of the war in the Netherlands

We need not occupy ourselves with views which are so clearly artificial and inspired by later political prejudice. The split was a disaster brought upon the Netherlands race by foreign domination. Time was to show what misfortunes lay hidden in the situation that resulted from it.

# 84 / THE THIRTY YEARS' WAR (1618-1648): THE TEARS OF GERMANY (1638)

*Despite some doubts raised in recent studies, it seems clear that the devastation of the Thirty Years' War—the most destructive war of modern history until World War II—was one of the chief causes of the later decline and backwardness of Germany, one of the more prosperous and culturally advanced parts of sixteenth-century Europe. The present extract is from a Protestant sermon, preached and printed at Nuremberg in 1638; it was at once translated into English and published as part of the Puritan campaign for intervention in a war in which Protestantism seemed to be fighting for its life.[19]*

Private miseries admit of remedies and are not so deplorable because they are limited; they are as little brooks and rivulets easily restrained in their own channels. But when they prove public and general they scorn restrainments and, as violent streams, break down all before them. These are as comets, never seen but with amazement; and whose effects, as theirs, produce ruins to whole states and nations. . . .

Take notice of the fearful issues and effects of war, what lamentable conclusions the sword makes; whose beginnings are blood, whose proceedings are fire and famine, whose upshot is utter destruction and desolation. What places could seem happier than God's Church, God's house? What commonwealth more blessed than that which enjoyed the house of God, public religion? And yet the Church, the house of God, burned up with fire; the state, with all the delights of it, laid waste. . . . War is a curse; and this appears plainly, for is not war accounted by God himself as a curse? So He threatens the rebellious

---

[19] From *Lacrymae Germaniae, or the Tears of Germany*, trans. S. Baker (London, 1638).

Jews if they would not obey His laws: amongst many other curses which should pursue them, and overtake them, and destroy them, God reckons up the sword of their enemies. . . .

How are our sacred temples pillaged, rifled, uncovered, laid waste, overthrown, made now a refuge for wild beasts. How are the priests, the ministers of God's word and sacrament, abused, plundered, prosecuted, proscribed, murdered, killed. How has the fury of the destroying soldiers broken into our colleges, cloisters, convents and public churches, and desperately have rifled and defaced those sacred oratories. Oh, how truly may it be said of our temples: they are made cages of unclean beasts and dens for thieves and robbers. What ravishings, rapes, violences have been offered in these our sacred courts, and even to grave matrons, virgins, young maidens of nine and ten years old. How are we debarred liberty to approach those holy courts. And how are our flocks and congregations scattered miserably. Where, oh where, can we have liberty without danger of our lives, to present ourselves in public before the Lord in his own house? . . . Our priests are forced to flee into other countries, and many hundreds of them have miserably perished with their wives and children. Many of our public schools of learning and many famous colleges of students are utterly consumed; and what worthy libraries have perished by fire. . . . Our dear country, that was once so rich, so full of plenty, so abounding with multitudes of people, so glorious for arts, so renowned for pleasantness, for strength, for our many, great and beautiful cities, for our large and graceful churches, for variety of all worldly delights! . . . What relief has our superfluity and plenty of things afforded to those that have been in want. What afflicted Churches have not tasted of Germany's liberality? Witness the relief and succour that English divines have found amongst us; witness Denmark, Poland, France, Spain, Italy. . . . What a bulwark and defence has it been against the common adversaries of Christians; what famous sieges has Germany endured for the defence of the gospel. . . . What country has outstripped her (O fair, beloved Germany) in any excellences or privileges?

But these times are gone; oh, how my soul mourns to see her excellence thus departed! . . . Where shall I begin to reckon up her troubles? What shall I speak of the lamentable extortions and exactions upon all estates? What shall I mention the tortures and torments inflicted upon all degrees, sexes, ages? What shall I insist upon the rapes and ravishings, without distinction of persons or places, unfit to be rehearsed? What need I relate the robberies, pillagings, plunderings of villages, cities, against promises and public oaths? What shall I mention the murders and bloodsheddings committed in every acre of ground in our land? What need I insist upon the general devastations by fire in every country as the armies have marched? You are all witnesses. . . . The sword has not marched without other judgments to accompany it, as heavy or heavier than itself; as fire, famine, pestilence; and not yet stinted, but going on as furiously as if it had scarce begun its work. . . .

Let us that are here present pray that the Lord would keep us, that here remain alive, from battle and murder and from sudden death; from plague, pestilence and from famine; from hardness of heart and contempt of His Word and commandment, good Lord, deliver us and [all] people on the face of the earth.

# 85 / TREATY OF WESTPHALIA (1648)

*This treaty not only ended the Thirty Years' War and the age of religious wars, but also marked a real stage in European history. It pronounced the death of Spain's predominance in affairs and of Italy's in culture; it acknowledged the end of the Holy Roman Empire and the decline of Germany; it heralded the ascendancy of France· and the emergence of Austria and Prussia. Of course, it also had more immediate and restricted applications, especially with regard to the internal religious divisions of Germany and the temporary power of Sweden. The treaty was the product of prolonged negotiations from January 1645 onward, carried on at Münster between the Empire and France (A) and at Osnabrück between the Empire on the one side and Sweden and the Protestant states of Germany on the other (B). Both treaties were signed at Münster on October 24, 1648.[20]*

A.

*Article 1*

There shall be a Christian, general and lasting peace, and true and genuine amity, between his sacred Imperial Majesty and his sacred

[20] Translated from *Sammlung der Reichsabschiede*, ed. E. A. Koch (Frankfurt, 1747), A at pp. 604–20, B at pp. 574–604.

Most Christian Majesty; [21] as also between each and all the allies and adherents of the said Imperial Majesty, the House of Austria, its heirs and successors, but chiefly the electors, princes and estates of the empire on the one hand; and each and all the allies and adherents of the said Most Christian Majesty, his heirs and successors, and primarily the most serene queen and the kingdom of Sweden, and the respective electors, princes and estates of the empire, on the other. And this peace shall be so honestly and earnestly preserved and cultivated that each party shall procure the advantage, honor and profit of the other, and that on all sides (both on the part of the whole Roman Empire as against the kingdom of France, and on the part of the kingdom of France towards the Roman Empire) true neighborly relations shall be resumed and the care of peace and amity shall flourish again. . . .

### Article 62

But to prevent in future any differences arising in political matters, all and every the electors, princes and estates of the Roman Empire shall in this treaty be confirmed and secured in all their rights, prerogatives, liberties, privileges, in the free exercise of territorial rights both in ecclesiastical and in political matters, in their lordships and sovereign rights, and in the possession of all these; so that they never can or ought to be molested therein by anyone under any pretext whatsoever.

### Article 63

They shall enjoy without contradiction the right of suffrage in all deliberations concerning the affairs of the empire, especially when the business in hand touches the making or interpreting of laws, the declaring of war, levying of taxes, raising or maintenance of troops, the erection on imperial behalf of new fortresses or the garrisoning of old in the territories of the states, also the conclusion of peace or of alliances, or similar matters. In these and like concerns nothing is in future to be done or admitted except by the common free choice and consent of all the imperial states. But particularly the individual states shall be for ever at liberty to enjoy the right of making alliances with each other and with other parties for their own support and security; always provided that such alliances shall not be directed against the emperor or empire, nor against the public peace of the empire, nor above all against the present treaty; and in everything without prejudice to the oath which everyone is bound to take to emperor and empire. . . .

[21] the king of France

**B.**

*Article 5*

Paragraph 1. . . . The Religious Peace of 1555,[22] as it was later confirmed . . . by various imperial diets, shall, in all its articles entered into and concluded by the unanimous consent of the emperor, electors, princes and estates of both religions, be confirmed and observed fully and without infringement. . . . In all matters there shall be an exact and mutual equality between all the electors, princes and states of either religion, as far as agrees with the constitution of the realm, the imperial decrees, and the present treaty; so that what is right for one side shall also be right for the other; all violence and other contrary proceedings being herewith between the two sides for ever prohibited. . . .

Paragraph 30. Whereas all immediate states enjoy, together with their territorial rights and sovereignty as hitherto used throughout the empire, also the right of reforming the practice of religion; and whereas in the Religious Peace the privilege of emigration was conceded to the subjects of such states if they dissented from the religion of their territorial lord; and whereas later, for the better preserving of greater concord among the states, it was agreed that no one should seduce another's subjects to his religion, or for that reason make any undertaking of defense or protection, or come to their aid for any reason; it is now agreed that all these be fully observed by the states of either religion, and that no state shall be hindered in the rights in matters of religion which belong to it by reason of its territorial independence and sovereignty. . . .

*Article 7*

Paragraphs 1 and 2. . . . It is agreed by the unanimous consent of His Imperial Majesty and all the estates of the empire that whatever rights and benefits are conferred upon the states and subjects attached to the Catholic and Augsburg[23] faiths, either by the constitutions of the empire, or by the Religious Peace and this public treaty, . . . shall also apply to those who are called reformed.[24] . . . Beyond the religions mentioned above, none shall be received or tolerated in the Holy Empire. . . .

[22] the Religious Peace of Augsburg, which recognised the rights of Lutheran states
[23] Lutheran (adherents of the Augsburg Confession of 1530)
[24] Calvinist

# VIII / THE EXPANSION OF EUROPE

*Medieval Europe was never entirely out of touch with other parts of the world, especially after the Crusades, which made the Eastern Mediterranean and the routes into Asia familiar to many from the Western countries. In the fourteenth and fifteenth centuries, travelers like Marco Polo reported the wonders of India and China, and the Portuguese opened up a sea route to India round the Cape of Good Hope. This European expansion eastward (which there is no room to illustrate here) had an immediate economic importance which on the whole outweighed the gains of the later westward expansion. Nevertheless, it was the discovery of a whole unknown continent, peopled by both savages and surprisingly advanced civilizations, that left the greater mark on the European imagination. It also initiated that characteristic European enterprise, the founding of colonies, whether exploitation colonies like Mexico, where a small European population established political and social dominance over a large native working population, or settlement colonies like New England, where European societies took hold in lands that were either found or rendered empty. With colonies came the multifarious problems of the imperial power: administration, control, protection of the natives, distant war, sea communications. The discoveries transferred the strategic center of Europe from the Mediterranean and Alpine regions to the Atlantic; they shifted power from the land mass to the seas, from the continental to the maritime nations. If the immediately most important contribution of America to Europe lay in her precious metals—whose influx disrupted the economy as surely as the discoveries themselves disrupted settled ideas about absolute truths—her ultimate importance as a part of Western civilization lay a long time in the future. So did Europe's profound influence on the ancient civilizations of the East. Yet the voyagers of the sixteenth century, vic-*

*torious through the superiority of European technology, already showed that the world, Old and New, would have to go to school with its smallest but most dynamic sector.*

# 86 / CHRISTOPHER COLUMBUS (C. 1450-1506): THE DISCOVERY OF AMERICA

*Columbus was born in Genoa, probably of Venetian parents. From an early date he seems to have developed an obsession about the west route to the wealth of East Asia; after many disappointments, he finally got a commission and ships from the Spanish sovereigns. Appointed admiral of three small vessels, he set out on August 3, 1492, to cross the unknown ocean; over two months (and much trouble with his crews) later, he sighted one of the Outer Antilles. Neither then nor in his later voyages (1493–6, 1498, and 1502) did Columbus ever reach the mainland, and to the end of his days he believed that his islands lay somewhere off China. Though a remarkable seaman, Columbus was only a moderate explorer and an indifferent colonial administrator; he was touchy and given to suspiciousness and wild hunches; an upstart Italian, he had much trouble with the out-at-elbows Spanish nobility whom he was supposed to manage. But whatever his weaknesses, nothing must detract from his deed of vision and courage. A, an entry in the journal of his original voyage, records the sighting of the new land.[1] B, a letter written on February 13, 1493, to the secretary of the Spanish treasury, shows some of the explorer's first impressions.[2]*

[1] From Columbus, *Journal of the First Voyage*, ed. C. R. Markham (London: Hakluyt Society, 1893), pp. 35–8.

[2] From *Select Letters of Christopher Columbus*, ed. R. H. Major, 2nd ed. (London: Hakluyt Society, 1870), pp. 1 ff.

## A. SIGHTING THE NEW LAND

[Thursday, 11 October] After sunset the Admiral returned to his
original west course, and they went along at the rate of 12 miles
an hour. Up to two hours after midnight they had gone 90 miles,
equal 22½ leagues. As the caravel *Pinto* was a better sailer, and
went ahead of the Admiral, she found the land and made the signals
ordered by the Admiral. The land was first seen by a sailor named
Rodrigo de Triana. But the Admiral, at ten in the previous night, being
on the castle of the poop, saw a light, though it was so uncertain that
he could not affirm it was land. He called Pero Gutierrez, a gentleman of the King's bedchamber, and said that there seemed to be a
light, and that he should look at it. He did so, and saw it. . . . It
seemed to few to be an indication of land; but the Admiral made
certain that land was close. When they said the *Salve*, which all the
sailors were accustomed to sing in their way, the Admiral asked and
admonished the men to keep a good look-out on the forecastle, and
to watch well for land; and to him who should first cry out that he
saw land, he would give a silk doublet, besides the other rewards
promised by the Sovereigns, which were 10,000 maravedis to him who
should first see it. At two hours after midnight the land was sighted
at a distance of two leagues. . . . The vessels were hove to, waiting
for daylight; and on Friday they arrived at a small island of the
Lucayos, called, in the language of the Indians, *Guanahani*.[3] Presently
they saw naked people. The Admiral went on shore in the armed boat,
and Martin Alonso Pinzon, and Vincente Yañez, his brother, who was
captain of the *Niña*. The Admiral took the royal standard, and the
captains went with two banners of the green cross, which the Admiral
took in all the ships as a sign. . . .

Presently many inhabitants of the island assembled. What follows
is in the actual words of the Admiral in his book of the first navigation
and discovery of the Indies. "I," he says, "that we might form a great
friendship, for I knew that they were a people who could more easily
be freed and converted to our holy faith by love than by force, gave
to some of them red caps, and glass beads to put round their necks,
and many other things of little value, which gave them great pleasure,
and made them so much our friends that it was a marvel to see. They
afterwards came to the ship's boats where we were, swimming and
bringing us parrots, cotton threads in skeins, darts and many other
things; and we exchanged them for other things that we gave them,

---

[3] Watling Island, named San Salvador by Columbus

such as glass beads and small bells. In fine, they took all, and gave what they had with good will. It appeared to me to be a race of people very poor in everything. They go as naked as when their mothers bore them, and so do the women, although I did not see more than one young girl. All I saw were youths, none more than thirty years of age. They are very well made, with very handsome bodies, and very good countenances. Their hair is short and coarse, almost like the hair of a horse's tail. They wear the hair brought down to the eyebrows, except a few locks behind, which they wear long and never cut. They paint themselves black, and they are the colour of the Canarians, neither black nor white. . . . They neither carry nor know anything of arms, for I showed them swords, and they took them by the blade and cut themselves through ignorance. They have no iron, their darts being wands without iron, some of them having a fish's tooth at the end, and others being pointed in various ways. . . . I saw some with marks of wounds on their bodies, and I made signs to ask what it was, and they gave me to understand that people from other adjacent islands came with the intention of seizing them, and that they defended themselves. I believed, and still believe, that they come here from the mainland to take them prisoners. They should be good servants and intelligent, for I observed that they quickly took in what was said to them, and I believe that they would easily be made Christians, as it appeared to me that they had no religion. I, our Lord being pleased, will take hence, at the time of my departure, six natives for your Highnesses, that they may learn to speak. I saw no beast of any kind except parrots, on this island."

## B. FIRST IMPRESSIONS OF THE INDIES

Sir,—Believing that you will take pleasure in hearing of the great success which our Lord has granted me in my voyage, I write you this letter, whereby you will learn how in thirty-seven days' time I reached the Indies with the fleet which the most illustrious King and Queen, our Sovereigns, gave to me, where I found very many islands thickly peopled, of all which I took possession without resistance for their Highnesses by proclamation made and with the royal standard unfurled. . . . When I reached Juana,[4] I followed its coast to the westward, and found it so large that I thought it must be the mainland,—the province of Cathay;[5] and, as I found neither towns nor villages on the sea-coast, but only a few hamlets, with the in-

[4] Cuba
[5] China

habitants of which I could not hold conversation because they all immediately fled, I kept on the same route, thinking that I could not fail to light upon some large cities and towns. At length . . . I resolved not to wait for a change in the weather, but returned to a certain harbour which I had remarked, and from which I sent two men ashore to ascertain whether there was any king or large cities in that part. They journeyed for three days and found countless small hamlets with numberless inhabitants, but with nothing like order; they therefore returned. In the meantime I had learned from some other Indians whom I had seized, that this land was certainly an island. . . . The lands are high and there are many very lofty mountains. . . . [The islands] are all most beautiful, of a thousand different shapes, accessible, and covered with trees of a thousand kinds of such great height that they seemed to reach the skies. . . . The nightingale was singing as well as other birds of a thousand different kinds; and that, in November, the month in which I myself was roaming amongst them. There are palm-trees of six or eight kinds, wonderful in their beautiful variety; but this is the case with all the other trees and fruits and grasses; trees, plants, or fruits filled us with admiration. It contains extraordinary pine groves, and very extensive plains. There is also honey, a great variety of birds, and many different kinds of fruits. In the interior there are many mines of metals and a population innumerable. . . . The inhabitants of this and of all the other islands I have found or gained intelligence of, both men and women, go as naked as they were born, with the exception that some of the women cover one part only with a single leaf of grass or with a piece of cotton, made for the purpose. They have neither iron, nor steel, nor arms, nor are they competent to use them, not that they are not well-formed and of handsome stature, but because they are timid to a surprising degree.

On my reaching the Indies, I took by force, in the first island that I discovered, some of these natives that they might learn our language and give me information in regard to what existed in these parts; and it so happened that they soon understood us and we them, either by words or signs, and they have been very serviceable to us. They are still with me, and, from repeated conversations that I have had with them, I find that they still believe that I come from heaven. And they were the first to say this wherever I went, and the others ran from house to house and to the neighbouring villages, crying with a loud voice: "Come, come, and see the people from heaven!" And thus they all, men as well as women, after their minds were at rest about us, came, both large and small, and brought us something to eat and drink, which they gave us with extraordinary kindness. . . .

They assure me that there is another island larger than Espaniola [6] in which the inhabitants have no hair. It is extremely rich in gold; and I bring with me Indians taken from these different islands, who will testify to all these things. Finally, and speaking only of what has taken place in this voyage . . . their Highnesses may see that I shall give them all the gold they require, if they will give me but a little assistance; spices also, and cotton, as much as their Highnesses shall command to be shipped; and mastic, hitherto found only in Greece . . . ; slaves, as many of these idolators as their Highnesses shall command to be shipped. I think also I have found rhubarb and cinnamon, and I shall find a thousand other valuable things. . . .

# 87 / FERDINAND MAGELLAN (C. 1480-1521): CIRCUMNAVIGATION

*Magellan, a Portuguese sailor and gentleman who saw service in the East Indies, broke with his king in 1514 and went over to Spain. In August, 1519, he started on the voyage which was to lead to the discovery of Magellan's Straits, the first European crossing of the Pacific (he was responsible for the singular misnomer), and his own death at Cebu in the Indian archipelago. The remainder of his fleet sailed on to Lisbon, to complete the first journey round the world. The account here printed is by an anonymous Portuguese member of the expedition; though neither as lively nor as romantic as several others, it is chosen because it shows how much these voyages were a matter of hard professionalism, of collecting and recording the information and charts which really opened up the oceans.[7]*

In the name of God and of good salvation. We departed from Seville with five ships on the tenth of August, in the year 1519, to go and discover the Molucca Islands. We commenced our voyage from San Lucar for the Canary Islands, and sailed south-west 960 miles, where

[6] Santo Domingo

[7] From *The First Voyage Round the World*, various accounts ed. by Lord Stanley of Alderney (London: Hakluyt Society, 1874), pp. 30–32.

we found ourselves at the island of Tenerife, in which is the harbour of Santa Cruz in twenty-eight degrees of north latitude. And from the island of Tenerife we sailed southwards 1680 miles, when we found ourselves in four degrees of north latitude. From these four degrees of north latitude we sailed southwest, until we found ourselves at the Cape of Saint Augustin, which is in eight degrees of south latitude, having accomplished 1200 miles. And from Cape Saint Augustin we sailed south and by southwest 864 miles, where we found ourselves near the river, whose mouth is 108 miles wide, and lies in thirty-five degrees of south latitude. We named it the river of Saint Christopher. From this river we sailed 1638 miles south-west by west, where we found ourselves at the point of the Lupi Marini, which is in forty-eight degrees of south latitude. And from the point of the Lupi Marini we sailed south-west 350 miles, where we found ourselves in the harbour of Saint Julian, and stayed there five months waiting for the sun to return towards us, because in June and July it appeared for only four hours each day. From this harbour of Saint Julian, which is in fifty degrees, we departed on the 14th of August 1520, and sailed westward a hundred miles, where we found a river to which we gave the name of River of Santa Cruz, and there we remained until the 18th of October. This river is in fifty degrees. We departed thence on the 18th of October, and sailed along the coast 378 miles south-west by west, where we found ourselves in a strait, to which we gave the name Strait of Victoria, because the ship *Victoria* was the first that had seen it: some called it the Strait of Magalhaens, because our captain was named Fernando de Magalhaens. The mouth of the strait is in fifty-three degrees and a half, and we sailed through it 400 miles to the other mouth, which is in the same latitude of fifty-three degrees and a half. We emerged from this strait on the 27th of November, 1520, and sailed between west and north-west 9858 miles, until we found ourselves upon the equinoctial line. In this course we found two uninhabited islands, the one of which was distant from the other 800 miles. To the first we gave the name of Saint Peter, and to the other the island of the Tiburones. Saint Peter is in eighteen degrees, the island of the Tiburones in fourteen degrees of south latitude. From the equinoctial line we sailed between west and north-west 2046 miles, and discovered several islands between ten and twelve degrees of north latitude. In these islands there were many naked people as well men as women, we gave the islands the name of the Ladrones, because the people had robbed our ship: but it cost them very dear. I shall not relate further the course that we made, because we lengthened it not a little. But I will tell you that to go direct from these islands of the Ladrones to the Moluccas it is necessary to sail south-west a 1000 miles, and there occur many islands, to which we gave the name of the Archipelago of Saint Lazarus. A little further there are the islands of the Moluccas, of which there are five, namely, Ternate, Tidor, Molir, Machiam, Bachian. In Ternate the Portuguese had built a very strong castle before I left. From the Molucca Islands to the islands of Banda there are three hundred miles, and one goes thither by different courses, because there are many islands in between, and one must sail by sight. In these islands until you reach the island of Banda, which are in four degrees and a half of south latitude, there are collected from thirty to forty thousand cantaros of nutmegs annually, and there is likewise collected much mastic; and if you wish to go to Calicut you must always sail amidst the islands as far as Malacca, which is distant from the Moluccas 2000 miles, and from Malacca to Calicut are 2000 miles more. If from the islands of Banda you wish to round the Cape of Good Hope, you must sail between west and south-west until you find yourself in thirty-four degrees and a half of south latitude, and from there you sail westward, always keeping a good look out at the prow not to run aground on the said Cape of Good Hope or its neighbourhood. From this Cape of Good Hope one sails north-west by west 2400 miles, and there finds the island of Saint Helena, where Portuguese ships go to take in water and wood, and other things. This island is in sixteen degrees south latitude, and there is no habitation except that of a Portuguese man, who has but one hand and one foot, no nose, and no ears, and is called Fornam-lopem.

Sailing 1600 miles north-west from this island of Saint Helena you will find yourself upon the equinoctial line: from which line you will sail 3534 miles north-west by north, until you find yourself in thirty-nine degrees north latitude. And if you wish to go from these thirty-nine degrees to Lisbon you will sail 950 miles eastward, where you will find the islands of the Azores, of which there are seven, namely, Terceira, San Jorge, Pico, Fayal, Graciosa, on the east, the island of Saint Michael, and the island of Saint Mary, all are between thirty-seven and forty degrees of north latitude. From the island of Terceira you will then sail eastward 1100 miles, where you will find yourself on the land of Lisbon.

# 88 / HERNÁN CORTÉZ (1485-1547): THE CONQUEST OF MEXICO

*Though Balboa put the Spaniards on the mainland by 1513, the credit for establishing colonies beyond the islands really belongs to Cortéz, a Spanish nobleman who in 1504 had come to the West Indies in search of his fortune. The conquest of Mexico and overthrow of the Aztec empire in some two and a half years (1519–21) was a tribute both to his superlative military and political skill and to the reckless courage of the small band of con-quistadores. Through well rewarded with lands and wealth, Cortéz was to experience the suspicion which the Spanish government reserved for potentially overmighty subjects. The conqueror of New Spain died frustrated in Old Spain.[8]*

On the following day I set out again and after half a mile entered upon a causeway which crosses the middle of the lake arriving finally at the great city of Tenochtitlan [9] which is situated at its centre. This causeway was as broad as two lances and very stoutly made such that eight horsemen could ride along it abreast, and in these two leagues either on the one hand or the other we met with three cities all containing fine buildings and towers, especially the houses of the chief men and the mosques and little temples in which they keep their idols. In these towns there is quite a brisk trade in salt which they make from the water of the lake and what is cast up on the land that borders it. . . . I accordingly proceeded along this causeway and half a league from the city of Tenochtitlan itself, at the point where another causeway from the mainland joins it, I came upon an extremely powerful fort with two towers, surrounded by a six-foot wall abutting on the two causeways, and having two gates and no more for going in and out. Here nearly a thousand of the chief citizens came out to greet me, all dressed alike and, as their custom is, very richly; on coming to speak with me each performed a ceremony very common among them, to wit, placing his hand on the ground and then kissing it, so

[8] From H. Cortéz, *Five Letters*, trans. J. Bayard Morris (London: Routledge & Kegan Paul Ltd., Broadway Travellers Series, 1928), pp. 68–70, 75–6, 86–94. By permission of the publisher.
[9] Mexico City

that for nearly an hour I stood while they performed this ceremony. Now quite close to the city there is a wooden bridge some ten paces broad, which cuts the causeway and under which the water can flow freely, for its level in the two parts of the lake is constantly changing: moreover, it serves as a fortification to the city, for they can remove certain very long and heavy beams which form the bridge whenever they so desire; and there are many such bridges throughout the city. . . .

When we had passed this bridge Muteczuma [10] himself came out to meet us with some two hundred nobles, all barefoot and dressed in some kind of uniform also very rich, in fact more so than the others. They came forward in two long lines keeping close to the walls of the street, which is very broad and fine and so straight that one can see from one end of it to the other, though it is some two-thirds of a league and lined on both sides with very beautiful, large houses, both private dwellings and temples. Muteczuma himself was borne along in the middle of the street with two lords one on his right hand and one on his left. . . . All three were dressed in similar fashion except that Muteczuma wore shoes whereas the others were barefoot. . . . While speaking to Muteczuma I took off a necklace of pearls and crystals which I was wearing and threw it round his neck; whereupon having proceeded some little way up the street a servant of his came back to me with two necklaces wrapped in a napkin, made from the shells of sea snails, which are much prized by them; and from each necklace hung eight prawns fashioned very beautifully in gold some six inches in length. The messenger who brought them put them round my neck and we then continued up the street in the manner described until we came to a large and very handsome house which Muteczuma had prepared for our lodging. . . .

[Some Spaniards having been killed by a chief called Qualpopoca] I thanked Muteczuma for the zeal he displayed in the capture of those who had killed the Spaniards, of which affair I should have to give a particular account to your Majesty. It but remained for him to come to my lodging until such time as the truth of the matter should be more manifest and he be shown free of blame; and I earnestly begged him to be in no way grieved at this, for he should not be there as a prisoner but in all liberty; I would place no impediment in the ordering and command of his dominions, and he should choose whatever room he liked in the palace. . . . He finally agreed to accompany me; and forthwith gave orders for rooms to be prepared, which was done in very elaborate and complete fashion. Upon this many

[10] Montezuma, king of the Aztecs

nobles presented themselves and removing their clothes which they placed under their arms they brought in barefoot a litter somewhat roughly decorated: weeping, they conveyed him in complete silence to the palace where I was lodged and without any actual disturbances in the city although there were some signs of agitation. But on this being known to Muteczuma he gave orders that it should cease; and thus there was complete calm as there had been before, and as, indeed, continued during the whole time that I kept Muteczuma prisoner. . . .

The great city of Tenochtitlan is built in the middle of this salt lake, and it is two leagues from the heart of the city to any point on the mainland. Four causeways lead to it all made by hand and some twelve feet wide. The city itself is as large as Seville or Cordova. The principal streets are very broad and straight, the majority of them being of beaten earth, but a few and at least half the smaller thoroughfares are waterways along which they pass in their canoes. . . . The city has many open squares in which markets are continually held and the general business of buying and selling proceeds. One square in particular is twice as big as that of Salamanca and and completely surrounded by arcades where there are daily more than sixty thousand folk buying and selling. Every kind of merchandise such as may be met with in every land is for sale there, whether of food and victuals, or ornaments of gold and silver, or lead, brass, copper, tin, precious stones, bones, shells, snails, and feathers; limestone for building is likewise sold there, stone both rough and polished, bricks burnt and unburnt, wood of all kinds and in all stages of preparation. . . . There is a street of herbsellers where there are all manner of roots and medicinal plants that are found in the land. There are houses as it were of apothecaries where they sell medicines made from these herbs, both for drinking and for use as ointments and salves. There are barbers' shops where you may have your hair washed and cut. There are other shops where you may obtain food and drink. . . . Each kind of merchandise is sold in its own particular street and no other kind may be sold there: this rule is very well enforced. All is sold by number and measure, but up till now no weighing by balance has been observed. A very fine building in the great square serves as audience chamber where ten or twelve persons are always seated, as judges, who deliberate on all cases arising in the market and pass sentence on evildoers. In the square itself there are officials who continually walk amongst the people, inspecting goods exposed for sale and the measures by which they are sold, and on certain occasions I have seen them destroy measures which were false. . . . Finally, to avoid prolixity in telling all the wonders of this city, I will simply say that the manner of living among the people is very similar to that in Spain, and considering that this is a barbarous nation shut off from a knowledge of the true God or communication with enlightened nations, one may well marvel at the orderliness and good government which is everywhere maintained. . . .

# 89 / FRANCISCO DE XÉRES: THE CONQUEST OF PERU (1533)

*Francisco Pizarro's (c. 1471–1541) conquest of the Inca empire was the most extravagantly improbable part of the whole Spanish story in America. A tiny army of adventurers in effect destroyed a highly organized military empire in remote mountain fastnesses in the course of the brief action described here; though, of course, much further work was necessary to exploit the victory. Within a few years the conquest was so complete that the Spaniards could indulge in vicious struggles amongst themselves without endangering their hold on New Granada, as the Andean empire was to be called. When all allowances for the internecine troubles of the Incas, for the firearms and horses of the Spaniards, and for Pizarro's efficient cruelty have been made, it still remains an unlikely story of successful termerity. Xéres was Pizarro's secretary; the offense to Christian feelings alleged to have set off the battle is a lie.[11]*

The monk told the Governor [12] what had passed between him and Atabaliba,[13] and that he had thrown the Scriptures to the ground. Then the Governor put on a jacket of cotton, took his sword and dagger, and, with the Spaniards who were with him, entered among the Indians most valiantly; and, with only four men who were able to follow him, he came to the litter where Atabaliba was, and fearlessly seized him by the arm, crying out *Santiago*. Then the guns were fired off, the trumpets were sounded, and the troops, both horse and foot,

[11] From *Reports on the Discovery of Peru,* ed. C. H. Markham (London: Hakluyt Society, 1872), pp. 55–61.
[12] Francisco Pizarro
[13] the Inca Atahualpa

sallied forth. On seeing the horses charge, many of the Indians who were in the open space fled, and such was the force with which they ran that they broke down part of the wall surrounding it, and many fell over each other. The horsemen rode them down, killing and wounding, and following in pursuit. The infantry made so good an assault upon those that remained that in a short time most of them were put to the sword. The Governor still held Atabaliba by the arm, not being able to pull him out of the littler because he was raised so high. Then the Spaniards made such slaughter amongst those who carried the litter that they fell to the ground, and, if the Governor had not protected Atabaliba, that proud man would there have paid for all the cruelties he had committed. The Governor, in protecting Atabaliba, received a slight wound in the hand. During the whole time no Indian raised his arms against a Spaniard. So great was the terror of the Indians at seeing the Governor force his way through them, at hearing the fire of the artillery, and beholding the charging of the horses, a thing never before heard of, that they thought more of flying to save their lives than of fighting. All those who bore the litter of Atabaliba appeared to be principal chiefs. They were all killed, as well as those who were carried in the other litters and hammocks. . . .

The Governor went to his lodging, with his prisoner Atabaliba, despoiled of his robes, which the Spaniards had torn off in pulling him out of the litter. It was a very wonderful thing to see so great a lord taken prisoner in so short a time, who came in such power. The Governor presently ordered native clothes to be brought, and when Atabaliba was dressed, he made him sit near him, and soothed his rage and agitation at finding himself so quickly fallen from his high estate. Among many other things, the Governor said to him: "Do not take it as an insult that you have been defeated and taken prisoners, for with the Christians who come with me, though so few in number, I have conquered greater kingdoms than yours, and have defeated other more powerful lords than you, imposing upon them the dominion of the Emperor, whose vassal I am, and who is King of Spain and of the universal world. We come to conquer this land by his command, that all may come to a knowledge of God, and of His Holy Catholic Faith; and by reason of our good object, God, the Creator of heaven and earth and of all things in them, permits this, in order that you may know him, and come out from the bestial and diabolical life you lead. It is for this reason that we, being so few in number, subjugate that vast host. . . ."

. . . The battle lasted only about half an hour, for the sun had already set when it commenced. If the night had not come on, few out of the thirty thousand men that came would have been left. It is the opinion of some, who have seen armies in the field, that there were more than forty thousand men. In the square and on the plain there were two thousand killed, besides wounded. A wonderful thing was observed in this battle. It was that the horses which, the day before, could scarcely move for the cold, were able to charge with such fury that they seemed as if nothing had ever ailed them. . . .

In this town of Caxamalca, certain houses were found full of cloth, packed in bales which reached the roof. They say that it was a depot to supply the army. The Christians took what they required, and yet the house remained so full that what was taken seemed hardly to be missed. The cloth was the best that had been seen in the Indies. The greater part of it is of very fine wool, and the rest of cotton of rich colours, beautifully variegated. The arms they found, with which they made war, and their manner of fighting were as follows. In the van of their armies came the sling-men, who hurled pebbles from slings. These sling-men carry shields, which they make from narrow boards very small. They also wear jackets of quilted cotton. Next came men armed with sticks having large knobs at one end, and axes; . . . some of the axes and clubs, used by chiefs, were of gold and silver. Behind these came men armed with hurling lances, like darts. In the rear were pikemen with lances thirty handbreadths in length. These men had sleeves with many folds of cotton, over which they worked the lances. They are all divided into squadrons, with their banners and captains who command them, with as much order as Turks. Some of them wear great head pieces of wood, with many folds of cotton, reaching to the eyes, which could not be stronger if they were of iron. . . .

The lodging of Atabaliba, which he had in the centre of his camp, was the best that had been seen in the Indies, though it was small. It consisted of four rooms, with a court in the centre, having a pond supplied with water by a tube, and this water was so warm that one could not bear to put a hand into it. This water rises out of an adjacent mountain. Another tube brought cold water, and the two united in one tube on the road, and flowed, mixed together, by a single tube, into the pond. When they wish to allow one sort to flow alone, they remove the tube of the other. The pond is large and paved with stone. Outside the house, in a part of the yard, there is another pond, not so well made. They both have their flights of stone steps, by which to go down and bathe. The room in which Atabaliba stayed during the day was a corridor looking into an orchard, and near it there is a chamber where he slept, with a window looking towards the court and the pond. The corridor also opens on the court. The walls were plastered with red bitumen, better than ochre, which shined much, and the wood, which formed the eaves of the house, was of the same colour. Another room is composed of four vaults, like bells, united into one.

This is plastered with lime, as white as snow. The other two are offices. A river flows in front of this palace. . . .

# 90 / WILLIAM STRACHEY (FL. 1609-1618): THE COLONY OF VIRGINIA (1612)

*English settlement on the North American continent started in 1584–5 when Sir Walter Raleigh's first colony was brought to Roanoke Island by Sir Richard Grenville. However, these early attempts came to nothing; permanent colonization began along Chesapeake Bay in 1607–10. William Strachey was secretary to the Virginia Company; he went out in 1609 and wrote an invaluable account of the country.*[14]

Although the country people are very barbarous, yet have they amongst them such government as that their magistrates for good commanding and their people for due subjection and obeying excel many places that would be counted civil. The form of their commonwealth, by what has already been declared, you may well gather to be a monarchical government where one as emperor rules over many kings. . . . You shall now understand how his kingdom descends not to his sons or children, but first to his brethren whereof he has (as you have heard) three, and after their decease to his sisters; first to his eldest sister, then to the rest, and after them to the heirs-male and female of the eldest sister, but never to the heirs male.

He nor any of his people understand how to express their minds by any kinds of letters, to write or read, in barks of trees or any other kind of way, which necessity or invention might have instructed them in, as do other barbarians and some even in these new discoveries; nor have they positive laws—only the law whereby he rules is custom. Yet when he pleases, his will is law and must be obeyed, not only as king but as half a god, his people esteem him so. His inferior kings are tied likewise to rule by like customs and have permitted them power of life and death over their people. . . .

As for their houses, who knows one of them knows them all, even

[14] From William Strachey, *The History of Travaile into Virginia Britannia*, ed. R. H. Major (London: Hakluyt Society, 1849), Part 1, Chapter 6.

the chief's house itself, for they be all alike built one to the other. They are like garden arbours, at best like our shepherds' cottages, made, yet handsomely enough, though without strength or gayness, of such young plants as they can pluck up, bow and make the green tops meet together in fashion of a round roof which they thatch with mats thrown over. The walls are made of barks of trees, but then those be principal houses, for so many barks which go to the making up of a house are long time of purchasing. In the midst of the house there is a louvre out of which the smoke issues, the fire being kept right under. Every house commonly has two doors, one before and a postern. The doors be hung with mats, never locked nor bolted. . . . Windows they have none, but the light comes in at the door and the louvre. . . . By their houses they have sometimes a . . . high stage, raised like a scaffold, of small spelts, reeds or dried osiers, covered with mats, which both gives a shadow and is a shelter and serves for such a covered place where men used in old time to sit and talk for recreation or pleasure . . . and where on a loft of hurdles they lay forth their corn and fish to dry. They eat, sleep, and dress their meat [15] all under one roof and in one chamber, as it were.

Round about the house on both sides are their bedsteads, which are thick short posts staked into the ground, a foot high and somewhat more, for the sides small poles laid along, with a hurdle of reeds cast over, wherein they roll down a fine white mat or two, as for a bed, when they go to sleep; and the which they roll up again in the morning when they rise, as we do our pallets; and upon these, round about the house, they lie, heads and points, one by the other, especially making a fire before them in the midst of the house . . . ; some of them, when they lie down to sleep, cover them with mats, some with skins, and some lie stark naked on the ground, from six to twenty in a house, as do the Irish. . . .

It is strange to see how their bodies alter with their diet; even as the deer and wild beasts, they seem fat and lean, strong and weak. [King] Powhatan and some others that are provident roast their fish and flesh upon hurdles and reserve of the same until scarce times. Commonly the fish and flesh they boil, either very tenderly, or broil it long on hurdles over the fire or else (after the Spanish fashion) put it on a spit and turn first the one side then the other, till it be as dry as their jerkin beef in the West Indies; and so they may keep it a month or more without putrefying. The broth of fish or flesh they sup up as ordinarily as they eat the meat. Their corn they eat in the ears green, roasted, and sometimes bruising it on a mortar of wood with a little

[15] cook their food

pestle; they lap it in rolls within the leaves of the corn and so boil it
for a dainty. . . .

The men bestow their time in fishing, hunting, wars and such like
manlike exercises, without the doors, scorning to be seen in any
effeminate labour, which is the cause that the women be very painful
and the men often idle.

Their fishing is much in boats. These they call "quintans," as the
West Indians call their canoes. They make them with one tree, by
burning and scraping away the coals with stones and shells, till they
have made them in form of a trough. Some of them are an ell deep
and forty or fifty foot in length, and some will transport forty men;
but the most ordinary are smaller and will ferry ten or twenty, with
some luggage, over their broadest rivers. Instead of oars, they use pad-
dles or sticks which they will row faster than we in our barges. They
have nets for fishing . . . and these are made of the barks of certain
trees, deer sinews, or a kind of grass which they call "pemmenaw" of
which their women, between their hands and thighs, spin a thread very
even and readily; and this thread serves for many uses, as about their
housing, their mantles of feathers, and their trousers; and they also
make with it lines for angles.[16] . . .

In the time of hunting they leave their habitations and gather themselves into companies, as do the Tartars, and go to the most desert
places with their families, where they pass the time with hunting and
fowling up towards the mountains, by the heads of their rivers, where
indeed there is plenty of game; for betwixt the rivers the land is not
so large below that therein breed sufficient to give them all content.
. . . At their hunting in the deserts [17] they are commonly two or three
hundred together. With the sun rising they call up one another and go
forth, searching after the herd; which when they have found, they
environ and circle it with many fires, and betwixt the fires they place
themselves, and there take up their stand, making the most terrible
noise they can. The deer, being thus feared by the fires and their
voices, betake them to their heels, whom they chase so long within that
circle that many times they kill six, eight, ten, or fifteen in a morning.
They use also to drive them into some narrow point of land, when
they find that advantage, and so force them into the river where with
their boats they have ambuscades to kill them. . . .

A kind of exercise they have often amongst them much like that
which boys call bandy [18] in English, and may be an ancient game, as

[16] fishing rods
[17] wilderness
[18] a form of hockey

it seems in Virgil. . . . Likewise they have the exercise of football, in which they only forcibly encounter with the foot to carry the ball from one to the other, and spurned it to the goal with a kind of dexterity and swift footmanship which is the honour of it; but they never strike up one another's heels, as we do, not accounting that praiseworthy to purchase a goal by such an advantage. Dice play or cards or lotto they know not; howbeit, they use a game upon rushes much like primero [19] wherein they card and discard, and lay a stake too, and so win and lose. They will play at this for their bows and arrows, their copper beads, hatchets and their leather coats.

If any great commander arrive at the habitation of a weroance [20] they spread a mat, as the Turks do a carpet, for him to sit upon; upon another right opposite they sit themselves. Then do they all, with a tunable voice of shouting, bid him welcome; after this do two or more of the chief men make several orations, testifying their love, which they do with such vehemency and so great earnestness of passion that they sweat till they drop and are so out of breath that they can scarce speak, in so much as a stranger would take them to be exceeding angry or stark mad. After this verbal entertainment they cause such victual as they have or can provide to be brought forth, with which they feast him fully and freely, and at night they bring him to the lodging appointed for him, whither upon their departure they send a young woman, fresh painted red with pochone and oil, to be his bedfellow. The void time between sleep and meat [21] they commonly bestow in revelling, dancing and singing and in their kind of music. . . . As for their dancing, the sport seems unto them, and the use, almost as frequent and necessary, as their meat and drink, in which they consume much time, and for which they appoint many and often meetings. . . . One of them stands by, with some fur or leather thing in his left hand, upon which he beats with his right hand, and sings withal as if he began the choir . . . ; when upon a certain stroke or more (as upon his cue or time to come in) one rises up and begins to dance. After he has danced a while steps forth another, as if he came in just upon his rest. And in this order all of them as many as there be, one after another, who then dance an equal distance from each other in ring, shouting, howling, and stamping their feet against the ground with such force and pain that they sweat again, and with all variety of strange mimic tricks and distorted faces; . . . and sure they will keep stroke with their feet to the time he gives, and just one with another, but with the hands, head, face, and body everyone has a several [22] gesture. . . .

[19] a primitive form of poker
[20] warrior
[21] eating
[22] individual

# 91 / MICHEL DE MONTAIGNE (1533-1592): ON CANNIBALS

*Born of a landed family in the neighborhood of Bordeaux and educated as a child in a rather precocious humanist fashion, Montaigne studied law and practiced as a magistrate in the Bordeaux* Parlament *(superior court) until 1571, when poor health forced his retirement. The rest of his life he devoted to study and writing. The inventor of the essay as a form of literature, he infused into his varied reflections, called forth by anything that took his fancy, a very personal spirit compounded of scepticism, humor, and tolerance, the whole amalgamated into a predominantly elegiac mood of great charm. His essay* On Cannibals *both shows the impression made by the new discoveries on one of the best minds of the age, and stands at the head of a long line of writings which extol the life of the "noble savage" above the corruptions of civilization.*[23]

The discovery of an enormous continent deserves consideration. I do not know that I can be sure that some other may not hereafter be added, seeing that so many great men have been deceived in this. . . .

I find . . . that there is nothing barbarous or savage about that people, as far as I have been able to learn, except that everybody will call anything barbarous that does not agree with what he is used to. Admittedly, we have no other test of truth and reason except the example and model of the notions and customs of our own country: the perfect religion, the perfect society, the perfect and complete employment of all things are naturally there. Those others are savages, just as we call those fruits wild which nature produces unassisted and by its ordinary processes; whereas by rights we ought to apply the term wild to those which we by our science have changed and perverted from their proper state. . . . Those peoples, therefore, seem barbarous to me because they have received very little conditioning by the human mind and are still close to their original simplicity. The laws of nature, but little bastardised by ours, still govern them, and in such pure form that I am sometimes distressed by the thought that the

[23] Translated from Michel de Montaigne, *Essais*, ed. H. Motheau and D. Jouaust (Paris, 1886), Vol. 2, pp. 125 ff.

knowledge of all this did not come sooner, at a time when there were men who could have brought greater insight to the matter than we can. I am sorry Lycurgus and Plato knew nothing of this; for it seems to me that what we have learned about those people there exceeds not only all the images with which poetry has embellished the golden age and all the fanciful inventions about a happy state for man, but also the arguments and even the desires of philosophers. These could not imagine so pure and simple a lack of artificiality as now we see before our eyes; they could not believe that our society could maintain itself with so little contrivance and human sweat. Those peoples, I would tell Plato, have no knowledge of trade or of letters, no science of numbers, not the name even of a magistrate, no superiors to rule them; no use of services, of wealth or poverty; no contracts, no inheritance, no property rights, no occupations except those of leisure; no respect for ancestry except that which they all share, no clothes, no agriculture, no metal, no use of wine or wheat. The very words signifying lies, treason, deceit, avarice, envy, slander, pardon—all unheard of! How far would he find that his imaginary republic differs from such perfection? . . .

They live in a country so very pleasant and temperate in climate that, as my information goes, it is rarely one sees a sick man; and they tell me they have never seen there anybody suffering from palsy, eye-trouble, toothlessness or bent old age. They live on a strip of land along the seashore, shut off on the land side by great and high mountains, there being about a hundred leagues of open plain between the two. They have great abundance of fish and meat which in no way resembles ours, and they eat this without any fancy tricks, just plain cooking it. The first man to bring a horse along, though he had on several earlier voyages had dealings with them, caused such terror in their settlement that they had shot him down with arrows before they managed to recognise him. . . . They rise with the sun and eat at once after rising, making this do for the day; for they have no other meal but that. They do not drink with their meal . . . but drink several times in the day, sometimes beyond the limit. Their drink is made of a root and has the color of our claret; they drink it lukewarm. . . . It has a sharpish taste, nothing heady, and is good for the stomach; a laxative to those not used to it, but a very pleasant drink to anyone accustomed to it. In place of bread they eat a certain white substance rather like coriander biscuits. I have tasted it: it is sweet and a trifle dull. All day long is spent in dancing. The younger men go hunting with bows and arrows, while some of their women in the meantime amuse themselves by warming up the drink, which is their chief occupation. . . .

They have a sort of priests and prophets who, living in the mountains, rarely show themselves to the people. When they come, there is a great feast and solemn assembly of several villages. . . . The prophet addresses them in public, calling them to virtue and to do their duty. The whole of their ethics is contained in these two articles: resolution in war and love of their women. He also foretells them what is to come and the outcome they are to expect of their enterprises; he encourages them to war or dissuades them from it; but all on condition that if his prophecy miscarries and things happen otherwise than he predicted he is hacked into a thousand pieces (if they can catch him) and damned for a false prophet. In consequence, one who has miscalculated is never seen again. . . .

Three of them, ignorant how dear their acquaintance with our corruption will one day cost their peace and happiness, and how this intercourse will bring about their ruin which, I suppose, is already well advanced (wretches, to have allowed themselves to be deluded by a desire for novelty, and to have left their joyous skies in order to come and see ours), were at Rouen when the late King Charles IX [24] was there. He talked a good while to them, and they were shown our manners, our pomp, the sight of a fair city. Afterwards somebody asked them what they thought of it and wished to know what they had found most surprising. They said three things, of which I have forgotten the third (for which I am sorry); but two remain in my memory. They said that in the first place they found it very strange that so many tall men, bearded, strong and armed, who stood around the king (very probably they meant his Swiss guards) should submit in obedience to a child; why was not one of them chosen to command? Secondly (they have a habit in their language of calling men halves of one another) they had perceived that there were among us men full and gorged with all sorts of good things to their heart's content, while their halves, haggard with hunger and poverty, stood begging at the doors; and they found it strange that these halves, so very much in need, should permit such injustice and did not seize the others by the throat and set fire to their houses.

I talked to one of them for quite a while, but I had an interpreter who followed me so badly and was so hampered by his stupidity in understanding my drift that I got little from the man. When I asked him what benefit he derived from his superior station among his people (for he was a chief, and our sailors called him king) he told me that it was to lead the advance into battle. How many men followed him? He showed me a stretch of ground to indicate so many as would fill that space—it might be, four or five thousand. Did all his authority end when the war was over? He said all that remained was that when

24 king of France, 1560–74

he visited the villages dependent on him they cleared paths for him through the undergrowth of their forests, so that he could pass at his ease. All this does not sound too bad: after all, they wear no sort of trousers.

# IX / ECONOMIC PROBLEMS

*The economic History of Europe between 1300 and 1648 is much too diverse and complicated to be properly dealt with here. All one can do is to present a few significant points; other points, equally significant, must be left out. One omission, however, is deliberate. As far as I can judge, there are really no satisfactory grounds for the famous thesis (associated especially with Max Weber's* The Protestant Ethic and the Spirit of Capitalism *and R. H. Tawney's* Religion and the Rise of Capitalism*) that a meaningful relationship exists between the spread of the Reformation and something to be called the origins of modern capitalism. Capitalism, however defined, was older than the Reformation, and, at least until the second half of the seventeenth century, reformed teaching did nothing to assist it.*

*The Europe of the period under review was predominantly agrarian. Most people worked on the land; the bulk of wealth came from the land; except in some German, Italian, and Flemish cities, land alone bestowed social prestige. The two centuries after the population disaster caused by the plague of c. 1350 witnessed an amelioration of the peasant's lot and growing difficulties for landlords, except in France where the Hundred Years' War caused general devastation and misery. Labor services disappeared; lands were leased out to peasant proprietors; nonfreedom was not so much abolished as allowed to be forgotten (especially in England). The peasants' risings which punctuated the period (the French Jacquerie of 1358, the English rising of 1381, the German unrest culminating in the Peasants' War of 1524–5) were essentially the protest of solid men eager to escape out-of-date and burdensome (though legal) obligations. Then in the sixteenth century the great inflation fed by the rapid influx of bullion, mostly from Spanish America, reversed the trend, drove many small proprietors to the wall, and assisted the businesslike landowner—especially the English gentry and the East German nobility who rationalized their enterprises by concentrating on sheep farming and the mass production of grain re-*

spectively. Survival and wealth depended on one's ability to produce for a rising market dominated by the upward curve in population and prices, and this meant enterprise and flexibility, which also meant some ruthlessness to the weaker.

European trade, resting on the raw materials (especially wool, grain, timber, leather, and metals) produced by certain areas and the industrial capacity of others (with Northern Italy, Flanders, and, for a time, South Germany predominating), was always quite as complex and sophisticated as that of the early seventeenth century, described in No. 99. Details, of course, changed. Thus the English near monopoly in the export of raw wool of the fourteenth century dwindled away as a native cloth industry came to absorb the bulk of the crop; by the sixteenth century the textile industries of the continent relied on Spanish wool. The discoveries enormously increased the range of trade. The manufacturing ascendancy of Italy and Flanders passed, by the early seventeenth century, to Holland, France, and England. Both industry and trade were quickened by the inflation of the sixteenth century. Behind them stood an international money market capable of collecting and redistributing capital with a fair degree of skill, though it was always seriously hampered by the machinations of governments whose military needs tended to absorb all the available resources to the detriment of economic activity.

Governments and politics also ruined one financial center after another. The Italian bankers of the fourteenth and fifteenth centuries (Lombards, succeeded by Genoese and Florentines), who were the first to develop techniques suitable for a traffic covering all Europe, saw their predominance pass to South Germans (especially the Augsburg Fuggers, risen to pre-eminence on what in the end ruined them—the needs of the Habsburg empire) and to Antwerp, the economic hub of Western Europe for the fifty years before its destruction by the Spaniards in 1576. Lyons and Lisbon provided subsidiary centers. Before the end of the period, Amsterdam had succeeded to Antwerp's role, and London was beginning to get ready to take over from Amsterdam.

# 92 / THE BLACK DEATH (1349)

*Bubonic plague, endemic in Europe from its first onset in about 1350 until the cycle had run its course some three hundred years later, struck at economies already in some decline from the prosperity of the thirteenth-century agricultural boom. The Black Death accelerated the breakup of the manorial economy of the high Middle Ages, advanced the serfs' emancipation from the rights of lords, and in general added to those economic problems of the upper classes (whose income from land rents depended on a large working population of peasants) which in great part accounted for the unstable politics of the time. The most serious long-term consequences of the Death did not lie in the immediate loss of life—which was made good with surprising speed—but in its repeated attacks; these weakened stamina and contributed to the spiritual malaise of the fifteenth century.[1]*

The grievous plague penetrated the sea coasts from Southampton and came to Bristol, and there almost the whole strength of the town died, struck as it were by sudden death; for there were few who kept their beds more than three days, or two days, or half a day; and after this the fell death broke forth on every side with the course of the sun. There died at Leicester in the small parish of St. Leonard more than 380; and in the parish of the Holy Cross more than 400; and so in each parish a great number. . . . In the same year there was a great plague of sheep everywhere in the realm, so that in one place there died in one pasturage more than 5000 sheep, and so rotted that neither beast nor bird would touch them. And there were small prices for everything on account of the fear of death. For there were very few who cared about riches or anything else. For a man could have a horse which before was worth 40s. for 6s.8d., a fat ox for 4s., a cow for 12d., a heifer for 6d., a fat wether for 4d., a sheep for 3d., a lamb for 2d., a big pig for 5d., a stone of wool for 9d. Sheep and cattle went wandering over fields and through crops and there was no one to go and drive or father them, so that the number cannot be reckoned which perished

---

[1] From the translation of Henry Knighton's *Chronicle* in R. B. Morgan, *Readings in English Social History* (Cambridge: Cambridge University Press, 1923), pp. 145–7. By permission of Cambridge University Press.

in the ditches in every district for lack of herdsmen; for there was such a lack of servants that no one knew what he ought to do.

In the following autumn no one could get a reaper for less than 8d. with his food, a mower for less than 12d. with his food. Wherefore, many crops perished in the fields for want of some one to gather them; but in the pestilence year, as is above said of other things, there was such abundance of all kinds of corn that no one much troubled about it.

. . . Priests were in such poverty that many churches were widowed and lacking the divine offices, masses, matins, vespers, sacraments, and other rites . . . but within a short time a very great multitude of those whose wives had died in the pestilence flocked into orders, of whom many were illiterate and little more than laymen, except so far as they knew how to read, although they could not understand.

Meanwhile the king sent proclamation into all the counties that reapers and labourers should not take more than they had been accustomed to take under the penalty appointed by statute. But the labourers were so lifted up and obstinate that they would not listen to the king's command, but if any wished to have them he had to give them what they wanted, and either lose his fruit and crops or satisfy the lofty and covetous desires of the workmen. . . . After the aforesaid pestilence many buildings, great and small, fell into ruins in every city, borough and village for lack of inhabitants, likewise many villages and hamlets became desolate, all having died who dwelt there.

# 93 / THE MEDICI BANK IN THE FIFTEENTH CENTURY

*These entries from the Medici ledger will have to do duty for all the many financial houses of these three and a half centuries. The Medici rose to affluence as bankers; by this time, thanks to Cosimo Medici (1389–1464), they were also the political heads of their native Florence, though Cosimo was wise enough to preserve the outward appearance of a republic and hold no title of power. The Lorenzo here mentioned was his brother (1395–1440). Cosimo's grandson, Lorenzo the Magnificent (1449–92), the poet and patron of arts and letters, overdid the power game; after his death the Medici were soon expelled, returning in 1512 to establish by degrees a frankly despotic rule in the city. The financial transactions of the bank were made possible by the invention of the bill of exchange, a document assigning to a payee money owed to the payer in some other, often distant, place; the actual and cumbersome transfer of cash was thus rendered unnecessary.*[2]

No. 71 (25 Feb., 1423). The Council of the city of Siena have acknowledged that they have received of Folco Adovardi dei Portinari of Florence, associate and commissary of Cosimo and Lorenzo dei Medici, 9616 gold florins, being paid in the name of Pope Martin V for the occupation of the castle and fortifications of the city of Spoleto.

No. 78 (31 May, 1424). Baldo Andrea Baldi of Piombino, unable to read or write, has appointed Gabriel and Benedict dei Borromei, merchants of Pisa, as his proxies, for the presentation to Andrea Bardi & Co. of Pisa of a bill of exchange for 100 florins, given to him by Cosimo and Lorenzo dei Medici.

No. 95 (16 Nov., 1433). Nicolaus Lasozski, canon of Cracow [Poland], has made recognisance for the receipt of 37 florins in exchange from Albici dei Medici, for a payment made by the same Albici to the person of master John de Laironio, representative for Stanislas Pawlowski, bishop of Plonsk; and has promised to repay either him [Albici], or Cosimo and Lorenzo Medici & Co. in the court of Rome.

No. 107 (5 August, 1435). Whereas Sigismund, Holy Roman Emperor, a few years ago granted to Frederick Deys letters of reprisal against certain citizens of Florence, on account of certain sums of money which were owing to him; [it is] now [ordered] that this reprisal shall not extend to the Medici Company of Florence at the Council of Basel and in all of Germany.

No. 123 (31 August, 1438). The president and prelates representing the German nation at the Council of Basel have agreed that of the indulgence money of the diocese of Padua 2000 florins shall be paid to Messrs. Cosimo and Lorenzo dei Medici, in settlement of the loan which they had made to the Holy Council on the occasion of the bringing over of the Greeks.

No. 134 (19 Feb., 1440). Ralph of Rüdesheim, auditor-general of the Holy Synod of Basel, publicly excommunicates Stacius Malsen, a

[2] Translated from *I documenti commerciali del fondo diplomatico mediceo*, ed. Giulia Camerari Massi (Florence: Leo S. Olschki, Editore, 1951), Vol 3. By permission of the publisher.

layman of the diocese of Cologne, debtor to Lorenzo and Cosimo dei Medici, because he has not paid or rendered to Giovanni de la Stapha, their factor, the 15 *salutiae* [3] in which he stands condemned.

No. 141 (19 April, 1441). Francesco Foscari, Doge of Venice, writes to Cosimo dei Medici that, in pursuance of the alliance with the pope and the agreement made by himself with Roberto Martelli,[4] he shall order 4000 ducats to be paid at Florence to the troops stationed in Tuscany and the Romagna. And encloses a bill of exchange for 4000 ducats.

# 94 / SIR ANTHONY FITZHERBERT (1470-1538): THE BOOK OF HUSBANDRY (1523)

*The agrarian boom of the sixteenth century demanded efficient management, and several writers applied themselves to instructing farmers in their tasks. Fitzherbert, an English lawyer promoted to a judgeship in 1522, is now preferred to his brother John as the probable author of this book; he was quite a prolific author of handbooks, producing also a systematic abstract of English law, a guide for justices of the peace, another for sheriffs, and a book on surveying.[5]*

The most general living that husbands [6] can have is by ploughing and sowing of their corn and rearing or breeding of their cattle; and not the one without the other. Then is the plough the most necessariest instrument that a husband can occupy, wherefore it is convenient to know how a plough should be made. . . .

It is to be known whether is better a plough of horses or a plough of oxen, and therein, me seems, ought to be made a distinction. For in some places an ox plough is better than a horse plough, and some places a horse plough is better. . . . Oxen will plough in tough clay and upon hilly ground, whereas horses will stand still. . . . Horses

---

[3] a French coin
[4] the Medici representative at Venice
[5] Taken from Sir Anthony Fitzherbert, *The Boke of Husbandry* (London, 1523).
[6] farmers

will go faster than oxen on even ground or light ground, and quicker in carriages, but they be far more costly to keep in winter. For they must have both hay and corn to eat, and straw for litter; they must be well shod on all four feet, and the gear that they shall draw with is more costly than for the oxen, and shorter while it will last. And the oxen will eat but straw and a little hay, the which is not half the cost that horses must have, and they have no shoes as horses have. And if any sorance [7] come to the horse (wax old, bruised, or blind), then he is little worth. And if any sorance come to an ox (wax old, bruised, or blind) . . . he may be fed and then he is man's meat and as good ox better than ever he was. And the horse, when he dies, is but carrion. And therefore me seems, all things considered, the plough of oxen is much more profitable than the plough of horses. . . .

An husband cannot well thrive by his corn without he has other cattle, nor by his cattle without corn; for else he shall be a buyer, borrower or beggar; and . . . sheep in my opinion is the most profitablest cattle [8] that a man can have. . . .

A shepherd should not go without his dog, his sheep-hook, a pair of shears, and his tar-box either with him or ready at his sheep-fold. And he must teach his dog to bark when he would have him, to run when he would have him, and to leave running when he would have him; or else he is not a cunning shepherd. The dog must learn it when he is a whelp, or else it will not be; for it is hard to make an old dog to stoop. . . .

Now, thou husband that hast both horses and mares, beasts and sheep, it were necessary also that thou have both swine and bees. For it is an old saying: he that has both sheep, swine and bees, sleep he, wake he, he may thrive. And that saying is because that they be those things that most profit rises [from] in shortest space with the least cost. . . .

[7] trouble
[8] here, any domestic animal

# 95 / THE GERMAN PEASANTS' WAR: THE MEMMINGEN ARTICLES (1525)

*Of the several sets of demands put forward by the great peasants' uprising in south and central Germany, the Twelve Articles agreed at Memmingen were both the most moderate and most representative. Their economic sections, dealing with peasants' payments and services and the common rights of villages, reflect similar points made in other parts of Europe in the previous 150 years. The religious articles, on the other hand, are novel and demonstrate Lutheran and Anabaptist influences.[9]*

It is our humble request and prayer, and also our general desire and intent, that in future we shall have power and authority for every congregation to elect and choose its own minister. Also to have power to remove him if he behaves in an unfitting manner. The said minister so chosen shall preach the holy gospel purely and clearly without any additions made by man, teach us the true faith, give us cause to ask God for His grace, and erect and confirm the true faith in us. For if His grace is not entered into us we remain always flesh and blood, which is no use: as Scripture clearly says, that we cannot come to grace but by faith alone and can be saved only by His mercy. . . .

2. Where the tithe is ordained in the Old Testament and released in the New, nevertheless we will gladly pay the proper tithe of corn, but only in due manner. Each man shall give to God and shall share his own with a true minister who preaches the word of God. . . . Our churchwardens shall make a general assessment, and shall collect and gather [the tithe]; out of it they shall pay to any minister elected by the congregation his sufficient maintenance according to the mind of the parish; and what is left shall be distributed to such poor and needy as may be in the village. . . . The small tithe [10] we will not

[9] Translated from H. Boehmer, *Urkunden zur Geschichte des Bauernkrieges und der Wiedertäufer* (Bonn, 1910), pp. 4 ff.

[10] The great tithe was payable on agrarian produce, the small on an increase in stock animals.

render at all, for the Lord God has provided beasts freely for men; we think it an improper tithe which men have invented. . . .

3. It has been the custom hitherto to hold us for bondmen, which is a pitiful matter, seeing that Christ with His precious blood has freed and bought us all, the hind as well as the highest, no man excepted. Therefore we assert that we are free and will be free; not that we wish to be free altogether and renounce all authority: so God does not teach us. We mean to live under the law, not under an arbitrary and carnal will. . . . God's command does not show and order us to refuse obedience to lordship; we are to be humble not only towards lordship but towards all men and to obey our chosen and appointed superiors (if appointed by God) in all proper and Christian matters. . . .

4. It has hitherto been the custom that no poor man has any right to catch game, fowl or fish in running water; which seems to us wrong and not brotherly, but only selfish and contrary to the Word of God. . . . When the Lord God created man He gave him dominion over all beasts, over the fowls of the air and the fish in the water. Therefore we demand this: if any man owns a river and can prove a proper bargain [with the village], we do not wish to take it from him by force, but it will be meet in brotherly love to use Christian charity therein; but if he cannot show sufficient proof, he must share it with the village, as is proper.

5. We make complaint concerning woods, for our lords have acquired sole rights of timber; and if the poor man needs any he has to pay for it twice over. . . .

6. We complain most heavily about the labor services which are daily increased and daily grow. We demand that this be looked to and that we be not so burdened beyond measure, but that mercy be shown to us according to our fathers' services. . . .

7. That in future no lord shall impose more burdens but as his lordship entitles him to, according to the agreement of lords and commons. The lord shall not force and extort more service nor make other demands, so that the peasant may use and enjoy his rights in peace; but if the lord needs service, the peasant shall willingly and obediently do it, but at a time that means no hardship to him; and shall receive for it his proper penny.

8. We complain, and that bitterly; where some hold manors, and the said estate cannot bear the rent [asked] and the peasants rot and decay, that the lords shall have men of worship survey the said manors and assess a convenient rent, so that the peasant may not have his work in vain, for the laborer is worthy of his hire.

9. We complain concerning justice in serious offences where new laws are always being made. They do not punish us after the facts of

the matter, but at times with too much severity and at other times with too much favor shown. It is our opinion that we should be punished according to the old penalties laid down in writing. . . .

10. We complain that some have taken over meadows and land which should be held in common; these we shall take back into common possession, unless the rights have been honestly acquired by purchase; but if they have been bought dishonestly there shall be made a decent and brotherly composition, according to the truth of the matter.

11. We desire to end altogether the custom called heriot.[11] We will not suffer nor permit that widows and orphans shall be shamefully robbed of their own, contrary to God and decency, as has happened in many a place. Those who should have guarded and warded them, have grieved and ground them down. . . . No man in future shall owe anything for this, neither little nor much.

12. We finally agree and conclude that, if any of these articles here written be not in accord with the Word of God (as we do not hold to any the same articles such as may be proved to be against the Word of God), we will omit them, provided it is so explained to us on grounds of Scripture. Even if any of these articles are granted and are later found to be unjust, the same shall from that hour be dead and void and shall have no more force. Similarly, if in truth any more articles be found of matters against God and to the burden of neighbors, we reserve such. And we are resolved to live in and use Christian doctrine; for which reason we pray to the Lord God Who can grant our request, and no one else. The peace of Christ be with us all.

# 96 / WILLIAM MARSHALL (FL. 1535): DRAFT OF A POOR LAW (1536)

*One of the problems which a rising population and the economic crisis of inflation made general in sixteenth-century Europe was unemployment or, as the age called it, the poor and the vagrant beggars. Various humanists wrote about it; various cities legislated for it; England produced in 1597–1601 the first national code for dealing with it. A draft act of 1536, of which*

---

[11] the lord's right to the serf's best beast or other property on his death

*only a small part became law, gave this lucid classification of the unemployed and unemployables; it offered to solve the first problem by means of state works financed by a graduated income tax, and the second by charity supported out of a compulsory local rate. The first point was too ambitious to be attempted anywhere; the second became the mainstay of the later English poor law. Almost certainly the draft was written by William Marshall, a printer and one of Thomas Cromwell's pamphleteers, who in 1535 produced a translation of Marsiglio of Padua as part of the propaganda campaign for Henry VIII's state church.*[12]

Forasmuch as the king's majesty has full and perfect notice that there be within this his realm as well a right great multitude of strong valiant beggars, vagabonds and idle persons of both kinds, men and women, which though they might well labour for their living if they would will not yet put themselves to it as divers other of his true and faithful subjects do, but give themselves to live idly by begging and procuring of alms of the people, to the high displeasure of Almighty God, hurt of their own souls, evil example of others, and to the great hurt of the commonwealth of this realm; as also divers others old, sick, lame, feeble and impotent persons not able to labour for their living but are driven of necessity to procure the alms and charity of the people. And his highness has perfect knowledge that some of them have fallen into such poverty only of the visitation of God through sickness and other casualties,[13] and some through their own default, whereby they have come finally to that point that they could not labour for any part of their living but of necessity are driven to live wholly by the charity of the people. And some have fallen to such misery through the default of their masters which have put them out of service in time of sickness and left them wholly without relief and comfort. And some be fallen thereto through default of their friends which in youth have brought them up in overmuch pleasure and idleness, and instructed them not in anything wherewith they might in age get their living. And some have set such as have been under their rule to procure their living by open begging even from childhood, so that they never knew any other way of living but only by begging. And so for lack of good oversight in youth many live in great misery in age. And some have come to such misery through their own default, as through sloth, pride, negligence, falsehood and such other ungraciousness, whereby their masters, lovers and friends have been driven to forsake

[12] From British Museum, Royal MS 18.C.vi.
[13] accidents

them and finally no man would take them to any service; whereby they have in process of time lain in the open streets and fallen to utter desolation. And divers other occasions have brought many to such poverty which were very long to rehearse here. But whatsoever the occasion be, charity requires that some way be taken to help and succour them that be in such necessity and also to prevent that others shall not hereafter fall into like misery. Therefore his highness, of his most blessed and godly disposition, like a virtuous prince and gracious head regarding as well the maintenance of the commonwealth of his realm, the good governance of his people and subjects being the members of his body, as the relief of the poor, wretched and miserable people whereof be a great multitude in this his realm, and the redress and avoiding of all valiant beggars and idle persons within the same . . . has by the advice of the lords spiritual and temporary and the commons in this present Parliament assembled . . . provided certain remedies as well for the help and relief of such idle, valiant beggars as has been before remembered, as of such poor and miserable people as be before rehearsed, in manner and form following. . . .

# 97 / JOHN HALES (D. 1571): ENCLOSURES AND INFLATION (1548)

*In England the rising prices were for a long time ascribed to the activities of monopolists and hoarders, and especially to the enclosing of arable land for sheep-farming which allegedly reduced the food supply. It is now accepted that contemporaries greatly exaggerated the extent and evil effects of enclosure, though the enclosing of village commons by landlords was a serious and justified grievance. For the rest, greed no doubt played its part in the story of distress, but the trouble lay essentially with the large economic movements which people could not understand. They preferred scapegoats. Hales, a government official, was very active in the attempt made in 1548–9 to arrest and reverse the enclosure movement; this passage comes from the address which he delivered during his proceedings as a commissioner of enquiry in the Midland counties. The commissions failed to overcome the resistance of the powerful gentry who thought enclosure necessary both to improve their lands and increase their pleasures; but a few years later the bottom dropped out of the wool market, and much sheep pasture went back under the plow.*[14]

As by natural experience we find it to be true that if any one part of man's body be grieved . . . it is a great pain to all the whole body . . . so ought we to consider and remember in the state of the body of the realm. If the poorest sort of the people, which be members of the same body as well as the rich, be not provided and cherished in their degree, it cannot but be a great trouble of the body and a decay of the strength of the realm. Surely, good people, methinks that if men would know how much this ungodly desire of worldly things, and the unlawful getting and heaping together of riches, were hated of God, how hurtful and dangerous for the commonwealth of the realm it is, and what a virtue the mean in all things is, these laws nor a great many more that be needed not. God's Word is full of threats and curses against these kind of greediness. . . . When men in a commonwealth go about to gather as much as they can, and to get it they care not how; not considering whether by their gain any hurt should come to their neighbours or to the commonwealth; not only others, but they themselves should shortly perish. What avails a man to have his house full of gold and be not able to keep it with his force against his enemies? So what shall all our goods avail us if we be not able to defend us from our enemies?

The force and puissance of the realm consists not only in riches but chiefly in the multitude of people. But it appears, good people, that the people of this realm, our native country, is greatly decayed through the greediness of a few men in comparison, and by this ungodly means of gathering together goods, by pulling down towns and houses, which we ought all to lament. Where there were in few years ten or twelve thousand people, there be now scarce four thousand. Where there were a thousand, now scarce three hundred, and in many places, where there were very many able to defend our country from landing of our enemies, now almost none. Sheep and cattle, that were ordained to be eaten of men, has eaten up the men, not of their own nature but by the help of men. Is it not a pitiful case that there should be so little charity among men? Is it not a sorrowful hearing that one Englishman should be set to destroy his countrymen? The places where poor men dwelt clearly destroyed; lands improved to so great rents,

[14] From J. Strype, *Ecclesiastical Memorials* (London, 1721), Vol. 2, Appendix of Documents, Doc. Q.

or so excessive fines [15] taken that the poor husbandman cannot live. All things at this present . . . be so dear as never they were—victual and other things that be necessary for man's use. And yet, as it is said, there was never more cattle, specially sheep, than there is at this present. But the cause of the dearth is that those have it that may choose whether they will sell it or not, and will not sell it but at their own prices. . . .

To declare unto you what is meant by this word, enclosures. It is not taken where a man does enclose and hedge in his own proper ground where no man has commons. For such enclosure is very beneficial to the commonwealth: it is a cause of great increase of wood. But it is meant thereby when any man has taken away and enclosed any other men's commons, or has pulled down houses of husbandry and converted the lands from tillage to pasture. This is the meaning of the word, and so we pray you remember it.

To defeat these statutes [against enclosure and depopulation] as we be informed, some have not pulled down their houses but maintain them; howbeit, no person dwells therein, or if there be it is but a shepherd or a milkmaid; and convert the lands from tillage to pasture. And some about one hundred acres of ground, or more or less, make a furrow and sow that, and the rest they till not but pasture with their sheep. And some take the lands from their houses and occupy them in husbandry, but let the houses out to beggars and old poor people. Some, to colour [16] the multitude of their sheep father them on their children, kinsfolk and servants. All which be but only crafts and subtleties to defraud the laws, such as no good man will use but rather abhor. . . .

Besides, it is not unlike but that these great fines for lands and improvement of rents shall abate, and all things wax better cheap —20 and 30 eggs for a penny, and the rest after the rate as has been in times past. And the poor craftsmen may live and set their wares at reasonable prices. And noblemen and gentlemen that have not improved nor enhanced their rents, nor were sheepmasters nor graziers but lived like noblemen and gentlemen, shall be the better able to keep good hospitality among you, and keep servants about them, as they have done in time past. . . .

---

[15] a sum payable by the incoming tenant on a new or renewed tenancy
[16] disguise

# 98 / THOMAS MUN (1571-1641): EXPORTS AND IMPORTS (C. 1635)

*Mun, a London merchant with interests in the Levant and East India trades, was one of the many who wrote on the subject of commerce. His works display much sound sense and are representative of the best—that is, the least doctrinaire—thinking along so-called mercantilist lines. The book from which this passage is taken was not published until 1664, but was written some thirty years earlier.[17]*

The revenue or stock of a kingdom by which it is provided of foreign wares is either natural or artificial. The natural wealth is so much only as can be spared from our own use and necessities to be exported unto strangers. The artificial consists in our manufactures and industrious trading with foreign commodities, concerning which I will set down such particulars as may serve for the cause we have in hand.

1. First, although this realm be already exceeding rich by nature, yet it might be much increased by laying the waste grounds . . . into such employment as should in no way hinder the present revenues of other manured lands, but hereby to supply ourselves and prevent the importations of hemp, flax, cordage, tobacco and divers other things which now we fetch from strangers to our great impoverishing.

2. We may likewise diminish our importations if we would soberly refrain from excessive consumption of foreign wares in our diet and raiment, with such often change of fashions as is used, so much the more to increase the waste and charge. . . .

3. In our exportations we must not only regard our own superfluities, but also we must consider our neighbours' necessities, that so upon the wares which they cannot want, nor yet be furnished thereof elsewhere, we may (beside the vent [18] of the materials) gain so much of the manufacture as we can; and also endeavour to sell them dear, so far forth as the high price cause not a less vent in the quantity. But the superfluities of our commodities which strangers use, and may also have the same from other nations . . . we must in this

[17] From Thomas Mun, *England's Treasure by Foreign Trade* (London, 1664), Chapter 3.
[18] sale

case strive to sell as cheap as possible. . . . When cloth is dear, other nations do presently practise clothing,[19] and we know they want neither art nor materials to this performance. But when by cheapness we drive them from this employment and so in time obtain our dear price again, then do they also use their former remedy. So that by these alterations we learn that it is in vain to expect a greater revenue of our wares than their condition will afford; but rather it concerns us to apply our endeavours to the times with care and diligence, to help ourselves the best we may by making our cloth and other manufactures without deceit, which will increase their estimation and use.

4. The value of our exportations likewise may be much advanced when we perform it ourselves in our own ships; for then we get only not the price of our wares as they are worth here, but also the merchants' gains, the charges of insurance and freight to carry them beyond the seas. . . .

6. The fishing in His Majesty's seas of England, Scotland and Ireland is our natural wealth and would cost nothing but labour, which the Dutch bestow willingly; and thereby draw yearly a very great profit to themselves by serving many places of Christendom with our fish, for which they return and supply their wants of foreign wares and money; besides the multitude of mariners and shipping which hereby are maintained. . . .

7. A staple or magazine for foreign corn, indigo, spices, raw silks, cottonwool or any other commodity whatsoever to be imported, will increase shipping, trade, treasure and the king's customs by exporting them again where need shall require. . . . For such purpose England stands most commodiously, wanting nothing to this performance but our own diligence and endeavour.

8. Also we ought to esteem and cherish those trades which we have in remote countries, for besides the increase of shipping and mariners thereby, the wares also sent thither and received from thence are far more profitable unto the kingdom than our trades near at hand. As for example: suppose pepper to be worth here two shillings the pound constantly, if it be brought from the Dutch at Amsterdam the merchant may give there twenty pence the pound and gain well by the bargain; but if he fetch this pepper from the East Indies he must not give above threepence the pound at the most. . . .

10. It were policy and profit for the state to suffer manufactures made of foreign materials to be exported custom-free. . . . It would employ very many poor people and much increase the value of the stock yearly issued into other countries. . . .

11. It is needful also not to charge the native commodities with

---

[19] cloth manufacture

too great customs, lest by endearing them to the strangers' use it hinder their vent. And especially foreign wares brought in to be transported again should be favoured, for otherwise that manner of trading . . . cannot prosper or subsist. . . . .

Lastly, in all things we must endeavour to make the most we can of our own, whether it be natural or artificial. And forasmuch as the people which live by the arts are far more in number than they who are masters of the fruits, we ought the more carefully to maintain those endeavours of the multitude in whom does consist the greatest strength and riches both of king and kingdom; for where the people are many and the arts good, there the traffic must be great and the country rich. The Italians employ a greater number of people and get more money by their industry and manufactures of the raw silks of the kingdom of Sicily than the king of Spain and his subjects have by the revenue of this rich commodity. But what need we fetch the example so far when we know that our own natural wares do not yield us so much profit as our industry? For iron ore in the mines is of no great worth when it is compared with the employment and advantage it yields being digged, tried, transported, bought, sold, cast into ordnance, muskets and many other instruments of war for offence and defence, wrought into anchors, bolts, spikes, nails and the like, for the use of ships, houses, carts, coaches, ploughs and other instruments for tillage. Compare our fleece wool with our cloth, which requires shearing, washing, carding, spinning, weaving, fulling, dyeing, dressing and other trimmings, and we shall find these arts more profitable than the natural wealth. . . .

# 99 / COMMENT: R. H. TAWNEY (1880-1961) ON THE PATTERN OF EUROPEAN TRADE (C. 1610)

*The dean of English economic historians, R. H. Tawney, devoted to the elucidation of the sixteenth and seventeenth centuries that part of his life which he spared from the labors of a sociopolitical writer on contemporary affairs and problems. This passage is taken from his last book,* Business and Politics under James I.[20]

The fundamental feature of the economy of Europe can be simply stated. It was a contrast of climate, of natural resources, and probably of population, between north and south, resembling in miniature that later to become important between Europe as a whole and the extra-European world. . . . At one end, the regions adjacent to the Baltic remained semi-colonial. Thinly settled, heavily wooded, with the trapper giving way to the lumberman, and lumbering to agriculture as the timber-line retreated and the cereal frontier advanced, they were a still unexhausted reservoir of raw materials and foodstuffs. At the other, Spain and Portugal, with a surplus of textile fibres, vegetable oils, dye-stuffs, iron ore and southern fruits, reinforced by colonial wares, supplied primary products complementary to those of the north. Commanding the resources of a more genial environment, a denser population and a more sophisticated civilisation than the first, and less disposed than the second to "employ themselves in arms, not in manufactures," the chief industrial areas of Europe lay between these two extremes. To such a statement there are, of course, numerous exceptions; but the larger currents of trade had their source in the regional differences which such contrasts caused. As in the Middle Ages, and indeed, well into the last century, they flowed south and north, from forest, corn land, territories rich in copper, lead or iron, and seas in fish, to vineyards, olive grove, sheep pasture, salt lagoon, textile workshop, smithy and shipyard, meeting, crossing and restarting in the great junction of the Netherlands, and, at different points, feeding or fed by subsidiary streams. Of these tributaries, some were themselves no trifling rivers; but the circulation depended on the pulse of the great north to south artery. If that were blocked or cut, the whole organism languished. The knot-points were Amsterdam and London: Danzig and Hamburg: Frankfurt-am-Main, Leipzig and Nürnberg: Rouen, Bordeaux and Marseilles: Venice and Leghorn. The international exchange, to which most staples found their way, was Amsterdam. The financial experts were Italians, in particular the Genoese, the South Germans and the Dutch, with the last gaining rapidly on the two first. The bullion on which their operations were based came, largely via Barcelona and Genoa, from Spain. The ligament which held the whole structure together was the shipping of the Dutch. . . .

As a clue to the nexus between nations, the character of the wares

[20] R. H. Tawney, *Business and Politics under James I* (Cambridge: Cambridge University Press, 1958), pp. 21–8. By permission of Cambridge University Press.

exchanged is . . . both less uncertain and more illuminating than official valuations put on them at ports. The venerable legend of medieval commerce as an affair of high values in small bulk has recently sustained . . . some corrective shocks. The infectious glamour of Milton's "barbaric pearls and gold," which clings to the first predatory phase of European expansion, requires, if to a somewhat less degree, the same deflating touch. The part played by costly superfluities . . . was, doubtless, more conspicuous than later it became . . . but, apart from the East Indian and South American fleets, bulk consignments were predominantly of a different stamp. Except for the virtual absence of crude minerals, and the paucity of capital goods other than timber, ships and guns, the international staples which kept tonnage moving were at once insignificant in number compared with those of today, and in kind not less prosaic. Handling, as it did, three essential foodstuffs, the raw materials of a dozen or so industries, and one large group of manufactures flanked by several minor ones, international commerce had as its backbone, not the luxuries of romantic legend, but commodities catering, if not for mass demand, which, outside a few cities, hardly yet existed, for the elementary needs of a large consuming public..

In an economy destitute of the auxiliaries and substitutes supplied by science, and in which production depends less on generalised technology than on traditional crafts, goods must be sought where nature supplies them. Hence the primary products of differently endowed regions occupied, it is probable, a larger space in freights than in the Europe of today. A catalogue would be tedious, and a handful of specimens must suffice. Corn is one example. The world's chief cereal-importing countries tend in our age to be those whose high population density and low acreage per head causes land to be dear; the chief cereal exporters those where the opposite conditions make it cheap. Except that rye, not wheat, was the principal export crop, a similar situation obtained in the past. Four permanent deficiency areas, the Netherlands, northern Italy, Spain and Portugal, the two first the most densely populated countries in Europe, the two last with natural disadvantages which made cereal-farming a gamble, depended regularly on imported grain, as at moments of emergency did several more. Poland with Prussia—with a climate and soil suitable for rye, if not for wheat, excellent river communications between the interior and the sea, and a population per square mile a third or less that of the Netherlands, prepared for the role of a European Middle West—was the principal source of the surplus which supplied them. Minor contributions came from Estonia; from Russia, described, when trade with it had been developed by Dutch capital, as "the Sicily of Holland"; and in southern Europe from Sicily itself, Sardinia and France. The export specialty of the last, wheat, not rye, went to Spain, the Netherlands, and, when the English harvest failed, across the Channel.

Fish—at a period whose agricultural technique made fresh meat almost the seasonal delicacy that game now is, not a supplement to fresh food, but a substitute for it—was another article in the same category. Cheap, easily packed, and standing transport well, it travelled from the "golden mines" of the North Sea as far as Venice in one direction, and Archangel in the other; entered eastern Germany by the Sound and western by the Rhine; set nations by the ears; reconciled Protestant sailors to Popish fasts; and produced for the edification of posterity a library of pamphlets unique even in economic literature for their singular blend of credulity and dullness. The reader, exasperated by the intolerable tedium of odes to the herring, must solace his sufferings with the princely aphorism that the humble kipper was the pebble in the sling with which the Dutch David laid at last the Spanish Goliath low.[21] . . .

All countries manufacturing textiles produced some of the raw materials required, but none produced all. Spanish silk was important to the French silk industry and essential to the Dutch. France and Holland relied mainly on home-grown flax, but also imported it. The exotic connections of the cotton industry are an old story. A trickle of wool found its way into trade from a dozen countries from Poland to Greece, but supplies from the one great specialist, Spain, were essential to the textile industries of not less than four. England, while buying abroad such indispensable subsidiaries as oils, alum, potash and dyestuffs, and producing minor specialties from Spanish wool, was the least dependent on foreign fibre. . . .

The student of mercantilist literature may be pardoned for some perplexity at the limelight lavished on [textiles], as though the grand end of economic statesmanship were to deluge with an ever-mounting flood of fabrics a world already wallowing in superfluous piece-goods. In reality, the industries concerned were not one, but five, and, if their subdivisions be included, not five, but legion. Italian looms supplied the larger part of the small demand for silks, satins and velvets. France rivalled Italy in the luxury trade, but her longest suit was based on flax, which then met the needs later served by cotton. . . . The specialty of south Germany was fustians; that of the Spanish Netherlands tapestries and carpets. The United Provinces shipped to London half-a-million yards of linens of their own production, together with three-quarters of a million yards of linen re-exports, at a time when they were themselves the second largest market for English woollens. England, while importing linen warps from the Netherlands and cotton

---

[21] The remark is ascribed to Prince Maurice [of Orange].

yarn from Turkey, supplied the former with the grey cloths which were the raw materials of its finishing industry, and sent kerseys to be dressed and dyed at Bremen and Nürnberg. Nor do these familiar examples stand alone. Venetian glass; French *bimbeloterie;* the products of Nürnberg's mechanical ingenuity, which were to be found . . . in every corner of Europe; above all, in spite of every disadvantage, the miraculous pre-eminence in shipbuilding of the Dutch, are further instances of a specialisation which owed less to nature than to art. . . .

# X / THE PREHISTORY OF MODERN SCIENCE

*However much the Renaissance may have believed in the use of the human reason, it did very little to advance men's understanding of their natural surroundings. The most favored "sciences" of the humanists were astrology and alchemy, and, contrary to the probabilities, the practitioners of these mysteries contributed almost nothing even to the development of astronomy and chemistry. Some fourteenth-century Franciscans like Nicole Oresme (d. 1382), starting from Aristotle, the Arabs, and independent observation, had been more searching scientists than nearly all the great humanist scholars; and the demands of ocean navigation produced more positive gain in knowledge than all the humanists together. Despite this curious blind spot, the fifteenth and sixteenth centuries were not entirely barren of scientific interest and investigation. The rediscovery of many Greek works increased the number of authorities relied upon, even if it did not induce independent study; and the invention of printing enabled men to use more, and more reliably produced, books.*

*While in general, therefore, men's ideas about the universe and their environment changed remarkably little before the end of the sixteenth century, a few isolated workers produced results and theories which, when in due course assimilated, were to be revolutionary. Copernicus' assertion that the sun, not the earth, was the center of the universe took a long time to attract widespread attention, especially because his exposition failed to answer certain commonsensical objections. But after the Dane, Tycho Brahe (1546–1601), had greatly improved celestial observation and collected a mass of data, and the German, Johannes Kepler (1571–1630), had broken the hold of the ancient doctrine that all planetary motion must be in perfect circles, the way was clear for the astronomical revolution. By 1600, as the debate really got under way, the Church of Rome took fright: a moving earth offended theological postulates. Giordano Bruno (1548–1600), who argued that perhaps the universe was infinite, was burned at the stake; some thirty years later Galileo had to recant his views. But this did not even delay progress; outside Italy, science was in no danger from the Inquisition. In other sciences, too, changes were being prepared. An excellent anatomical textbook like that of Andreas Vesalius (1514–64) pointed the way to the revolutionary discoveries of William Harvey. Medical needs developed the technique of distillation, ultimately to be useful to chemistry; the haphazard collecting of information in natural history began to assemble the materials for a systematic study of botany and zoology. By the end of the sixteenth century, scientific knowledge was a curious amalgam of inherited lore (some of it sound enough), of superstition and pseudoscience, and of some fruitful new ideas not yet properly considered. The work was to be done in the following century, and mostly after the period with which we are concerned. But the achievements of Galileo, the speculations of Bacon, and the system of Descartes all made their appearance before the age of Newton opened.*

# 100 / NICHOLAS COPERNICUS (1473-1543): ON THE REVOLUTIONS OF CELESTIAL BODIES (1543)

*Copernicus, the son of a Polish merchant, went to Cracow University, developed an interest in astronomy which grew during a long spell of study in Italy, and after his return to Poland began to grow dissatisfied with the Ptolemaic and Aristotelian system, according to which the earth stood still at the center of the universe, while the heavens, composed of concentric spheres to which the sun, the planets and the fixed stars were attached, revolved around it. The immediate response was moderate; for one thing, Copernicus' mathematics were not sufficient to make his theory stick. But some eighty years later, after fresh work had made his fundamental discovery more convincing, his theory became the center of a sharp controversy. And then, almost overnight, doctrines of great antiquity just evaporated.*[1]

For these and similar reasons it is claimed that the earth is at rest in the center of the universe and that this is undoubtedly true. But one who believes that the earth rotates will also certainly be of the opinion that this motion is natural and not violent. . . . Whatever happens in the course of nature remains in good condition and in its best arrangement. Without cause, therefore, Ptolemy[2] feared that the earth and earthly things if set in rotation would be dissolved by the action of nature, for the functioning of nature is something entirely different from artifice, or from that which could be contrived by the human mind. But why did he not fear the same, and indeed in much higher degree, for the universe, whose motion would have to be as much more rapid as the heavens are larger than the earth? . . . It is said that outside of the heavens there is no body, nor place, nor empty space, in fact, that nothing at all exists, and that, therefore, there is no space in which the heavens could expand. . . . Now whether the world[3] is finite or infinite, we will leave to the quarrels of the natural philosophers; for us remains the certainty that the earth, contained between poles, is bounded by a spherical surface. Why should we hesitate to grant it a motion, natural and corresponding to its form; rather than assume that the whole world, whose boundary is not known and cannot be known, moves? And why are we not willing to acknowledge that the *appearance* of a daily revolution belongs to the heavens, its *actuality* to the earth? . . . For when a ship is sailing along quietly, everything which is outside of it will appear to those on board to have a motion corresponding to the movement of the ship, and the voyagers are of the erroneous opinion that they with all that they have with them are at rest. . . .

Since nothing stands in the way of the movability of the earth, I

[1] From the translation of *De Revolutionibus Orbium Coelestium* in *A Source Book of Astronomy*, ed. Harlow Shapley and Helen E. Howarth (Cambridge, Mass.: Harvard University Press, 1929), pp. 7–12. By permission of Harvard University Press.

[2] Greek astronomer (second century A.D.), whose geocentric system dominated astronomy until the triumph of Copernican ideas in the seventeenth century

[3] the universe

believe we must now investigate whether it also has several motions, so that it can be considered one of the planets. That it is not the center of all the revolutions is proved by the irregular motions of the planets, and their varying distances from the earth, which cannot be explained as concentric circles with the earth at the center. Therefore, since there are several central points, no one will without cause be uncertain whether the center of the universe is the center of gravity of the earth or some other central point. I, at least, am of the opinion that gravity is nothing else than a natural force planted by the divine providence of the Master of the World into its parts, by means of which they, assuming a spherical shape, form a unity and a whole. And it is to be assumed that the impulse is also inherent in the sun and the moon and the other planets, and that by the operation of this force they remain in the spherical shape in which they appear; while they, nevertheless, complete their revolutions in diverse ways. If then the earth, too, possesses other motions beside that around its center, then they must be of such a character as to become apparent in many ways and in appropriate manners; and among such possible effect we recognise the yearly revolution. If one admits the motionlessness of the sun, and transfers the annual revolution from the sun to the earth, there would result, in the same manner as actually observed, the rising and setting of the constellations and the fixed stars; and it will thus become ·apparent that also the haltings and the backward and forward motion of the planets are not motions of these but of the earth, which lends the appearance of being actual planetary motions. Finally, one will be convinced that the sun itself occupies the center of the universe. And all this is taught us by the law of sequence in which things follow one upon another, and the harmony of the universe; that is, if we only (so to speak) look at the matter with both eyes. . . .

# 101 / THOMAS VICARY (C. 1490-1562): THE CRAFT OF SURGERY

*Vicary was one of the most prominent medical men of the reign of Henry VIII, chief surgeon to the King from 1530 and responsible for the refounding and renewal of St. Bartholomew's Hospital in London after 1548. However, he was a surgeon, not a physician, and as such he was regarded as totally inferior—a mere artisan rather than a member of a profession. In consequence he introduced his influential handbook on surgery (largely a summary of traditional Galenic medicine but embodying some personal observation, too) with a defense of his craft that emphasized its complexity, difficulty, and respectability.*[4]

In the name of God, amen. Here I shall declare unto you shortly and briefly the sayings and determinations of diverse ancient authors in three points, very expedient for all men to know that intend to use or exercise the mystery or art of surgery. The first is to know what thing surgery is; the second how that a surgeon should be chosen; and the third is, with what properties a surgeon should be endowed.

The first is to know what thing surgery is. Herein I do note the saying of Lanfranc, whereas he sayeth: all things that a man would know may be known by one of these three things—that is to say, by his name, or by his working, or else by his very being and showing of his properties. So then it followeth that we may know what surgery is by three things. First by his name, as thus: the interpreters write that surgery is derived out of these words, *Apo tes chiros kai tou ergou*,[5] that is to be understanded, a hand-working, and so it may be taken for all handy arts. But noble Hypocras sayeth that surgery is hand-working in man's body; for the very end and profit of surgery is hand-working. Now the second manner of knowing what surgery is, it is . . . to be known by his being; for it is verily a medicinal science; and as Galen says, he that will know the certainty of a thing, let him not busy himself to know only the name of that thing but also the working and effect of the same thing. Now the third way of knowing what thing surgery is, it is also to be known by his being or declaring of his own properties, the which teacheth us to work in man's body with hands, as thus: in cutting or opening those parts that be whole, and in healing those parts that be broken or cut, and in taking away that that is superfluous, as warts, wens, scrofulas and other like. But further to declare what Galen sayeth surgery is, it is the last instrument of medicine: that is to say, diet, potion and surgery; of the which three, he sayeth, diet is the noblest and the most virtuous. And thus he sayeth, whereas a man may be cured with diet only, let there be given no manner of medicine. The second instrument is potion: for and if a man may be cured with diet and potion, let there not be ministered any surgery. And this suffices for us for that point. Now it is known what thing surgery is, there must also be chosen a man apt and meet to minister surgery, or to be

[4] From Thomas Vicary, *A Profitable Treatise of the Anatomy of a Man's Body* (1548), ed. F. J. and P. Furnivall (London, 1888), pp. 12–17.

[5] from the words *hand* and *labor*

a surgeon. And in this point all authors do agree that a surgeon should be chosen by his complexion,[6] and that his complexion be very temperate and all his members well proportioned. For . . . whose face is not seemly, it is impossible for him to have good manners. And Aristotle, the great philosopher, writeth in his epistles to the noble king Alexander (as in those epistles more plainly doth appear) how he should choose all such persons as should serve him, by the form and shape of the face and all other members of the body. And furthermore, they say, he that is of an evil complexion, there must needs follow like conditions. Wherefore it agreeth that a surgeon must be both of a good and temperate complexion, as is afore rehearsed. And principally that he be a good liver and a keeper of the holy commandments of God, of whom cometh all cunning [7] and grace, and that his body be not quaking and his hands steadfast, his fingers long and small and not trembling, and that his left hand be as ready as his right hand, with all his limbs able to fulfil the good works of the soul. Now here is a man meet to be made a surgeon. And though he have all these good qualities before rehearsed, yet is he no good surgeon but a man very fit and meet therefore.

Now, then, to know what properties and conditions this man must have before he be a perfect surgeon. And I do note four things most specially that every surgeon ought for to have. The first, that he be learned; the second, that he be expert; the third, that he be ingenious; the fourth, that he be well-mannered. The first (I said), he ought to be learned, and that he know his principles not only in surgery but also in physic,[8] that he may the better defend his surgery. Also he ought to be seen in natural philosophy and in grammar, that he speak congruity in logic that teacheth him to prove his proportions with good reason. In rhetoric, that teacheth him to speak seemly and eloquently; also in theory that teacheth him to know things natural and not natural, and things against nature. Also he must know the anatomy, for all authors write against those surgeons that work in man's body, not knowing the anatomy; for they be likened to a blind man that cutteth a vine tree, for he taketh more or less than he ought to do. And here we note well the saying of Galen, the prince of philosophers, in his *Histories*, that it is as possible for a surgeon not knowing the anatomy to work in man's body without error as it is for a blind man to carve an image and make it perfect. The second, I said, he must be expert; . . . he ought to know and to see other men work, and after to have use and exercise. The third, that he be ingenious or witty,[9] for all things

6 appearance
7 knowledge
8 medicine
9 intelligent

belonging to surgery may not be written nor with letters set forth. The fourth, I said, that he must be well mannered and that he have all these good conditions here following: first, that he be no spouse-breaker [10] nor no drunkard. For the philosophers say, amongst all other things beware of those persons that follow drunkenness, for they be accounted for no men because they live a life bestial; wherefore amongst all other sorts of people they ought to be sequestered from the ministering of medicine. Likewise a surgeon must take heed that he deceive no man with his vague promises, for to make of small matter a great, because he would be counted the more famous. And amongst other things, they may neither be flatterers nor mockers nor privy backbiters [11] of other men. Likewise they must not be proud nor presumptuous nor detractors of other men. Likewise they ought not to be too covetous nor no niggard, and namely amongst their friends or men of worship; but let them be honest, courteous and free, both in word and deed. Likewise they shall give no counsel except they be asked and then say their advice by good deliberation; and that they be well advised before they speak, chiefly in the presence of wise men. Likewise they must be as privy and as secret as any confessor of all things that they shall either hear or see in the house of their patient. They shall not take into their cure any manner of person except he will be obedient unto their precepts; for he cannot be called a patient unless he be a sufferer. Also that they do their diligence as well to the poor as to the rich. They shall never discomfort their patient and shall command all that be about him that they do the same; but to his friends speak truth, as the case standeth. They must also be bold in those things whereof they be certain, and as dreadful [12] in all perils. They may not chide with the sick, but be always pleasant and merry. They must not covet any woman by way of villainy and especially in the house of their patient. They shall not, for covetousness of money, take in hand those cures that be uncurable, nor never set any certain day of the sick man's health, for it lieth not in their power: following the distinct counsel of Galen. . . . "Oportet seipsum non solum." [13] By this Galen meaneth that to the cure of every sore there belongeth four things of which the first and principal belongeth to God, the second to the surgeon, the third to the medicine, and the fourth to the patient. Of the which four, and if any one do fail, the patient cannot be healed; then they to whom belongeth but the fourth part shall not promise the whole but be first well advised. They must also be gracious and good to the poor, and of the rich take liberally for both. And see they never praise themselves, for that

[10] adulterer
[11] talkers behind men's backs
[12] circumspect
[13] "Nothing is sufficient to itself."

redoundeth more to their shame and discredit then to their fame and
worship; for a cunning and skilful surgeon need never vaunt of his
doings, for his works will ever get credit enough. Likewise that they
despise no other surgeon without a great cause; for it is meet that one
surgeon should love another, as Christ loveth us all. And in thus doing
they shall increase both in virtue and cunning, to the honour of God
and worldly fame. To whom he bring us all. Amen.

# 102 / PARACELSUS: HERMETICAL OR MYSTICAL SCIENCE

*Theophrastus Bombastus von Hohenheim, surnamed Para-*
*celsus (c. 1490–1541), a Swiss student of science and medicine,*
*was the leading exponent of a movement in science that stemmed*
*from a neo-Platonic reaction against Aristotelian reason and rested*
*much of its case on the writings of Hermes Trismegistus, a late-*
*Hellenic mystic falsely believed to have been an ancient Egyptian.*
*The heart of Paracelsus' thinking was a cloudy concept of the*
*oneness of all things—the permeation of all creation by something*
*that at times sounds like a "life force" and at other times more*
*substantially like some basic and universal form of matter. Views*
*such as these lie behind the practice of alchemy, which tried not*
*only to transform matter from one manifestation into another but*
*also to isolate the inner principle of both matter and spirit by*
*chemical experiments. Paracelsus' alchemical research led him to*
*denounce the established traditions of Galenic medicine and to*
*advocate the use of metallic compounds for curative purposes.*
*Recent modern scholarship, reacting against the positivism of*
*earlier historians of science, has revived an interest in these magi-*
*cal preoccupations and professes to find much virtue in them;*
*and one may concede to Paracelsus some merit in that he advanced*
*our knowledge of drugs and took medicine away from books and*
*back to nature. However, the exalted content of his teaching was*
*incurably muddled and fuddled (A), whereas his experimentation*
*lacked the scepticism and precision (especially accurate measure-*
*ment) that alone could have turned these alchemical outpourings*
*into a foundation for scientific understanding (B). In his credulity*

*and self-satisfaction, Paracelsus was essentially an ass—an influential ass in that age of alchemy, but because of his reckless playing about with metallic poisons sometimes a dangerous ass.*[14]

## A. CONCERNING THE ARCANUM OF THE PRIMAL MATTER

Since we have sufficiently pointed out concerning the Primal Matter, whence it proceeds or what it is, we must understand that it is based not only on men, but on all bodily creatures, that is, on everything that is born from any seed. Whence it may be inferred that if it has its operations in any created body and perfects it, as we have before declared, it is able also to preserve trees from corruption, herbs from being dried up, and also metals from rust, concerning which the same thing must be understood of men and brute beasts. So, then, a tree which is now almost consumed with age, and daily verging more and more on its own corruption, not from defect of root or of nutriment, but of its own proper virtue, can be renewed by its own primal matter. . . . On this principle virtues are to contribute to it, namely, in order that the corruption and destruction may be now and again renewed in a long process of time. No less is this to be understood of herbs, which last only for a single year, because their predestination is no longer. For they, even when they begin to be dried up are renewed by their primal matter; so that they remain green and fresh for another annual period, or for a third, a fourth, or more. The same thing understand of brute beasts, as, for instance, old sheep and other animals. They can be renewed for a fresh period of life, having received their virtues, such as milk and wool, like young sheep. Equally, too, can men be led on from one age to another, as we have said before. From this it ought to be known that the primal matter is according to its essence. In created things, such as have no sensation, it is their seed; but in created beings endowed with sensation, it is their sperm. For it must be known that the primal matter is not to be taken from the thing out of which this created body is produced, but out of the produced and generated material. For the primal matter has in it such virtues that it will not allow the body which is born of it to go into corruption, but abundantly affords whatever is necessary for the supply of every requirement. Indeed, death only arises from the destruction or infection of the living spirit. Now, that spirit grows out of the sperm, or out of the seed, and is altogether a spermatic substance; therefore it can be helped by its like. For wherever the like is given as a help,

[14] From *The Hermetical and Alchemical Writings of Paracelsus*, ed. and trs. A. E. Waite (London, 1894), ii, pp. 40–1, 140.

there is introduced a new period of life. . . . The quintessence of the seed of the nettle (otherwise the lavender) if it be poured on any root of its own herb, so that this herb may receive its tincture and be affected by it, it remains another year as in the former year, not putrefying until that second year shall have been completed.

### B. OIL OF MARS

Pound up crocus of Mars [15] into a most minute and delicate powder. Wash this with fresh water. Pour out the water of the lotion. Let it stand until it sinks. Then separate the water from that which sinks and let the crocus be dried up. Take any quantity of this, and make a paste with the yolk of eggs. Let it be again thoroughly dried. At last beat it into powder, and spread on a smooth glass slab. Place in a wine cellar, and it will be dissolved into a clear oil. This is the oil of Mars, suitable for all external ulcers.

# 103 / ROBERT FLUDD (1574-1637): SCIENCE AS MAGIC

*Fludd, a medical doctor with an Oxford degree (1605), fell under the spell of magic and the occult early in his life. He was much influenced by the great John Dee (1527–1608), a man who combined high scientific attainments with a profound and often credulous attachment to astrology and necromancy. Dee's eccentric genius will excuse his extravagances; Fludd, an early devotee of the nonexistent mysteries of the nonexistent society of the Rosicrucians, became merely an absurdity. Justly attacked by a sceptical adversary on the subject of a salve that allegedly healed wounds when applied not to the injured place but to the instrument that had caused the injury, he fought back with the arguments delineated here. However, he is worth notice because he reminds us of the powerful magical tradition in science that persisted by the side of the equally strong rational movement into the age of Newton.[16]*

[15] crocus: orange-coloured compound; Mars: iron; i.e., iron oxide?

[16] From Robert Fludd, *Answer to Mr. Foster: or Squeezing of Parson Foster's sponge, ordained by him for the wiping away of the weapon-salve* (London, 1631).

[pp. 108–9] There is a knight dwelling in Kent, a man judicious, religious and learned, called Sir Nicholas Gilbourne, one (I say) with whom I both am and have been long familiar. For he married my sister. This knight, having good acquaintance with one Captain Stiles, forasmuch as in time past he was his tenant, was with the said captain in the company of very good and learned divines at the making of the said ointment, who saw all the ingredients apart and after beheld an apothecary to compound them together without any kind of superstitious action, where it was generally adjudged to be a lawful medicine and no way superstitious or diabolical. A box of this ointment was bestowed on this my brother-in-law; what wholesome effects it has wrought, I will in a word relate unto you, and that *verbatim,* as I have it under his own hand.

The first (says he) was at Chatham in Kent where the servant of one Popper, a shipwright, was cut with his axe into the instep, so deep as it could pass and not cut it off; upon the hurt (which was in the afternoon) he was brought unto me, but I refused to meddle with it; only I advised him to wash his wound with his own urine, which he did. The next morning early I did dress the axe, and after dressing it I did send to know how the fellow did. Answer was made that he had been in great pain all night, but now lately was at ease. The next morning, coming into my study, I struck my rapier down upon the axe the hilt whereof struck the ointment off from the axe, which when I found I sent to understand how he did. And had answer that he had been exceeding well that night, but this morning was in great pain, and so continued. I therefore anointed the axe again and then sent again unto him, and heard that he was then at great ease—and within seven days perfectly cured.

[Part II, pp. 26–29: Against Foster's denial "that any spirits remain in separated blood"] I will prove that . . . his assertion is erroneous, by three manner of ways. Namely, first, by philosophical reason: for being that every amputated creature, even from the lively stock of his growth, is filled with a balsamic salt of the nature of the tree or plant from which it sprang, by which it does exist (such as indeed it *is*), it is not possible but that it should have of the spirit of his wonted life in it, although it does not act but rest in its centre.

Next, by holy scripture: for (as is proved abundantly before) the blood spilled and flesh killed is full of lively spirits, though they remain potentially in them; or else why should the Israelites be commanded not to eat the fat and blood? For it is said: "because the blood is the seat of the soul or spirit of life." For if that spirit were fled from it, what sin had it been to have eaten it? But the text says, "for it is the seat of life," and therefore it is commanded that "they should pour it out on the earth. . . ."

And lastly by common experience: for we find that fat and blood

and mummy have singular properties of healing, which they could not
have if all the spirits which they did receive from the living body were
exhaled, "but it is the office only of the incorruptible Spirit and Word
to heal" (I Cor. 12); and therefore, being these ingredients have a
healing property, they must needs in this their existence participate or
communicate with this good spirit whose nature is to expel and take
away all corruption and sickness and other unnatural impediments.
. . . Moreover I know and with mine eyes have seen abundance of
spirits which by the activity of the least fire have been excited out of
the essence of corrupted blood and fat, insomuch that with the natural
heat of the hand they, in form of little atoms, have been observed to
dance and caper in the air: which is an evident token that there is the
spirit of life lurking in the dead blood. . . . Again, if this were not, is
it possible that dead blood, flesh and fat could nourish the living, being
that like is nourished by like? . . . I have observed that the balsam of
wheat so aboundeth in it that if it be put into rainwater in a short space
it produceth long worms of a white colour. . . .

# 104 / GALILEO GALILEI (1564-1642): ON MOTION (1636)

*Galileo brought two powerful aids to his study of physics:
a great experimental skill (he virtually invented the telescope)
and an open mind. The best-known part of his career concerns
his clash with the Roman Inquisition, which arose from his public
defense of the Copernican system after the Church had condemned it (Dialogue of the Two Chief World Systems, 1633).
His defeat and recantation left him free to continue his more
fundamental studies in mechanics, in which he overthrew Aristotle's impulse theory (that motion is produced by a quality introduced by the moving force into the object moved) and laid
the foundations of modern physics.*[17]

My purpose is to set forth a very new science dealing with a very

[17] From *Dialogues concerning Two New Sciences*, by Galileo Galilei, trans.
Henry Crew and Alfonso de Salvio (New York: Dover Publications, Inc., 1914),
pp. 153, 160–2.

ancient subject. There is, in nature, perhaps nothing older than motion, concerning which the books written by philosophers are neither few nor small; nevertheless I have discovered by experiment some properties of it which are worth knowing and which have not hitherto been either observed or demonstrated. Some superficial observations have been made, as, for instance, that the free motion of a heavy falling body is continuously accelerated; but to just what extent this acceleration occurs has not yet been announced; for so far as I know, no one has yet pointed out that the distances traversed, during equal intervals of time, by a body falling from rest, stand to one another in the same ratio as the odd numbers beginning with unity. . . .

Accelerated motion remains to be considered. And first of all it seems desirable to find a definition best fitting natural phenomena. For anyone may invent an arbitrary type of motion and discuss its properties; thus, for instance, some have imagined helices and conchoids as described by certain motions which are not met with in nature, and have very commendably established the properties which these curves possess in virtue of their definitions; but we have decided to consider the phenomena of bodies falling with an acceleration such as actually occurs in nature and to make this definition of accelerated motion exhibit the essential features of observed accelerated motions. And this, at last, after repeated efforts we trust we have succeeded in doing, In this belief we are confirmed mainly by the consideration that experimental results are seen to agree with and exactly correspond with those properties which have been, one after another, demonstrated by us. Finally, in the investigation of naturally accelerated motion we were led, by hand as it were, in following the habit and custom of nature herself, in all her various other processes, to employ only those means which are most common, simple and easy. . . .

When, therefore, I observe a stone initially at rest falling from an elevated position and continually acquiring new increments of speed, why should I not believe that such increases take place in a manner which is exceedingly simple and rather obvious to everybody? If now we examine the matter carefully we find no addition or increment more simple than that which repeats itself in the same manner. This we readily understand when we consider the intimate relationship between time and motion; for just as uniformity of motion is defined by and conceived through equal times and equal spaces ( thus we call a motion uniform when equal distances are traversed during equal timeintervals ), so also we may, in a similar manner, through equal timeintervals, conceive additions of speed as taking place without complication; thus we may picture to our mind a motion as uniformly and continuously accelerated when, during any equal intervals of time whatever, equal increments of speed are given to it. Thus if any equal intervals of time have elapsed, counting from the time at which the moving body left its position of rest and began to descend, the amount of speed acquired during the first time-intervals will be double that acquired during the first time-interval alone; so the amount added during three of these time-intervals will treble; and that in four, quadruple that of the first time-interval. To put the matter more clearly, if a body were to continue its motion with the same speed which it had acquired during the first time-interval and were to retain this same uniform speed, then its motion would be twice as slow as that which it would have if its velocity had been acquired during *two* time-intervals.

And thus, it seems, we shall not be far wrong if we put the increment of speed as proportional to the increment of time; hence the definition of motion which we are about to discuss may be stated as follows: A motion is said to be uniformly accelerated, when starting from rest, it acquires, during equal time-intervals, equal increases of speed. . . .

# 105 / WILLIAM HARVEY (1578-1657): ON THE MOTION OF THE HEART AND BLOOD (1628)

*Harvey spent a long life as a very successful doctor, but he is remembered for two magnificent pieces of research. In addition to his discovery of the circulation of the blood, published a good twelve years after he had described it to his students at the London College of Physicians, he also did most valuable work on the sexual reproduction of animals* (De Generatione Animalium, *1651*). *However, it is the first achievement, the basis of all scientific physiology, which deserves the highest praise.*[18]

Thus far I have spoken of the passage of the blood from the veins into the arteries, and of the manner in which it is transmitted and distributed by the action of the heart. . . . What remains to be said upon the quantity and source of the blood is of so novel and unheard-

[18] From Harvey's *Works*, trans. Robert Willis (London, 1847), pp. 45–7.

of character, that I do not only fear injury to myself from the envy of a few, but I tremble lest I have mankind at large for enemies, so much does wont and custom, that become as another nature, and doctrine once sown . . . and respect for antiquity influence all men: still, the die is cast, and my trust is in my love of truth. . . .

When I surveyed my mass of evidence, whether derived from vivisections, and my various reflections on them, or from the ventricles of the heart and the vessels that enter into and issue from them, the symmetry and size of these conduits—for nature doing nothing in vain would never have given them so large a relative size without a purpose —or from the arrangement and intimate structure of the valves in particular, and of the other parts of the heart in general, with many things besides, I frequently and seriously bethought me, and long revolved in my mind, what might be the quantity of blood which was transmitted, in how short a time its passage might be effected, and the like; and not finding it possible that this could be supplied by the juices of the ingested aliment without the veins on the one hand becoming drained, and the arteries on the other getting ruptured through the excessive charge of blood, unless the blood should somehow find its way from the arteries into the veins, and so return to the right side of the heart; I began to think whether there might not be *a motion, as it were, in a circle.* Now this I afterwards found to be true; and I finally saw that the blood, forced by the action of the left ventricle into the artéries, was distributed to the body at large, and its several parts, in the same manner as it is sent through the lungs, impelled by the right ventricle into the pulmonary artery, and that it then passed through the veins and along the vena cava, and so round to the left ventricle in the manner already indicated. Which motion we may be allowed to call circular. . . . The various parts are nourished, cherished, quickened by the warmer, more perfect, vaporous, spirituous, and, as I may say, alimentative blood; which, on the contrary, in contact with these parts becomes cooled, coagulated, and, so to speak, effete; whence it returns to its sovereign the heart, as if to its source, or to the inmost home of the body, there to recover its state of excellence or perfection. . . . The heart, consequently, is the beginning of life; the sun of the microcosm, even as the sun in his turn might well be designated the heart of the world; for it is the heart by whose virtue and pulse the blood is moved, perfected, made apt to nourish, and is preserved from corruption and coagulation. . . .

# 106 / FRANCIS BACON (1561-1626): NOVUM ORGANUM (1620)

*Bacon was certainly many-sided enough. The lawyer and politician who reached the high place of lord chancellor, only to fall over a charge of corruption, also wrote on politics, economics, and religion and imitated Montaigne's essays. His own chief ambition was to be a universal philosopher, and he planned a great general system which would present the world with an original key to the secrets of the mind and the universe. Such systems were fashionable in philosophy, and the surviving fragments of Bacon's suggest that he might have produced a very interesting one if his other preoccupations had not taken so much of his time. The* Novum Organum, *intended as Part Two of the enterprise, presented a new method of reasoning based on induction from data. The work is written in numbered aphorisms, a method which hides its close construction. Though Bacon was never an experimental scientist, and shows both some ignorance of the true nature of experiments and some failure to grasp the importance of working hypotheses, his aphorisms contain some very penetrating analysis of scientific method and probably exercised a certain amount of influence among the men who founded the Royal Society later in the century.[19]*

XIV. A syllogism consists of propositions, propositions consist of words, words are tokens for ideas. If therefore the ideas themselves (the foundation of the matter) are confused and rashly deduced from things, there is no sort of firmness in the superstructure. Therefore the only true hope lies in *induction*.

XVIII. All that has so far been discovered in the sciences pretty well remains subject to vulgar notions; if we are to penetrate to the heart and limits of nature, we shall have to find a more certain and better fortified way of inferring both ideas and axioms from things. Altogether, a better and more certain method of reasoning will have to be brought into use.

XIX. There are, and can only be, two methods of enquiry and

[19] Translated from Bacon's *Works*, ed. J. Spedding (London, 1857), Vol. 2, pp. 157 ff.

the discovery of truth. One flies upward from sense-data and particulars to extremely general axioms and causes, and discovers from these principles and their unchanging truth the intermediate axioms; this is the method now in use. The other deduces axioms from sense-data and particulars by steadily and gradually climbing higher, coming at the last to the most universal generalisations; this is the true method, but one not yet tried.

XXI. The intellect, left to itself, in a sober, patient and serious condition (especially if not impeded by received teaching), tends markedly towards the second and right way, but a very slow rate of progress; since the intellect, unless directed and assisted, is an inadequate weapon and altogether unable to overcome the obscurity of things.

XXII. Both methods begin with sense-data and particulars, and culminate in generalisations of a universal order, but they nevertheless differ enormously. For the one only just touches on experiment and the particular, while the other employs these properly and by rote; the one from the first posits certain abstract and useless generalisations, while the other by stages arrives at the truly knowable aspects of nature.

XXIV. It can in no way happen that axioms arrived at by reasoning should result in the discovery of new facts; for the subtlety of nature by many degrees exceeds the subtlety of reasoning. But axioms arrived at properly and by rote easily indicate and describe new particulars; thus they activate science.

XXVIII. Anticipation[20] is not in the least more useful for the establishment of agreed fact than is interpretation [of phenomena]. Gathered from a few facts—and those as a rule the ones that occur familiarly—it only dazzles the intellect and stimulates the fancy. Interpretation, on the other hand, gathered all over the place from very varied and far separated data, cannot strike the mind with such sudden force; the facts must be treated, like opinions, as hard and discordant, not unlike the mysteries of the faith.

XXX. If all the geniuses of all the ages co-operated in conflating and transmitting their labours, no great progress would be possible in the sciences by the use of hypotheses; for radical errors, contained in the first dispositions of the mind, are not cured by the excellence of subsequent steps and corrections.

XXXI. It is vain to expect great additions in the sciences from the superimposition and insertion of new facts among the old; the building must start from the very foundations, unless one likes to move in circles for ever, with negligible and despicable advances only.

XCV. All practitioners of science have been either empiricists or

[20] Bacon's word for hypothesis

dogmatists. Empiricists, like ants, only collect and put to use; dogmatic reasoners, like spiders, spin webs from within themselves. The bee's is the middle way: it extracts matter from the flowers of garden and field, but, using its own faculties, converts and digests it. The true operation of philosophy is not unlike this. It neither relies exclusively on the powers of the mind, nor simply deposits untouched in the memory the material provided by natural history and physical experiment. Rather it transforms and works on this material intellectually. Therefore we may have hopes of great results from an alliance, so far unconcluded, between the experimental and rational methods.

# 107 / RENÉ DESCARTES (1596-1650): DISCOURSE ON METHOD (1637)

*Where the Englishman Bacon demanded experiment, the Frenchman Descartes identified mathematics as the only true method of natural and metaphysical philosophy. He was himself an outstanding mathematician, the inventor of coordinate geometry. His immediate influence was overwhelming: Cartesianism became the characteristic philosophy of the later seventeenth century. In the sciences, the progress of physics seemed to bear out his devotion to mathematics. But in fact, Newton got at the truth by discarding Descartes' cosmic physics, and another universal system bit the dust. The* Discourse *is an autobiographical account of his search for a single unifying method and his arrival in due course at mathematics.*[21]

When I was younger, I had devoted a little study to logic, among philosophical matters, and to geometrical analysis and to algebra, among mathematical matters—three arts or sciences which, it seemed, ought to be able to contribute something to my design. But on examining them I noticed that the syllogisms of logic and the greater part of the rest of its teachings serve rather for explaining to other people the things we already know, or even . . . for speaking without judgment of things we know not, than for instructing us of them. And although

[21] From René Descartes, *Discourse on Method*, trans. G. B. Rawlings (London, n.d.), pp. 20–4.

they indeed contain many very true and very good precepts, there are always so many others mingled therewith that it is almost as difficult to separate them as to extract a Diana or a Minerva from a block of marble not yet rough-hewn. Then, as to the analysis of the ancients and the algebra of the moderns, besides that they extend only to extremely abstract matters and appear to have no other use, the first is always so restricted to the consideration of figures that it cannot exercise the understanding without greatly fatiguing the imagination, and in the other one is so bound down to certain rules and ciphers that it has been made a confused and obscure art which embarrasses the mind, instead of a science which cultivates it. This made me think that some other method must be sought, which, while combining the advantages of these three, should be free from their defects. And as a multitude of laws often furnishes excuses for vice, so that a state is much better governed when it has but few, and those few strictly observed, so in place of the great number of precepts of which logic is composed, I believed that I should find the following four sufficient, provided that I made a firm and constant resolve not once to omit to observe them.

The first was, never to accept anything as true when I did not recognise it clearly to be so, that is to say, to carefully avoid precipitation and prejudice, and to include in my opinions nothing beyond that which should present itself so clearly and so distinctly to my mind that I might have no occasion to doubt it.

The second was, to divide each of the difficulties which I should examine into as many portions as were possible, and as should be required for its better solution.

The third was, to conduct my thoughts in order, by beginning with the simplest objects, and those most easy to know, so as to mount little by little, as if by steps, to the most complex knowledge, and even assuming an order amongst those which do not naturally precede one another.

And the last was, to make everywhere enumerations so complete, and surveys so wide, that I should be sure of omitting nothing.

The long chains of perfectly simple and easy reasons which geometers are accustomed to employ in order to arrive at their most difficult demonstrations, had given me reason to believe that all things which can fall under the knowledge of man succeed each other in the same way, and that provided only we abstain from receiving as true any opinions which are not true, and always observe the necessary order in deducing one from the other, there can be none so remote that they may not be reached, or so hidden that they may not be discovered. And I was not put to much trouble to find out which it was necessary to begin with, for I knew already that it was with the simplest and most easily known; and considering that of all those who have heretofore sought truth in the sciences it is the mathematicians alone who have been able to find demonstrations, that is to say, clear and certain reasons, I did not doubt that I must start with the same things that they have considered, although I hoped for no other profit from them than that they would accustom my mind to feed on truths and not to content itself with false reasons. But I did not therefore design to try to learn all those particular sciences which bear the general name of mathematics: and seeing that although their objects were different, they nevertheless all agree, in that they consider only the various relations or proportions therein, I thought it would be better worth while if I merely examined these proportions in general, supposing them only in subjects which would serve to render the knowledge of them more easy to me, and even also, without in any wise restricting them thereto, in order to be the better able to apply them subsequently to every other subject to which they should be suitable. Then, having remarked that in order to know them I should sometimes need to consider each separately, I had to suppose them in lines, because I found nothing more simple, or which I could more distinctly represent to my imagination and to my senses; but to retain them, or to comprehend many of them together, it was necessary that I should express them by certain ciphers as short as possible, and in this way I should borrow all the best in geometrical analysis, and in algebra, and correct all the faults of the one by means of the other. . . . What satisfied me most with this method, was that by it I was assured of always using my reason, if not perfectly, at least to the best of my power. . . .

# 108 / COMMENT: HERBERT BUTTERFIELD (B. 1900) ON THE SCIENTIFIC REVOLUTION

*Professor Butterfield, since 1944 professor of modern history at the University of Cambridge, and since 1955 Master of Peterhouse, has shown a quite unusual versatility of interests. His books include technical studies of diplomacy and politics, but he is perhaps best known for his reflections on the nature of history and for the impetus he has given to two only recently established branches of scientific historiography: the study of both the historical writing and the science of the past as aspects of its intellectual structure. This passage is taken from his* The Origins of Modern Science.[22]

Now it was Bacon's firm principle that if men wanted to achieve anything new in the world, it was of no use attempting to reach it on any ancient method—they must realise that new practices and policies would be necessary. He stressed above all the need for the direction of experiments—an end to the mere haphazard experimenting—and he insisted that something far more subtle and far-reaching could be achieved by the proper organisation of experiments. It is quite clear that he realised how science could be brought to a higher power altogether by being transported away from that ordinary world of common-sense phenomena in which so much of the discussion had hitherto been carried on. He insisted on the importance of the actual recording of experiments, a point which . . . was now coming to be of some significance. He insisted that experiments in different fields should get together, because they would knock sparks off one another; and things done in one field would give hints to people working in another field. . . . Suggestions which are scattered in various parts of

[22] Herbert Butterfield, *The Origins of Modern Science* (London: G. Bell & Sons, Ltd.; New York: The Macmillan Co., 1949), pp. 87–9, 162–3. By permission of the publishers.

Bacon's work seem to have served as an inspiration to some of the men who founded the Royal Society.

It often happens that when a philosopher comes to deal with the position of a man like Bacon in the history of thought, he lays great stress either upon the internal inconsistencies that may exist in the intellectual system in question, or on the actual correctness—from a modern point of view—of the man's conclusions, which in the present case would mean the correctness of Bacon's predictions concerning the character and the method which modern science was going to take upon itself. A modern critic may lay about him right and left on the subject of the philosophy of the nineteenth-century Utilitarians, if that teaching merits the name of philosophy; but the historian who remembers all the inhibitions that restricted parliamentary action at the beginning of the nineteenth century, and who has in mind the vast flood of legislation that began to appear in the second quarter of that century, can hardly help realising that on a lower level altogether—in a sub-philosophical field—it required a first-class campaign to get rid of the inhibitions and to persuade people of the commonplace fact that laws could be regarded as mere ministers to ordinary utility, that anachronistic legislation was not a thing to be preserved for semi-mystical reasons. It is at this lower level of analysis—in this sub-philosophical realm—that Bacon is so interesting and so important in history, and we must not ask ourselves: How many people adopted the Baconian system literally and *in toto*? We must not be surprised that even in the seventeenth century it was precisely the people in the same line of thought as Bacon—the logicians—who were the least influenced by his teaching. We must not be disconcerted if even at the very heart of his teaching, where he purported to show exactly how the results of experiments could be turned into generalisations, he was on occasion less original than he intended to be, and on occasion actually mistaken. In the days when the grand campaign against Aristotle was coming to its height he produced a programme and manifesto, and some of the most important things that he said are dead to us but were quivering with life in the seventeenth century, because they were right and so happen to have become commonplaces today. He did not produce Baconians taking over his whole system, but rather stimulated people in a piecemeal way—people who apparently did not always even read his works in their entirety. . . .

A primary aspect of the Renaissance . . . is the fact that it completes and brings to its climax the long process by which the thought of antiquity was being recovered and assimilated in the middle ages. It even carries to what at times is a ludicrous extreme the spirit of an exaggerated subservience to antiquity, the spirit that helped to turn Latin into a dead language. Ideas may have appeared in new combinations, but we cannot say that essentially new ingredients were introduced into our civilisation at the Renaissance. We cannot say that here were intellectual changes calculated to transform the character and structure of our society or civilisation. Even the secularisation of thought which was locally achieved in certain circles at this time was not unprecedented and was a hot-house growth, soon to be overwhelmed by the fanaticism of the Reformation and the Counter-Reformation. During much of the seventeenth century itself we can hardly fail to be struck, for example, by the power of religion in thought and politics.

People have talked sometimes as though nothing very new happened in the seventeenth century either, since natural science itself came to the modern world as a legacy from ancient Greece. More than once in the course of our survey we ourselves have even been left with the impression that the scientific revolution could not take place—that significant developments were held up for considerable periods—until a further draft had been made upon the thought of antiquity and a certain minimum of Greek science had been recovered. Against all this, however, it might be said that the course of the seventeenth century as we have studied it represents one of the great episodes in human experience, which ought to be placed—along with the exile of the ancient Jews or the building-up of the universal empires of Alexander the Great and of Ancient Rome—amongst the epic adventures that have helped to make the human race what it is. It represents one of those periods when new things are brought into the world and into history out of men's own creative activity, and their own wrestlings with truth. There does not seem to be any sign that the ancient world, before its heritage had been dispersed, was moving towards anything like the scientific revolution, or that the Byzantine Empire, in spite of the continuity of its classical tradition, would ever have taken hold of ancient thought and so remoulded it by a great transforming power. The scientific revolution we must regard, therefore, as a creative product of the West—depending on a complicated set of conditions which existed only in Western Europe, depending partly also perhaps on a certain dynamic quality in the life and the history of this half of the continent. And not only was a new factor introduced into history at this time amongst other factors, but it proved to be so capable of growth, and so many-sided in its operations, that it consciously assumed a directing role from the very first, and, so to speak, began to take control of the other factors—just as Christianity in the middle ages had come to preside over everything else, percolating into every corner of life and thought. And when we speak of Western civilisation being carried to an oriental country like Japan in recent generations, we do not mean Graeco-Roman philosophy and humanist ideals, we do not mean the Christianising of Japan, we mean the science, the modes of thought and all that apparatus of civilisation which were beginning to change the face of the West in the latter half of the seventeenth century.